Management Accounting
for Decision Makers

Visit the *Management Accounting for Decision Makers, fourth edition*
Companion Website at **www.pearsoned.co.uk/atrillmclaney** to find
valuable **student** learning material including:

- Learning objectives for each chapter
- Multiple choice questions to help test your learning
- Additional exercises and revision questions
- Solutions to end of chapter review questions
- Links to relevant sites on the web
- An online glossary to explain key terms
- Flashcards to test your knowledge of key terms and definitions

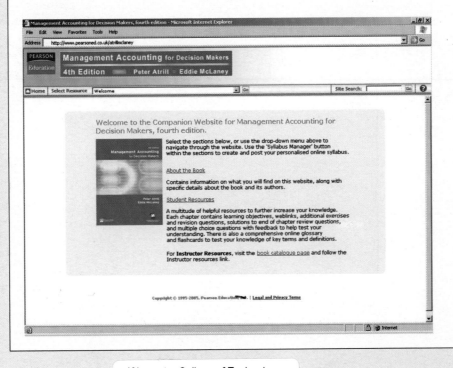

We work with leading authors to develop the strongest educational materials in accounting, bringing cutting-edge thinking and best learning practice to a global market.

Under a range of well-known imprints, including Financial Times Prentice Hall, we craft high quality print and electronic publications which help readers to understand and apply their content, whether studying or at work.

To find out more about the complete range of our publishing please visit us on the World Wide Web at:
www.pearsoned.co.uk

4th Edition

Management Accounting
for Decision Makers

Peter Atrill

and

Eddie McLaney

FT Prentice Hall
FINANCIAL TIMES

An imprint of **Pearson Education**
Harlow, England • London • New York • Boston • San Francisco • Toronto
Sydney • Tokyo • Singapore • Hong Kong • Seoul • Taipei • New Delhi
Cape Town • Madrid • Mexico City • Amsterdam • Munich • Paris • Milan

Pearson Education Limited

Edinburgh Gate
Harlow
Essex CM20 2JE
England

and Associated Companies throughout the world

Visit us on the World Wide Web at:
www.pearsoned.co.uk

First published 1995 by Prentice Hall Europe
Second edition published 1999 by Prentice Hall Europe
Third edition published 2002 by Pearson Education Limited
Fourth edition published 2005

ISBN 0 273 68867 7

British Library Cataloguing-in-Publication Data
A catalogue record for this book is available from the British Library

Library of Congress Cataloging-in-Publication Data
Atrill, Peter.
    Management accounting for decision makers / Peter Atrill and Eddie McLaney. – 4th ed.
        p. cm
    Rev ed. of: Management accounting for non-specialists / Peter Atrill and Eddie McLaney.
3rd ed. 2002
    Includes bibliographical references and index.
    ISBN 0-273-68867-7 (alk. paper)
    1. Managerial accounting. 2. Decision making. I. McLaney, E. J. II. Atrill, Peter.
Management accounting for non-specialists. III. Title.
HF5657.4.A873 2004
658.15'11—dc22

                                                                    2004057759

10 9 8 7 6 5 4 3 2 1
09 08 07 06 05

Typeset in 9.5/12.5pt Stone Serif by 35
Printed and Bound by Mateu Cromo Artes Graficas, Spain

The publisher's policy is to use paper manufactured from sustainable forests.

Contents

5 Costing and pricing in a competitive environment

8 Making capital investment decisions   211

9   Managing working capital

Companion Website and instructor resources

Visit **www.pearsoned.co.uk/atrillmclaney** to find valuable online resources

For students
- Learning objectives for each chapter
- Multiple choice questions to help test your learning
- Additional exercises and review questions
- Solutions to end of chapter review questions
- Links to relevant sites on the web
- An online glossary to explain key terms
- Flashcards to test your knowledge of key terms and definitions

For lecturers
- Complete, downloadable Instructor's Manual
- PowerPoint slides that can be downloaded and used as OHTs
- Case study material with solutions
- Progress tests, consisting of various questions and exercise material with solutions
- Tutorial/seminar questions and solutions
- Solutions to end of chapter review questions

Also: The Companion Website provides the following features

- Search tool to help locate specific items of content
- E-mail results and profile tools to send results of quizzes to instructors
- Online help and support to assist with website usage and troubleshooting

For more information please contact your local Pearson Education sales representative or visit **www.pearsoned.co.uk/atrillmclaney**

Guided tour of the book

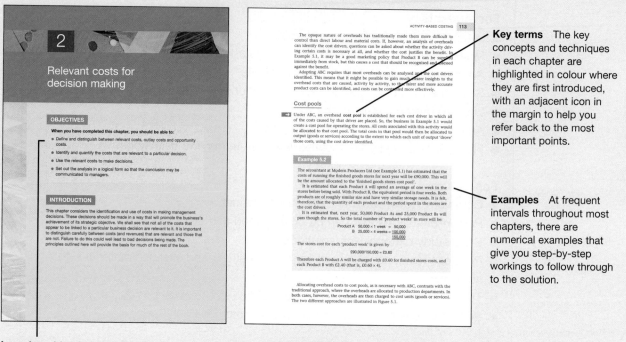

Learning objectives Bullet points at the start of each chapter show what you can expect to learn from that chapter, and highlight the core coverage.

Key terms The key concepts and techniques in each chapter are highlighted in colour where they are first introduced, with an adjacent icon in the margin to help you refer back to the most important points.

Examples At frequent intervals throughout most chapters, there are numerical examples that give you step-by-step workings to follow through to the solution.

Activities These short questions, integrated throughout each chapter, allow you to check your understanding as you progress through the text. They comprise either a narrative question requiring you to review or critically consider topics, or a numerical problem requiring you to deduce a solution. A suggested answer is given immediately after each activity.

'Real World' illustrations Integrated throughout the text, these illustrative examples highlight the practical application of accounting concepts and techniques by real businesses, including extracts from company reports and financial statements, survey data and other interesting insights from business.

Self-assessment questions   Towards the end of most chapters you will encounter one of these questions, allowing you to attempt a comprehensive question before tackling the end-of-chapter assessment material. To check your understanding and progress, solutions are provided in Appendix C.

INVESTMENT APPRAISAL IN PRACTICE   235

Self-assessment question 8.1

Beacon Chemicals plc is considering buying some equipment to produce a chemical named X14. The new equipment's capital cost is estimated at £100,000. If its purchase is approved now, the equipment can be bought and production can commence by the end of this year. £50,000 has already been spent on research and development work. Estimates of revenues and costs arising from the operation of the new equipment appear below:

	Year 1	Year 2	Year 3	Year 4	Year 5
Sales price (£ per litre)	100	120	120	100	80
Sales volume (litres)	800	1,000	1,200	1,000	800
Variable costs (£ per litre)	50	50	40	30	40
Fixed costs (£000)	30	30	30	30	30

If the equipment is bought, sales of some existing products will be lost, and this will result in a loss of contribution of £15,000 a year over its life.

The accountant has informed you that the fixed costs include depreciation of £20,000 a year on the new equipment. They also include an allocation of £10,000 for fixed overheads. A separate study has indicated that if the new equipment were bought, additional overheads, excluding depreciation, arising from producing the chemical would be £8,000 a year. Production would require additional working capital of £30,000.

For the purposes of your initial calculations ignore taxation.

Required:
(a) Deduce the relevant annual cash flows associated with buying the equipment.
(b) Deduce the payback period.
(c) Calculate the net present value using a discount rate of 8 per cent.

Hint: You should deal with the investment in working capital by treating it as a cash outflow at the start of the project and an inflow at the end.

Investment appraisal in practice

Many surveys have been conducted in the UK into the methods of investment appraisal used in practice. They have tended to show the following features:

● businesses using more than one method to assess each investment decision, increasingly so over time;
● an increased use of the discounting methods (NPV and IRR) over time, with these two becoming the most popular in recent years;
● continued popularity of ARR and PP, despite their theoretical shortcomings and the rise in popularity of the discounting methods;
● a tendency for larger businesses to use the discounting methods and to use more than one method in respect of each decision.

Real World 8.4 shows the results of the most recent (1997) survey conducted of UK businesses regarding their use of investment appraisal methods.

---

102   CHAPTER 4 FULL COSTING

SUMMARY

The main points in this chapter may be summarised as follows:

Full cost = the total amount of resources sacrificed to achieve a particular objective.

Single-product operations
● Where all the units of output are identical, the full cost can be calculated as follows:

$$\text{cost per unit} = \frac{\text{total cost of output}}{\text{number of units produced}}$$

Multi-product operations – job costing
● Where units of output are not identical, it is necessary to divide the costs into two categories: direct costs and indirect costs.
● Direct costs = costs that can be identified with specific cost units (for example, labour of a garage mechanic).
● Indirect costs (overheads) = costs that cannot be directly measured in respect of particular cost units (for example, the rent of a garage).
● Full cost = direct cost + indirect cost.
● Direct/indirect is not linked to variable/fixed.
● Indirect costs are difficult to relate to individual cost units – arbitrary bases are used and there is no single correct method.
● Traditionally, indirect costs are seen as the costs of providing a 'service' to cost units.
● Direct labour hour basis of applying indirect costs to cost units is the most popular in practice.

Dealing with overheads on a departmental basis
● Indirect costs can be segmented – usually on departmental basis – each department has its own overhead recovery rate.
● Each department is a separate cost centre – that is an area, activity or function for which costs are separately collected.
● Overheads must be allocated or apportioned to cost centres.
● Service cost centre costs must then be apportioned to product cost centres and product cost centre overheads absorbed by cost units (jobs).

Batch costing
● A variation of job costing where each job consists of a number of identical (or near identical) cost units:

$$\text{Cost per unit} = \frac{\text{Cost of the batch (direct + indirect)}}{\text{Number of units in the batch}}$$

If the full cost is charged as the sales price and things go according to plan, the business will break even.

Uses of full cost information
● Pricing (full cost) on a cost-plus basis.
● Income measurement.

Full cost information is seen by some as not very useful because it can be backward looking; it includes information irrelevant to decision making, but excludes some relevant information.

Bullet point chapter summary   Each chapter ends with a 'bullet-point' summary. This highlights the material covered in the chapter and can be used as a quick reminder of the main issues.

Key terms summary   At the end of each chapter, there is a listing (with page reference) of all the key terms, allowing you to refer back easily to the most important points.

REFERENCES   103

➤ Key terms

Full costing p. 77	Cost unit p. 82
Full cost p. 77	Overhead absorption (recovery)
Process costing p. 78	rate p. 83
Direct costs p. 78	Cost centre p. 90
Indirect costs p. 79	Product cost centre p. 91
Overheads p. 79	Service cost centre p. 91
Common costs p. 79	Cost allocation p. 92
Job costing p. 79	Cost apportionment p. 92
Cost behaviour p. 81	Batch costing p. 99
Total cost p. 81	Cost-plus pricing p. 100

Further reading

If you would like to explore the topics covered in this chapter in more depth, we recommend the following books:

Management Accounting, *Atkinson A., Banker R., Kaplan R. and Young S.*, 3rd edn, Prentice Hall, 2001, chapter 4.

Management and Cost Accounting, *Drury C.*, 5th edn, Thomson Learning Business Press, 2000, chapters 3, 4 and 5.

Cost Accounting: A managerial emphasis, *Horngren C., Foster G. and Datar S.*, 11th edn, Prentice Hall International, 2002, chapter 4.

Cost and Management Accounting, *Williamson D.*, Prentice Hall International, 1996, chapters 6, 8 and 10.

References

1   *Cost Systems Design and Profitability Analysis in UK Manufacturing Companies, Drury C. and Tayles M.*, CIMA Publishing, 2000.
2   *2003 Survey of Management Accounting, Ernst and Young*, Ernst and Yong, 2003.
3   *A Survey of Management Accounting Practices in UK Manufacturing Companies, Drury C., Braund S., Osborne P. and Tayles M.*, Chartered Association of Certified Accountants, 1993.

EXERCISES   37

REVIEW QUESTIONS

Answers to these questions can be found on the students' side of the Companion Website at www.booksites.net/atrillmclaney.

2.1   To be relevant to a particular decision, a cost must have two attributes. What are they?

2.2   Distinguish between a sunk cost and an opportunity cost.

2.3   Define the word 'cost' in the context of management accounting.

2.4   What is meant by the expression 'committed cost'? How do committed costs arise?

EXERCISES

Exercises 2.7 and 2.8 are more advanced than 2.1 to 2.6. Those with coloured numbers have answers at the back of the book.

2.1   Lombard Ltd has been offered a contract for which there is available production capacity. The contract is for 20,000 identical items, manufactured by an intricate assembly operation, to be produced and delivered in the next financial year at a price of £80 each. The specification for one item is as follows:

Assembly labour	4 hours
Component X	4 units
Component Y	3 units

There would also be the need to hire equipment, for the duration of the contract, at an outlay cost of £200,000.

The assembly is a highly skilled operation and the workforce is currently underutilised. It is the business's policy to retain this workforce on full pay in anticipation of high demand in a few years' time, for a new product currently being developed. Skilled workers are paid £10 an hour.

Component X is used in a number of other subassemblies produced by the business. It is readily available. A stock (inventory) of 50,000 units of component X is currently held. Component Y was a special purchase in anticipation of an order that did not in the end materialise. It is, therefore, surplus to requirements and 100,000 units that are in stock may have to be sold at a loss. An estimate of alternative values for components X and Y provided by the materials planning department is as follows:

	X £/unit	Y £/unit
Historic cost	4	10
Replacement cost	5	11
Net realisable value	3	8

Review questions These short questions encourage you to review and/or critically discuss your understanding of the main topics covered in each chapter, either individually or in a group. Solutions to these questions can be found on the Companion Website at **www.pearsoned.co.uk/atrillmclaney**.

Further reading This section comprises a listing of relevant chapters in other textbooks that you might refer to in order to pursue a topic in more depth or gain an alternative perspective.

References Provides full details of sources of information referred to in the chapter.

Exercises   There are eight of these comprehensive questions at the end of most chapters. The more advanced questions are separately identified. Solutions to five of the questions (those with coloured numbers) are provided in Appendix D, enabling you to assess your progress. Solutions to the remaining questions are available for lecturers only. An additional exercise for each chapter can be found on the Companion Website at **www.pearsoned.co.uk/atrillmclaney**.

Guided tour of the Companion Website

Extra material has been prepared to help you study using *Management Accounting for Decision Makers*. This material can be found on the book's Companion Website at **www.pearsoned.co.uk/atrillmclaney**. You will find links to websites of interest, as well as a range of material including:

Interactive quizzes

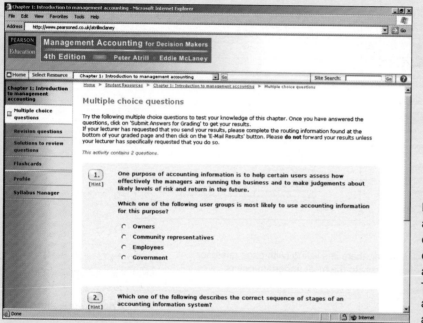

For each chapter there is a set of interactive multiple choice questions, plus a set of fill-in-the blanks questions and an extra exercise. Test your learning and get automatic grading on your answers.

Revision questions

Sets of questions covering the whole book are designed to help you check your overall learning whilst you are revising.

Review questions solutions

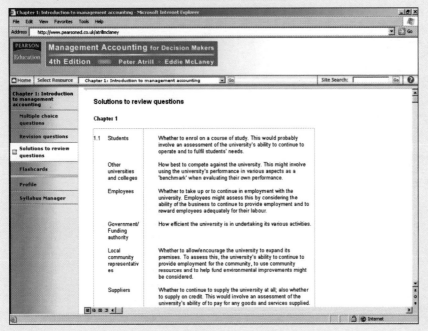

Answers to the end-of-chapter review questions that appear in the book are to be found on the website, so you can check your progress.

Glossary and flashcards

Full version of the book's glossary to help you check definitions while you are online. Flashcards help you to learn and test yourself on definitions of key terms. A term is displayed on each card: 'flip over' for the definition. 'Shuffle' the cards to randomly test your knowledge.

Preface

Management accounting is concerned with the provision and use of information that should help managers to make better decisions and try to ensure that what has been decided actually occurs. This book seeks to introduce management accounting, particularly to those people who wish or need to have an understanding of the subject, without going into a lot of unnecessary technical detail.

The book is directed primarily at those who are following an introductory course in management accounting. Some readers may be majoring in accounting and will go on to study management accounting at a higher level. They should also find the book useful as an introduction to the principles of management accounting, which can be used as a foundation for deeper study. Other readers may be taking a management accounting course, perhaps as part of a university or college course majoring in some other area, such as business studies, tourism or engineering. The book is also directed at readers who are studying independently, perhaps with no qualification in mind.

In writing the book, we have been mindful of the fact that most of the book's readers will not have studied management accounting before. We have therefore tried to write in an accessible style, avoiding technical jargon. Where technical terminology is unavoidable, we have tried to give clear explanations. At the end of the book there is a glossary of technical terms, which readers can use to refresh their memory if they come across a term whose meaning is in doubt.

The book is written in an 'open learning' style. That is to say, it aims to involve the reader in a way not traditionally found in textbooks. The book tries to approach its contents much as a good lecturer would do. We have tried to introduce topics gradually, explaining everything as we go. We have also included a number of questions and tasks of various types to try to help readers to understand the subject fully, in much the same way as a good lecturer would do in lectures and tutorials. More detail of the nature and use of these questions and tasks is given in the 'How to use this book' section immediately following this preface.

The open learning style has been adopted because we believe it to be more 'user friendly' to readers. Whether they are using the book as part of a taught course or for personal study, we feel that the open learning approach makes it easier for readers to learn.

Chapter 1 provides a broad introduction to the nature and purpose of management accounting. Chapters 2, 3, 4 and 5 are concerned with identifying cost information and using it to make short-term and medium-term decisions. Chapters 6 and 7 deal with the use of management accounting in the process of planning and trying to ensure that plans are actually achieved. Chapter 8 considers the use of management accounting information in making investment decisions, typically long-term ones. Chapter 9 looks at the way in which management accounting can help in the control of short-term assets, like stock and cash. Chapter 10 deals with the role of management accounting in trying to deal with the problems which arise from managing businesses which operate, as most businesses do, through a divisional structure. Finally, Chapter 11, a completely new chapter in this edition, deals with 'strategic management accounting'. This is an increasingly important area of management accounting that focuses on factors outside the organisation but which have a significant effect on the success of the organisation.

In this fourth edition, we have changed the title to highlight the decision-making focus of the book, but broadly the content has remained the same. The opportunity has been taken to improve the book. We have increased the emphasis on the need for businesses to operate within a framework of strategic planning and decision making. We have highlighted the role of management accountants' in this and their place at the centre of the decision-making and planning process. We have included more material that relates to management accounting in practice.

We should like to thank those at Pearson Education who were involved with this book, for their support and encouragement. Without their help it would not have materialised.

We hope that readers will find the book readable and helpful.

Peter Atrill
Eddie McLaney

How to use this book

Whether you are using the book as part of a lecture/tutorial-based course or as the basis for a more independent mode of study, the same approach should be broadly followed.

Order of dealing with the material

The contents of the book have been ordered in what is meant to be a logical sequence. For this reason, it is suggested that you work through the book in the order in which it is presented. Every effort has been made to ensure that earlier chapters do not refer to concepts or terms which are not explained until a later chapter. If you work through the chapters in the 'wrong' order, you may encounter points that have been explained in an earlier chapter and which you have not read.

Working through the chapters

You are advised to work through the chapters, from start to finish, but not necessarily in one sitting. Activities are interspersed within the text. These are meant to be like the sort of questions which a good lecturer will throw at students during a lecture or tutorial. Activities seek to serve two purposes:

1 To give you the opportunity to check that you understand what has been covered so far.
2 To try to encourage you to think beyond the topic that you have just covered, sometimes so that you can see a link between that topic and others with which you are already familiar. Sometimes, activities are used as a means of linking the topic just covered to the next one.

You are strongly advised to do all the activities. The answers are provided immediately after the activity. These answers should be covered up until you have arrived at a solution, which should then be compared with the suggested answer provided.

Towards the end of Chapters 2–11 there is a 'self-assessment question'. This is rather more demanding and comprehensive than any of the activities. It is intended to give you an opportunity to see whether you understand the main body of material covered in the chapter. The solutions to the self-assessment questions are provided at the end of the book. As with the activities, it is very important that you make a thorough attempt at the question before referring to the solution. If you have real difficulty with a self-assessment question you should go over the chapter again, since it should be the case that careful study of the chapter will enable completion of the self-assessment question.

End-of-chapter assessment material

At the end of each chapter, there are four 'review' questions. These are short questions requiring a narrative answer and intended to enable you to assess how well you can recall main points covered in the chapter. Suggested answers to these questions are included on the student website. Again, a serious attempt should be made to answer these questions before referring to the solutions.

At the end of each chapter, there are normally eight exercises. These are more demanding and extensive questions, mostly computational, and should further reinforce your knowledge and understanding. We have attempted to provide questions of varying complexity.

Answers to five out of the eight exercises in each chapter are provided at the end of the book. These exercises are marked with a coloured number. Answers to the three exercises that are not marked with a coloured number are given in a separate teacher's manual. Yet again, a thorough attempt should be made to answer these questions before referring to the answers.

Supplements and website

A comprehensive range of supplementary materials is available to lecturers adopting this text at **www.pearsoned.co.uk/atrillmclaney**.

Acknowledgements

We are grateful to the following for permissions to reproduce copyright material:

Figure 5.1 reprinted from *Activity-based Costing – A Review With Case Studies*, CIMA Publishing (Innes, J. and Mitchell, F. 1990) with permission from Elsevier; Real World 6.1, 6.4, 7.2, 7.3, 10.5 and 10.8 from *A Survey of Management Accounting Practices in UK Manufacturing Companies*, Chartered Association of Accountants (Drury, C., Braund, S., Osbourne, P. and Tayles, M. 1993); Figure 6.5 from *Financial Management and Working Capital Practices in UK SMEs*, Manchester Business School (Chittenden, F., Poutziouris, P. and Michaelas, N. 1998); Figure 6.6 from www.bbrt.org. Copyright and source Beyond Budgeting Round Table (BBRT) – www.bbrt.org; Real World 8.4 from The theory-practice gap in capital budgeting: evidence from the United Kingdom in *Journal of Business Finance and Accounting*, June/July, Blackwell Publishing (Arnold, G. C. and Hatzopoulos, P. 2000); Figure 11.4 reprinted by permission of Harvard Business School Press from *The Balanced Scorecard* by Kaplan, R. and Norton, D., Boston, MA, 1996. Copyright © 1996 by Harvard Business School Publishing Corporation, all rights reserved.

Real World 1.3 Profit without honour from *The Financial Times Limited*, 29/30 June 2002, © John Kay; Tesco Stores Ltd for an extract (Real World 11.7) from the 2003 Tesco Annual Report and Financial Statements; and Harvard Business School Publishing Corporation for an extract (Real World 11.8) from the article 'The Balanced Scorecard' by R. Kaplan and D. Norton © The Harvard Business School Publishing Corporation 1996.

We are grateful to the Financial Times Limited for permission to reprint the following material:

Real World 1.2 Goodbye to a little bit of history, © *Financial Times*, 28 May 2003; Real World 5.2 Sony and Microsoft in European console price war, FT.com, © *Financial Times*, 28 August 2002.

In some instances we have been unable to trace the owners of copyright material and we would appreciate any information that would enable us to do so.

1

Introduction to management accounting

OBJECTIVES

When you have completed this chapter, you should be able to:

● Explain the role and nature of accounting.

● Explain the distinction between management and financial accounting.

● Identify the main users of accounting information and discuss their needs.

● Explain how management accounting can fulfil the needs of managers.

● Discuss the key financial objective of a business.

INTRODUCTION

Welcome to the world of management accounting! In this first chapter, we shall begin by considering the role and nature of accounting in general. We shall identify the main users of accounting information and discuss the ways in which accounting can improve the quality of the decisions that they make. We shall then go on to consider the needs of managers and the role of management accounting information in meeting those needs. As this book is concerned with management accounting for private sector businesses, we shall also consider what the key financial objective of a business is likely to be. The particular objective chosen will exert an important influence on what is reported and how it is reported. Despite the book's primary concentration on private sector businesses, most of the issues covered apply equally well to other types of organisation, including public sector ones and charities.

What is accounting?

→ **Accounting** exists to help people make informed financial decisions. It is concerned with collecting and analysing financial information and then communicating this information to those making decisions. Sometimes the impression is given that the purpose of accounting is simply to prepare financial reports on a regular basis. While it is true that accountants undertake this kind of work, it does not represent an end in itself. The ultimate purpose of the accountant's work is to improve the quality of financial decisions. This decision-making perspective of accounting fits in with the theme of this book and shapes the way that we shall deal with each topic.

Who are the users?

For accounting information to be useful, the accountant must be clear about *for whom* the information is being prepared and *for what purpose* the information will be used. There are likely to be various groups of people (known as 'user groups') with an interest in a particular organisation, in the sense of needing to make decisions about that organisation. For the typical private sector business, the most important of these groups are shown in Figure 1.1.

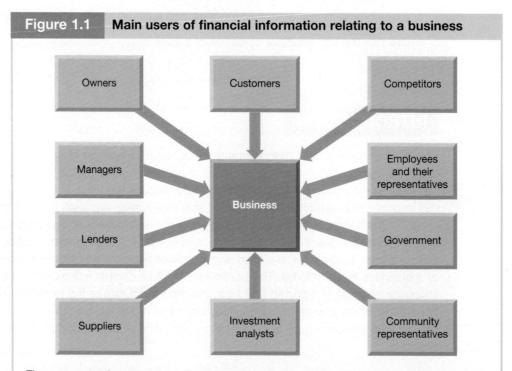

Figure 1.1   Main users of financial information relating to a business

There are several user groups with an interest in the accounting information relating to a business. The majority of these are outside the business but, nevertheless, they have a stake in the business. The above is not meant to be an exhaustive list of potential users; however, the groups identified are normally the most important.

Activity 1.1

Ptarmigan Insurance plc (PI) is a large motor insurance business. Taking the user groups identified above, suggest what sort of decisions each one is likely to make about PI.

Your answer may be as follows:

User group	Decision
Customers	Whether to buy motor policies from PI. This would probably involve an assessment of PI's ability to continue in business, to meet claims and generally to supply customers' needs.
Competitors	How best to compete against PI or, perhaps, whether to leave the market on the grounds that it is not possible to compete profitably with PI. This might involve using PI's performance in various aspects as a 'benchmark' when evaluating their own performance. They might also try to assess PI's competitive strength and to identify significant changes that may signal PI's future actions (for example, expanding its ability to provide its insurance service as a prelude to market expansion).
Employees	Whether to take up or to continue in employment with PI. Employees might assess this by considering the ability of the business to continue to provide employment and to reward employees adequately for their labour.
Government	Whether PI should pay tax and, if so, how much, whether it complies with agreed pricing policies, whether financial support is needed and so on. In making these decisions an assessment of its profits, sales and financial strength would be made.
Community representatives	Whether to allow PI to expand its premises or whether to provide economic support for PI. To assess these, PI's ability to continue to provide employment for the community, to use community resources and to help fund environmental improvements might be considered.
Investment analysts	Whether or not to advise clients to buy shares in PI. This would involve an assessment of the likely risks and returns associated with PI's business.
Suppliers	Whether to continue to supply PI at all; also whether to supply on credit. This would involve an assessment of PI's ability to pay for any goods and services supplied.
Lenders	Whether to lend money to PI and/or whether to require repayment of any existing loans. To assess this, PI's ability to meet its obligations to pay interest and to repay the principal would be considered.
Managers	Whether the performance of the business requires improvement. Here performance to date would be compared with earlier plans or some other 'benchmark' to decide whether action needs to be taken and whether there should be a change in PI's future direction. In making such decisions, management will need to look at PI's ability to perform and at the opportunities available to it.
Owners (shareholders)	Whether to buy additional shares in PI or to sell some or all of those currently held. This would involve an assessment of the likely risks and returns associated with PI. Owners would also be involved with decisions on the employment of senior managers. Here past performance would be assessed.

You may have thought of other reasons why each group would find accounting information useful.

Accounting for managers

This book is concerned with providing accounting information for the penultimate group mentioned above, that is, managers. This is a particularly important group. Managers have day-to-day responsibility for running the business and so their decisions and actions will influence its financial health. We shall see in later chapters how planning for the future and exercising day-to-day control over a business involves a wide range of decisions being made. For example, managers may need information to help them decide whether to:

● develop new products or services (such as a computer manufacturer developing a new range of computers);
● increase or decrease the price or quantity of existing products or services (such as a telecommunications business changing its mobile phone call and text charges);
● borrow money to help finance the business (such as a supermarket wishing to increase the number of stores it owns);
● increase or decrease the operating capacity of the business (such as a beef farming business reviewing the size of its herd);
● change the methods of purchasing, production or distribution (such as a clothes retailer switching from UK to overseas suppliers).

As management decisions are broad in scope, the accounting information provided to managers must also be wide-ranging. Accounting information should help in identifying and assessing the financial consequences of decisions such as those listed above. In later chapters, we shall consider each of the types of decisions in the list and see how their financial consequences can be assessed.

Not-for-profit organisations

Though the focus of this book is accounting as it relates to private sector businesses, there are many organisations that do not exist mainly for the pursuit of profit yet produce accounting information for decision-making purposes. Examples of such organisations include charities, clubs and associations, universities, national and local government authorities, churches and trade unions. User groups need accounting information about these types of organisation to help them to make decisions. These groups are often the same as, or similar to, those identified for private sector businesses. They may have a stake in the future viability of the organisation and may use accounting information to check that the wealth of the organisation is being properly controlled and used in a way that is consistent with its objectives.

How useful is accounting information?

No one would seriously claim that accounting information fully meets all of the needs of each of the various user groups. Accounting is still a developing subject and we still have much to learn about user needs and the ways in which these needs should be met. Nevertheless, the information contained in accounting reports should help users make decisions relating to the business. The information should reduce uncertainty over the financial position and performance of the business. It should help to answer questions concerning the availability of cash to pay owners a return for their investment or to repay loans and so on. Typically, there is no other source of the information that is provided by accounting statements. This is to say that if managers do not get this information from accounting statements, they simply will not have access to it.

The evidence on the usefulness of accounting

There are arguments and convincing evidence that accounting information is at least perceived as being useful to users. There have been numerous research surveys that asked users to rank the importance of accounting information, in relation to other sources of information, for decision-making purposes. Generally speaking, these studies have found that users rank accounting information very highly. There is also considerable evidence that businesses choose to produce accounting information that far exceeds the minimum requirements imposed by accounting regulations. (For example, businesses often produce a considerable amount of accounting information for managers, which is not required by any regulations.) Presumably, the cost of producing this additional accounting information is justified on the grounds that users believe it to be useful to them. Such arguments and evidence, however, leave unanswered the question as to whether the information produced is actually being used for decision-making purposes, that is, does it affect people's behaviour?

It is normally very difficult to assess the impact of accounting on decision making. One situation arises, however, where the impact of accounting information can be observed and measured. This is where the shares (portions of ownership of a business) are traded on a stock exchange. The evidence reveals that, when a business makes an announcement concerning its accounting profits, the prices at which shares are traded and the volume of shares traded often change significantly. This suggests that investors are changing their views about the future prospects of the business as a result of this new information available to them and that this, in turn, leads them to make a decision either to buy or sell shares in the business.

Thus, we can see that there is evidence that accounting reports are perceived as being useful and are used for decision-making purposes. It is impossible, however, to measure just how useful accounting reports are to users and whether the cost of producing those reports represents value for money.

Accounting information and the decision-making process

Accounting information will usually represent only one input to a particular decision and the precise weight attached to the accounting information by the decision maker and the benefits which flow as a result cannot be accurately assessed. We shall see below, however, that it is at least possible to identify the kinds of qualities which accounting information must possess in order to be useful. Where these qualities are lacking, the usefulness of the information will be diminished.

Accounting as a service function

One way of viewing accounting is as a form of service. Accountants provide economic information to their 'clients', who are the various users identified in Figure 1.1 (see p. 2). The quality of the service provided would be determined by the extent to which the information needs of the various user groups have been met. It can be argued that, to be useful, accounting information should possess certain key qualities, or characteristics. These are:

- → ● **Relevance**. Accounting information must have the ability to influence decisions. Unless this characteristic is present, there is really no point in producing the information. The information may be relevant to the prediction of future events (for example, in predicting how much profit is likely to be earned next year) or relevant in helping confirm past events (for example, in establishing how much profit was earned last year). The role of accounting in confirming past events is important because users often wish to check on the accuracy of earlier predictions that they have made. The accuracy (or inaccuracy) of earlier predictions may enable users to judge the likely accuracy of current predictions.
- → ● **Reliability**. Accounting should be free from significant errors or bias. It should be capable of being relied upon by users to represent what it is supposed to represent. Though both relevance and reliability are very important, the problem that we often face in accounting is that information that is highly relevant may not be very reliable, and that which is reliable may not be very relevant.

Activity 1.2

To illustrate this last point, let us assume that a manager has to sell a custom-built machine owned by the business and has recently received a bid for it. What information would be relevant to the manager when deciding whether to accept the bid? How reliable would that information be?

The manager would probably like to know the current market value of the machine before deciding whether or not to accept the bid. The current market value would be highly relevant to the final decision, but it might not be very reliable because the machine is unique and there is likely to be little information concerning market values.

Where a choice has to be made between providing information that has either more relevance or more reliability, the maximisation of relevance tends to be the guiding rule.

- → ● **Comparability**. This quality will enable users to identify changes in the business over time (for example, the trend in sales over the past five years). It will also help users to evaluate the performance of the business in relation to other similar businesses. Comparability is achieved by treating items that are basically the same in the same manner for accounting purposes. Comparability tends also to be enhanced by making clear the policies that have been adopted in measuring and presenting the information.
- → ● **Understandability**. Accounting reports should be expressed as clearly as possible and should be understood by those at whom the information is aimed.

Activity 1.3

Do you think that accounting reports should be understandable to those who have not studied accounting?

It would be very useful if everyone could understand accounting reports, but it seems not possible for this to be the case. The complexity of financial events and transactions cannot normally be so easily reported. It is probably best that we regard accounting reports in the same way as we regard a report written in a foreign language. To understand either of these, we need to have had some preparation. Generally speaking, accounting reports assume that the user not only has a reasonable knowledge of business and accounting but is also prepared to invest some time in studying the reports.

The threshold of materiality

The qualities, or characteristics, that have just been described will help us to decide whether financial information is potentially useful. If a particular piece of information has these qualities then it may be useful. However, in making a final decision, we also have to consider whether the information is material, or significant. This means that we should ask whether its omission or misrepresentation in the financial reports would really alter the decisions that users make. Thus, in addition to possessing the characteristics mentioned above, financial information must also achieve a threshold of **materiality**. If the information is not regarded as material, it should not be included within the reports as it will merely clutter them up and, perhaps, interfere with the users' ability to interpret the financial results. The type of information and amounts involved will normally determine whether it is material.

Costs and benefits of accounting information

Having read the previous sections you may feel that, when considering a piece of financial information, provided the four main qualities identified are present and it is material it should be included in the financial reports. Unfortunately, there is one more hurdle to jump. Something may still exclude a piece of financial information from the financial reports even when it is considered to be useful. Consider Activity 1.4 below.

Activity 1.4

Suppose an item of information is capable of being provided. It is relevant to a particular decision, it is also reliable, comparable, can be understood by the decision maker concerned and is material.
Can you think of a reason why, in practice, you might choose not to produce the information?

The reason that you may decide not to produce, or discover, the information is that you judge the cost of doing so to be greater than the potential benefit of having the information. This cost–benefit issue will limit the extent to which accounting information is provided.

Figure 1.2	Relationship between costs and the value of providing additional financial information

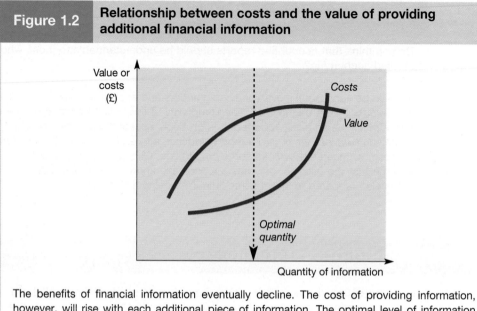

The benefits of financial information eventually decline. The cost of providing information, however, will rise with each additional piece of information. The optimal level of information provision is where the gap between the value of the information and the cost of providing it is at its greatest.

In theory, financial information should only be produced if the costs of providing a particular item of information are less than the benefits, or value, to be derived from its use. Figure 1.2 shows the relationship between the costs and value of providing additional financial information. The figure shows how the value of information received by the decision maker eventually begins to decline. This is, perhaps, because additional information becomes less relevant, or because of the problems that a decision maker may have in processing the sheer quantity of information provided. The costs of providing the information, however, will increase with each additional piece of information. The broken line indicates the point at which the gap between the value of information and the cost of providing that information is at its greatest. This represents the optimal amount of information that can be provided. This theoretical model, however, poses a number of problems in practice, as discussed below.

To illustrate the practical problems of establishing the value of information, suppose that we wish to buy a particular DVD system that we have seen in a local shop for sale at £250. We believe that other local shops may have the same system on offer for a lower price. The only ways of finding out the prices at other shops are either to telephone them or to visit them. Telephone calls cost money and involve some of our time. Visiting the shops may not involve the outlay of money, but more of our time will be involved. Is it worth the cost of finding out the price of the system at various shops? The answer, as we have seen, is that if the cost of discovering the price is less than the potential benefit, it is worth having that information.

To identify the various selling prices of the DVD system, there are various points to be considered, including:

● How many shops shall we telephone or visit?
● What is the cost of each telephone call?
● How long will it take to make all the telephone calls or visits?
● How much do we value our time?

The economic benefit of having the information on the price of the system is probably even harder to assess, and the following points need to be considered:

● What is the cheapest price that we might be quoted for the DVD system?
● How likely is it that we shall be quoted prices cheaper than £250?

As we can imagine, the answers to these questions may be far from clear. When assessing the value of accounting information we are confronted with similar problems.

The provision of accounting information can be very costly; however, the costs are often difficult to quantify. The direct, out-of-pocket, costs such as salaries of accounting staff are not really a problem, but these are only part of the total costs involved. There are also less direct costs such as the costs of the manager's time spent on analysing and interpreting the information contained in reports. In addition, costs will also be incurred if users employ the accounting information to the disadvantage of the business. For example, if suppliers discovered from the accounting reports that the business was in a poor financial state, they might decide to refuse to supply further goods or to impose strict conditions.

The economic benefit of having accounting information is even harder to assess. It is possible to apply some 'science' to the problem of weighing the costs and benefits, but a lot of subjective judgement is likely to be involved. Whilst no one would seriously advocate that the typical business should produce no accounting information, at the same time, no one would advocate that every item of information that could be seen as possessing one or more of the key characteristics should be produced, irrespective of the cost of producing it.

When weighing the costs of providing additional financial information against the benefits, there is also the problem that those who bear the burden of the costs may not be the ones who benefit from the additional information. The costs of providing accounting information are usually borne by the owners, but other user groups may be the beneficiaries.

The characteristics that influence the usefulness of accounting information and which have been discussed in this section and the preceding section are set out in Figure 1.3.

Accounting as an information system

We have already seen that accounting can be seen as the provision of a service to 'clients'. Another way of viewing accounting is as a part of the business's total information system. Users, both inside and outside the business, have to make decisions concerning the allocation of scarce economic resources. To try to ensure that these resources are allocated in an efficient manner, users require economic information on which to base decisions. It is the role of the accounting system to provide that information and this will involve information gathering and communication.

→ The **accounting information system** has certain features that are common to all information systems within a business. These are:

● identifying and capturing relevant information (in this case economic information);
● recording the information collected in a systematic manner;
● analysing and interpreting the information collected;
● reporting the information in a manner that suits the needs of users.

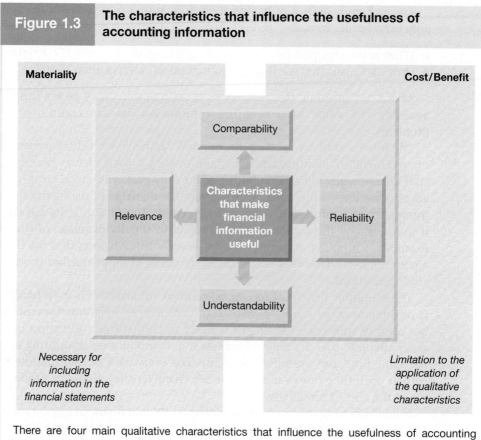

Figure 1.3   **The characteristics that influence the usefulness of accounting information**

There are four main qualitative characteristics that influence the usefulness of accounting information. In addition, however, accounting information should be material and the benefits of providing the information should outweigh the costs.

The relationship between these features is set out in Figure 1.4.

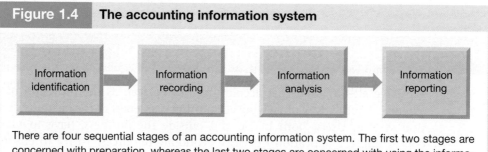

Figure 1.4   **The accounting information system**

There are four sequential stages of an accounting information system. The first two stages are concerned with preparation, whereas the last two stages are concerned with using the information collected.

Given the decision-making emphasis of this book, we shall be concerned primarily with the final two elements of the process – the analysis and reporting of financial information. We shall consider the way in which information is used by, and is useful to, managers rather than the way in which it is identified and recorded. In this context, information technology is playing an increasingly important role. It has created opportunities for analysis and reporting that were not possible before. The role of information technology in management accounting will be discussed in more detail later in the chapter.

Management and financial accounting

Accounting is usually seen as having two distinct strands. These are:

- **Management accounting**, which seeks to meet the needs of managers; and
- **Financial accounting**, which seeks to meet the accounting needs of all of the other users that were identified earlier in Figure 1.1 (see p. 2).

The differences between the two types of accounting reflect the different user groups that they address. Briefly, the major differences are as follows:

- *Nature of the reports produced*. Financial accounting reports tend to be general-purpose. That is, they contain financial information that will be useful for a broad range of users and decisions rather than being specifically designed for the needs of a particular group or set of decisions. Management accounting reports, on the other hand, are often specific-purpose reports. They are designed either with a particular decision in mind or for a particular manager.

- *Level of detail*. Financial accounting reports provide users with a broad overview of the performance and position of the business for a period. As a result, information is aggregated and detail is often lost. Management accounting reports, however, often provide managers with considerable detail to help them with a particular operational decision.

- *Regulations*. Financial reports, for many businesses, are subject to accounting regulations that try to ensure they are produced with standard content and in a standard format. Law and the accounting profession impose these regulations. As management accounting reports are for internal use only, there are no regulations from external sources concerning the form and content of the reports. They can be designed to meet the needs of particular managers.

- *Reporting interval*. For most businesses, financial accounting reports are produced on an annual basis, though large businesses may produce half-yearly reports, and a few produce quarterly ones. Management accounting reports may be produced as frequently as required by managers. In many businesses, managers are provided with certain reports on a weekly or monthly basis, which allows them to check progress frequently. In addition, special-purpose reports will be prepared when required (for example, to evaluate a proposal to purchase a piece of machinery).

- *Time horizon*. Financial accounting reports reflect the performance and position of the business for the past period. In essence, they are backward looking. Management accounting reports, on the other hand, often provide information concerning future performance as well as past performance. It is an oversimplification, however, to suggest that financial accounting reports never incorporate expectations concerning the future. Occasionally, businesses will release projected information to other users in an attempt to raise capital or to fight off unwanted takeover bids.

- *Range and quality of information*. Financial accounting reports concentrate on information that can be quantified in monetary terms. Management accounting also produces such reports, but is also more likely to produce reports that contain information of a non-financial nature such as measures of physical quantities of stocks (inventories) and output. Financial accounting places greater emphasis on the use of objective, verifiable evidence when preparing reports. Management accounting reports may use information that is less objective and verifiable, but they provide managers with the information they need.

We can see from this that management accounting is less constrained than financial accounting. It may draw from a variety of sources and use information that has varying degrees of reliability. The only real test to be applied when assessing the value of the information produced for managers is whether or not it improves the quality of the decisions made.

Activity 1.5

Are the information needs of managers and those of other users so very different? Is there any overlap between the information needs of managers and the needs of other users?

The distinction between management and financial accounting suggests that there are differences between the information needs of managers and those of other users. Whilst differences undoubtedly exist, there is also a good deal of overlap between these needs. For example, managers will, at times, be interested in receiving an historical overview of business operations of the sort provided to other users. Equally, the other users would be interested in receiving information relating to the future, such as the planned level of profits and non-financial information such as the state of the sales order book and the extent of product innovations.

The distinction between the two areas reflects, to some extent, the differences in access to financial information. Managers have much more control over the form and content of information they receive. Other users have to rely on what managers are prepared to provide or what the financial reporting regulations state must be provided. Though the scope of financial accounting reports has increased over time, fears concerning loss of competitive advantage and user ignorance concerning the reliability of forecast data have led businesses to resist providing other users with the detailed and wide-ranging information available to managers.

How are businesses managed?

As we have already seen, management accounting is concerned with providing managers with information that will help them to manage. This leads to the questions as to how businesses are managed and, therefore, what information managers will find most useful.

Over the past two decades, the environment in which businesses operate has become increasingly turbulent and competitive. Various reasons have been identified to explain these changes, including:

- the increasing sophistication of customers;
- the development of a global economy where national frontiers become less important;
- rapid changes in technology;
- the deregulation of domestic markets (for example, electricity, water and gas);
- increasing pressure from owners (shareholders) for competitive economic returns; and
- the increasing volatility of financial markets.

The effect of these environmental changes has been to make the role of managers more complex and demanding. It has meant that managers have had to find new ways to manage their business. This has increasingly led to the introduction of strategic management.

Strategic management

Strategic management is an approach where the business seeks to reach its objectives by taking advantage of its strengths, such as having a skilled workforce, but at the same time avoiding exposing its weaknesses, such as being short of investment finance. This involves strategic plans or strategies that take account of the business's strengths and weaknesses, and also of the opportunities offered and threats posed by the outside world. Access to a new, expanding market is an example of an opportunity; the decision of a major competitor to reduce prices is an example of a threat.

Strategic management involves five steps, described below.

1 Establish mission and objectives

The mission statement is usually a brief statement of the overall aims of the business. This is usually established on a 'once and for all' basis. It is relatively rare for businesses to alter their mission statements. Businesses often publish their mission statements on their websites and in their annual reports. Real World 1.1 provides two examples of a mission statement.

REAL WORLD 1.1

On a mission

Mission statements usually reflect high ideals or goals to be achieved for the business. Two examples of mission statements are set out below.

BT, the multinational telecommunications business, states its mission as follows:

> BT's strategy is to create value for shareholders through being the best provider of communications services and solutions for everybody in the UK, and for corporate customers in Europe, achieving global reach through partnership.

Source: BT Group plc Annual Report 2003.

The Great North Eastern Railway (GNER) has a mission to:

> . . . create a golden era of rail travel by setting the highest standards of service, speed and quality in the UK.

Source: 'Looks wonderful shame about the taste', FT.com, 10 July 2002.

As we can see, the mission statements of both businesses are very broad. Both mission statements set out what the business is seeking to do (create value for shareholders (BT) or create a golden age of rail travel (GNER)) and how it intends to do it (by being the best provider of telecommunications services and solutions (BT) or by setting the highest standards in service, speed and quality (GNER)).

The objectives are rather more specific than the mission and need to be both quantifiable and consistent with the mission or aims. Objectives need to be quantifiable so that an assessment can be made as to whether they have been achieved or are being achieved. Businesses tend not to make their statement of objectives public. Examples of the types of objectives used in practice include:

● a specified percentage share of the market in which the business is involved; and
● a specified percentage net profit margin.
● a specified percentage return on capital employed.

We shall consider what is likely to be the key financial objective shortly.

2 Undertake a position analysis

With the **position analysis**, the business is seeking to establish how it is placed relative to its environment (competitors, markets, technology, the economy, political climate, and so on) given the business's mission and objectives. This is often approached within the framework of an analysis of the business's strengths, weaknesses, opportunities and threats (a **SWOT analysis**). Strengths and weaknesses are internal factors that are attributes of the business itself, whereas opportunities and threats are factors expected to be present in the environment in which the business operates.

Activity 1.6

Try to suggest some factors that could be strengths, weaknesses, opportunities and threats for a business. Try to think of two for each of these (eight in all).

Strengths could include such things as:

● a loyal, skilled workforce
● a strong financial position
● access to markets.

Weaknesses might include:

● lack of experience
● lack of access to new finance
● lack of access to raw materials.

Opportunities could be such things as:

● new markets opening up for the business
● a competitor leaving the market
● the development of some new technology.

Threats to the business might come from:

● a new competitor entering the market
● a decline in the size of the market
● a change in the law making it harder for the business to operate.

You may have thought of others.

A SWOT analysis involves identifying the business's strengths and weaknesses as well as the opportunities provided and threats posed by the world outside the business. The SWOT framework is not the only possible approach to undertaking a position analysis, but it seems to be a very popular one.

3 Identify and assess the strategic options

This involves attempting to identify possible courses of action that will enable the business to reach its objectives through using its strengths to exploit opportunities, at the same time avoiding exposing its weaknesses to threats. The strengths, weaknesses, opportunities and threats are, of course, those identified by the SWOT analysis.

4 Select strategic options

Here the business will select what seems to be the best of the courses of action or strategies (identified in step 3) and formulating a strategic plan. The plan is normally broken down into a series of plans, one for each element of the business. The plans are normally expressed partially in financial terms.

REAL WORLD 1.2

Reviewing the options   FT

Sometimes a business may select a strategic option that results in the sale of a part, or all, of its operations. One example of this is described below.

Goodbye to a little piece of history

GUS yesterday sold its history. In offloading its home shopping business to the Barclay brothers, the retail and financial information group made a decisive break with the past.

The group was founded in 1900 as a mail order business, and one of the catalogues which changed hands yesterday – Great Universal – was the only part of the group that still retains part of the original name.

But there was no sentiment involved. According to David Tyler, finance director, it was simply a question of return on capital. The group makes far more money from its Argos high street business and the Experian financial information arm, as well as its 77 per cent stake in Burberry, the luxury goods group.

'In investment terms, home shopping just did not make an adequate return on capital,' said Mr Tyler.

The group has tried most strategic options in terms of running home shopping over the years. More recently, according to people close to the group, it looked at all the possibilities for exit – from joint ventures to closure – before opting for the sale to the Barclays.

Source: 'Goodbye to a little bit of history', *Financial Times*, 28 May 2003.

5 Perform, review and control

Here the business pursues the plans derived in step 4. By comparing the actual outcome with the plans, managers can see if things are going according to plan or not. Steps would be taken to exercise control where actual performance appears not to be matching plans.

As the book develops, we shall look at how the business's mission links, through objectives and long-term plans, to detailed budgets.

Figure 1.5 shows the strategic planning framework in diagrammatic form.

It seems that all successful businesses are now managed on strategic lines. As we have just seen, strategic management is very much concerned with the world outside the business. With the more traditional approach to management, this has been less the case. In seeking to provide a useful service to managers, management accounting tends also to look outside as well as at what is happening internally.

Figure 1.5	**The strategic management framework**

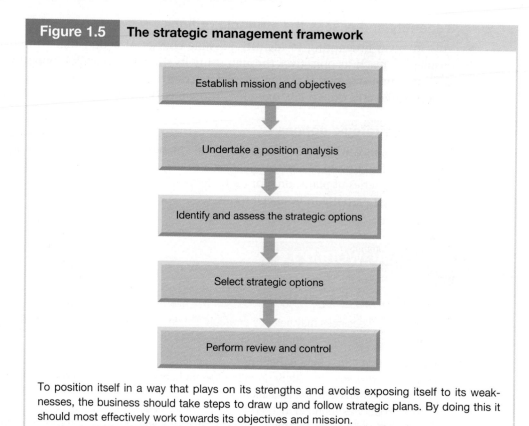

To position itself in a way that plays on its strengths and avoids exposing itself to its weaknesses, the business should take steps to draw up and follow strategic plans. By doing this it should most effectively work towards its objectives and mission.

The key financial objective

We have seen that managers can only work towards the business's mission through the achievement of identified objectives. We have also seen that these objectives need to be quantifiable.

The key financial objective of businesses seems to be to seek to enhance the wealth of their owners. Certainly, many businesses state wealth enhancement as a key point in their mission statements. Real World 1.1 (see p. 13) provides an example of this, where BT includes the phrase 'create shareholder value' in its short mission statement. This is far from an isolated example.

Does this mean that the needs of other groups associated with the business (employees, customers, suppliers, the community and so on) are not really important? The answer to this question is almost certainly no, if the business wishes to survive and prosper over the longer term. Satisfying the needs of other groups will normally be consistent with increasing the wealth of the owners over the longer term. A dissatisfied workforce, for example, may result in low productivity, strikes and so forth, which will in turn have an adverse effect on the wealth of the owners. Similarly, a business that upsets the local community by polluting the environment may attract bad publicity, resulting in a loss of customers and heavy fines.

Real World 1.3 provides an example of a well-known retailer that suffered from not paying sufficient attention to these other groups. It also raises questions about businesses in other industries.

REAL WORLD 1.3

Short-term gains, long-term problems   **FT**

In recent years, many businesses have been criticised for failing to consider the long-term implications of their policies on the wealth of the owners. John Kay argues that some businesses have achieved growth and short-term increases in wealth by sacrificing their longer-term prosperity. He points out that:

> . . . The business of Marks and Spencer, the retailer, was unparalleled in reputation but mature. To achieve earnings growth consistent with a glamour rating the company squeezed suppliers, gave less value for money, spent less on stores. In 1998, it achieved the highest (profit) margin in sales in the history of the business. It had also compromised its position to the point where sales and profits plummeted.
>
> Banks and insurance companies have taken staff out of branches and retrained those that remain as sales people. The pharmaceuticals industry has taken advantage of mergers to consolidate its research and development facilities. Energy companies have cut back on exploration.
>
> We know that these actions increased corporate earnings. We do not know what effect they have on the long-run strength of the business – and this is the key point – do the companies themselves know? Some rationalisations will genuinely lead to more productive businesses. Other companies will suffer the fate of Marks and Spencer.

Source: 'Profit without honour', John Kay, *Financial Times Weekend*, 29/30 June 2002.

In the case of large businesses, the owners are often divorced from day-to-day control of the business, and professional managers are employed to act on their behalf. This means that the wealth objectives of the owners should become the managers' objectives. However, there is always a risk that these managers will pursue their own interests, such as increasing their pay and 'perks' (for example, expensive cars and lavish offices) at the expense of the owners' interests. This can be a problem for the owners, which may be dealt with, at least in part, by monitoring carefully the actions of managers through the use of regular financial reports. Thus accounting has an important role to play in helping the owners to assess whether the wealth enhancement objective is being pursued.

Though enhancing the wealth of the owners may not be a perfect description of what businesses seek to achieve, it is certainly something that businesses cannot ignore. Unless the owners feel that their wealth is being enhanced there would be little reason for them to continue the business.

For the remainder of this book enhancement/maximisation of owners' wealth is treated as the key objective against which decisions will be assessed. There will usually be other non-financial/non-economic factors that will also tend to bear on decisions. The final decision may well involve some compromise.

Management accounting information and management decisions

If we view accounting as a form of service, then managers can be viewed as the 'clients' of management accounting information. This raises the question as to what kind of information these 'clients' require. Management accounting information is usually required to help managers make decisions that fall within the following broad areas:

● *Developing strategic plans.* Managers are responsible for establishing the mission and objectives of the business and then developing strategic plans to achieve these objectives. Management accounting information can play a valuable role in providing projections that set out the likely financial outcomes from the proposed courses of action. Managers can then use these reports to evaluate each course of action. They can then go on to select the appropriate course(s) of action for inclusion in the strategic plans.

● *Performance evaluation and control.* Having set a particular course of action, managers need to know whether things are going to plan. Actual outcomes will, therefore, be compared with plans to see whether the performance is better or worse than expected. Where there is a significant difference, some investigation should be carried out and corrective action taken where necessary. In this way, the managers may control performance more effectively.

● *Allocating resources.* Resources available to a business are limited and it is the responsibility of managers to try to ensure that they are used in an efficient and effective manner. Decisions concerning such matters as the optimum level of output, the optimum mix of products and the appropriate type of investment in new equipment will all require management accounting information.

● *Determining costs and benefits.* Many management decisions require a knowledge of the costs and benefits of pursuing a particular course of action such as providing a service, or producing a new product or closing down a department. The decision will involve weighing the costs against the benefits. The management accountant can help managers by providing details of particular costs and benefits. In some cases, costs and benefits may be extremely difficult to quantify; however, some approximation is usually better than nothing at all.

These areas of management decision making are set out in Figure 1.6.

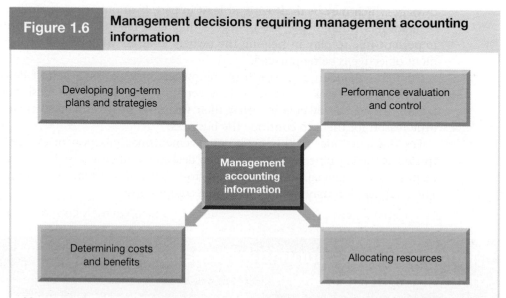

Figure 1.6 **Management decisions requiring management accounting information**

Management accounting information is required to help managers to make decisions in four broad areas: developing long-term plans and strategies, performance evaluation and control, allocating resources and determining costs and benefits.

The changing nature of management accounting

Changes in management practice and the move to strategic management have inevitably led to changes in management accounting. It has had to respond to the changing needs of managers.

Increasingly, successful businesses are those that are able to secure and maintain competitive advantage over their rivals. To obtain such advantage, businesses have become more 'customer driven' (that is, concerned with satisfying customer needs). This has led to a need for management accounting information that provides details of customers and the market such as customer evaluation of services provided and market share. Customer focus has also led to greater concern for quality and for developing new, innovative products.

Many types of management accounting information are not expressed in financial terms.

Activity 1.7

Imagine that you are the manager of a service-providing business. What kinds of non-financial information (that is, information not containing monetary values) may be relevant to help you evaluate:

- The quality of the output (services provided)?
- The level of innovation in developing new products?

The quality of the output may be assessed using the following information:

- Customer perception surveys
- Unsatisfactory services provided as a percentage of total output
- Percentage of services that require reworking.

The level of innovation may be assessed using the following information:

- New products launched over the past two years compared with competitors
- Percentage of total revenue generated by new products
- Time taken to develop new products
- New products launched as a percentage of new product proposals.

You may have thought of other information that may be relevant.

To compete successfully, businesses must also find ways of reducing costs. The cost base of modern businesses is under continual review and this, in turn, has created a need to develop more sophisticated methods of measuring and controlling costs. It has also created a need for information about the costs incurred by rival businesses. These costs can be used as 'benchmarks' by which to gauge competitiveness.

The changes described above have meant that management accounting has become more outward-looking in its focus. In the past, information provided to managers has been largely restricted to that collected within the business. However, the attitude and behaviour of customers and rival businesses have now become the object of much information gathering. The changes have also meant that management accounting has become increasingly concerned with non-financial reporting such as quality, product innovation, product cycle times, delivery times and so on.

Activity 1.8

It can be argued that non-financial measures, such as those mentioned above, do not, strictly speaking, fall within the scope of accounting information and, therefore, could (or should) be provided by others. What do you think?

It is true that this kind of information need not be collected by the management accounting system. The reason for it to be regarded as management accounting is, perhaps, that the accounting system is often regarded as the most important element of the management information system and it can be readily adapted so as to provide a broad range of information necessary for economic decisions. The boundaries of accounting are not fixed and so it is possible to argue that this kind of information should be collected by the management information system, as it is often linked inextricably to financial outcomes.

Management accounting and human behaviour

It is important to appreciate that management accounting information is intended to have an effect on the behaviour of those working in the business. Unfortunately, the behaviour change caused by management accounting is not always beneficial. One possible effect is that managers and employees will concentrate their attention and efforts on the aspects of the business that are being measured and will give much less attention to the items that are not. It is said that 'the things that count are the things that get counted'. This rather narrow view, however, can have undesirable consequences for the business.

Undesirable consequences can often arise where a particular measure is being used, or is perceived as being used, as a basis for evaluating performance (see Activity 1.9).

The management accountant must be aware of the impact of accounting measures of performance on human behaviour. When designing accounting measures, it is important to try to ensure that all key aspects of performance are taken into account, even though certain aspects may be difficult to measure. When operating an accounting measurement system, it is important to be alert to behaviour aimed at manipulating particular measures rather than achieving the goals to which they relate.

Activity 1.9

The manager of a department has been allocated an amount of money to spend on staff training. How might the manager's focus on 'the things that get counted' result in undesirable consequences?

To demonstrate cost consciousness, the manager may underspend during the period by cutting back on staff training and development. Though the effect on expenditure incurred may be favourable, the effect on staff morale and longer-term profitability may be extremely unfavourable for the business. These unfavourable effects may go unrecognised, at least in the short term, where the expenditure limit is the focus of attention.

Attempts may be made to manipulate a particular measure where it is seen as important. For example, a manager may continue to use old, fully depreciated, pieces of equipment to keep depreciation charges low and, therefore, boost profits. This may be done despite knowledge that the purchase of new equipment would produce higher-quality products and help to increase sales over the longer term. Attempts at manipulation are often related to managers' rewards. For example, profit-related bonuses may provide the incentive to manipulate reported profits in the way described.

In some cases, the particular targets against which performance is measured are the objects of manipulation. For example, a sales manager may provide a deliberately low forecast of the size of the potential market for the next period if he or she believes that the forecast will form the basis of future sales targets. This may be done either to increase rewards (for example, where bonuses are awarded for exceeding sales targets) or to ensure that future sales targets can be achieved with relatively little effort.

Management accounting and information technology

The impact of information technology on the development of management accounting is difficult to overstate. The ability of information technology to process large amounts of information means that routine reports can be produced quickly and accurately. This is vital to businesses operating in a competitive environment as they cannot risk the damage to competitive advantage that may occur where decisions are based on inaccurate and misleading information.

Information technology has allowed management reports to be produced in greater detail and in greater variety than could be contemplated under a manual system. In addition, it has allowed sophisticated measurement systems to be provided at relatively low cost. Managers can use information technology to help assess proposals by allowing variables (such as product price, output, product cost and so on) to be changed easily. By pressing a few keys on a computer keyboard, managers can increase or decrease the size of key variables to create a range of possible scenarios.

The information revolution is gathering pace and so information technology is likely to play an increasingly important role in management accounting in the future. Particularly interesting developments are occurring in the area of financial information evaluation. Computers are becoming more capable of making sophisticated judgements that, in the past, only humans were considered capable of doing. Increasingly, information technology in management accounting is viewed not only as a means of improving the timeliness and accuracy of management reports but also as an important source of competitive advantage.

The changing role of the management accountant

Given the changes described above, it is not surprising that the traditional role of the management accountant within a business has changed. Information technology has released the management accountant from much of the routine work associated with preparation of financial reports. In the past, the management accountant's role has been confined to assisting managers by providing information in the areas discussed earlier. Whilst this role is still vital, management accountants are increasingly seen as part of the management team. As a team member, the management accountant is directly involved in the planning and decision-making process. Thus, management accountants are now working more closely with other managers to improve profit performance.

This expanded role for the management accountant has benefits for the development of management accounting as a discipline. It provides the management accountant with a greater awareness of operational matters and the information needs of managers that can, in turn, improve the quality of information provided by the management accounting system. As a consequence, we can see increasing evidence that management accounting systems are being designed to fit the particular structure and processes of the business rather than the other way round.

The changes identified are largely in response to changes in the external environment in which management accounting exists. Given the increasing rate of change in the external environment, we can expect management accounting to change at an even faster pace in the future.

SUMMARY

The main points of this chapter may be summarised as follows:

What is accounting?

● Accounting provides financial information for a range of users to help them make better judgements and decisions concerning a business.

Accounting and user needs

● For accounting to be useful, there must be a clear understanding of *for whom* and *for what purpose* the information will be used.
● Accounting can be viewed as a form of service as it involves providing financial information required by the various users.
● To provide a useful service, accounting must possess certain qualities, or characteristics. These are relevance, reliability, comparability and understandability. In addition, accounting information must be material.
● Providing a service to users can be costly and financial information should be produced only if the cost of providing the information is less than the benefits gained.

Accounting information

● Accounting is part of the total information system within a business. It shares the features that are common to all information systems within a business, which are the identification, recording, analysis and reporting of information.
● Managers are among the most important users of financial information, and they use financial information in planning and controlling business activities.

Management and financial accounting

● Accounting has two main strands – management accounting and financial accounting.
● Management accounting seeks to meet the needs of the business's managers and financial accounting seeks to meet the needs of the other user groups.
● These two strands differ in terms of the types of reports produced, the level of reporting detail, the time horizon, the degree of standardisation and the range and quality of information provided.

Strategic management

● The move to strategic management has been caused by the changing and more competitive nature of business.

- Strategic management involves five steps:
  1 Establish mission and objectives.
  2 Undertake a position analysis (for example, a SWOT analysis).
  3 Identify and assess strategic options.
  4 Select strategic options.
  5 Perform, review and control.

A key financial objective is to enhance/maximise owners' (shareholders') wealth.

Role of management accounting

- Develop strategic plans.
- Performance evaluation and control.
- Allocating resources.
- Determining costs and benefits.

Changing nature of management accounting

- More externally focused.
- Uses more non-financial information.
- Focuses on cost control.

Management accounting and human behaviour

- The main purpose of accounting is to affect people's behaviour.
- This effect is not always beneficial.

Management accounting and IT

- IT has a major impact on the feasibility of providing information.

Changing role of management accountant

- Less time is spent preparing reports.
- The management accountant is now a key member of the management team.

→ Key terms

Accounting p. 2	Accounting information system p. 9
Relevance p. 6	Management accounting p. 11
Reliability p. 6	Financial accounting p. 11
Comparability p. 6	Strategic management p. 13
Understandability p. 6	Position analysis p. 14
Materiality p. 7	SWOT analysis p. 14

Further reading

If you would like to explore the topics covered in this chapter in more depth, we recommend the following books:

Management Accounting, *Atkinson A., Banker R., Kaplan R. and Young S.*, 3rd edn, Prentice Hall, 2001, chapter 1.

Management and Cost Accounting, *Drury C.*, 5th edn, Thomson Learning, 2000, chapter 1.

Cost Accounting: A managerial emphasis, *Horngren C., Foster G. and Datar S.*, 11th edn, Prentice Hall, 2002, chapter 1.

REVIEW QUESTIONS

Answers to these questions can be found on the students' side of the Companion Website at www.pearsoned.co.uk/atrillmclaney.

1.1 Identify the main users of accounting information for a university. Do these users differ very much from the users of accounting information for private-sector businesses? Is there a difference in the ways in which accounting information for a university would be used compared with that of a private-sector business?

1.2 Management accounting has been described as 'the eyes and ears of management'. What do you think this expression means?

1.3 Assume that you are a manager considering the launch of a new service. What accounting information might be useful to help in making a decision?

1.4 'Accounting information should be understandable. As some managers have a poor knowledge of accounting we should produce simplified financial reports to help them.' To what extent do you agree with this view?

EXERCISES

Exercise 1.2 is more advanced than 1.1. Both have answers at the back of the book.

1.1 You have been speaking to a friend who owns a small business and she has said that she has read something about strategic management and that no modern business can afford not to get involved with it. Your friend has little idea what strategic management involves.

Required:
Briefly outline the steps in strategic management, summarising what each step tends to involve.

1.2 Jones Dairy Ltd (Jones) operates a 'doorstep' fresh milk delivery service. Two brothers carried on the business that they inherited from their father in the early 1960s. They are the business's only directors. The business operates from a yard on the outskirts of Trepont, a substantial town in mid-Wales.

Jones expanded steadily from when the brothers took over until the early 1980s, by which time it employed 25 full-time rounds staff. This was achieved because of four factors: (i) some expansion of the permanent population of Trepont, (ii) expanding Jones's geographical range to the villages surrounding the town, (iii) an expanding tourist trade in the area and (iv) through a positive attitude to 'marketing'.

As an example of the marketing effort, when new residents move into the area, the member of the rounds staff concerned reports this back. One of the directors immediately visits the potential customer with an introductory gift, usually a bottle of milk, a bottle of wine and a bunch of flowers, and attempts to obtain a regular milk order. Similar methods are used to persuade existing residents to place orders for delivered milk.

By the mid-1980s Jones had a monopoly of doorstep delivery in the Trepont area. A combination of losing market share to Jones and the town's relative remoteness had discouraged the national doorstep suppliers. The little, locally-based competition there once was had gone out of business.

Supplies of milk come from a bottling plant, owned by one of the national dairy companies, which is located 50 miles from Trepont. The bottlers deliver nightly, except Saturday nights, to Jones's depot. Jones delivers daily, except on Sundays.

Profits, after adjusting for inflation, have fallen since the early 1980s. Sales volumes have fallen by about a third, compared with a decline of about 50 per cent for doorstep deliveries nationally over the same period. New customers are increasingly difficult to find, despite a continuing policy of encouraging them. Many existing customers tend to have less milk delivered. A sufficient profit has been made to enable the directors to enjoy a reasonable income compared with their needs, but only by raising prices. Currently Jones charges 40p for a standard pint, delivered. This is fairly typical of doorstep delivery charges around the UK. The Trepont supermarket, which is located in the centre of town, charges 26p a pint and other local stores charge between 35p and 40p.

Currently Jones employs 15 full-time rounds staff, a van maintenance mechanic, a secretary/ bookkeeper and the two directors. Jones is regarded locally as a good employer. Regular employment opportunities in the area are generally few. Rounds staff are expected to, and generally do, give customers a friendly, cheerful and helpful service.

The two brothers continue to be the only shareholders and directors and comprise the only level of management. One of the directors devotes most of his time to dealing with the supplier and with issues connected with details of the rounds. The other director looks after administrative matters, such as the accounts and personnel issues. Both directors undertake rounds to cover for sickness and holidays.

Required:
As far as the information given in the question will allow, undertake an analysis of the strengths, weaknesses, opportunities and threats (SWOT analysis) of the business.

2

Relevant costs for decision making

OBJECTIVES

When you have completed this chapter, you should be able to:

● Define and distinguish between relevant costs, outlay costs and opportunity costs.

● Identify and quantify the costs that are relevant to a particular decision.

● Use the relevant costs to make decisions.

● Set out the analysis in a logical form so that the conclusion may be communicated to managers.

INTRODUCTION

This chapter considers the identification and use of costs in making management decisions. These decisions should be made in a way that will promote the business's achievement of its strategic objective. We shall see that not all of the costs that appear to be linked to a particular business decision are relevant to it. It is important to distinguish carefully between costs (and revenues) that are relevant and those that are not. Failure to do this could well lead to bad decisions being made. The principles outlined here will provide the basis for much of the rest of the book.

What is meant by 'cost'?

Let us begin this chapter by asking 'what is meant by cost?' The answer to this question may seem, at first sight, very obvious. Many people might say that **cost** is how much was paid for an item of goods being supplied or a service being provided. However, the following activity illustrates that the definition of 'cost' is not always as obvious as might first be thought.

Activity 2.1

Let us assume that you own a motor car, for which you paid a purchase price of £5,000 – much below the list price – at a recent car auction. You have just been offered £6,000 for this car.

What is the cost to you of keeping the car for your own use? *Note*: Ignore running costs and so on; just consider the 'capital' cost of the car.

By retaining the car, you are forgoing an offer of £6,000. Thus, the real sacrifice, or cost, incurred by keeping the car for your own use is £6,000. Any decision that you make with respect to the car's future should logically take account of this figure. This cost is known as the 'opportunity cost' since it is the value of the opportunity forgone in order to pursue the other course of action. (In this case, the other course of action is to retain the car.)

We can see that the cost of retaining the car is not the same as the purchase price. In one sense, of course, the cost of the car in Activity 2.1 is £5,000 because that is how much was paid for it. However, this cost, which for obvious reasons is known as the **historic cost**, is only of academic interest. It cannot logically ever be used to make a decision on the car's future. If we disagree with this point, we should ask ourselves how we should assess an offer of £5,500, from another person, for the car. The answer is that we should compare the offer price of £5,500 with the **opportunity cost** of £6,000. This should lead us to reject the offer as it is less than the £6,000 opportunity cost. In these circumstances, it would not be logical to accept the offer of £5,500 on the basis that it was more than the £5,000 that we originally paid. (The only other figure that should concern us is the value to us, in terms of pleasure, usefulness and so on, of retaining the car. If we valued this more highly than the £6,000 opportunity cost, we should reject both offers.)

We may still feel, however, that the £5,000 is relevant here because it will help us in assessing the profitability of the decision. If we sold the car, we will make a profit of either £500 (£5,500 – £5,000) or £1,000 (£6,000 – £5,000) depending on which offer we accept. Since we should seek to make the higher profit, the right decision is to sell the car for £6,000. However, we do not need to know the historic cost of the car to make the right decision. What decision should we make if the car cost us £4,000 to buy? Clearly we should still sell the car for £6,000 rather than for £5,500 as the important comparison is between the offer price and the opportunity cost. We should reach the same conclusion whatever the historic cost of the car.

To emphasise the above point, let us assume that the car cost £10,000. Even in this case the historic cost would still be irrelevant. Had we just bought a car for £10,000 and found that shortly after it is only worth £6,000, we may well be fuming with rage at our mistake, but this does not make the £10,000 a **relevant cost**. The only relevant factors, in a decision on whether to sell the car or to keep it, are the £6,000 opportunity cost and the value of the benefits of keeping it. Thus, the historic cost can never be relevant to a future decision.

Historic cost is normally used in accounting statements, like the balance sheet and the profit and loss account (income statement). This is logical, however, since these statements are intended to be accounts of what has actually happened and are drawn up after the event. In the context of decision making, which is always related to the future, historic cost is always irrelevant.

Real World 2.1 gives an example of a decision made by Manchester United.

REAL WORLD 2.1

Transferring players: a game of two halves

In August 2003, Manchester United Football Club transferred one of its midfield players, Juan Sebastian Veron, to Chelsea Football Club for a reported £15m. Manchester United had purchased the player's services two years earlier for a reported club transfer record of £28.1m. As the transfer price to Chelsea Football Club was only a little more than half of the amount originally paid, Manchester United made a huge loss on the transaction. However, the offer of £15m from Chelsea must have been greater than the sacrifice, or cost, of losing Veron's services for Manchester United to agree to the transfer. The original amount paid for the player's services should not have been an issue in arriving at the agreed transfer price.

To say that historic cost is an **irrelevant cost** is not to say that *the effects of having incurred that cost* are always irrelevant. The fact that we own the car, and are thus in a position to exercise choice as to how to use it, is not irrelevant.

It might be useful to formalise what we have discussed so far.

A definition of cost

Cost may be defined as the amount of resources, usually measured in monetary terms, sacrificed to achieve a particular objective.

The objective might be to retain a car, to buy a particular house, to make a particular product or to render a particular service.

Relevant costs: opportunity and outlay costs

We have just seen that, when we are making decisions concerning the future, **past costs** (that is, historic costs) are irrelevant. It is future opportunity costs and future **outlay costs** that are of concern. An opportunity cost can be defined as the value in monetary terms of being deprived of the next best opportunity in order to pursue the particular objective. An outlay cost is an amount of money that will have to be spent to achieve that objective. We shall shortly meet plenty of examples of both of these types of future cost.

To be relevant to a particular decision, a future outlay cost, or opportunity cost, must satisfy both of the following criteria:

- *It must relate to the objectives of the business.* Most businesses have maximising owners' (shareholders') wealth as their key strategic objective. That is to say, they are seeking to become richer (see Chapter 1). Thus, to be relevant to a particular decision, a cost must have an effect on the wealth of the business.
- *It must differ from one possible decision outcome to the next.* Only costs (and revenues) that are different between outcomes can be used to distinguish between them. Thus the reason that the historic cost of the car that we discussed earlier, is irrelevant, is that it is the same whichever decision is taken about the future of the car. This means that all past costs are irrelevant because what has happened in the past must be the same for all possible future outcomes.

It is not only past costs that are the same from one decision outcome to the next; some future costs may also be the same. Take, for example, a road haulage business that has decided that it will buy a new lorry and the decision lies between two different models. The load capacity, the fuel and maintenance costs are different for each lorry. The potential costs and revenues associated with these are relevant items. The lorry will require a driver, so the business will need to employ one, but a suitably qualified driver could drive either lorry equally well, for the same wage. The cost of employing the driver is thus irrelevant to the decision as to which lorry to buy. This is despite the fact that this cost is a future one.

If, however, the decision did not concern a choice between two models of lorry but rather whether to operate an additional lorry or not, the cost of employing the additional driver would be relevant, because it would then be a cost that would vary with the decision made.

Activity 2.2

A garage has an old car that it bought several months ago for £3,000. The car needs a replacement engine before it can be sold. It is possible to buy a reconditioned engine for £300. This would take seven hours to fit by a mechanic who is paid £8 an hour. At present the garage is short of work, but the owners are reluctant to lay off any mechanics or even to cut down their basic working week because skilled labour is difficult to find and an upturn in repair work is expected soon.

Without the engine the car could be sold for an estimated £3,500. What is the minimum price at which the garage should sell the car with a reconditioned engine fitted?

The minimum price is the amount required to cover the relevant costs of the job. At this price, the business will make neither a profit nor a loss. Any price lower than this amount will mean that the wealth of the business is reduced. Thus, the minimum price is:

	£
Opportunity cost of the car	3,500
Cost of the reconditioned engine	300
Total	3,800

The original cost of the car is irrelevant for reasons that have already been discussed: it is the opportunity cost of the car that concerns us. The cost of the new engine is relevant

Activity 2.2 continued

because, if the work is done, the garage will have to pay £300 for the engine; but will pay nothing if the job is not done. The £300 is an example of a future outlay cost.

The labour cost is irrelevant because the same cost will be incurred whether the mechanic undertakes the work or not. This is because the mechanic is being paid to do nothing if this job is not undertaken; thus the additional labour cost arising from this job is zero.

It should be emphasised that the garage will not seek to sell the car with its reconditioned engine for £3,800; it will attempt to charge as much as possible for it. However, any price above the £3,800 will make the garage better off financially than not undertaking the engine replacement.

Activity 2.3

Assume exactly the same circumstances as in Activity 2.2, except that the garage is quite busy at the moment. If a mechanic is to be put on the engine-replacement job, it will mean that other work that the mechanic could have done during the seven hours, all of which could be charged to a customer, will not be undertaken. The garage's labour charge is £20 an hour, though the mechanic is only paid £8 an hour.

What is the minimum price at which the garage should sell the car, with a reconditioned engine fitted, under these altered circumstances?

The minimum price is:

	£
Opportunity cost of the car	3,500
Cost of the reconditioned engine	300
Labour cost (7 × £20)	140
Total	3,940

We can see that the opportunity cost of the car and the cost of the engine are the same as in Activity 2.2 but now a charge for labour has been added to obtain the minimum price. The relevant labour cost here is that which the garage will have to sacrifice in making the time available to undertake the engine replacement job. While the mechanic is working on this job, the garage is losing the opportunity to do work for which a customer would pay £140. Note that the £8 an hour mechanic's wage is still not relevant. The mechanic will be paid £8 an hour irrespective of whether it is the engine-replacement work or some other job that is undertaken.

Activity 2.4

A business is considering making a bid to undertake a contract. Fulfilment of the contract will require the use of two types of raw material, both of which are held in stock by the business. All of the stock (inventory) of these two raw materials will need to be used on the contract. Information on the stock required is as follows:

Stock item	Quantity units	Historic cost £/unit	Sales value £/unit	Replacement cost £/unit
A1	500	5	3	6
B2	800	7	8	10

Stock item A1 is in frequent use in the business on a variety of work. The stock of item B2 was bought a year ago for a contract that was abandoned. It has recently become obvious that there is no likelihood of ever using this stock if the contract currently being considered does not proceed.

Management wishes to deduce the minimum price at which the business could undertake the contract without reducing its wealth as a result. This can be used as the baseline in deducing the bid price.

How much should be included in the minimum price in respect of the two stock items detailed above?

The relevant costs to be included in the minimum price are:

Stock (inventory) item: A1   £6 × 500 = £3,000
                             B2   £8 × 800 = £6,400

We are told that the stock of item A1 is in frequent use and so, if it is used on the contract, it will need to be replaced. Sooner or later, the business will have to buy 500 units (currently costing £6 a unit) additional to those which would have been required had the contract not been undertaken.

We are told that the stock of item B2 will never be used by the business unless the contract is undertaken. Thus, if the contract is not undertaken, the only reasonable thing for the business to do is to sell the stock. This means that if the contract is undertaken and the stock is used, it will have an opportunity cost equal to the potential proceeds from disposal, which is £8 a unit.

Note that the historic cost information about both materials is irrelevant and this will always be the case.

Activity 2.5

HLA Ltd is in the process of preparing a quotation for a special job for a customer. The job will have the following material requirements:

Material	Units required	Units currently held in stock		
		Quantity held	Historic cost £/unit	Sales value £/unit	Replacement cost £/unit

Material	Units required	Quantity held	Historic cost £/unit	Sales value £/unit	Replacement cost £/unit
P	400	0	–	–	40
Q	230	100	62	50	64
R	350	200	48	23	59
S	170	140	33	12	49
T	120	120	40	0	68

→

Activity 2.5 continued

Material Q is used consistently by the business on various jobs. Materials R, S and T are in stock as the result of previous overbuying. No other use can be found for R, but the 140 units of S could be used in another job as a substitute for 225 units of material V that are about to be purchased at a price of £10 a unit. Material T has no other use, it is difficult to store and the business has been informed that it will cost £160 to dispose of the material currently in stock.

What is the relevant cost of the materials for the job specified above?

The relevant cost is as follows:

	£
Material P	
This will have to be purchased at £40 a unit (400 × £40)	16,000
Material Q	
This will have to be replaced, therefore, the relevant price is (230 × £64)	14,720
Material R	
200 units of this are in stock and could be sold. The relevant price of these is the sales revenue foregone (200 × £23)	4,600
The remaining 150 units of R would have to be purchased (150 × £59)	8,850
Material S	
This could be sold or used as a substitute for material V.	
The existing stock (inventory) could be sold for £1,680 (140 × £12), however, the saving on material V is higher and therefore should be taken as the relevant amount (225 × £10)	2,250
The remaining units of material S must be purchased (30 × £49)	1,470
A saving on disposal will be made if material T is used	(160)
Total relevant cost	47,730

Sunk costs and committed costs

When trying to identify relevant costs for a particular decision, we may come across the terms **sunk cost** and **committed cost**. In order to deal with such costs we need to understand what these terms mean. A sunk cost is simply another way of saying past cost and the two expressions can be used interchangeably. A committed cost is also, in effect, a past cost to the extent that an irrevocable decision has been made to incur the cost because, for example, the business has entered into a binding contract. As a result, it is more or less a past cost despite the fact that the cash may not be paid in respect of it until some point in the future. Since the business has no choice as to whether it incurs the cost or not, a committed cost can never be a relevant cost.

It is important to remember that, to be relevant, a cost must be capable of varying according to the decision made. If the business is already committed by a legally binding contract to a cost, that cost cannot vary with the decision.

Figure 2.1 summarises the relationship between relevant, irrelevant, opportunity, outlay and past costs.

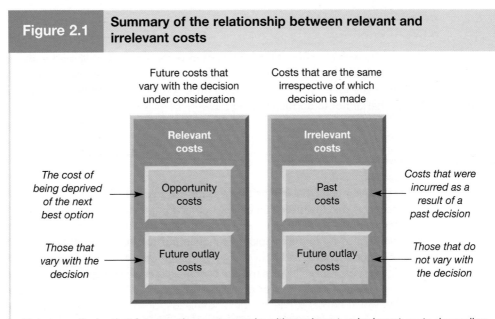

| Figure 2.1 | **Summary of the relationship between relevant and irrelevant costs** |

Note in particular that future outlay costs may be either relevant or irrelevant costs depending on whether they vary with the decision. Future opportunity costs and outlay costs, which vary with the decision, are relevant; future outlay costs, which do not vary with the decision, and all past costs, are irrelevant.

Activity 2.6

Past costs are irrelevant costs. Does this mean that what happened in the past is irrelevant?

No, it does not mean this. The fact that the business has an asset that it can deploy in the future is highly relevant. What is not relevant is how much it cost to acquire that asset. This point was examined in the discussion that followed Activity 2.1.

Another reason why the past is not irrelevant is that it generally – though not always – provides us with our best guide to the future. Suppose that we need to estimate the cost of doing something in the future to help us to decide whether it is worth doing. In these circumstances our own experience, or that of others, on how much it has cost to do the thing in the past may provide us with a valuable guide to how much it is likely to cost in the future.

Qualitative factors of decisions

Though businesses must look closely at the obvious financial effects when making decisions, they must also consider factors that are not directly economic. These are likely to be factors that have a broader, but less immediate, impact on the business. Ultimately, however, these factors are likely to have economic effect – that is, to affect the wealth of the business.

Activity 2.7

Activity 2.3 was concerned with the cost of putting a car into a marketable condition. Apart from whether the car could be sold for more than the relevant cost of doing this, are there any other factors that should be taken into account in making a decision as to whether or not to do the work?

We can think of three points:

- Turning away another job in order to do the engine replacement may lead to customer dissatisfaction.
- On the other hand, having the car available for sale may be useful commercially for the garage, beyond the profit that can be earned from that particular car sale. For example, having a good stock (inventory) of second-hand cars may attract potential customers.
- There is also a more immediate economic point. It has been assumed that the only labour opportunity cost is the charge-out rate for the seven hours concerned. In practice, most car repairs involve the use of some materials and spare parts. These are usually charged to customers at a profit to the garage. Any such profit from a job turned away would be lost to the garage, and this lost profit would be an opportunity cost of the engine replacement and should, therefore, be included in the calculation of the minimum price to be charged for the sale of the car.

You may have thought of additional points.

It is important to consider 'qualitative' factors carefully. They can seem unimportant because they are virtually impossible to assess in terms of their ultimate economic effect. This effect can nevertheless be very significant.

Self-assessment question 2.1

JB Limited is a small specialist manufacturer of electronic components. Makers of aircraft, for both civil and military purposes, use much of its output. One of the aircraft makers has offered a contract to JB Limited for the supply, over the next 12 months, of 400 identical components. The data relating to the production of each component are as follows:

(i) *Material requirements*:
   3 kg of material M1 (see note 1 below)
   2 kg of material P2 (see note 2 below)
   1 part no. 678 (see note 3 below)

   Note 1: Material M1 is in continuous use by the business; 1,000 kg are currently held in stock. Their original cost was £4.70/kg, but it is known that future purchases will cost £5.50/kg.

   Note 2: 1,200 kg of material P2 are held in stock. The original cost of this material was £4.30/kg. The material has not been required for the last two years. Its scrap value is £1.50/kg. The only foreseeable alternative use is as a substitute for material P4 (in constant use) but this would involve further processing costs of £1.60/kg. The current cost of material P4 is £3.60/kg.

   Note 3: It is estimated that part no. 678 could be bought in for £50 each.

(ii) *Labour requirements*: Each component would require five hours of skilled labour and five hours of semi-skilled. A skilled employee is available and is currently paid £7/hour. A replacement would, however, have to be obtained at a rate of £6/hour for the work, which would otherwise be done by the skilled employee. The current rate for semi-skilled work is £5/hour and an additional employee could be appointed for this work.

(iii) *General manufacturing costs*: It is JB Limited's policy to charge a share of the general costs (rent, heating and so on) to each contract undertaken at the rate of £20 for each machine-hour used on the contract. If the contract is undertaken, the general costs are expected to increase as a result of undertaking the contract by £3,200.

Spare machine capacity is available and each component would require four machine hours. A price of £150 a component has been offered by the potential customer.

Required:

(a) Should the contract be accepted? Support your conclusion with appropriate figures to present to management.

(b) What other factors ought management to consider that might influence the decision?

SUMMARY

The main points in this chapter may be summarised as follows:

Cost = amount of resources, usually measured in monetary terms, sacrificed to achieve a particular objective.

Relevant costs must

- Relate to the objective being pursued by the business.
- Differ from one possible decision output to the next.

Relevant costs therefore include

- Opportunity costs.
- Differential future outlay costs.

Irrelevant costs therefore include

- All past (or sunk) costs.
- All committed costs.
- Non-differential outlay costs.

Financial/economic decisions almost inevitably have qualitative aspects that financial analysis cannot really handle, despite their importance.

→ Key terms

Cost p. 27	**Past cost** p. 28
Historic cost p. 27	**Outlay cost** p. 28
Opportunity cost p. 27	**Sunk cost** p. 32
Relevant cost p. 27	**Committed cost** p. 32
Irrelevant cost p. 28	

Further reading

If you would like to explore the topics covered in this chapter in more depth, we recommend the following books:

Accounting for Management Decisions, *Arnold J. and Turley S.*, 3rd edn, Prentice Hall International, 1996, chapter 9.

Management and Cost Accounting, *Drury C.*, 5th edn, Thomson Learning Business Press, 2000, chapter 9.

Cost Accounting: A managerial emphasis, *Horngren C., Foster G. and Datar S.*, 11th edn, Prentice Hall International, 2002, chapter 11.

Cost and Management Accounting, *Williamson D.*, Prentice Hall International, 1996, chapter 12.

REVIEW QUESTIONS

Answers to these questions can be found on the students' side of the Companion Website at **www.pearsoned.co.uk/atrillmclaney**.

2.1 To be relevant to a particular decision, a cost must have two attributes. What are they?

2.2 Distinguish between a sunk cost and an opportunity cost.

2.3 Define the word 'cost' in the context of management accounting.

2.4 What is meant by the expression 'committed cost'? How do committed costs arise?

EXERCISES

Exercises 2.7 and 2.8 are more advanced than 2.1 to 2.6. Those with coloured numbers have answers at the back of the book.

2.1 Lombard Ltd has been offered a contract for which there is available production capacity. The contract is for 20,000 identical items, manufactured by an intricate assembly operation, to be produced and delivered in the next financial year at a price of £80 each. The specification for one item is as follows:

Assembly labour	4 hours
Component X	4 units
Component Y	3 units

There would also be the need to hire equipment, for the duration of the contract, at an outlay cost of £200,000.

The assembly is a highly skilled operation and the workforce is currently underutilised. It is the business's policy to retain this workforce on full pay in anticipation of high demand in a few years' time, for a new product currently being developed. Skilled workers are paid £10 an hour.

Component X is used in a number of other subassemblies produced by the business. It is readily available. A stock (inventory) of 50,000 units of component X is currently held. Component Y was a special purchase in anticipation of an order that did not in the end materialise. It is, therefore, surplus to requirements and 100,000 units that are in stock may have to be sold at a loss. An estimate of alternative values for components X and Y provided by the materials planning department is as follows:

	X £/unit	Y £/unit
Historic cost	4	10
Replacement cost	5	11
Net realisable value	3	8

It is estimated that any additional relevant costs associated with the contract (beyond the above) will amount to £8 an item.

Required:

Analyse the information in order to advise Lombard Ltd on the desirability of the contract.

2.2   The local authority of a small town maintains a theatre and arts centre for the use of a local repertory company, other visiting groups and exhibitions. Management decisions are taken by a committee that meets regularly to review the financial statements and to plan the use of the facilities.

The theatre employs a full-time staff and a number of artistes at costs of £4,800 and £17,600 a month, respectively. They mount a new production every month for 20 performances. Other monthly costs of the theatre are as follows:

	£
Costumes	2,800
Scenery	1,650
Heat and light	5,150
A share of the administration costs of local authority	8,000
Casual staff	1,760
Refreshments	1,180

On average the theatre is half full for the performances of the repertory company. The capacity and seat prices in the theatre are:

200 seats at £12 each
500 seats at £8 each
300 seats at £6 each

In addition, the theatre sells refreshments during the performances for £3,880 a month. Programme sales cover their costs but advertising in the programme generates £3,360 a month.

The management committee has been approached by a popular touring group, which would like to take over the theatre for one month (25 performances). The group is prepared to pay half of its ticket income for the booking. It expects to fill the theatre for 10 nights and achieve two-thirds capacity on the remaining 15 nights. The prices charged are £1 less than normally applies in the theatre.

The local authority will pay for heat and light costs and will still honour the contracts of all artistes and pay the full-time employees who will sell refreshments, programmes and so on. The committee does not expect any change in the level of refreshments or programme sales if they agree to this booking.

Note: The committee includes the share of the local authority administration costs when making profit calculations. It assumes occupancy applies equally across all seat prices.

Required:

(a) On financial grounds should the management committee agree to the approach from the touring group? Support your answer with appropriate workings.

(b) What other factors may have a bearing on the decision by the committee?

2.3   Andrews and Co. Ltd has been invited to tender for a contract. It is to produce 10,000 metres of a cable in which the business specialises. The estimating department of the business has produced the following information relating to the contract:

● *Materials*:   The cable will require a steel core, which the business buys in. The steel core is to be coated with a special plastic, also bought in, using a special process. Plastic for the covering will be required at the rate of 0.10 kg/metre of completed cable.

● *Direct labour*: – Skilled: 10 minutes/metre
                        – Unskilled: 5 minutes/metre

The business already has sufficient stock of each of the materials required, to complete the contract. Information on the cost of the stock is as follows:

	Steel core £/metre	Plastic £/kg
Historic cost	1.50	0.60
Current buying-in cost	2.10	0.70
Scrap value	1.40	0.10

The steel core is in constant use by the business for a variety of work that it regularly undertakes. The plastic is a surplus from a previous contract where a mistake was made and an excess quantity ordered. If the current contract does not go ahead, this plastic will be scrapped.

Unskilled labour, which is paid at the rate of £5 an hour, will need to be taken on specifically to undertake the contract. The business is fairly quiet at the moment which means that a pool of skilled labour exists that will still be employed at full pay of £7 an hour to do nothing if the contract does not proceed. The pool of skilled labour is sufficient to complete the contract.

Required:
Indicate the minimum price at which the contract could be undertaken, such that the business would be neither better nor worse off as a result of doing it.

2.4 SJ Services Ltd has been asked to quote a price for a special contract to render a service that will take the business one week to complete. Information relating to labour for the contract is as follows:

Grade of labour	Hours required	Basic rate/hour
Skilled	27	£9
Semi-skilled	14	£7
Unskilled	20	£5

A shortage of skilled labour means that the necessary staff to undertake the contract would have to be moved from other work that is currently yielding an excess of sales revenue over labour and other costs of £8 an hour.

Semi-skilled labour is currently being paid at semi-skilled rates to undertake unskilled work. If the relevant members of staff are moved to work on the contract, unskilled labour will have to be employed for the week to replace them.

The unskilled labour actually needed to work on the contract will be specifically employed for the week of the contract.

All labour is charged to contracts at 50 per cent above the rate paid to the employees, so as to cover the contract's fair share of the business's overheads. It is estimated that these will increase by £50 as a result of undertaking the contract.

Undertaking the contract will require the use of a specialised machine for the week. The business owns such a machine, which it depreciates at the rate of £120 a week. This machine is currently being hired out to another business at a weekly rental of £175 on a week-by-week contract.

To derive the above estimates, the business has had to spend £300 on a specialised study. If the contract does not proceed, the results of the study can be sold for £250.

An estimate of the contract's fair share of the business's rent is £150 a week.

Required:
Deduce the minimum price at which SJ Services Ltd could undertake the contract such that it would be neither better nor worse off as a result of undertaking it.

2.5 A business in the food industry is currently holding 2,000 tonnes of material in bulk storage. This material deteriorates with time, and so in the near future it needs to be repackaged for sale or sold in its present form.

The stock was acquired in two batches: 800 tonnes at a price of £40 a tonne and 1,200 tonnes at a price of £44 a tonne. The current market price of any additional purchases is £48 a tonne. If the business were to dispose of the material, it could sell any quantity but only for £36 a tonne; it does not have the contacts or reputation to command a higher price.

Repackaging this bulk material may be undertaken to develop either Product A or Product X. No weight loss occurs with repackaging, that is, one tonne of material will make one tonne of A or X. For Product A, there is an additional cost of £60 a tonne, after which it will sell for £105 a tonne. The marketing department estimates that 500 tonnes could be sold in this way.

In the development of Product X, the business incurs additional costs of £80 a tonne for repackaging. A market price for X is not known and no minimum price has been agreed. The management is currently engaged in discussions over the minimum price that may be charged for Product X in the current circumstances.

Required:
Identify the relevant unit cost for pricing the increments of Product X, given sales volumes of X of:

(a) up to 1,500 tonnes
(b) over 1,500 tonnes, up to 2,000 tonnes
(c) over 2,000 tonnes.

Explain your answer.

2.6   A local education authority is faced with a predicted decline in the demand for school places in its area. It is believed that some schools will have to close in order to remove up to 800 places from current capacity levels. The schools that may face closure are referenced as A, B, C or D. Their details are as follows:

● *School A*. (capacity 200) was built 15 years ago at a cost of £1.2m. It is situated in a 'socially disadvantaged' community area. The authority has been offered £14m for the site by a property developer.
● *School B*. (capacity 500) was built 20 years ago and cost £1m. It was renovated only two years ago at a cost of £3m to improve its facilities. An offer of £8m has been made for the site by a business planning a shopping complex in this affluent part of the town.
● *School C*. (capacity 600) cost £5m to build five years ago. The land for this school is rented from a local business for an annual cost of £300,000.
● *School D*. (800 capacity) cost £7m to build eight years ago; last year £1.5m was spent on an extension. It offers considerable space, which is currently used for sporting events. This factor makes it popular with developers, who have recently offered £9m for the site.

In the accounting system, the local authority depreciates non-current (fixed) assets based on 2 per cent a year on the original cost. It also differentiates between one-off, large items of capital expenditure or revenue, and annually recurring items.

The land rented for School C is based on a 100-year lease. If the school closes, the property reverts immediately to the owner. If School C is not closed, it will require a £3m investment to improve safety at the school.

If School D is closed, it will be necessary to pay £1.8m to adapt facilities at other schools to accommodate the change.

The local authority has a central staff, which includes administrators for each school costing £200,000 a year each, and a chief education officer costing £40,000 a year in total.

Required:
(a) Prepare a summary of the relevant cash flows (costs and revenues, relative to not making any closures) under the following options:
   (i)   closure of D only
   (ii) closure of A and B
   (iii) closure of A and C.

Show separately the one-off effects and annually recurring items, rank the options open to the local authority, and briefly interpret your answer. *Note*: Various approaches are acceptable provided that they are logical.

(b) Identify and comment on any two different types of irrelevant cost contained in the information given.

(c) Discuss other factors that might have a bearing on the decision.

2.7 Rob Otics Ltd, a small business that specialises in building electronic-control equipment, has just received an order from a customer for eight identical robotic units. These will be completed using Rob Otic's own labour force and factory capacity. The product specification prepared by the estimating department shows the following:

- Material and labour requirements for each robotic unit:

Component X	2 a unit
Component Y	1 a unit
Component Z	4 a unit

- Other miscellaneous items:

Assembly labour	25 hours a unit (but see below)
Inspection labour	6 hours a unit

As part of the costing exercise, the business has collected the following information:

- *Component X*. This is a stock item normally held by the business as it is in constant demand. The 10 units currently in stock were invoiced to Rob Otics at £150 a unit, but the sole supplier has announced a price rise of 20 per cent effective immediately. Rob Otics has not yet paid for the items in stock.
- *Component Y*. 25 units are in stock. This component is not normally used by Rob Otics but is in stock because of a cancelled order following the bankruptcy of a customer. The stock originally cost the business £4,000 in total, although Rob Otics has recouped £1,500 from the liquidator. As Rob Otics can see no use for it, the finance director proposes to scrap the 25 units (zero proceeds).
- *Component Z*. This is in regular use by Rob Otics. There is none in stock but an order is about to be sent to a supplier for 75 units, irrespective of this new proposal. The supplier charges £25 a unit on small orders but will reduce the price by 20 per cent to £20 a unit for all units on any order over 100 units.
- *Other miscellaneous items*. These are expected to cost £250 in total.

Assembly labour is currently in short supply in the area and is paid at £10 an hour. If the order is accepted, all necessary labour will have to be transferred from existing work, and other orders will be lost. It is estimated that for each hour transferred to this contract £38 will be lost (calculated as lost sales revenue £60, less materials £12 and labour £10). The production director suggests that, owing to a learning process, the time taken to make each unit will reduce, from 25 hours to make the first one, by one hour a unit made.

Inspection labour can be provided by paying existing personnel overtime which is at a premium of 50 per cent over the standard rate of £12 an hour.

When the business is working out its contract prices, it normally adds an amount equal to £20 for each assembly hour to cover its general costs (such as rent and electricity). To the resulting total, 40 per cent is normally added as a profit mark-up.

Required:

(a) Prepare an estimate of the minimum price that you would recommend Rob Otics Ltd to charge for the proposed contract, and provide explanations for any items included.

(b) Identify any other factors that you would consider before fixing the final price.

2.8 A business places substantial emphasis on customer satisfaction and, to this end, delivers its product in special protective containers. These containers have been made in a department within the business. Management has recently become concerned that this internal supply of containers is very expensive. As a result, outside suppliers have been invited to submit tenders for the provision of these containers. A quote of £250,000 a year has been received for a volume that compares with current internal supply.

An investigation into the internal costs of container manufacture has been undertaken and the following emerges:

(a) The annual cost of material is £120,000, according to the stores records maintained, at actual historic cost. Three-quarters (by cost) of this represents material that is regularly stocked and replenished. The remaining 25 per cent of the material cost is a special foaming chemical that is not used for any other purpose. There are 40 tonnes of this chemical currently held in stock. It was bought in bulk for £750 a tonne. Today's replacement price for this material is £1,050 a tonne but it is unlikely that the business could realise more than £600 a tonne if it had to be disposed of owing to the high handling costs and special transport facilities required.

(b) The annual labour cost is £80,000 for this department, however, most are casual employees or recent starters, and so, if an outside quote was accepted, little redundancy would be payable. There are, however, two long-serving employees who would each accept as a salary £15,000 a year until they reached retirement age in two years' time.

(c) The department manager has a salary of £30,000 a year. The closure of this department would release him to take over another department for which a vacancy is about to be advertised. The salary, status and prospects are similar.

(d) A rental charge of £9,750 a year, based on floor area, is allocated to the containers department. If the department was closed, the floor space released would be used for warehousing and, as a result, the business would give up the tenancy of an existing warehouse for which it is paying £15,750 a year.

(e) The plant cost £162,000 when it was bought five years ago. Its market value now is £28,000 and it could continue for another two years, at which time its market value would have fallen to zero. (The plant depreciates evenly over time.)

(f) Annual plant maintenance costs are £9,900 and allocated general administrative costs £33,750 for the coming year.

Required:
Calculate the annual cost of manufacturing containers for comparison with the quote using relevant figures for establishing the cost or benefit of accepting the quote. Indicate any assumptions or qualifications you wish to make.

3

Cost–volume–profit analysis

OBJECTIVES

When you have completed this chapter, you should be able to:

- Distinguish between fixed costs and variable costs and use this distinction to explain the relationship between costs, volume and profit.

- Prepare a break-even chart and deduce the break-even point for some activity.

- Discuss the weaknesses of break-even analysis.

- Demonstrate the way in which marginal analysis can be used when making short-term decisions.

INTRODUCTION

This chapter is concerned with the relationship between volume of activity, costs and profit. Broadly, costs can be analysed between those that are fixed, relative to the volume of activity, and those that vary with the volume of activity. We shall consider how we can use knowledge of this relationship to make decisions and to assess risk, particularly in the context of short-term decisions. This continues the theme of Chapter 2, but in this chapter we shall be looking at situations where a whole class of costs – fixed costs – can be treated as being irrelevant for decision-making purposes.

The behaviour of costs

We saw in the previous chapter that costs represent the resources that have to be sacrificed to achieve a business objective. The objective may be to make a particular product, to provide a particular service and so on. The costs incurred by a business may be classified in various ways and one important way is according to how they behave in relation to changes in the volume of activity. There are:

● those that are fixed (stay the same) when changes occur to the volume of activity; and
● those that vary according to the volume of activity.

→   These are known as **fixed costs** and **variable costs** respectively.

A restaurant manager's salary would normally provide an example of a fixed cost of operating the restaurant. The cost to the restaurant of buying the raw food would be a typical variable cost of operating the restaurant.

We shall see in this chapter that knowledge of how much of each type of cost is associated with some particular activity can be of great value to the decision maker.

Fixed costs

The way in which fixed costs behave can be shown by preparing a graph that plots the fixed costs of a business against the level of activity, as in Figure 3.1. The distance 0F represents the amount of fixed costs, and this stays the same irrespective of the volume of activity.

Activity 3.1

A business operates a small chain of hairdressing salons. Can you give some examples of costs that are likely to be fixed for this business?

We came up with the following:

● rent
● insurance
● cleaning costs
● staff salaries.

These costs seem likely to be the same irrespective of the number of customers having their hair cut or styled.

Staff salaries and wages are sometimes automatically assumed always to be variable costs. In practice, they tend to be fixed. People are generally not paid according to the volume of output, and it is not normal to dismiss staff when there is a short-term downturn in activity. If there is a long-term downturn in activity, or at least if it looks that way to management, redundancies may occur, with fixed-cost savings. This, however, is true of all costs. If there is seen to be a likely reduction in demand, the business may decide to close some branches and make rental cost savings. Thus 'fixed' does not mean set in stone for all time; it usually means fixed over the short to medium term.

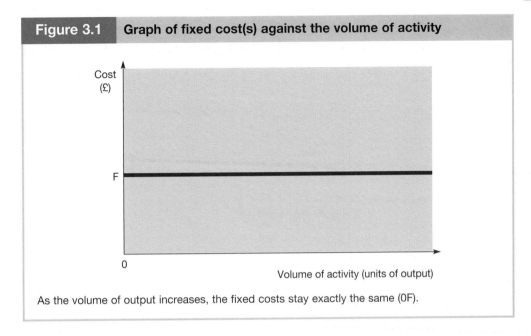

| Figure 3.1 | Graph of fixed cost(s) against the volume of activity |

As the volume of output increases, the fixed costs stay exactly the same (0F).

Nevertheless, in some circumstances, labour costs are variable (for example, where employees are paid according to how much output they produce), but this is unusual.

It is important to be clear that 'fixed', in this context, means only that the cost is not altered by changes in the volume of activity. Fixed costs are likely to be affected by inflation. If rent (a typical fixed cost) goes up because of inflation, a fixed cost will have increased, but not because of a change in the volume of activity.

The level of fixed costs does not stay the same, irrespective of the time period involved. Fixed costs are almost always *time-based*: that is, they vary with the length of time concerned. The rental charge for two months is normally twice that for one month. Thus fixed costs normally vary with time, but (of course) not with the volume of output. We should note that when we talk of fixed costs being, say, £1,000, we must add the period concerned, say, £1,000 a month.

Activity 3.2

Do fixed costs stay the same irrespective of the volume of output, even where there is a massive rise in that volume?
Think in terms of the rent cost for the hairdressing business.

In fact, the rent is only fixed over a particular range (known as the 'relevant' range). If the number of people wanting to have their hair cut by the business increased, and the business wished to meet this increased demand, it would eventually have to expand its physical size. This might be achieved by opening additional branches, or perhaps by moving existing branches to larger premises in the vicinity. It may be possible to cope with relatively minor increases in activity by using existing space more efficiently, or by having longer opening hours. If activity continued to expand, increased rent charges would seem inevitable, however.

In practice, the situation described in Activity 3.2 would look something like Figure 3.2.

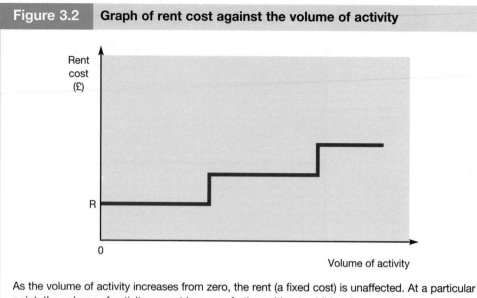

Figure 3.2 **Graph of rent cost against the volume of activity**

As the volume of activity increases from zero, the rent (a fixed cost) is unaffected. At a particular point, the volume of activity cannot increase further without additional space being rented. The cost of renting the additional space will cause a 'step' in the rent cost. The higher rent cost will continue unaffected if volume rises further until eventually another step point is reached.

At lower volumes of activity, the rent cost shown in Figure 3.2 would be 0R. As the volume of activity expands, the accommodation becomes inadequate and further expansion requires an increase in premises and, therefore, cost. This higher level of accommodation provision will enable further expansion to take place. Eventually, further costs will need to be incurred if further expansion is to occur. Fixed costs that behave like this are often referred to as **stepped fixed costs**.

Variable costs

We saw earlier that variable costs are costs that vary with the volume of activity. In a manufacturing business, for example, this would include raw materials used.

Variable costs can be represented graphically as in Figure 3.3. At zero volume of activity the variable cost is zero. The cost increases in a straight line as activity increases.

Activity 3.3

Can you think of some examples of variable costs in the hairdressing business?

We can think of a couple:

● lotions and other materials used;
● laundry costs to wash towels used to dry customers' hair.

As with many types of business activity, variable costs of hairdressers tend to be relatively light in comparison with fixed costs: that is, fixed costs tend to make up the bulk of total costs.

| Figure 3.3 | Graph of variable costs against the volume of activity |

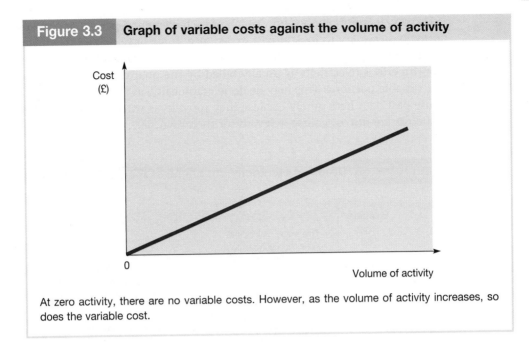

At zero activity, there are no variable costs. However, as the volume of activity increases, so does the variable cost.

The straight line for variable cost on this graph implies that the variable cost will normally be the same per unit of activity, irrespective of the volume of activity concerned. We shall consider the practicality of this assumption a little later in this chapter.

Semi-fixed (semi-variable) costs

In some cases, costs have an element of both fixed and variable cost. These can be described as **semi-fixed (semi-variable) costs**. An example might be the electricity cost for the hairdressing business. Some of this will be for heating and lighting, and this part is probably fixed, at least until the volume of activity expands to a point where longer opening hours or larger premises are necessary. The other part of the cost will vary with the volume of activity. Here we are talking about such things as power for hairdryers, and so on.

Activity 3.4

Can you suggest another cost for a hairdressing business that is likely to be semi-fixed (semi-variable)?

We thought of telephone charges for landlines. These tend to have a rental element, which is fixed, and there may also be certain calls that have to be made irrespective of the volume of activity involved. However, increased business would be likely to lead to the need to make more telephone calls and so increased call charges.

Usually, it is not obvious how much of each element a particular cost contains. It is normally necessary to look at past experience. If we have data on what the electricity cost has been for various volumes of activity, say the relevant data over several three-month periods (electricity is usually billed by the quarter), we can estimate the fixed and variable portions. This may be done graphically, as shown in Figure 3.4. We tend to use past data here purely because they provide us with an estimate of future costs; past costs are not, of course, relevant for their own sake.

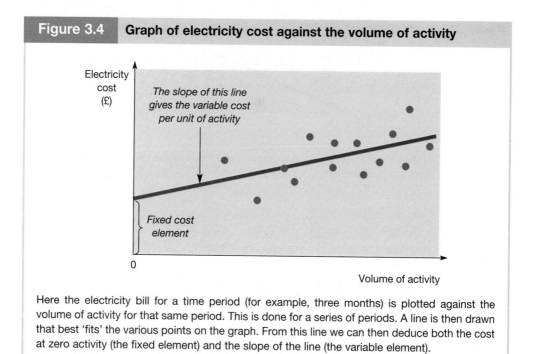

Figure 3.4   Graph of electricity cost against the volume of activity

Here the electricity bill for a time period (for example, three months) is plotted against the volume of activity for that same period. This is done for a series of periods. A line is then drawn that best 'fits' the various points on the graph. From this line we can then deduce both the cost at zero activity (the fixed element) and the slope of the line (the variable element).

Each of the dots in Figure 3.4 is the electricity charge for a particular quarter plotted against the volume of activity (probably measured in terms of sales revenue) for the same quarter. The diagonal line on the graph is the *line of best fit*. This means that this was the line that best seemed (to us, at least) to represent the data. A better estimate can usually be made using a statistical technique (*least squares regression*), which does not involve drawing graphs and making estimates. In practice though, it probably makes little difference which approach is taken.

From the graph we can say that the fixed element of the electricity cost is the amount represented by the vertical distance from the origin at zero (bottom left-hand corner) to the point where the line of best fit crosses the vertical axis of the graph. The variable cost per unit is the amount that the graph rises for each increase in the volume of activity.

By breaking down semi-fixed costs in this way into their fixed and variable elements, we are left with just two types of cost: fixed costs and variable costs.

Now that we have considered the nature of fixed and variable costs, we can go on to do something useful with that knowledge – carry out a **break-even analysis**.

Break-even analysis

If, in respect of a particular activity, we know the total fixed costs for a period and the total variable cost per unit, we can produce a graph like the one shown in Figure 3.5.

The bottom part of Figure 3.5 shows the fixed cost area. Added to this is the variable cost, the wedge-shaped portion at the top of the graph. The uppermost line represents the total cost at any particular volume of activity. This total is the vertical distance between the graph's horizontal axis and the uppermost line for the particular volume of activity concerned. Logically enough, the total cost at zero activity is the amount of the fixed costs. This is because, even where there is nothing going on, the business will still be paying rent, salaries, and so on, at least in the short term. The total cost is augmented by the amount of the relevant variable costs, as the volume of activity increases.

| Figure 3.5 | Graph of total cost against volume of activity |

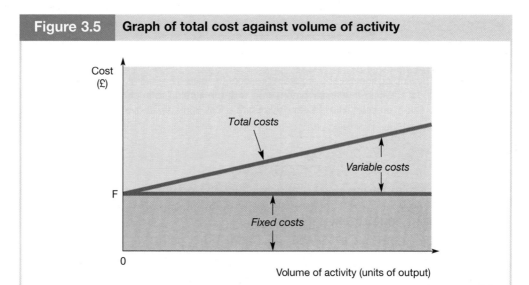

The bottom part of the graph represents the fixed cost element. To this is added the wedge-shaped top portion, which represents the variable costs. The two parts together represent total cost. At zero activity, the variable costs are zero, so total costs equal fixed costs. As activity increases so does total cost, but only because variable costs increase. We are assuming that there are no steps in the fixed costs.

If we take this total cost graph in Figure 3.5, and superimpose on it a line representing total revenue for each volume of activity, we obtain the **break-even chart**. This is shown in Figure 3.6.

Note in Figure 3.6 that, at zero volume of activity (zero sales), there is zero sales revenue. The profit (loss), which is the difference between total sales revenue and total cost, for a particular volume of activity is the vertical distance between the total sales revenue line and the total cost line at that volume of activity. Where the volume of activity is at **break-even point (BEP)**, there is no vertical distance between these two lines (total sales revenue equals total costs) and so there is no profit or loss; that is, the activity breaks even. Where the volume of activity is below BEP, a loss will be incurred because total costs exceed total sales revenue. Where the business operates at a volume of activity above BEP, there will be a profit because total sales revenue will exceed total costs. The further below BEP, the higher the loss: the further above BEP, the higher the profit.

Figure 3.6	**Break-even chart**

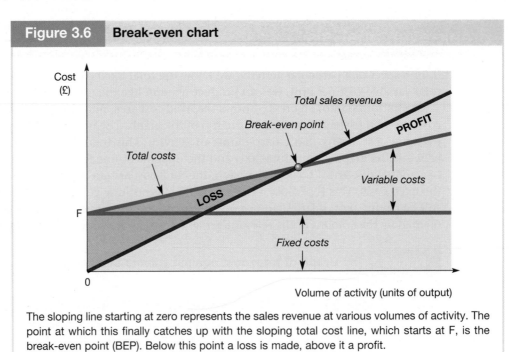

The sloping line starting at zero represents the sales revenue at various volumes of activity. The point at which this finally catches up with the sloping total cost line, which starts at F, is the break-even point (BEP). Below this point a loss is made, above it a profit.

As may be imagined, deducing BEPs by graphical means is a laborious business. However, since the relationships in the graph are all linear (that is, the lines are all straight), it is easy to calculate the BEP.

We know that at BEP (but not at any other point):

Total sales revenue = Total costs

(At all other points except the BEP, either total sales revenue will exceed total cost or the other way round. Only at BEP are they equal.) That is,

Total sales revenue = Fixed costs + Total variable costs

If we call the number of units of output at BEP b, then

b × Sales revenue per unit = Fixed costs + (b × Variable costs per unit)

Thus:

(b × Sales revenue per unit) − (b × Variable costs per unit) = Fixed costs

and:

b × (Sales revenue per unit − Variable costs per unit) = Fixed costs

giving:

$$b = \frac{\text{Fixed costs}}{\text{Sales revenue per unit} - \text{Variable costs per unit}}$$

If we look back at the break-even chart in Figure 3.6, this seems logical. The total cost line starts off at point F, higher than the starting point for the total sales revenues line (zero) by amount F (the amount of the fixed costs). Because the sales revenue per unit is greater than the variable cost per unit, the sales revenue line will gradually catch up with the total cost line. The rate at which it will catch up is dependent on the relative steepness of the two lines and the amount that it has to catch up (the fixed costs). Bearing in mind that the slopes of the two lines are the variable cost per unit and the selling price per unit, the above equation for calculating b looks perfectly logical.

Though the BEP can be calculated quickly and simply, as shown, it does not mean that the graphical approach of the break-even chart is without value. The chart shows the relationship between cost, volume and profit over a range of output and in a form that can easily be understood by non-financial managers. The break-even chart can therefore be a useful device for explaining this relationship.

Example 3.1

Cottage Industries Ltd makes baskets. The fixed costs of operating the workshop for a month total £500. Each basket requires materials that cost £2. Each basket takes two hours to make, and the business pays the basket makers £5 an hour. The basket makers are all on contracts such that if they do not work for any reason, they are not paid. The baskets are sold to a wholesaler for £14 each.

What is the BEP for basket making for the business?

The BEP (in number of baskets):

$$= \frac{\text{Fixed costs}}{(\text{Sales revenue per unit} - \text{Variable costs per unit})}$$

$$= \frac{£500}{£14 - (£2 + £10)}$$

$$= 250 \text{ baskets per month}$$

Note that the BEP must be expressed with respect to a period of time.

Real World 3.1 shows information on the BEPs of three well-known businesses.

Activity 3.5

Can you think of reasons why the managers of a business might find it useful to know the BEP of some activity that they are planning to undertake?

The usefulness of being able to deduce the BEP is that it makes it possible to compare the planned or expected volume of activity with the BEP and so make a judgement about risk. Planning to operate only just above the volume of activity necessary in order to break even may indicate that it is a risky venture, since only a small fall from the planned volume of activity could lead to a loss. Real World 3.1, below reveals that Ryanair's operations look rather less risky than those of the other two airlines in that the difference between its load factor and its BEP is largest.

REAL WORLD 3.1

BEP at BA, Ryanair and easyJet

Commercial airlines seem to pay a lot of attention to their BEPs and their 'load factors', that is, their actual level of activity. Figure 3.7 shows the BEP and load factor for three well-known airlines operating from the UK. British Airways (BA) is a traditional airline. Ryanair and Easyjet are 'no frills' carriers, which means that passengers receive lower levels of service in return for lower fares. All three operate flights within the UK and from the UK to other European countries. Only BA operates flights beyond Europe. We can see that all three airlines are making operating profits as each has a load factor greater than its BEP.

Figure 3.7	Break even and load factors in the airline industry

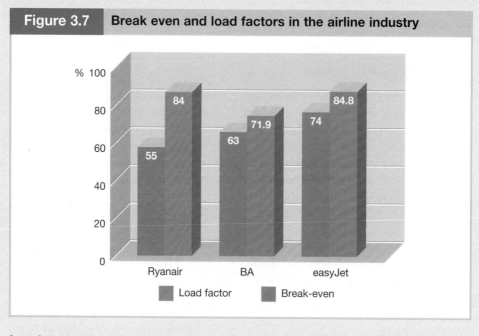

Source: Derived from information contained in 'Ryanair alert hits shares' by Jon Ashworth, *The Times*, 4 June 2003, p. 21. The data in the article are based on the year ended 31 March 2003.

Activity 3.6

Cottage Industries Ltd (see Example 3.1) expects to sell 500 baskets a month. The business has the opportunity to rent a basket-making machine. Doing so would increase the total fixed costs of operating the workshop for a month to £3,000. Using the machine would reduce the labour time to one hour per basket. The basket makers would still be paid £5 an hour.

(a) How much profit would the business make each month from selling baskets (i) assuming that the basket-making machine is not rented and (ii) assuming that it is rented?
(b) What is the BEP if the machine is rented?
(c) What do you notice about the figures that you calculate?

(a) Estimated monthly profit from basket making:

	Without the machine		With the machine	
	£	£	£	£
Sales (500 × £14)		7,000		7,000
Less Materials (500 × £2)	1,000		1,000	
Labour (500 × 2 × £5)	5,000			
(500 × 1 × £5)			2,500	
Fixed costs	500		3,000	
		6,500		6,500
Profit		500		500

(b) The BEP (in number of baskets) with the machine:

$$= \frac{\text{Fixed costs}}{\text{Sales revenue per unit} - \text{Variable costs per unit}}$$

$$= \frac{£3,000}{£14 - (£2 + £5)}$$

$$= 429 \text{ baskets a month}$$

The BEP without the machine is 250 baskets per month (see Example 3.1).

(c) There seems to be nothing to choose between the two manufacturing strategies regarding profit, at the estimated sales volume. There is, however, a distinct difference between the two strategies regarding the BEP. Without the machine, the actual volume of sales could fall by a half of that which is expected (from 500 to 250) before the business would fail to make a profit. With the machine, however, a 14 per cent fall (from 500 to 429) would be enough to cause the business to fail to make a profit. On the other hand, for each additional basket sold above the estimated 500, an additional profit of only £2 (that is, £14 – (£2 + £10)) would be made without the machine, whereas £7 (that is, £14 – (£2 + £5)) would be made with the machine. (Note that knowledge of the BEP and the planned volume of activity gives some basis for assessing the riskiness of the activity.)

We shall take a closer look at the relationship between fixed costs, variable costs and break-even together with any advice that we might give the management of Cottage Industries Ltd after we have briefly considered the notion of contribution.

Contribution

The bottom part of the break-even formula (sales revenue per unit less variable costs per unit) is known as the **contribution per unit**. Thus for the basket-making activity, without the machine the contribution per unit is £2, and with the machine it is £7. This can be quite a useful figure to know in a decision-making context. It is called 'contribution' because it contributes to meeting the fixed costs and, if there is any excess, it also contributes to profit.

We shall see, a little later in this chapter, how knowing the amount of the contribution generated by a particular activity can be valuable in making short-term decisions of various types, as well as being useful in the BEP calculation.

Margin of safety and operating gearing

→ The **margin of safety** is the extent to which the planned volume of output or sales lies above the BEP. Going back to Activity 3.6, we saw that the following situation exists:

	Without the machine (number of baskets)	With the machine (number of baskets)
Expected volume of sales	500	500
BEP	250	429
Difference (margin of safety):		
Number of baskets	250	71
Percentage of estimated volume of sales	50%	14%

Activity 3.7

What advice would you give Cottage Industries Ltd about renting the machine, on the basis of the values for margin of safety?

It is a matter of personal judgement, which in turn is related to individual attitudes to risk, as to which strategy to adopt. Most people, however, would prefer the strategy of not renting the machine, since the margin of safety between the expected volume of activity and the BEP is much greater. Thus, for the same level of return the risk will be lower without renting the machine.

The relative margins of safety are directly linked to the relationship between the selling price per basket, the variable costs per basket, and the fixed costs per month. Without the machine the contribution (selling price less variable costs) per basket is £2; with the machine it is £7. On the other hand, without the machine the fixed costs are £500 a month; with the machine they are £3,000. This means that, with the machine, the contributions have more fixed costs to 'overcome' before the activity becomes profitable. However, the rate at which the contributions can overcome fixed costs is higher with the machine, because variable costs are lower. This means that one more, or one less, basket sold has a greater impact on profit than it does if the machine is not rented. The contrast between the two scenarios is shown graphically in Figures 3.8(a) and 3.8(b).

→ The relationship between contribution and fixed costs is known as **operating gearing**. An activity with relatively high fixed costs compared with its variable costs is said to have high operating gearing. Thus, Cottage Industries Ltd is more highly operationally geared using the machine than not using it. Renting the machine increases the level of operating gearing quite dramatically because it causes an increase in fixed costs, but at the same time it leads to a reduction in variable costs per basket.

The reason why the word 'gearing' is used in this context is that, as with intermeshing gear wheels of different circumferences, a movement in one of the factors (volume of output) causes a more-than-proportionate movement in the other (profit) as illustrated by Figure 3.9.

Figure 3.8	Break-even charts for Cottage Industries' basket-making activities (a) without the machine and (b) with the machine

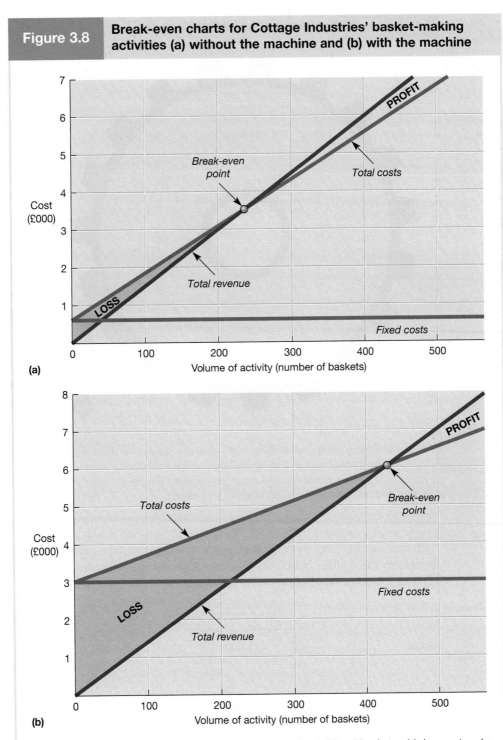

Without the machine the contribution is low. Thus, each additional basket sold does not make a dramatic difference to the profit or loss. With the machine, however, the opposite is true, and small increases or decreases in the sales volume will have a marked effect on the profit or loss.

Figure 3.9	The effect of operating gearing

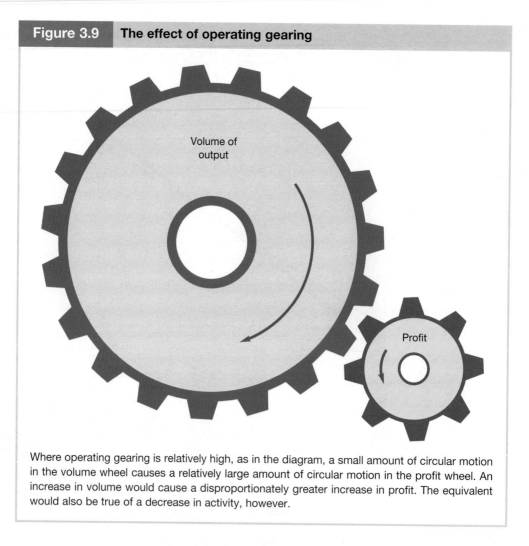

Where operating gearing is relatively high, as in the diagram, a small amount of circular motion in the volume wheel causes a relatively large amount of circular motion in the profit wheel. An increase in volume would cause a disproportionately greater increase in profit. The equivalent would also be true of a decrease in activity, however.

Increasing the level of operating gearing tends to make profits more sensitive to changes in the volume of activity. We can demonstrate operating gearing with Cottage Industries Ltd's basket-making activities as follows:

	Without the machine			With the machine		
Volume	500	1,000	1,500	500	1,000	1,500
	£	£	£	£	£	£
Contributions*	1,000	2,000	3,000	3,500	7,000	10,500
Less Fixed costs	500	500	500	3,000	3,000	3,000
Profit	500	1,500	2,500	500	4,000	7,500

* £2 per basket without the machine and £7 per basket with it.

Note that, without the machine (low operating gearing), a doubling of the output from 500 to 1,000 units brings a trebling of the profit. With the machine (high operating gearing), doubling output causes profit to rise by eight times. At the same time, reductions in the volume of output tend to have a more damaging effect on profit where the operating gearing is higher.

Activity 3.8

In general terms, what types of business activity tend to be most highly operationally geared? (*Hint*: Cottage Industries Ltd might give you some idea.)

In general, activities that are capital intensive tend to be more highly operationally geared. This is because renting or owning capital equipment gives rise to additional fixed costs, but it can also give rise to lower variable costs. **Real World 3.2** shows how a very well-known business has benefited from high operating gearing.

REAL WORLD 3.2

Sky-high operating gearing

British Sky Broadcasting Group plc (Sky), the satellite television broadcaster, is an obvious example of a business with high operating gearing. Nearly all of its costs are fixed in that they do not vary with the number of subscribers that it has or the value of its advertising revenues. This means that any increase in total revenues is likely to have a strong favourable effect on profit. The business acknowledged this in its 2003 annual report where it said, 'Sky continues to benefit from strong operational gearing', before going on to explain how a 15 per cent increase in revenues led to an increase of 94 per cent in operating profit.

Source: British Sky Broadcasting Group plc Annual Report 2003.

Profit–volume charts

A slight variant of the break-even chart is the **profit–volume (PV) chart**. A typical PV chart is shown in Figure 3.10.

The profit–volume chart is obtained by plotting loss or profit against volume of activity. The slope of the graph is equal to the contribution per unit, since each additional unit sold decreases the loss, or increases the profit, by the sales revenue per unit less the variable cost per unit. At zero volume of activity there are no contributions, so there is a loss equal to the amount of the fixed costs. As the volume of activity increases, the amount of the loss gradually decreases until BEP is reached. Beyond BEP, profits increase as activity increases.

As we can see, the profit–volume chart does not tell us anything not shown by the break-even chart. On the other hand, information is perhaps more easily absorbed from the profit–volume chart. This is particularly true of the profit (loss) at any volume of activity. The break-even chart shows this as the vertical distance between the total cost and total sales revenue lines. The profit–volume chart, in effect, combines the total sales revenue and total variable cost lines, which means that profit (or loss) is plotted directly.

Figure 3.10	Profit–volume chart

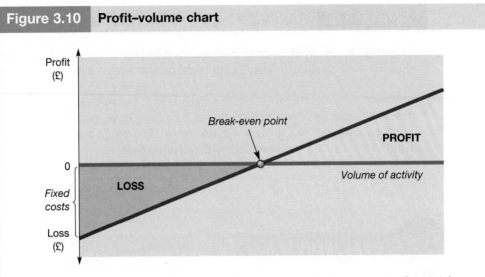

The sloping line is profit (loss) plotted against activity. As activity increases, so does total contribution (sales revenue less variable costs). At zero activity there are no contributions, so there will be a loss equal in amount to the total fixed costs.

The economist's view of the break-even chart

So far in this chapter we have treated all the relationships as linear – that is, all of the lines in the graphs have been straight. This is typically the approach taken in accounting, though it may not be strictly valid.

Consider, for example, the variable cost line in the break-even chart; accountants would normally treat this as being a straight line. Strictly, however, the line perhaps should not be straight because at high levels of output **economies of scale** may be available to an extent not available at lower levels. For example, a raw material (a typical variable cost) may be able to be used more efficiently with higher volumes of activity. Similarly, the relatively large quantities of material and services bought may enable the business to benefit from bulk discounts and general power in the marketplace to negotiate lower prices.

There is also a general tendency for sales revenue per unit to reduce as volume is expanded, since to sell more units of the product or service, it will probably be necessary to lower the selling price.

Economists tend to recognise that, in real life, the relationships portrayed in the break-even chart are usually non-linear. The typical economist's view of the chart is shown in Figure 3.11.

Note, in Figure 3.11, that the variable costs start to increase quite steeply with volume but, around point A, economies of scale start to take effect. After this point, further increases in volume do not cause such a large increase, for each additional unit of output, in variable costs. These economies of scale continue to have a benign effect on costs until a point is reached where the business will be operating towards the end of its efficient range. Here the business may have problems with finding supplies of the variable-cost elements, which will normally adversely affect their price. Also,

Figure 3.11 The economist's view of the break-even chart

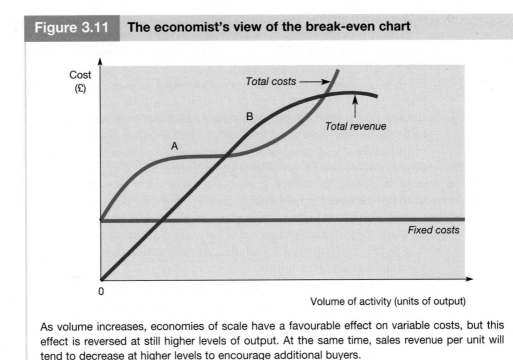

As volume increases, economies of scale have a favourable effect on variable costs, but this effect is reversed at still higher levels of output. At the same time, sales revenue per unit will tend to decrease at higher levels to encourage additional buyers.

the business may find it more difficult to produce, there may be machine breakdowns, and so on.

At low levels of output, sales may be made at a relatively high price per unit. To increase sales output beyond point B it may be necessary to lower the average sales price per unit.

Note how this 'curvilinear' representation of the break-even chart can easily lead to the existence of two break-even points.

Accountants justify their approach to this topic by the fact that, though the lines may not, in practice, be perfectly straight, this defect is probably not worth taking into account in most cases. This is partly because all of the information used in the analysis is based on estimates of the future. As this will inevitably be flawed, it seems pointless to be pedantic about minor approximations, such as treating the total cost and total revenue lines as straight when strictly this is not so. Only where significant economies or diseconomies of scale are involved should the non-linearity of the variable costs be taken into account. Also, for most businesses, the range of possible volumes of activity at which they are capable of operating (the **relevant range**) is pretty narrow. Over very short distances, it is perfectly reasonable to treat a curved line as being straight.

Weaknesses of break-even analysis

As we have seen, break-even analysis can provide some useful insights to the important relationship between fixed costs, variable costs and the volume of activity. It does, however, have its weaknesses. There are three general problems:

- *Non-linear relationships*. The normal approach to break-even analysis assumes that the relationships between sales revenues, variable costs and volume are strictly straight-line ones. In real life this is unlikely to be so. This is probably not a major problem, since, as we have just seen:
  - break-even analysis is normally conducted in advance of the activity actually taking place. Our ability to predict future costs, revenues and so on is somewhat limited: hence what are probably minor variations from strict linearity are unlikely to be significant, compared with other forecasting errors;
  - most businesses operate within a narrow range of volume of activity. Over short ranges, curved lines tend to be relatively straight.
- *Stepped fixed costs*. Most fixed costs are not fixed over all volumes of activity. They tend to be 'stepped' in the way depicted in Figure 3.2. This means that, in practice, great care must be taken in making assumptions about fixed costs. The problem is particularly heightened because most activities will probably involve fixed costs of various types (rent, supervisory salaries, administration costs), all of which are likely to have steps at different points.
- *Multi-product businesses*. Most businesses do not offer just one product or service. This is a problem for break-even analysis since it raises the question of the effect of additional sales of one product or service on sales of another of the business's products or services. There is also the problem of identifying the fixed costs of one particular activity. Fixed costs tend to relate to more than one activity – for example, two activities may be carried out in the same rented premises. There are ways of dividing fixed costs between activities, but these tend to be arbitrary, which calls into question the value of the break-even analysis.

Despite some problems, the notions of break-even analysis and BEP seem to be widely used. The media frequently refer to the BEP for businesses and activities. For example, there was much discussion at the turn of this century about the BEP, in terms of the number of visitors, for the London Millennium Dome. Eurotunnel's BEP, and whether it will be reached, also seems to be a much-reported topic. Similarly, the number of people regularly needed to pay to watch a football team so that the club breaks even often seems to be referred to. **Real World 3.3** provides an insight to the extent that break-even analysis is used by managers in practice.

REAL WORLD 3.3

Break-even analysis in practice

A survey of management accounting practice in the United States was conducted in 2003. Nearly 2,000 businesses replied to the survey. These tended to be larger businesses, of which about 40 per cent were manufacturers and about 16 per cent financial services; the remainder were across a range of other industries.

The survey revealed that 62 per cent use break-even analysis extensively, with a further 22 per cent considering using the technique in the future.

Though the survey relates to the US, in the absence of UK evidence, it provides some insight to what is likely also to be practice in the UK and elsewhere in the developed world.

Source: Taken from the *2003 Survey of Management Accounting* by Ernst and Young, 2003.

Marginal analysis

If we cast our minds back to Chapter 2, where we discussed relevant costs for decision making, we should recall that when we are trying to decide between two or more possible courses of action, *only costs that vary with the decision should be included in the decision analysis.*

For many decisions that involve:

● relatively small variations from existing practice, and/or
● relatively limited periods of time,

fixed costs are not relevant to the decision, because they will be the same irrespective of the decision made, because either:

● fixed costs tend to be impossible to alter in the short term, or
● managers are reluctant to alter them in the short term.

Activity 3.9

Ali plc occupies premises that it owns in order to provide a service. There is a downturn in demand for the service, and it would be possible for Ali plc to carry on the business from smaller, cheaper premises.

Can you think of any reasons why the business might not immediately move to smaller, cheaper premises?

....

We thought of broadly three reasons:

1 It is not usually possible to find a buyer for premises at very short notice.
2 It may be difficult to move premises quickly where there is, say, delicate equipment to be moved.
3 Management may feel that the downturn might not be permanent, and would thus be reluctant to take such a dramatic step and deny itself the opportunity to benefit from a possible revival of trade.

The business's premises in Activity 3.9 may provide an example of one of the more inflexible types of cost, but most fixed costs tend to be broadly similar in this context.

We shall now consider some types of decisions where fixed costs can be regarded as irrelevant. In making these decisions, we should have as our key strategic objective the maximisation of owners' (shareholders') wealth. Since these decisions are short-term in nature, this means that wealth will normally be maximised by trying to generate as much net cash inflow as possible.

 In **marginal analysis** we concern ourselves just with costs and revenues that vary with the decision and so this usually means that fixed costs are ignored. Marginal analysis tends to assume that the variable cost per unit will be equal to the **marginal cost**, which is the additional cost of producing one more unit of output. Although this is normally the case, there may be times when producing one more unit will involve a step in the fixed costs. If this occurs, the marginal cost is not just the variable cost, it will include the increment, or step, in the fixed costs as well.

Marginal analysis may be used in four key areas of decision making:

● accepting/rejecting special contracts;
● determining the most efficient use of scarce resources;
● make-or-buy decisions;
● closing or continuation decisions.

We shall now consider each of these areas in turn.

Accepting/rejecting special contracts

To understand how marginal analysis may be used in decisions as to whether to accept or reject special contracts, let us consider the following activity.

Activity 3.10

Cottage Industries Ltd (see Example 3.1) has spare capacity in that its basket makers have some spare time. An overseas retail chain has offered the business an order for 300 baskets at a price of £13 each.

Without considering any wider issues, should the business accept the order? (Assume that the business does not rent the machine.)

Since the fixed costs will be incurred in any case, they are not relevant to this decision. All we need to do is see whether the price offered will yield a contribution. If it will, the business will be better off by accepting the contract than by refusing it.

	£
Additional revenue per unit	13
Less Additional cost per unit	12
Additional contribution per unit	1

For 300 units, the additional contribution will be £300 (that is, 300 × £1). Since no fixed cost increase is involved, irrespective of what else is happening to the business, it will be £300 better off by taking this contract than by refusing it.

As ever with decision making, there are other factors that are either difficult or impossible to quantify. These should be taken into account before reaching a final decision. In the case of Cottage Industries Ltd's decision on the overseas customer, these could include the following:

● The possibility that spare capacity will have been 'sold off' cheaply when there might be another potential customer who will offer a higher price, but, by which time, the capacity will be fully committed. It is a matter of commercial judgement as to how likely this will be.
● Selling the same product, but at different prices, could lead to a loss of customer goodwill. The fact that a different price will be set for customers in different countries (that is, in different markets) may be sufficient to avoid this potential problem.

- If the business is going to suffer continually from being unable to sell its full production potential at the 'regular' price, it might be better, in the long run, to reduce capacity and make fixed cost savings. Using the spare capacity to produce marginal benefits may lead to the business failing to address this issue.
- On a more positive note, the business may see this as a way of breaking into the overseas market. This is something that might be impossible to achieve if the business charges its regular price.

The most efficient use of scarce resources

We tend to think in terms of the size of the market being the brake on output. This is to say that the ability of a business to sell will limit production, rather than the ability to produce will limit sales. In some cases, however, it is a limit on what can be produced that limits sales. Limited production might stem from a shortage of any factor of production – labour, raw materials, space, machinery and so on. Such scarce factors are often known as *key* or *limiting* factors.

The most profitable combination of products will occur where the *contribution per unit of the scarce factor* is maximised. Example 3.2 should illustrate this point.

Example 3.2

A business provides three different services, the details of which are as follows:

Service (code name)	AX107	AX109	AX220
	£	£	£
Selling price per unit	50	40	65
Variable cost per unit	(25)	(20)	(35)
Contribution per unit	25	20	30
Labour time per unit	5 hours	3 hours	6 hours

Within reason, the market will take as many units of each service as can be provided, but the ability to provide the service is limited by the availability of labour, all of which needs to be skilled. Fixed costs are not affected by the choice of service provided because all three services use the same facilities.

The most profitable service is AX109 because it generates a contribution of £6.67 (£20/3) an hour. The other two generate only £5.00 each an hour (£25/5 and £30/6). So, to maximise profit, priority should be given to the production that maximises the contribution per unit of limiting factor.

Our first reaction may have been that the business should provide only service AX220, because this is the one that yields the highest contribution per unit sold. If so, we should have been making the mistake of thinking that it is the ability to sell that is the limiting factor. If the above analysis is not convincing, we can take an imaginary number of available labour hours and ask ourselves what is the maximum contribution (and, therefore, profit) that could be made by providing each service exclusively. Bear in mind that there is no shortage of anything else, including market demand, just a shortage of labour.

Activity 3.11

A business makes three different products, the details of which are as follows:

Product (code name)	B14	B17	B22
Selling price per unit (£)	25	20	23
Variable cost per unit (£)	10	8	12
Weekly demand (units)	25	20	30
Machine time per unit (hours)	4	3	4

Fixed costs are not affected by the choice of product because all three products use the same machine. Machine time is limited to 148 hours a week.

Which combination of products should be manufactured if the business is to produce the highest profit?

Product (code name)	B14	B17	B22
	£	£	£
Selling price per unit	25	20	23
Variable cost per unit	(10)	(8)	(12)
Contribution per unit	15	12	11
Machine time per unit	4 hours	3 hours	4 hours
Contribution per machine hour	£3.75	£4.00	£2.75
Order of priority	2nd	1st	3rd

Therefore:

Produce		
20 units of product B17 using		60 hours
22 units of product B14 using		88 hours
		148 hours

This leaves unsatisfied the market demand for a further 3 units of product B14 and 30 units of product B22.

Activity 3.12

What steps could be contemplated that could lead to a higher level of contribution for the business in Activity 3.11?

The possibilities for improving matters that occurred to us are as follows:

● Consider obtaining additional machine time. This could mean obtaining a new machine, subcontracting the machining to another business, or perhaps squeezing a few more hours a week out of the business's own machine. Perhaps a combination of two or more of these is a possibility.
● Redesign the products in a way that requires less time per unit on the machine.
● Increase the price per unit of the three products. This might well have the effect of dampening demand, but the existing demand cannot be met at present, and it may be more profitable in the long run to make a greater contribution on each unit sold than to take one of the other courses of action to overcome the problem.

Activity 3.13

Going back to Activity 3.11, what is the maximum price that the business concerned would logically be prepared to pay to have the remaining B14s machined by a sub-contractor, assuming that no fixed or variable costs would be saved as a result of not doing the machining in-house?

Would there be a different maximum if we were considering the B22s?

If the remaining three B14s were subcontracted at no cost, the business would be able to earn a contribution of £15 a unit, which it would not otherwise be able to gain. Therefore, any price up to £15 a unit would be worth paying to a subcontractor to undertake the machining. Naturally, the business would prefer to pay as little as possible, but anything up to £15 would still make it worthwhile subcontracting the machining.

This would not be true of the B22s because they have a different contribution per unit; £11 would be the relevant figure in their case.

Make-or-buy decisions

Businesses are frequently confronted by the need to decide whether to produce the product or service that they sell themselves, or to buy it in from some other business. Thus, a producer of electrical appliances might decide to subcontract the manufacture of one of its products to another business, perhaps because there is a shortage of production capacity in the producer's own factory, or because it believes it to be cheaper to subcontract than to make the appliance itself.

It might just be part of a product or service that is subcontracted. For example, the producer may have a component for the appliance made by another manufacturer. In principle, there is hardly any limit to the scope of make-or-buy decisions. Virtually any part, component or service that is required in production of the main product or service, or the main product or service itself, could be the subject of a make-or-buy decision. So, for example, the personnel function of a business, which is normally performed in-house, could be subcontracted. At the same time, electrical power, which is typically provided by an outside electrical utility business, could be generated in-house. Obtaining services or products from a subcontractor is often called **outsourcing**.

Real World 3.4 provides an example of outsourcing by a well-known UK business.

REAL WORLD 3.4

Outsourcing at Boots

During 2002, Boots Company plc, the UK health-care manufacturer and retailer, decided to subcontract or 'outsource' its IT activities. Now, instead of employing its own IT staff, it has a contract for another business to run Boots' IT facility. Boots estimates that this will save it £100 million over a ten-year period. Outsourcing this type of activity is becoming very common in the UK and elsewhere.

Source: Boots Company plc Annual Report 2003.

Example 3.3

Shah Ltd needs a component for one of its products. It can subcontract production of the component to a subcontractor who will provide the components for £20 each. The business can produce the components internally for total variable costs of £15 per component. Shah Ltd has spare capacity.

Should the component be subcontracted or produced internally?

The answer is that Shah Ltd should produce the component internally, since the variable cost of subcontracting is greater by £5 than the variable cost of internal manufacture.

Activity 3.14

Now assume that Shah Ltd (Example 3.3) has no spare capacity, so it can only produce the component internally by reducing its output of another of its products. While it is making each component, it will lose contributions of £12 from the other product.

Should the component be subcontracted or produced internally?

The answer is to subcontract.

The relevant cost of internal production of each component is:

	£
Variable cost of production of the component	15
Opportunity cost of lost production of the other product	12
	27

This is obviously more costly than the £20 per component that will have to be paid to the subcontractor.

Activity 3.15

What factors, other than the immediately financially quantifiable, would you consider when making a make-or-buy decision?

We feel that there are two major factors:

1 The general problems of subcontracting:

(a) loss of control of quality;

(b) potential unreliability of supply.

2 Expertise and specialisation. It is possible for most businesses, with sufficient determination, to do virtually everything in-house. This may, however, require a level of skill and facilities that most businesses neither have nor feel inclined to acquire. For example, though it is true that most businesses could generate their own electricity, their managements tend to take the view that this is better done by a specialist generator business. Specialists can often do things more cheaply, with less risk of things going wrong.

Closing or continuation decisions

It is quite common for businesses to produce separate financial statements for each department or section, to try to assess the relative effectiveness of each one.

Example 3.4

Goodsports Ltd is a retail shop that operates through three departments, all in the same premises. The three departments occupy roughly equal-sized areas of the premises. The trading results for the year just finished showed the following:

	Total	Sports equipment	Sports clothes	General clothes
	£000	£000	£000	£000
Sales	534	254	183	97
Costs	(482)	(213)	(163)	(106)
Profit/(loss)	52	41	20	(9)

It would appear that if the general clothes department were to close, the business would be more profitable, by £9,000 a year, assuming last year's performance to be a reasonable indication of future performance.

When the costs are analysed between those that are variable and those that are fixed, however, the contribution of each department can be deduced and the following results obtained:

	Total	Sports equipment	Sports clothes	General clothes
	£000	£000	£000	£000
Sales	534	254	183	97
Variable costs	(344)	(167)	(117)	(60)
Contribution	190	87	66	37
Fixed costs (rent and so on)	(138)	(46)	(46)	(46)
Profit/(loss)	52	41	20	(9)

Now it is obvious that closing the general clothes department, without any other developments, would make the business worse off by £37,000 (the department's contribution). The department should not be closed, because it makes a positive contribution. The fixed costs would continue whether the department were closed or not. As can be seen from the above analysis, distinguishing between variable and fixed costs, and deducing the contribution, can make the picture a great deal clearer.

Activity 3.16

In considering Goodsports Ltd (in Example 3.4), we saw that the general clothes department should not be closed 'without any other developments'.

What 'other developments' could affect this decision, making continuation either more attractive or less attractive?

The things that we could think of are as follows:

- Expansion of the other departments or replacing the general clothes department with a completely new activity. This would make sense only if the space currently occupied by the general clothes department could generate contributions totalling at least £37,000 a year.
- Subletting the space occupied by the general clothes department. Once again, this would need to generate a net rent greater than £37,000 a year to make it more financially beneficial than keeping the department open.
- Keeping the department open, even if it generated no contribution whatsoever (assuming that there is no other use for the space), may still be beneficial. If customers are attracted into the shop because it has general clothing, they may then buy something from one of the other departments. In the same way, the activity of a sub-tenant might attract customers into the shop. (On the other hand, it might drive them away!)

Self-assessment question 3.1

Khan Ltd can render three different types of service (Alpha, Beta and Gamma) using the same staff. Various estimates for next year have been made as follows:

Service	Alpha £/unit	Beta £/unit	Gamma £/unit
Selling price	30	39	20
Variable material cost	15	18	10
Other variable costs	6	10	5
Share of fixed costs	8	12	4
Staff time required (hours)	2	3	1

Fixed costs for next year are expected to total £40,000.

Required:
(a) If the business were to render only service Alpha next year, how many units of the service would it need to provide in order to break even? (Assume for this part of the question that there is no effective limit to market size and staffing level.)
(b) If the business has a maximum of 10,000 staff hours next year, in which order of preference would the three services come?
(c) If the maximum market for next year for the three services is as follows:

Alpha	3,000 units
Beta	2,000 units
Gamma	5,000 units

what quantities of which service should the business provide next year and how much profit would this be expected to yield?

SUMMARY

The main points in this chapter may be summarised as follows:

Behaviour of costs

- Fixed costs are those that are independent of the level of activity (for example, rent).
- Variable costs are those that vary with the level of activity (for example, raw materials).
- Semi-fixed (semi-variable) costs are a mixture of the two (for example, electricity).

Break-even analysis

- The break-even point (BEP) is the level of activity (in units of output or sales revenue) at which total costs (fixed + variable) = total sales revenue.
- Calculation of BEP is as follows:

$$\text{BEP (in units of output)} = \frac{\text{Fixed costs for the period}}{\text{Contribution per unit}}$$

- Use of knowledge of BEP for a particular activity – risk assessment.
- Contribution per unit = sales revenue per unit less variable cost per unit.
- Margin of safety = excess of planned volume of activity over BEP.
- Operating gearing = the extent to which the total costs of some activity are fixed rather than variable.
- Profit–volume (PV) chart is an alternative approach to BE chart.
- Economists tend to take a different approach to BE, taking account of economies (and diseconomies) of scale and of the fact that, generally, to be able to sell large volumes, price per unit tends to fall.

Weaknesses of BE analysis

- Non-linear relationships.
- Stepped fixed costs.
- Multi-product businesses.

Marginal analysis (ignores fixed costs where these are not affected by the decision)

- Accepting/rejecting special contracts – consider only the effect on contributions.
- Using scarce resources – the limiting factor is most effectively used by maximising its contribution per unit.
- Make-or-buy decisions – take the action that leads to the highest total contributions.
- Closing/continuing an activity – should be assessed by net effect on total contributions.

➔ **Key terms**

Further reading

If you would like to explore the topics covered in this chapter in more depth, we recommend the following books:

Management Accounting, *Atkinson A., Banker R., Kaplan R. and Young S. M.*, 3rd edn, Prentice Hall, 2001, chapter 3.

Management and Cost Accounting, *Drury C.*, 5th edn, Thomson Learning Business Press, 2000, chapter 8.

Cost Accounting: A managerial emphasis, *Horngren C., Foster G. and Datar S.*, 11th edn, Prentice Hall International, 2002, chapter 3.

Cost and Management Accounting, *Williamson D.*, Prentice Hall International, 1996, chapters 3 and 11.

REVIEW QUESTIONS

Answers to these questions can be found on the students' side of the Companion Website at **www.pearsoned.co.uk/atrillmclaney**.

3.1 Define the terms *fixed cost* and *variable cost.* Explain how an understanding of the distinction between fixed costs and variable costs can be useful to managers.

3.2 What is meant by the *BEP* for an activity? How is the BEP calculated? Why is it useful to know the BEP?

3.3 When we say that some business activity has *high operating gearing*, what do we mean? What are the implications for the business of high operating gearing?

3.4 If there is a scarce resource that is restricting sales, how will the business maximise its profit? Explain the logic of the approach that you have identified for maximising profit.

EXERCISES

Exercises 3.4 to 3.8 are more advanced than 3.1 to 3.3. Those with a coloured number have answers at the back of the book.

3.1 The management of a business is concerned about its inability to obtain enough fully trained labour to enable it to meet its present budget projection.

Service:	Alpha	Beta	Gamma	Total
	£000	£000	£000	£000
Variable costs				
Materials	6	4	5	15
Labour	9	6	12	27
Expenses	3	2	2	7
Allocated fixed costs	13	8	12	33
Total cost	31	20	31	82
Profit	8	9	2	19
Sales revenue	39	29	33	101

The amount of labour likely to be available amounts to £20,000. All of the variable labour is paid at the same hourly rate. You have been asked to prepare a statement of plans ensuring that at least 50 per cent of the budget sales are achieved for each service, and the balance of labour is used to produce the greatest profit.

Required:
(a) Prepare a statement, with explanations, showing the greatest profit available from the limited amount of skilled labour available, within the constraint stated. *Hint*: Remember that all labour is paid at the same rate.
(b) What steps could the business take in an attempt to improve profitability, in the light of the labour shortage?

3.2 Lannion and Co. is engaged in providing and marketing a standard advice service. Summarised results for the past two months reveal the following:

	October	November
Sales (units of the service)	200	300
Sales revenue (£)	5,000	7,500
Operating profit (£)	1,000	2,200

There were no price changes of any description during these two months.

Required:
(a) Deduce the BEP (in units of the service) for Lannion and Co.
(b) State why the business might find it useful to know its BEP.

3.3 A hotel group prepares financial statements on a quarterly basis. The senior management is reviewing the performance of one hotel and making plans for next year.

The managers have in front of them the results for this year (based on some actual results and some forecasts to the end of this year):

Quarter	Sales	Profit/(loss)
	£000	£000
1	400	(280)
2	1,200	360
3	1,600	680
4	800	40
Total	4,000	800

The total estimated number of visitors (guest nights) for this year is 50,000. The results follow a regular pattern; there are no unexpected cost fluctuations beyond the seasonal trading pattern shown above. The management intends to incorporate into its plans for next year an anticipated increase in unit variable costs of 10 per cent and a profit target for the hotel of £1 million.

Required:
(a) Calculate the total variable and total fixed costs of the hotel for this year. Show the provisional annual results for this year in total, showing variable and fixed costs separately. Show also the revenue and costs per visitor.
(b) (i) If there is no increase in visitors for next year, what will be the required revenue rate per hotel visitor to meet the profit target?
   (ii) If the required revenue rate per visitor is not raised above this year's level, how many visitors will be required to meet the profit target?
(c) Outline and briefly discuss the assumptions that are made in typical PV or break-even analysis, and assess whether they limit its usefulness.

3.4 Motormusic Ltd makes a standard model of car radio, which it sells to car manufacturers for £60 each. Next year the business plans to make and sell 20,000 radios. The business's costs are as follows:

Manufacturing	
Variable materials	£20 per radio
Variable labour	£14 per radio
Other variable costs	£12 per radio
Fixed costs	£80,000 per year
Administration and selling	
Variable	£3 per radio
Fixed	£60,000 per year

Required:

(a) Calculate the break-even point for next year, expressed both in quantity of radios and sales value.

(b) Calculate the margin of safety for next year, expressed both in quantity of radios and sales value.

3.5 A business makes three products, A, B and C. All three products require the use of two types of machine: cutting machines and assembling machines. Estimates for next year include the following:

Product	A	B	C
Selling price (£ per unit)	25	30	18
Sales demand (units)	2,500	3,400	5,100
Material cost (£ per unit)	12	13	10
Variable production cost (£ per unit)	7	4	3
Time required per unit on cutting machines (hours)	1.0	1.0	0.5
Time required per unit on assembling machines (hours)	0.5	1.0	0.5

Fixed costs for next year are expected to total £42,000. It is the business's policy for each unit of production to absorb these in proportion to its total variable costs.

The business has cutting machine capacity of 5,000 hours a year and assembling machine capacity of 8,000 hours a year.

Required:

(a) State, with supporting workings, which products in which quantities the business should plan to make next year on the basis of the above information. *Hint*: First determine which machines will be a limiting factor (scarce resource).

(b) State the maximum price per product that it would be worth the business paying to a sub-contractor to carry out that part of the work that could not be done internally.

3.6 Darmor Ltd has three products, which require the same production facilities. Information about the production costs for one unit of its products is as follows:

Product	X	Y	Z
	£	£	£
Labour: Skilled	6	9	3
Unskilled	2	4	10
Materials	12	25	14
Other variable costs	3	7	7
Fixed costs	5	10	10

All labour and materials are variable costs. Skilled labour is paid £6 an hour, and unskilled labour is paid £5 an hour. All references to labour costs above, are based on basic rates of pay. Skilled labour is scarce, which means that the business could sell more than the maximum that it is able to make of any of the three products.

Product X is sold in a regulated market, and the regulators have set a price of £30 per unit for it.

Required:

(a) State, with supporting workings, the price that must be charged for products Y and Z, such that the business would find it equally profitable to make and sell any of the three products.

(b) State, with supporting workings, the maximum rate of overtime premium that the business would logically be prepared to pay its skilled workers to work beyond the basic time.

3.7 Intermediate Products Ltd produces four types of water pump. Two of these (A and B) are sold by the business. The other two (C and D) are incorporated, as components, into other of the business's products. Neither C nor D is incorporated into A or B. Costings (per unit) for the products are as follows:

	A	B	C	D
	£	£	£	£
Variable materials	15	20	16	17
Variable labour	25	10	10	15
Other variable costs	5	3	2	2
Other fixed costs	20	8	8	12
	£65	£41	£36	£46
Selling price (per unit)	£70	£45		

There is an outside supplier who is prepared to supply unlimited quantities of products C and D to the business, charging £40 per unit for product C and £55 per unit for product D.

Next year's estimated demand for the products, from the market (in the case of A and B) and from other production requirements (in the case of C and D) is as follows:

	Units
A	5,000
B	6,000
C	4,000
D	3,000

For strategic reasons, the business wishes to supply a minimum of 50 per cent of the above demand for products A and B.

Manufacture of all four products requires the use of a special machine. The products require time on this machine as follows:

	Hours per unit
A	0.5
B	0.4
C	0.5
D	0.3

Next year there are expected to be a maximum of 6,000 special-machine hours available. There will be no shortage of any other factor of production.

Required:
(a) State, with supporting workings and assumptions, which products the business should plan to make next year.
(b) Explain the maximum amount that it would be worth the business paying per hour to rent a second special machine.
(c) Suggest ways, other than renting an additional special machine, that could solve the problem of the shortage of special machine time.

3.8 Gandhi Ltd renders a promotional service to small retailing businesses. There are three levels of service: the 'basic', the 'standard' and the 'comprehensive'. On the basis of past experience, the business plans next year to work at absolute full capacity as follows:

Service	Number of units of the service	Selling price £	Variable cost per unit £
Basic	11,000	50	25
Standard	6,000	80	65
Comprehensive	16,000	120	90

The business's fixed costs total £660,000 a year. Each service takes about the same length of time, irrespective of the level.

One of the accounts staff has just produced a report that seems to show that the standard service is unprofitable. The relevant extract from the report is as follows:

Standard service cost analysis

	£	
Selling price per unit	80	
Variable cost per unit	(65)	
Fixed cost per unit	(20)	(£660,000/(11,000 + 6,000 + 16,000))
Net loss	(5)	

The producer of the report suggests that the business should not offer the standard service next year.

Required:

(a) Should the standard service be offered next year, assuming that the quantity of the other services could not be expanded to use the spare capacity?

(b) Should the standard service be offered next year, assuming that the released capacity could be used to render a new service, the 'nova', for which customers would be charged £75, and which would have variable costs of £50 and take twice as long as the other three services?

(c) What is the minimum price that could be accepted for the basic service, assuming that the necessary capacity to expand it will come only from not offering the standard service?

4

Full costing

OBJECTIVES

When you have completed this chapter, you should be able to:

- Deduce the full cost of a unit of output in a single-product environment.
- Distinguish between direct and indirect costs and use this distinction to deduce the full cost of a job in a multi-product environment.
- Discuss the problem of charging overheads to jobs in a multi-product environment.
- Deduce the overheads to be charged to a job in a departmental-costing environment.

INTRODUCTION

In this chapter we are going to look at a widely used approach for deducing the cost of a unit of output, which takes account of all of the costs. The precise approach taken tends to depend on whether each unit of output is identical to the next or whether each job has its own individual characteristics. It also tends to depend on whether or not the business accounts for overheads on a departmental basis. We shall look at how full costing is achieved and then we shall consider its usefulness for management purposes.

In this chapter we shall look at the traditional, but widely used, form of full costing. In Chapter 5 we shall go on to consider activity-based costing, which represents an alternative form of full costing.

The nature of full costing

→ With **full costing** we are concerned with all costs involved with achieving some objective, such as providing a particular service. The logic of full costing is that all of the costs of running a particular facility, say an office, are part of the cost of the output of that office. For example, the rent may be a cost that will not alter merely because we provide one more unit of the service, but if the office were not rented there would be nowhere for providing the service to take place, so rent is an important element of the cost of each unit of output.

→ **Full cost** is the total amount of resources, usually measured in monetary terms, sacrificed to achieve a particular objective. It takes account of all resources sacrificed to achieve the objective. Thus, if the objective were to supply a customer with a product or service, all costs relating to the production of the product or provision of the service would be included as part of the full cost. To derive the full cost figure, we must accumulate the costs incurred and then assign them to the particular product or service. In the sections that follow we shall first see how this is done for a single product operation and then see how it is done for a multi-product operation.

Deriving full costs in a single-product operation

The simplest case for which to deduce the full cost per unit is where the business has only one product line, that is, each unit of its product is identical. Here it is simply a question of adding up all the costs of production incurred in the period (materials, labour, rent, fuel and power and so on) and dividing this total by the total number of units of output for the period.

Activity 4.1

Fruitjuice Ltd has just one product, a sparkling orange drink that is marketed as 'Orange Fizz'. During last month the business produced 7,300 litres of the drink. The costs incurred were as follows:

	£
Ingredients (oranges and so on)	390
Fuel	85
Rent of premises	350
Depreciation of equipment	75
Labour	880

What is the full cost per litre of producing 'Orange Fizz'?

This figure is found by simply adding together all of the costs incurred and then dividing by the number of litres produced:

$$£(390 + 85 + 350 + 75 + 880)/7,300 = £0.24 \text{ per litre}$$

In practice, there can be problems in deciding exactly how much cost was incurred. In the case of Fruitjuice Ltd, for example, how is the cost of depreciation deduced? It is certainly an estimate, and so its reliability is open to question. The cost of raw materials may also be a problem. Should we use the 'relevant' cost of the raw materials (almost certainly the replacement cost), or the actual price paid for the stock (inventory) used? If it is worth calculating the cost per litre, it must be because this information will be used for some decision-making purpose, so the replacement cost is probably more logical. In practice, however, it seems that historic costs are more often used to deduce full costs.

There can also be problems in deciding precisely how many units of output there were. If making Orange Fizz is not a very fast process, some of the drink will be in the process of being made at any given moment. This, in turn, means that some of the costs incurred last month were for some Orange Fizz that was work in progress at the end of the month, so is not included in the output quantity of 7,300 litres. Similarly, part of the 7,300 litres was started and incurred costs in the previous month, yet all of those litres were included in the 7,300 litres that we used in our calculation of the cost per litre. Work in progress is not a serious problem, but some adjustment for opening and closing work in progress for a period needs to be made if reliable full cost information is to be obtained.

The approach to full costing described above, which can be taken with identical, or near identical units of output, is often referred to as **process costing**.

Deriving full costs in multi-product operations

Most businesses produce more than one type of product or service. In this situation, the units of output of the product, or service, will not be identical and so the approach that we used with litres of 'Orange Fizz' in Activity 4.1 cannot be used. Although it is reasonable to assign an identical cost to units of output that are identical; it is not reasonable to do this where the units of output are obviously different. It would not be reasonable, for example, to assign the same costs to each car repair carried out by a garage, irrespective of the complexity and size of the repair.

Direct and indirect costs

To provide full cost information, we need to have a systematic approach to accumulating costs and then assigning these costs to particular units of product or service on some reasonable basis. Where units of output are not identical, the starting point is to separate costs into two categories: direct costs and indirect costs.

● **Direct costs**. These are costs that can be identified with specific cost units. That is to say, the effect of the cost can be measured in respect of each particular unit of output. The main examples of these are direct materials and direct labour. Thus, in costing a motor car repair by a garage, both the cost of spare parts used in the repair and the cost of the mechanic's time would be direct costs. Collecting direct costs is a simple matter of having a cost-recording system that is capable of capturing the cost of direct materials used on each job and the cost, based on the hours worked and the rate of pay, of direct workers.

● **Indirect costs** (or **overheads**). These are all other costs, that is, those that cannot be directly measured in respect of each particular unit of output. Thus the rent of the garage premises would be an indirect cost of a motor car repair.

We shall use the terms 'indirect costs' and 'overheads' interchangeably for the remainder of this book. Overheads are sometimes known as **common costs** because they are common to all outputs of the production unit (for example, factory or department) for the period.

Real World 4.1 provides some insight to the direct/indirect cost balance in practice.

REAL WORLD 4.1

Direct and indirect costs in practice

A survey of 176 fairly large UK businesses, conducted during 1999, revealed that, on average, total costs of businesses are in the following proportions:

● Direct costs   70 per cent
● Indirect costs   30 per cent

Perhaps surprisingly, these proportions did not vary greatly among manufacturers, retailers and service businesses. The only significant variation from the 70/30 proportions was with financial and commercial businesses, which had an average 52/48 split.

Source: Based on information taken from Drury and Tayles (see reference 1 at the end of the chapter).

An extensive (nearly 2,000 responses) and more recent (2003) survey of management accounting practice in the US showed similar results. Like the 1999 UK survey, this tended to relate to larger businesses. About 40% were manufacturers and about 16% financial services; the remainder were from a range of other industries.

This survey revealed that, of total costs, indirect costs accounted for between:

● 34 per cent   for retailers (lowest) and
● 42 per cent   for manufacturers (highest),

with other industries' proportion of indirect costs falling within the 34 per cent to 42 per cent range. Financial and commercial businesses showed an indirect cost percentage of 38 per cent.

Source: Ernst and Young (see reference 2 of the end of the chapter).

The differences between the UK and the US could be accounted for by a higher level of capital intensity in US industry, which would tend to increase indirect costs relative to direct ones.

Job costing

The term **job costing** is used to describe the way in which we identify the full cost per unit of output (job) where the units of output differ. To cost (that is, deduce the full cost of) a particular unit of output (job), we first identify the direct costs of the job, which, by the definition of direct costs, is capable of being done. We then seek to 'charge' each unit of output with a fair share of indirect costs. This is shown graphically in Figure 4.1.

Figure 4.1   The relationship between direct costs and indirect costs

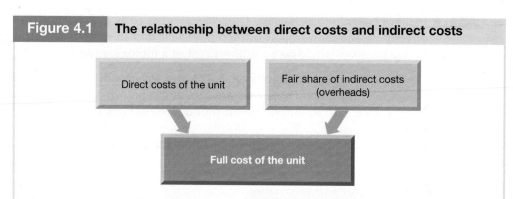

The full cost of any particular job is the sum of those costs that can be measured specifically in respect of the job (direct costs) and a share of those costs that create the environment in which production (of an object or service) can take place, but which do not relate specifically to any particular job (overheads).

Activity 4.2

Sparky Ltd is a business that employs a number of electricians. The business undertakes a range of work for its customers, from replacing fuses to installing complete wiring systems in new houses.

In respect of a particular job done by Sparky Ltd, into which category (direct or indirect) would each of the following costs fall?

● the wages of the electrician who did the job;
● depreciation (wear and tear) of the tools used by the electrician;
● the salary of Sparky Ltd's accountant;
● the cost of cable and other materials used on the job;
● rent of the premises where Sparky Ltd stores its stock (inventory) of cable and other materials.

Only the electrician's wages earned while working on the particular job and the cost of the materials used on the job are direct costs. This is because it is possible to measure how much time (and therefore the labour cost) was spent on the particular job and the amount of materials used in the job.

All of the other costs are general costs of running the business and, as such, must form part of the full cost of doing the job, but they cannot be directly measured in respect of the particular job.

It is important to note that whether a cost is direct or indirect depends on the item being costed – the cost objective. People tend to refer to overheads without stating what the cost objective is; this is incorrect.

Activity 4.3

Into which category, direct or indirect, would each of the costs listed in Activity 4.2 fall if we were seeking to find the cost of operating the entire business of Sparky Ltd for a month?

The answer is that all of them will be direct costs, since they can all be related to, and measured in respect of, running the business for a month.

Naturally, broader-reaching cost units, such as operating Sparky Ltd for a month, tend to include a higher proportion of direct costs than do more limited ones, such as a particular job done by Sparky Ltd. As we shall see shortly, this makes costing broader cost units rather more straightforward than costing narrower ones, since direct costs are easier to deal with than indirect ones.

Full costing and the behaviour of costs

We saw in Chapter 3 that the full cost of doing something (or total cost, as it is usually known in the context of marginal analysis) can be analysed between the fixed and the variable elements. This is illustrated in Figure 4.2.

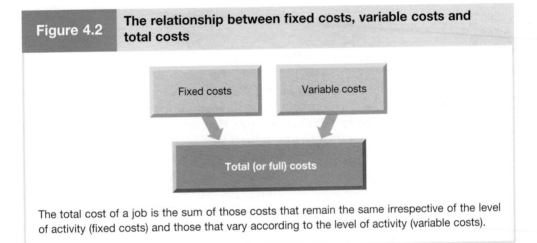

| Figure 4.2 | The relationship between fixed costs, variable costs and total costs |

The total cost of a job is the sum of those costs that remain the same irrespective of the level of activity (fixed costs) and those that vary according to the level of activity (variable costs).

The similarity of what is shown in Figure 4.2 to that depicted in Figure 4.1 seems to lead some people to believe, mistakenly, that variable costs and direct costs are the same and that fixed costs and overheads are the same. This is incorrect.

The notions of fixed and variable are concerned entirely with **cost behaviour** in the face of changes to the volume of activity. Directness of costs, on the other hand, is entirely concerned with collecting together the elements that make up full cost, that is, with the extent to which costs can be measured directly in respect of particular units of output or jobs. These are two entirely different concepts. Though it may be true that there is a tendency for fixed costs to be indirect costs (overheads) and for variable costs to be direct costs, there is no link, and there are many exceptions to this tendency. For example, most activities have variable overheads. Labour is a major element of direct cost in most types of business activity but is usually a fixed cost, at least over the short term.

The relationship between the reaction of costs to volume changes (cost behaviour), on the one hand, and how costs need to be gathered to deduce the full cost (cost collection), on the other, in respect of a particular job is shown in Figure 4.3.

Total cost is the sum of direct and indirect costs. It is also the sum of fixed and variable costs. These two facts are independent of one another. Thus a particular cost may, for example, be fixed relative to the level of output on the one hand, and be either direct or indirect on the other.

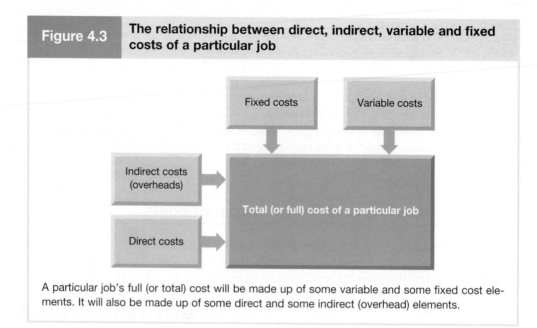

Figure 4.3   **The relationship between direct, indirect, variable and fixed costs of a particular job**

A particular job's full (or total) cost will be made up of some variable and some fixed cost elements. It will also be made up of some direct and some indirect (overhead) elements.

The problem of indirect costs

Distinguishing between direct and indirect costs is related only to deducing full cost in a job-costing environment, that is, where units of output differ. When we were considering costing a litre of 'Orange Fizz' drink in Activity 4.1, whether particular elements of cost were direct or indirect was of absolutely no consequence, because all costs were shared equally between the litres of 'Orange Fizz'. However, where we have units of output that are not identical, we have to look more closely at the make-up of the costs to achieve a fair measure of the full cost of a particular job.

Indirect costs of any activity must form part of the cost of each unit of output. By definition, however, they cannot be directly related to individual **cost units**. This raises a major practical issue: how are indirect costs to be apportioned to individual cost units?

Overheads as service renderers

It is reasonable to view the overheads as rendering a service to the cost units. A legal case undertaken by a firm of solicitors can be seen as being rendered a service by the office in which the work is done. In this sense, it is reasonable to charge each case (cost unit) with a share of the costs of running the office (rent, lighting, heating, cleaning, building maintenance, and so on). It also seems reasonable to relate the charge for the 'use' of the office to the level of service that the particular case has received from the office.

The next step is the difficult one. How might the cost of running the office, which is a cost of all work done by the firm, be divided between individual cases that are not similar in size and complexity?

One possibility is sharing this overhead cost equally between each case handled by the firm within the period. Most of us would not propose this method unless the cases were close to being identical in terms of the extent to which they had 'benefited' from the overheads.

If we are not to propose equal shares, we must identify something observable and measurable about the cases that we feel provides a reasonable basis for distinguishing between one case and the next in this context. In practice, time spent working on the cost unit by direct labour is the basis that is most popular. It must be stressed that this is not the 'correct' way, and it certainly is not the only way.

Job costing: a worked example

To see how job costing (as it is usually called) works, let us consider Example 4.1.

Johnson Ltd, a business that provides a television repair service to its customers, has overheads of £10,000 each month. Each month 1,000 direct labour hours are worked and charged to units of output (repairs carried out by the business). A particular repair undertaken by the business used direct materials costing £15. Direct labour worked on the repair was 3 hours and the wage rate is £8 an hour. Overheads are charged to jobs on a direct labour hour basis. What is the full cost of the repair?

Solution

First, let us establish the **overhead absorption (recovery) rate**, that is, the rate at which individual repairs will be charged with overheads. This is £10 (that is, £10,000/1,000) per direct labour hour.

Thus, the full cost of the repair is:

	£
Direct materials	15
Direct labour (3 × £8)	24
	39
Overheads (3 × £10)	30
Full cost of the job	69

Note, in Example 4.1, that the number of labour hours (3 hours) appears twice in deducing the full cost: once to deduce the direct labour cost and a second time to deduce the overheads to be charged to the repair. These are really two separate issues, though they are both based on the same number of labour hours.

Note also that if all of the repair jobs that are undertaken during the month are assigned overheads in a similar manner, all £10,000 of overheads will be charged to the jobs between them. Jobs that involve a lot of direct labour will be assigned a large share of overheads, and those that involve little direct labour will be assigned a small share of overheads.

Can you think of reasons why direct labour hours is regarded as the most logical basis for sharing overheads between cost units?

The reasons that occurred to us are as follows:

- Large jobs should logically attract large amounts of overheads because they are likely to have been rendered more 'service' by the overheads than small ones. The length of time that they are worked on by direct labour may be seen as a rough and ready way of measuring relative size, though other means of doing this may be found – for example, relative physical size, where the cost unit is a physical object, like a manufactured product.
- Most overheads are related to time. Rent, heating, lighting, non-current (fixed) asset depreciation, supervisors' and managers' salaries and loan interest, which are all typical

Activity 4.4 continued

overheads, are all more or less time based. That is to say that the overhead cost for one week tends to be about half of that for a similar two-week period. Thus, a basis of apportioning overheads to jobs that takes account of the length of time that the units of output benefited from the 'service' rendered by the overheads seems logical.

● Direct labour hours are capable of being measured for each job. They will normally be measured to deduce the direct labour element of cost in any case. Thus, a direct labour hour basis of dealing with overheads is practical to apply in the real world.

It cannot be emphasised enough that there is no 'correct' way to apportion overheads to jobs. Overheads (indirect costs), by definition, do not naturally relate to individual jobs. If, nevertheless, we wish to take account of the fact that overheads are part of the cost of all jobs, we must find some acceptable way of including a share of the total overheads in each job. If a particular means of doing this is accepted by those who use the full cost deduced, then the method is as good as any other method. Accounting is concerned only with providing useful information to decision makers. In practice, the method that seems to be regarded as being the most useful is the direct labour hour method. Real World 4.2, which we shall consider later in the chapter, provides some evidence of this.

Activity 4.5

Marine Suppliers Ltd undertakes a range of work, including making sails for small sailing boats on a made-to-measure basis.

The business expects to incur the following costs during the next month:

Direct labour costs	£60,000
Direct labour time	6,000 hours
Indirect labour cost	£9,000
Depreciation of machinery	£3,000
Rent and rates	£5,000
Heating, lighting and power	£2,000
Machine time	2,000 hours
Indirect materials	£500
Other miscellaneous indirect costs	£200
Direct materials cost	£3,000

The business has received an enquiry about a sail, and it is estimated that the sail will take 12 direct labour hours to make and will require 20 square metres of sailcloth, which costs £2 per square metre.

The business normally uses a direct labour hour basis of charging overheads to individual jobs.

What is the full cost of making the sail?

The direct costs of making the sail can be identified as follows:

	£
Direct materials (20 × £2)	40.00
Direct labour (12 × (£60,000/6,000))	120.00
	160.00

To deduce the indirect cost element that must be added to derive the full cost of the sail, we first need to total these costs as follows:

	£
Indirect labour	9,000
Depreciation	3,000
Rent and rates	5,000
Heating, lighting and power	2,000
Indirect materials	500
Other miscellaneous indirect costs	200
Total indirect costs	19,700

Since the business uses a direct labour hour basis of charging overheads to jobs, we need to deduce the indirect cost, or overhead recovery rate, per direct labour hour. This is simply:

$$£19,700/6,000 = £3.28 \text{ per direct labour hour}$$

Thus, the full cost of the sail would be expected to be:

	£
Direct materials (20 × £2)	40.00
Direct labour (12 × (£60,000/6,000))	120.00
Indirect costs (12 × £3.28)	39.36
Full cost	199.36

Activity 4.6

Suppose that Marine Suppliers Ltd (see Activity 4.5) used a machine hour basis of charging overheads to jobs. What would be the cost of the job detailed if it was expected to take 5 machine hours (as well as 12 direct labour hours)?

The total overheads of the business will of course be the same irrespective of the method of charging them to jobs. Thus, the overhead recovery rate, on a machine hour basis, will be:

$$£19,700/2,000 = £9.85 \text{ per machine hour}$$

Thus, the full cost of the sail would be expected to be:

	£
Direct materials (20 × £2)	40.00
Direct labour (12 × (£60,000/6,000))	120.00
Indirect costs (5 × £9.85)	49.25
Full cost	209.25

Selecting a basis for charging overheads

A question now presents itself as to which of the two costs for this sail is the correct one, or simply the better one. The answer is that neither is correct, as was pointed out earlier. Which is the better one is a matter of judgement. This judgement is concerned entirely with usefulness of information, which in this context is probably concerned with the attitudes of those who will be affected by the figure used. Thus, reasonableness, as those people perceive it, is likely to be the important issue.

Most people would probably feel that the nature of the overheads should influence the choice of the basis of charging the overheads to jobs. Where the operation is capital-intensive and overheads are primarily machine-based (such as depreciation, machine maintenance, power and so on), machine hours might be favoured. Otherwise direct labour hours might be preferred.

It could appear that one of these bases might be preferred to the other one simply because it apportions either a higher or a lower amount of overheads to a particular job. This would probably be irrational, however. Since the total overheads are the same irrespective of the method of dividing that total between individual jobs, a method that gives a higher share of overheads to one particular job must give a lower share to the remaining jobs. There is one cake of fixed size. If one person is to be given a relatively large slice, the other people, between them, must receive relatively small slices. To illustrate further this issue of apportioning overheads, consider Example 4.2.

Example 4.2

A business, that provides a service, expects to incur overheads totalling £20,000 next month. The total direct labour time worked is expected to be 1,600 hours and machines are expected to operate for a total of 1,000 hours.

During the next month, the business expects to do just two large jobs. Information concerning each job is as follows:

	Job 1	Job 2
Direct labour hours	800	800
Machine hours	700	300

How much of the total overheads will be charged to each job if overheads are to be charged on:

(a) a direct labour hour basis; and
(b) a machine hour basis?

What do you notice about the two sets of figures that you calculate?

(a) Direct labour hour basis

Overhead recovery rate = £20,000/1,600 = £12.50 per direct labour hour.

$$
\begin{array}{lll}
\text{Job 1} & £12.50 \times 800 = & \underline{£10,000} \\
\text{Job 2} & £12.50 \times 800 = & \underline{£10,000}
\end{array}
$$

(b) Machine hour basis

Overhead recovery rate = £20,000/1,000 = £20.00 per machine hour.

$$
\begin{array}{lll}
\text{Job 1} & £20.00 \times 700 = & \underline{£14,000} \\
\text{Job 2} & £20.00 \times 300 = & \underline{£\ \ 6,000}
\end{array}
$$

It is clear from these calculations that the total of the overheads charged to jobs is the same (that is, £20,000) whichever method is used. So, whereas the machine hour basis gives Job 1 a higher share than does the direct labour hour method, the opposite is true for Job 2.

It is not practical to charge overheads on one basis to one job and on the other basis to the other job. This is because either total overheads will not be fully charged to the jobs, or the jobs will be overcharged with overheads. For example, using the direct labour hour method for Job 1 (£10,000) and the machine hour basis for Job 2 (£6,000) will mean that only £16,000 of a total £20,000 of overheads will be charged to jobs. As a result, the objective of full costing, which is to charge all overheads to jobs done, will not be achieved. In this particular case, if selling prices are based on full costs, the business may not charge high enough prices to cover all of its costs.

Activity 4.7

The point was made above that it would normally be irrational to prefer one basis of charging overheads to jobs simply because it apportions either a higher or a lower amount of overheads to a particular job. This is because the total overheads are the same irrespective of the method of charging the total to individual jobs. Can you think of any circumstances where it would not necessarily be so irrational?

This might apply where, for a particular job, a customer has agreed to pay a price based on full cost plus an agreed fixed percentage for profit. Here it would be beneficial to the producer for the total cost of the job to be as high as possible. This would be relatively unusual, but sometimes public sector organisations, particularly central and local government departments, have entered into contracts to have work done, with the price to be deduced, after the work has been completed, on a cost-plus basis. Such contracts are pretty rare these days, probably because they are open to abuse in the way described. Usually, contract prices are agreed in advance, typically in conjunction with competitive tendering.

Real World 4.2 provides some insight to the basis of overhead recovery in the practice.

 **REAL WORLD 4.2**

Overhead recovery rates in practice

A survey of 303 UK manufacturing businesses, published in 1993, showed that the direct labour hour basis of charging overheads to cost units was overwhelmingly the most popular, used by 73 per cent of the respondents to the survey. Where the work has a strong labour element this seems reasonable, but the survey also showed that 68 per cent of businesses used this basis for automated activities. It is surprising that direct labour hours should have been used as the basis of charging overheads in an environment dominated by machines and machine-related costs.

Though this survey is not very recent and applied only to manufacturing businesses, in the absence of other information it provides some impression of what happens in practice. There is no reason to believe that current practice is very different from that which applied at the beginning of the 1990s.

Source: Based on information taken from Drury *et al*. (see reference 3 at the end of the chapter).

Segmenting the overheads

As we have just seen, charging the same overheads to different jobs on different bases is not possible. It is possible, however, to charge one segment of the total overheads on one basis and another segment, or other segments, on another basis.

Activity 4.8

Taking the same business as in Example 4.2, on closer analysis we find that of the overheads totalling £20,000 next month, £8,000 relate to machines (depreciation, maintenance, rent of the space occupied by the machines and so on) and the remaining £12,000 to more general overheads. The other information about the business is exactly as it was before.

How much of the total overheads will be charged to each job if the machine-related overheads are to be charged on a machine hour basis and the remaining overheads are charged on a direct labour hour basis?

Direct labour hour basis

Overhead recovery rate = £12,000/1,600 = £7.50 per direct labour hour

Machine hour basis

Overhead recovery rate = £8,000/1,000 = £8.00 per machine hour

Overheads charged to jobs

	Job 1 £	Job 2 £
Direct labour hour basis		
£7.50 × 800	6,000	
£7.50 × 800		6,000
Machine hour basis		
£8.00 × 700	5,600	
£8.00 × 300		2,400
Total	11,600	8,400

We can see from this that the expected overheads of £20,000 are charged in total.

Segmenting the overheads in this way may well be seen as providing a better basis of charging overheads to jobs. This is quite often found in practice, usually by dividing a business into separate 'areas' for costing purposes, charging overheads differently from one area to the next.

Remember that there is no correct basis of charging overheads to jobs, so our frequent reference to the direct labour and machine hour bases should not be taken to imply that these are the correct methods. However, it should be said that these two methods do have something to commend them and are popular in practice. As we have already discussed, a sensible method does need to identify something about each job that can be measured and which distinguishes it from other jobs. There is also a lot to be said for methods that are concerned with time, because most overheads are time related.

Dealing with overheads on a departmental basis

In general, all but the smallest businesses are divided into departments. Normally, each department deals with a separate activity. The reasons for dividing a business into departments include the following:

- Many businesses are too large and complex to be managed as a single unit. It is usually more practical to operate each business as a series of relatively independent units (departments) with each one having its own manager.
- Each department normally has its own area of specialism and is managed by a specialist.
- Each department can have its own accounting records that enable its performance to be assessed. This can lead to greater management control and motivation among the staff.

Very many businesses deal with charging overheads to cost units on a department-by-department basis. They do this in the expectation that it will give rise to a more useful way of charging overheads. It is probably often the case that it does not lead to any great improvement in the usefulness of the resulting full costs. Though it may not be of enormous benefit in many cases, it is probably not an expensive exercise to apply overheads on a departmental basis. Since costs are collected department by department for other purposes (particularly control), to apply overheads on a department-by-department basis is a relatively simple matter.

We shall now take a look at how the departmental approach to deriving full costs works, in a service-industry context, through Example 4.3.

Example 4.3

Autosparkle Ltd offers a motor vehicle paint-respray service. The jobs that it under-takes range from painting a small part of a saloon car, usually following a minor accident, to a complete respray of a double-decker bus.

Each job starts life in the Preparation Department, where it is prepared for the Paintshop. In the Preparation Department the job is worked on by direct workers, in most cases taking some direct materials from the stores with which to treat the old paintwork to render the vehicle ready for respraying. Thus the job will be charged with direct materials, direct labour and with a share of the Preparation Department's overheads. The job then passes into the Paintshop Department, already valued at the costs that it picked up in the Preparation Department.

In the Paintshop, the staff draw direct materials from the stores and direct workers spend time respraying the job, using a sophisticated spraying apparatus as well as working by hand. So, in the Paintshop, the job is charged with direct materials, direct labour plus a share of that department's overheads. The job now passes into the Finishing Department, valued at the cost of the materials, labour and overheads that it accumulated in the first two departments.

In the Finishing Department, jobs are cleaned and polished ready to go back to the customers. Further direct labour and, in some cases, materials are added. All jobs also pick up a share of that department's overheads. The job, now complete, passes back to the customer.

→

Example 4.3 continued

Figure 4.4 shows graphically how this works for a particular job.

The basis of charging overheads to jobs (for example, direct labour hours) might be the same for all three departments, or it might be different from one department to another. It is possible that spraying apparatus costs dominate the Paintshop costs, so overheads might well be charged to jobs on a machine hour basis. The other two departments are probably labour intensive, so that direct labour hours may be seen as being appropriate there.

Figure 4.4 **A cost unit (Job A) passing through Autosparkle Ltd's process**

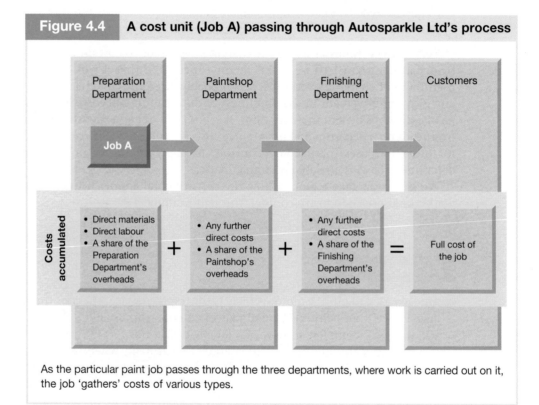

As the particular paint job passes through the three departments, where work is carried out on it, the job 'gathers' costs of various types.

The passage of the job through the departments can be compared to a snowball being rolled across snow: as it rolls, it picks up more and more snow.

Where costs are dealt with departmentally, each department is known as a **cost centre**. This can be defined as some physical area or some activity or function for which costs are separately identified. Charging direct costs to jobs, in a departmental system, is exactly the same as where the whole business is one single cost centre. It is simply a matter of keeping a record of:

● the number of hours of direct labour worked on the particular job and the grade of labour, assuming that there are different grades with different rates of pay;
● the cost of the direct materials taken from stores and applied to the job; and
● any other direct costs, for example some subcontracted work, associated with the job.

This record-keeping will normally be done departmentally in a departmental system.

It is obviously necessary to break down the production overheads of the entire business on a departmental basis. This means that the total overheads of the business must be divided between the departments, such that the sum of the departmental overheads equals the overheads for the entire business. By charging all of their overheads to jobs, the departments will, between them, charge all of the overheads of the business to jobs. **Real World 4.3** provides an indication of the number of different cost centres that businesses tend to use in practice.

REAL WORLD 4.3

Cost centres in practice

It is not unusual for a large business to have several cost centres. The survey of large UK businesses by Drury and Tayles referred to earlier (see Real World 4.1), revealed the following:

Figure 4.5	Analysis of the number of cost centres within a business

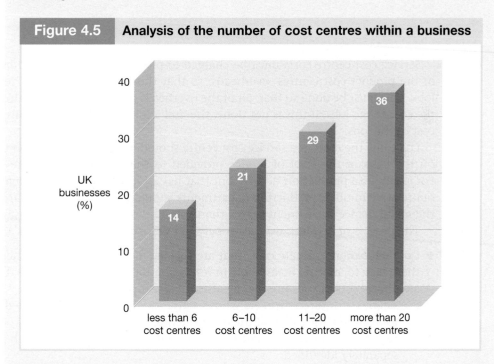

We can see from Figure 4.5 that 86 per cent of businesses surveyed had 6 or more cost centres and that 36 per cent of businesses had more than 20 cost centres. Though not shown on the diagram, 3 per cent of businesses surveyed had a single cost centre (that is, there was business-wide or overall overhead rate only used).

Source: Based on information taken from Drury and Tayles (see reference 1 at the end of the chapter).

For purposes of cost assignment, it is necessary to distinguish between **product cost centres** (or departments) and **service cost centres** (or departments). Product cost centres are departments in which jobs are worked on by direct workers and/or where direct materials are added. Here jobs can be charged with a share of their overheads. The Preparation, Paintshop and Finishing Departments, discussed above in Example 4.3, are all examples of product cost centres.

Activity 4.9

Can you guess what the definition of a service cost centre is? Can you think of an example of a service cost centre?

A service cost centre is one where no direct costs are involved. It renders a service to other cost centres. Examples include:

- General administration
- Accounting
- Stores
- Maintenance
- Personnel
- Catering.

All of these render services to product cost centres and, possibly, to other service cost centres.

Service cost centre costs must be charged to product cost centres, and become part of the product cost centres' overheads, so that those overheads can be recharged to jobs. This must be done so that, all of the overheads of the business find their way into the cost of the jobs. If this is not done, the 'full' cost derived will not really be the full cost of the jobs.

Logically, the costs of a service cost centre should be charged to product cost centres on the basis of the level of service provided to the product cost centre concerned. For example, a production department that has a lot of machine maintenance carried out relative to other production departments should be charged with a larger share of the maintenance department's costs than should those other product cost centres.

The process of dividing overheads between departments is as follows:

- **Cost allocation**. Allocate costs that are specific to the departments. These are costs that relate to, and are measurable in respect of, individual departments, that is, they are direct costs of running the department. Examples include:
  (a) salaries of indirect workers whose activities are wholly within the department, for example the salary of the departmental manager;
  (b) rent, where the department is housed in its own premises for which rent can be separately identified;
  (c) electricity, where it is separately metered for each department.
- **Cost apportionment**. Apportion the more general overheads to the departments. These are overheads that relate to more than one department, perhaps to them all. These would include:
  (a) rent, where more than one department is housed in the same premises;
  (b) electricity, where it is not separately metered;
  (c) salaries of cleaning staff who work in a variety of departments.

These costs would be apportioned to departments on some fair basis, such as by square metres of floor area, in the case of rent, or by level of mechanisation, for electricity used to power machinery. As with charging overheads to individual jobs, usefulness is the issue; there is no correct basis of apportioning general overheads to departments.

● Having totalled, allocated and apportioned costs to all departments, it is now necessary to apportion the total costs of service cost centres to production departments. Logically, the basis of apportionment should be the level of service rendered by the individual service department to the individual production department. With personnel department costs, for example, the basis of apportionment might be the number of staff in each production department, because it could be argued that the higher the number of staff, the more benefit the production department has derived from the personnel department. This is, of course, rather a crude approach. A particular production department may have severe personnel problems and a high staff turnover rate, which may make it a user of the personnel service that is way out of proportion to the number of staff in the production department.

The final total for each product cost centre is that cost centre's overheads. These can be charged to jobs as they pass through. We shall now go on to consider an example dealing with overheads on a departmental basis (Example 4.4).

Example 4.4

A business consists of four departments:

● Preparation department
● Machining department
● Finishing department
● General administration (GA) department.

The first three are product cost centres and the last renders a service to the other three. The level of service rendered is thought to be roughly in proportion to the number of employees in each production department.

Overhead costs, and other data, for next month are expected to be as follows:

	£
Rent	10,000
Electricity to power machines	3,000
Electricity for heating and lighting	800
Insurance of premises	200
Cleaning	600
Depreciation of machines	2,000

Salaries of each of the indirect workers are as follows:

	£000
Preparation department	2,000
Machining department	2,400
Finishing department	1,800
General administration department	1,800

The general administration department has a staff consisting of only indirect workers (including managers). The other departments have both indirect workers (including managers) and direct workers. There are 100 indirect workers within each of the four departments and none do any 'direct' work.

Example 4.4 continued

Each direct worker is expected to work 160 hours next month. The number of direct workers in each department is:

Preparation department	600
Machining department	900
Finishing department	500

Machining department direct workers are paid £12 an hour; other direct workers are paid £10 an hour.

All of the machinery is in the machining department. Machines are expected to operate for 120,000 hours next month.

The floorspace (in square metres) occupied by the departments is as follows:

	Sq m
Preparation department	16,000
Machining department	20,000
Finishing department	10,000
General administration department	2,000

Deducing the overheads department by department can be done, using a schedule, as follows:

	Total £000	Prep'n £000	Mach'g £000	Fin'g £000	GA £000
	£000				
Allocated costs:					
Machine power		3,000		3,000	
Machine depreciation		2,000		2,000	
Indirect salaries		8,000	2,000	2,400	1,800	1,800
Apportioned costs					
Rent	10,000				
Heating and lighting	800				
Insurance of premises	200				
Cleaning	600				
Apportioned by floor area		11,600	3,867	4,833	2,417	483
Departmental overheads		24,600	5,867	12,233	4,217	2,283
Reapportion GA costs by number of staff (including the indirect workers)			695	993	595	(2,283)
		24,600	6,562	13,226	4,812	–

Activity 4.10

Assume that the machining department overheads (in Example 4.4) are to be charged to jobs on a machine hour basis, but that the direct labour hour basis is to be used for the other two departments. What will be the full cost of a job with the following characteristics?

	Preparation	Machining	Finishing
Direct labour hours	10	7	5
Machine hours	–	6	–
Direct materials (£)	85	13	6

Hint: This should be tackled as if each department were a separate business, then departmental costs are added together for the job so as to arrive at the total full cost.

Firstly, we need to deduce the overhead recovery rates for each department:
  Preparation department (direct labour hour based):

$$\frac{£6,562,000}{600 \times 160} = £68.35$$

Machining department (machine hour based):

$$\frac{£13,226,000}{120,000} = £110.22$$

Finishing department (direct labour hour based):

$$\frac{£4,812,000}{500 \times 160} = £60.15$$

The cost of the job is as follows:

	£	£
Direct labour:		
Preparation department (10 × £10)	100.00	
Machining department (7 × £12)	84.00	
Finishing department (5 × £10)	50.00	
		234.00
Direct materials:		
Preparation department	85.00	
Machining department	13.00	
Finishing department	6.00	
		104.00
Overheads:		
Preparation department (10 × £68.35)	683.50	
Machining department (6 × £110.22)	661.32	
Finishing department (5 × £60.15)	300.75	
		1,645.57
Full cost of the job		1,983.57

Activity 4.11

The manufacturing costs for Buccaneers Ltd for next year are expected to be as follows:

	£000
Direct materials:	
Forming department	450
Machining department	100
Finishing department	50
Direct labour:	
Forming department	180
Machining department	120
Finishing department	75
Indirect materials:	
Forming department	40
Machining department	30
Finishing department	10
Administration department	10
Indirect labour:	
Forming department	80
Machining department	70
Finishing department	60
Administration department	60
Maintenance costs	50
Rent and rates	100
Heating and lighting	20
Building insurance	10
Machinery insurance	10
Depreciation of machinery	120
Total manufacturing costs	1,645

The following additional information is available:

(i)   All direct labour is paid £6 an hour for all hours worked.
(ii) The administration department renders personnel and general services to the production departments.
(iii) The area of the premises in which the business manufactures amounts to 50,000 square metres, divided as follows:

	Sq m
Forming department	20,000
Machining department	15,000
Finishing department	10,000
Administration department	5,000

(iv) The maintenance employees are expected to divide their time between the production departments as follows:

	%
Forming department	15
Machining department	75
Finishing department	10

(v) Machine hours are expected to be as follows:

	Hours
Forming department	5,000
Machining department	15,000
Finishing department	5,000

On the basis of this information:

(a) Allocate and apportion overheads to the three production departments.
(b) Deduce overhead recovery rates for each department using two different bases for each department's overheads.
(c) Calculate the full cost of a job with the following characteristics:

Direct labour hours:	
Forming department	4 hours
Machining department	4 hours
Finishing department	1 hour
Machine hours:	
Forming department	1 hour
Machining department	2 hours
Finishing department	1 hour
Direct materials:	
Forming department	£40
Machining department	£9
Finishing department	£4

Use whichever of the two bases of overhead recovery, deduced in (b), that you consider more appropriate.

(d) Explain why you consider the basis used in (c) to be the more appropriate.

(a) Overheads can be allocated and apportioned as follows:

Cost	Basis of apport't	Total £000	Forming £000	Machining £000	Finishing £000	Admin. £000
Indirect materials	Specifically allocated	90	40	30	10	10
Indirect labour	Specifically allocated	270	80	70	60	60
Maintenance	Staff time	50	7.5	37.5	5	–
Rent/rates		100				
Heat/light		20				
Buildings insurance		10				
	Area	130	52	39	26	13
Machine insurance		10				
Machine depreciation		120				
	Machine hours	130	26	78	26	–
		670	205.5	254.5	127	83
Admin.	Direct labour		39.84	26.56	16.6	(83)
		670	245.34	281.06	143.6	–

Note: Direct costs are not included in the above because they are allocated *directly* to jobs.

→

Activity 4.11 continued

(b) Overhead recovery rates are as follows:

Basis 1: direct labour hours

$$\text{Forming} = \frac{£245,340}{180,000/6} = £8.18 \text{ per direct labour hour}$$

$$\text{Machining} = \frac{£281,060}{120,000/6} = £14.05 \text{ per direct labour hour}$$

$$\text{Finishing} = \frac{£143,600}{75,000/6} = £11.49 \text{ per direct labour hour}$$

Basis 2: machine hours

$$\text{Forming} = \frac{£245,340}{5,000} = £49.07 \text{ per machine hour}$$

$$\text{Machining} = \frac{£281,060}{15,000} = £18.74 \text{ per machine hour}$$

$$\text{Finishing} = \frac{£143,600}{5,000} = £28.72 \text{ per machine hour}$$

(c) Full cost of job – on direct-labour-hour basis of overhead recovery

	£	£
Direct labour cost (9 × £6)		54.00
Direct materials (£40 + £9 + £4)		53.00
Overheads:		
Forming (4 × £8.18)	32.72	
Machining (4 × £14.05)	56.20	
Finishing (1 × £11.49)	11.49	100.41
Full cost		£207.41

(d) The reason for using the direct labour hour basis rather than the machine hour basis was that labour is more important, in terms of the number of hours applied to output, than is machine time. Strong arguments could have been made for the use of the alternative basis; certainly, a machine hour basis could have been justified for the machining department.

It would be possible, and it may be reasonable, to use one basis in respect of one department's overheads and a different one for those of another department. For example, machine hours could have been used for the machining department and a direct labour hours basis for the other two.

Batch costing

The production of many types of goods and services (particularly goods) involves producing in a batch of identical, or nearly identical, units of output, but where each batch is distinctly different from other batches. For example, a theatre may put on a production whose nature (and therefore costs) is very different from that of other productions. On the other hand, ignoring differences in the desirability of the various types of seating, all of the individual units of output (tickets to see the production) are identical.

In these circumstances, we should normally deduce the cost per ticket by using a job costing approach (taking account of direct and indirect costs and so on) to find the cost of mounting the production and then we should simply divide this by the expected number of tickets to be sold to find the cost per ticket. This is known as **batch costing**.

Full cost as the break-even price

We should recognise that if all goes according to plan (so that direct costs, overheads and the basis of charging overheads, for example direct labour hours, prove to be as expected), then selling the output for its full cost should cause the business to break even exactly. Therefore, whatever profit (in total) is loaded onto full cost to set actual selling prices will result in that level of profit being earned for the period.

The forward-looking nature of full costing

Though deducing full costs can be done after the work has been completed, it is often done in advance. In other words, costs are frequently predicted. Where, for example, full costs are needed as a basis on which to set selling prices, it is usually the case that prices need to be set before the customer will accept the job being done. Even where no particular customer has been identified, some idea of the ultimate price will need to be known before the business will be able to make a judgement as to whether potential customers will buy the product, and in what quantities. There is a risk, of course, that the actual outcome will differ from that which was predicted. If this occurs, corrections are subsequently made to the full costs originally calculated.

Self-assessment question 4.1

Hector and Co. Ltd has been invited to tender for a contract to produce 1,000 clothes hangers. The following information relates to the contract.

- *Materials*: The clothes hangers are made of metal wire covered with a padded fabric. Each hanger requires 2 metres of wire and 0.5 square metres of fabric.
- *Direct labour*: – Skilled: 10 minutes per hanger
  – Unskilled: 5 minutes per hanger.

The business already has sufficient stock of each of the materials required to complete the contract. Information on the cost of the stock is as follows:

	Metal wire £/m	Fabric £/m²
Historic cost	2.20	1.00
Current buying-in cost	2.50	1.10
Scrap value	1.70	0.40

The metal wire is in constant use by the business for a range of its products. The fabric has no other use for the business and is scheduled to be scrapped.

Unskilled labour, which is paid at the rate of £5.00 an hour, will need to be taken on specifically to undertake the contract. The business is fairly quiet at the moment, which means that a pool of skilled labour exists that will still be employed at full pay of £7.50 an hour to do nothing if the contract does not proceed. The pool of skilled labour is sufficient to complete the contract.

Self-assessment question 4.1 continued

The business charges jobs with overheads on a direct labour hour basis. The production overheads of the entire business for the month in which the contract will be undertaken are estimated at £50,000. The estimated total direct labour hours that will be worked are 12,500. The business tends not to alter the established overhead recovery rate to reflect increases or reductions to estimated total hours arising from new contracts. The total overhead cost is not expected to increase as a result of undertaking the contract.

The business normally adds 12.5 per cent profit loading to the job cost to arrive at a first estimate of the tender price.

Required:
(a) Price this job on a traditional job-costing basis.
(b) Indicate the minimum price at which the contract could be undertaken such that the business would be neither better nor worse off as a result of doing it.

Uses of full-cost information

Why do we need to deduce full-cost information? There are probably two main reasons:

- *For pricing purposes*. In some industries and circumstances, full costs are used as the basis of pricing. Here, the full cost is deduced and a percentage is added for profit. This is known as **cost-plus pricing**. Garages, carrying out vehicle repairs, typically operate in this way. Solicitors and accountants doing work for clients often use this approach as well.

  In many circumstances, suppliers are not in a position to deduce prices on a cost-plus basis, however. Where there is a competitive market, a supplier will usually have to accept the price that the market offers: that is, most suppliers are *price takers* not *price makers*. We shall take a closer look at pricing, and the place of full costs in it, in Chapter 5.

- *For income measurement purposes*. To provide a valid means of measuring a business's income it is necessary to match expenses with the revenues realised in the same accounting period. Where a service is partially rendered in one accounting period but the revenue is realised in the next, or where manufactured stock (inventory) is made or partially made in one period but sold in the next, the full cost (including an appropriate share of overheads) must be carried from the first accounting period to the second one. Unless we are able to identify the full cost of work done in one period that is the subject of a sale in the next, the profit figures of the periods concerned will become meaningless. This will mean that users of accounting information will not have a reliable means of assessing the effectiveness of the business as a whole, or the effectiveness of individual parts of it. This second reason for needing full cost information can be illustrated by Example 4.5.

Example 4.5

During the accounting year that ended on 31 December last year, Engineers Ltd made a special machine for a customer. At the beginning of this year, after having a series of tests successfully completed by a subcontractor, the machine was delivered

CRITICISMS OF FULL COSTING

to the customer. The business's normal practice (typical of most businesses and following the realisation convention) is to take account of sales when the product passes to the customer. The sale price of the machine was £25,000.

During last year, materials costing £3,500 were used on making the machine and 1,200 hours of direct labour, costing £9,300, were worked on the machine. The business uses a direct labour hour basis of charging overheads to jobs, which is believed to be fair because most of its work is labour intensive. The total manufacturing overheads for the business for last year were £77,000, and the total direct labour hours worked were 22,000. Testing the machine cost £1,000.

How much profit or loss did the business make on the machine during last year? How much profit or loss did the business make on the machine during this year? At what value should the business have included the machine on its balance sheet at the end of last year so that the correct profit will be recorded for each of the two years?

No profit or loss was made during last year, following the business's (and the generally accepted) approach to recognising revenues (sales). If the sale were not to be recognised until this year it would be illogical (and in contravention of the matching convention) to treat the costs of making the machine as expenses until that time.

During this year, the sale would be recognised and all of the costs, including a reasonable share of overheads, would be set against it in this year's profit and loss account (income statement) as follows:

	£	£
Sales price		25,000
Costs:		
Direct labour	(9,300)	
Direct materials	(3,500)	
Overheads (1,200 × (£77,000/22,000))	(4,200)	
Total incurred last year	(17,000)	
Testing cost	(1,000)	
Total cost		(18,000)
This year's profit from the machine		7,000

The machine needs to be shown as an asset of the business (valued at £17,000) in the balance sheet as at 31 December last year.

Unless all production costs are charged in the same accounting period as that in which the sale is recognised in the profit and loss account (income statement), distortions will occur that will render the profit and loss account much less useful. Thus it is necessary to deduce the full cost of any production undertaken completely or partially in one accounting period, but sold in a subsequent one.

Criticisms of full costing

Full costing has been criticised because, in practice, it tends to use past costs and to restrict its consideration of future costs to outlay costs. It can be argued that past costs are irrelevant, irrespective of the purpose for which the information is to be used. This is basically because it is not possible to make decisions about the past, only about the future. Advocates of full costing would argue that it provides an informative long-run average cost.

Despite the criticisms that are made of full costing, it is, according to research evidence, very widely practised.

SUMMARY

The main points in this chapter may be summarised as follows:

Full cost = the total amount of resources sacrificed to achieve a particular objective.

Single-product operations

- Where all the units of output are identical, the full cost can be calculated as follows:

$$\text{Cost per unit} = \frac{\text{Total cost of output}}{\text{Number of units produced}}$$

Multi-product operations – job costing

- Where units of output are not identical, it is necessary to divide the costs into two categories: direct costs and indirect costs.
- Direct costs = costs that can be identified with specific cost units (for example, labour of a garage mechanic).
- Indirect costs (overheads) = costs that cannot be directly measured in respect of particular cost units (for example, the rent of a garage).
- Full cost = direct cost + indirect cost.
- Direct/indirect is not linked to variable/fixed.
- Indirect costs are difficult to relate to individual cost units – arbitrary bases are used and there is no single correct method.
- Traditionally, indirect costs are seen as the costs of providing a 'service' to cost units.
- Direct labour hour basis of applying indirect costs to cost units is the most popular in practice.

Dealing with overheads on a departmental basis

- Indirect costs can be segmented – usually on departmental basis – each department has its own overhead recovery rate.
- Each department is a separate cost centre – that is an area, activity or function for which costs are separately collected.
- Overheads must be allocated or apportioned to cost centres.
- Service cost centre costs must then be apportioned to product cost centres and product cost centre overheads absorbed by cost units (jobs).

Batch costing

- A variation of job costing where each job consists of a number of identical (or near identical) cost units:

$$\text{Cost per unit} = \frac{\text{Cost of the batch (direct + indirect)}}{\text{Number of units in the batch}}$$

If the full cost is charged as the sales price and things go according to plan, the business will break even.

Uses of full cost information

- Pricing (full cost) on a cost-plus basis.
- Income measurement.

Full cost information is seen by some as not very useful because it can be backward looking: it includes information irrelevant to decision making, but excludes some relevant information.

→ Key terms

Full costing p. 77	**Cost unit** p. 82
Full cost p. 77	**Overhead absorption (recovery)**
Process costing p. 78	**rate** p. 83
Direct costs p. 78	**Cost centre** p. 90
Indirect costs p. 79	**Product cost centre** p. 91
Overheads p. 79	**Service cost centre** p. 91
Common costs p. 79	**Cost allocation** p. 92
Job costing p. 79	**Cost apportionment** p. 92
Cost behaviour p. 81	**Batch costing** p. 99
Total cost p. 81	**Cost-plus pricing** p. 100

Further reading

If you would like to explore the topics covered in this chapter in more depth, we recommend the following books:

Management Accounting, *Atkinson A., Banker R., Kaplan R. and Young S. M.*, 3rd edn, Prentice Hall, 2001, chapter 4.

Management and Cost Accounting, *Drury C.*, 5th edn, Thomson Learning Business Press, 2000, chapters 3, 4 and 5.

Cost Accounting: A managerial emphasis, *Horngren C., Foster G. and Datar S.*, 11th edn, Prentice Hall International, 2002, chapter 4.

Cost and Management Accounting, *Williamson D.*, Prentice Hall International, 1996, chapters 6, 8 and 10.

References

1 **Cost Systems Design and Profitability Analysis in UK Manufacturing Companies**, *Drury C. and Tayles M.*, CIMA Publishing, 2000.

2 **2003 Survey of Management Accounting**, *Ernst and Young*, Ernst and Young, 2003.

3 **A Survey of Management Accounting Practices in UK Manufacturing Companies**, *Drury C., Braund S., Osborne P. and Tayles M.*, Chartered Association of Certified Accountants, 1993.

REVIEW QUESTIONS

Answers to these questions can be found on the students' side of the Companion Website at www.pearsoned.co.uk/atrillmclaney.

4.1 What problem does the existence of work in progress cause in process costing?

4.2 What is the point of distinguishing direct costs from indirect ones? Why is this not necessary in process costing environments?

4.3 Are direct costs and variable costs the same thing? Explain your answer.

4.4 It is sometimes claimed that the full cost of pursuing some objective represents the long-run break-even selling price. Why is this said, and what does it mean?

EXERCISES

Exercises 4.4 to 4.8 are more advanced than 4.1 to 4.3. Those with a coloured number have answers at the back of the book.

4.1 Bodgers Ltd, a business that provides a market research service, operates a job costing system. Towards the end of each financial year, the overhead recovery rate (the rate at which overheads will be charged to jobs) is established for the forthcoming year.

(a) Why does the business bother to predetermine the recovery rate in the way outlined?
(b) What steps will be involved in predetermining the rate?
(c) What problems might arise with using a predetermined rate?

4.2 Athena Ltd is an engineering business doing work for its customers to their particular requirements and specifications. It determines the full cost of each job taking a 'job costing' approach, accounting for overheads on a departmental basis. It bases its prices to customers on this full cost figure. The business has two departments: a Machining Department, where each job starts, and a Fitting Department, which completes all of the jobs. Machining Department overheads are charged to jobs on a machine hour basis and those of the Fitting Department on a direct labour hour basis. The budgeted information for next year is as follows:

Heating and lighting	£25,000	(allocated equally between the two departments)
Machine power	£10,000	(all allocated to the Machining Department)
Direct labour	£200,000	(£150,000 allocated to the Fitting Department and £50,000 to the Machining Department. All direct workers are paid £5 an hour)
Indirect labour	£50,000	(apportioned to the departments in proportion to the direct labour cost)
Direct materials	£120,000	(all applied to jobs in the Machining Department)
Depreciation	£30,000	(all relates to the Machining Department)
Machine time	200,000 hours	(all worked in the Machining Department)

Required:

(a) Prepare a statement showing the budgeted overheads for next year, analysed between the two departments. This should be in the form of three columns: one for the total figure for each type of overhead and one column each for the two departments, where each type of overhead is analysed between the two departments. Each column should also show the total of overheads for the year.

(b) Derive the appropriate rate for charging the overheads of each department to jobs (that is, a separate rate for each department).

(c) Athena Ltd has been asked by a customer to specify the price that it will charge for a particular job that will, if the job goes ahead, be undertaken early next year. The job is expected to use direct materials costing Athena Ltd £1,200, to need 50 hours of machining time, 10 hours of Machine Department direct labour and 40 hours of Fitting Department direct labour. Athena Ltd charges a profit loading of 20% to the full cost of jobs to determine the selling price.

Show workings to derive the proposed selling price for this job.

4.3 Pieman Products Ltd makes road trailers to the precise specifications of individual customers. The following are predicted to occur during the forthcoming year, which is about to start:

Direct materials cost	£50,000
Direct labour costs	£80,000
Direct labour time	16,000 hours
Indirect labour cost	£25,000
Depreciation of machine	£8,000
Rent and rates	£10,000
Heating, lighting and power	£5,000
Indirect materials	£2,000
Other indirect costs	£1,000
Machine time	3,000 hours

All direct labour is paid at the same hourly rate.

A customer has asked the business to build a trailer for transporting a racing motorcycle to races. It is estimated that this will require materials and components that will cost £1,150. It will take 250 direct labour hours to do the job, of which 50 will involve the use of machinery.

Required:

Deduce a logical cost for the job, and explain the basis of dealing with overheads that you propose.

4.4 Promptprint Ltd, a printing business, has received an enquiry from a potential customer for the quotation of a price for a job. The pricing policy of the business is based on the plans for the next financial year shown below.

	£
Sales (billings to customers)	196,000
Materials (direct)	(38,000)
Labour (direct)	(32,000)
Variable overheads	(2,400)
Advertising (for business)	(3,000)
Depreciation	(27,600)
Administration	(36,000)
Interest	(8,000)
Profit (before tax)	49,000

A first estimate of the direct costs for the job are:

	£
Direct materials	4,000
Direct labour	3,600

Required:

(a) Prepare a recommended price for the job based on the plans, commenting on your method, ignoring the information given in the Appendix (below).

(b) Comment on the validity of using financial plans in pricing, and recommend any improvements you would consider desirable for the pricing policy used in (a).

(c) Incorporate the effects of the information shown in the Appendix (below) into your estimates of direct material costs, explaining any changes you consider it necessary to make to the above direct material cost of £4,000.

Appendix to Exercise 4.4

Based on historic costs, direct material costs were computed as follows:

	£
Paper grade 1	1,200
Paper grade 2	2,000
Card (zenith grade)	500
Inks and other miscellaneous items	300
	4,000

Paper grade 1 is in stock and in regular use. Because it is imported, it is estimated that if it is used for this job, a new stock order will have to be placed shortly. Sterling has depreciated against the foreign currency by 25 per cent since the last purchase.

Paper grade 2 is purchased from the same source as grade 1. However, current stock was bought in for a special order. This order was cancelled, although the defaulting customer was required to pay £500 towards the cost of the paper. The accountant has offset this against the original cost to arrive at the figure of £2,000 shown above. This paper is rarely used, and due to its special chemical coating will be unusable if it is not used on the job in question.

The card is another specialist item currently in stock. There is no use foreseen, and it would cost £750 to replace if required. However, the stock controller had planned to spend £130 on overprinting to use the card as a substitute for other materials costing £640.

Inks and other items are in regular use in the print shop.

4.5   Bookdon plc manufactures three products, X, Y and Z, in two production departments: a machine shop and a fitting section; it also has two service departments: a canteen and a machine maintenance section. Shown below are next year's planned production data and manufacturing costs for the business.

	X	Y	Z
Production	4,200 units	6,900 units	1,700 units
Direct materials	£11/unit	£14/unit	£17/unit
Direct labour			
Machine shop	£6/unit	£4/unit	£2/unit
Fitting section	£12/unit	£3/unit	£21/unit
Machine hours	6 hr/unit	3 hr/unit	4 hr/unit

Planned overheads are as follows:

	Machine shop	Fitting section	Canteen	Machine maintenance section	Total
Allocated overheads	£27,660	£19,470	£16,600	£26,650	£90,380
Rent, rates, heat and light					£17,000
Depreciation and insurance of equipment					£25,000
Additional data:					
Gross book value of equipment	£150,000	£75,000	£30,000	£45,000	
Number of employees	18	14	4	4	
Floor space occupied	3,600 m²	1,400 m²	1,000 m²	800 m²	

All machining is carried out in the machine shop. It has been estimated that approximately 70 per cent of the machine maintenance section's costs are incurred servicing the machine shop and the remainder servicing the fitting section.

Required:
(a) Calculate the following planned overhead absorption rates:
   (i) A machine-hour rate for the machine shop.
   (ii) A rate expressed as a percentage of direct wages for the fitting section.
(b) Calculate the planned full cost per unit of product X.

4.6 Shown below is an extract from next year's plans for a business manufacturing three products, A, B and C, in three production departments.

	A	B	C
Production	4,000 units	3,000 units	6,000 units
Direct material cost	£7 per unit	£4 per unit	£9 per unit
Direct labour requirements:			
Cutting department:			
Skilled operatives	3 hr/unit	5 hr/unit	2 hr/unit
Unskilled operatives	6 hr/unit	1 hr/unit	3 hr/unit
Machining department	½ hr/unit	¼ hr/unit	⅓ hr/unit
Pressing department	2 hr/unit	3 hr/unit	4 hr/unit
Machine requirements:			
Machining department	2 hr/unit	1½ hr/unit	2½ hr/unit

The skilled operatives employed in the cutting department are paid £8 per hour and the unskilled operatives are paid £5 per hour. All the operatives in the machining and pressing departments are paid £6 per hour.

(continued over)

	Production departments			Service departments	
	Cutting	Machining	Pressing	Engineering	Personnel
Planned total overheads	£154,482	£64,316	£58,452	£56,000	£34,000
Service department costs incurred for the benefit of other departments, as follows:					
Engineering services	20%	45%	35%	–	–
Personnel services	55%	10%	20%	15%	–

The business operates a full absorption costing system.

Required:

Calculate, as equitably as possible, the total planned cost of:

(a) One completed unit of product A.

(b) One incomplete unit of product B, which has been processed by the cutting and machining departments but which has not yet been passed into the pressing department.

4.7   'In a job costing system, it is necessary to divide up the business into departments. Fixed costs (or overheads) will be collected for each department. Where a particular fixed cost relates to the business as a whole, it must be divided between the departments. Usually this is done on the basis of area of floor space occupied by each department relative to the entire business. When the total fixed costs for each department have been identified, this will be divided by the number of hours that were worked in each department to deduce an overhead recovery rate. Each job that was worked on in a department will have a share of fixed costs allotted to it according to how long it was worked on. The total cost for each job will therefore be the sum of the variable costs of the job and its share of the fixed costs. It is essential that this approach is taken in order to deduce a selling price for the business's output.'

You are required to prepare a table of two columns. In the first column you should show any phrases or sentences in the above statement with which you do not agree, and in the second column you should show your reason for disagreeing with each one.

4.8   Many businesses charge overheads to jobs on a departmental basis.

Required:

(a) What is the advantage that is claimed for charging overheads to jobs on a departmental basis, and why is it claimed?

(b) What circumstances need to exist to make a difference to a particular job whether overheads are charged on a business-wide basis or on a departmental basis. (Note that the answer to this part of the question is not specifically covered in the chapter. You should, nevertheless, be able to deduce the reason from what you know.)

5

Costing and pricing in a competitive environment

OBJECTIVES

When you have completed this chapter, you should be able to:

● Describe the nature of the modern costing and pricing environment.

● Discuss the principles and practicalities of activity-based costing.

● Explain the theoretical underpinning of pricing decisions and discuss the issues involved in reaching a pricing decision in real-world situations.

● Explain how new developments such as total life-cycle costing and target costing can be used to manage costs.

INTRODUCTION

In recent years we have witnessed major changes in the business world, such as deregulation, privatisation, the growing expectations of shareholders and the impact of new technology. These have led to a much more fast-changing and competitive environment that has radically changed the way in which businesses need to be managed. In this chapter we consider some of the financial techniques that are being used to manage in this new era.

We begin by considering the impact of this new, highly competitive environment on the full-costing approach that we considered in Chapter 4. We shall see that activity-based costing, which is a development of the traditional full-costing approach, takes a much more enquiring, much less accepting attitude towards overheads. We shall see how, in theory and in practice, a business can use costing information to aid pricing decisions. This will pick up some of the points on relevant cost and cost–volume–profit relationships that we considered in Chapters 2 and 3. Some recent approaches to costing are also examined that can lower costs and, therefore, increase the ability of a business to compete on price will also be examined.

Costing and the changed business environment

The background to traditional costing and pricing

The traditional, but still widely used, approach to costing and pricing productive output first developed when the notion of trying to determine the cost of industrial production originally emerged. This was around the time of the Industrial Revolution when industry showed the following features:

- *Direct-labour-intensive and direct-labour-paced production.* Labour was at the heart of production. To the extent that machinery was used, it was to support the efforts of direct labour, and the speed of production was dictated by direct labour.
- *A low level of overheads relative to direct costs.* Little was spent on power, personnel services, machinery (leading to low depreciation charges) and other areas typical of the overheads of modern businesses.
- *A relatively uncompetitive market.* Transport difficulties, limited industrial production worldwide and a lack of knowledge by customers of competitors' prices meant that businesses could prosper without being too scientific in costing and pricing their output.

Since overheads then represented a pretty small element of total costs, it was acceptable and practical to deal with them in a fairly arbitrary manner. Not too much effort was devoted to trying to control the cost of overheads because the rewards of better control were relatively small, certainly when compared with the rewards from controlling direct labour and material costs. It was also reasonable to charge overheads to individual jobs on a direct labour hour basis. Most of the overheads were incurred directly in support of direct labour: providing direct workers with a place to work, heating and lighting that workplace, employing people to supervise the direct workers and so on. Direct workers, perhaps aided by machinery, carried out all production.

At that time, service industries were a relatively unimportant part of the economy and would have largely consisted of self-employed individuals. These individuals would probably have been uninterested in trying to do more than work out a rough hourly/daily rate for their time and to try to base prices on this.

The current full costing and pricing environment

In more recent years, the world of industrial production has fundamentally altered. Most of it is now characterised by:

- *Capital-intensive and machine-paced production.* Machines are at the heart of much production, including service provision. Most labour supports the efforts of machines, for example, technically maintaining them, and the pace of production is often dictated by machines.
- *A higher level of overheads relative to direct costs.* Modern businesses tend to have very high depreciation, servicing and power costs. There are also high costs of a nature scarcely envisaged in the early days of industrial production, such as personnel and staff welfare costs. At the same time, there are very low (sometimes no) direct labour costs. Although direct material cost often remains an important element of total cost, more efficient production methods lead to less waste and, therefore, less total material cost, again tending to make overheads more dominant.

- *A highly competitive international market.* Production, much of it highly sophisticated, is carried out worldwide. Transport, including fast airfreight, is relatively cheap. Fax, telephone and the Internet ensure that potential customers can quickly and cheaply find the prices of a range of suppliers. So the market is likely to be highly competitive. This means that businesses need to know their costs with a greater degree of accuracy than historically has been the case. Businesses also need to take a considered and informed approach to pricing their output.

In the UK, service industries now dominate the economy, employing the great majority of the workforce and producing most of the value of productive output. Though there are many self-employed individuals supplying services, many service providers are vast businesses such as banks, insurance companies and cinema operators. For most of these larger service providers, the activities very closely resemble modern manufacturing activity. They too are characterised by high capital intensity, overheads dominating direct costs and a competitive international market.

Activity-based costing

In Chapter 4 we considered the traditional approach to job costing (deriving the full cost of output where one unit of output differs from another). This approach is to collect those costs for each job, which can be unequivocally linked to and measured in respect of the particular job (direct costs). All other costs (overheads) are thrown into a pool of costs and charged to individual jobs according to some formula. As we saw in Chapter 4, survey evidence indicates that this formula has usually been on the basis of the number of direct labour hours worked on each particular job.

In the past, overhead recovery rates (that is, rates at which overheads are absorbed by jobs) were typically much less for each direct labour hour than the actual rate paid to direct workers. It is now, however, becoming increasingly common for overhead recovery rates to be between five and ten times the hourly rate of pay, because overheads are now much more significant. When production is dominated by direct labour paid, say, £8 an hour, it might be reasonable to have an overhead recovery rate of, say, £1 an hour. When, however, direct labour plays a relatively small part in production, to have overhead recovery rates of, say, £50 for each direct labour hour is likely to lead to very arbitrary costing. Even a small change in the amount of direct labour worked on a job could massively affect the total cost deduced. This is not because the direct worker is very highly paid, but because of the effect of the direct labour change on the overhead loading. Overheads are charged on a direct labour hour basis even though they may not be particularly related to direct labour.

An alternative approach to full costing

As a result of changes in the business environment, the whole question of overheads, what causes them and how they are charged to jobs, has been receiving much closer attention. Historically, businesses have been content to accept that overheads exist and, therefore, for costing purposes they must be dealt with in as practical a way as possible. In recent years, however, there has been an increasing realisation that overheads do not just happen; they must be caused by something. To illustrate this point, let us consider Example 5.1.

Example 5.1

Modern Producers Ltd has, like virtually all manufacturers, a storage area that is set aside for finished goods. The costs of running the stores include a share of the factory rent and other establishment costs, such as heating and lighting. They also include the salaries of staff employed to look after the stock (inventory), and the cost of financing the stock held in the stores.

The business has two product lines: A and B. Product A tends to be made in small batches, and low levels of finished stock are held. The business prides itself on its ability to supply Product B in relatively large quantities instantly. As a consequence, much of the finished goods store is filled with finished Product Bs ready to be despatched immediately an order is received.

Traditionally, the whole cost of operating the stores would have been treated as a general overhead and included in the total of overheads charged to jobs on a direct labour hour basis. This means that when assessing the cost of Products A and B, the cost of operating the stores has fallen on them according to the number of direct labour hours worked on each one. In fact, most of the stores cost should be charged to Product B, since this product causes (and benefits from) the stores cost much more than is true of Product A. Failure to account more precisely for the cost of running the stores is masking the fact that Product B is not as profitable as it seems to be. It may even be leading to losses as a result of the relatively high stores-operating cost that it causes. So far, much of this cost has been charged to Product A, without regard to the fact that Product A causes little of it. The products absorb the stores cost in proportion to the direct labour hour content, a factor that has nothing to do with storage.

Cost drivers

Realisation that overheads do not just occur, but that they are caused by activities – such as holding products in stores – that 'drive' the costs, is at the heart of **activity-based costing (ABC)**. The traditional approach is that direct labour hours are the **cost driver**, which probably used to be true. ABC recognises that this is often not the case.

There is a basic philosophical difference between the traditional and the ABC approaches. Traditionally we tend to think of overheads as *rendering a service to cost units*, the cost of which must be charged to those units. ABC sees overheads as being *caused by cost units*, and those cost units must be charged with the costs that they cause.

Activity 5.1

Can you think of any other purpose that identification of the cost drivers serves, apart from deriving more accurate costs?

Identification of the activities that cause costs puts management in a position where it may well be able to control them.

The opaque nature of overheads has traditionally made them more difficult to control than direct labour and material costs. If, however, an analysis of overheads can identify the cost drivers, questions can be asked about whether the activity driving certain costs is necessary at all, and whether the cost justifies the benefit. In Example 5.1, it may be a good marketing policy that Product B can be supplied immediately from stock, but this causes a cost that should be recognised and assessed against the benefit.

Adopting ABC requires that most overheads can be analysed and the cost drivers identified. This means that it might be possible to gain much clearer insights to the overhead costs that are caused, activity by activity, so that fairer and more accurate product costs can be identified, and costs can be controlled more effectively.

Cost pools

→ Under ABC, an overhead **cost pool** is established for each cost driver in which all of the costs caused by that driver are placed. So, the business in Example 5.1 would create a cost pool for operating the stores. All costs associated with this activity would be allocated to that cost pool. The total costs in that pool would then be allocated to output (goods or services) according to the extent to which each unit of output 'drove' those costs, using the cost driver identified.

Example 5.2

The accountant at Modern Producers Ltd (see Example 5.1) has estimated that the costs of running the finished goods stores for next year will be £90,000. This will be the amount allocated to the 'finished goods stores cost pool'.

It is estimated that each Product A will spend an average of one week in the stores before being sold. With Product B, the equivalent period is four weeks. Both products are of roughly similar size and have very similar storage needs. It is felt, therefore, that the quantity of each product and the period spent in the stores are the cost drivers.

It is estimated that, next year, 50,000 Product As and 25,000 Product Bs will pass though the stores. So the total number of 'product weeks' in store will be:

$$
\begin{array}{llll}
\text{Product A} & 50,000 \times 1 \text{ week} & = & 50,000 \\
\text{B} & 25,000 \times 4 \text{ weeks} & = & \underline{100,000} \\
& & & \underline{150,000}
\end{array}
$$

The stores cost for each 'product week' is given by

$$£90,000/150,000 = £0.60$$

Therefore each Product A will be charged with £0.60 for finished stores costs, and each Product B with £2.40 (that is, £0.60 × 4).

Allocating overhead costs to cost pools, as is necessary with ABC, contrasts with the traditional approach, where the overheads are allocated to production departments. In both cases, however, the overheads are then charged to cost units (goods or services). The two different approaches are illustrated in Figure 5.1.

| Figure 5.1 | Traditional versus activity-based costing |

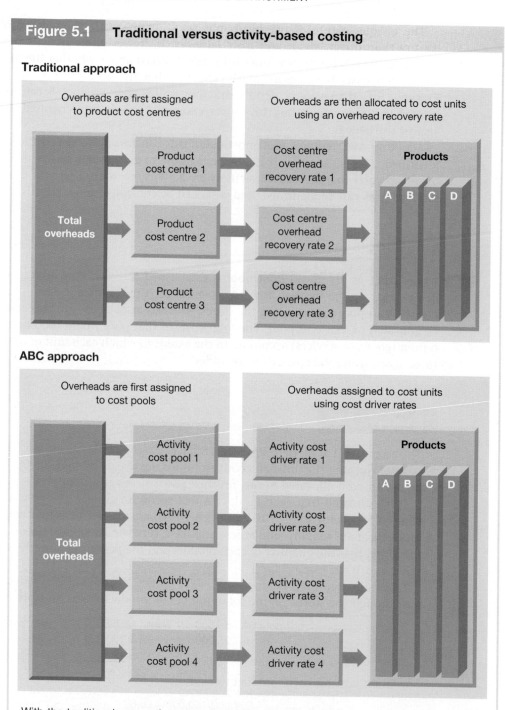

With the traditional approach, overheads are first assigned to product cost centres and then overheads are absorbed by cost units based on an overhead recovery rate (using direct labour hours worked on the cost units or some other approach) for each department. With activity-based costing, overheads are assigned to cost pools and then cost units are charged with overheads to the extent that they drive the costs in the various pools.

Source: Adapted from Innes and Mitchell (see reference 1 at the end of the chapter).

With the traditional approach, overheads are apportioned to product departments. Each department would then derive an overhead recovery rate, typically overheads per direct labour hour. Overheads would then be applied to units of output according to how many direct labour hours were worked on them.

With ABC, the overheads are analysed into cost pools, with one cost pool for each cost driver. The overheads are then charged to units of output, through activity cost driver rates. These rates are an attempt to represent the extent to which each particular cost unit is believed to cause the particular part of the overheads.

ABC and service industries

Much of our discussion of ABC has concentrated on manufacturing industry, perhaps because early users of ABC were manufacturing businesses. In fact, ABC is possibly even more relevant to service industries because, in the absence of a direct material element, a service business's total costs are likely to be largely made up of overheads. There is certainly evidence that ABC has been adopted more readily by businesses that sell services rather than goods, as we shall see later.

Activity 5.2

What is the difference in the way in which direct costs are accounted for when using ABC, relative to their treatment taking a traditional approach to full costing?

The answer is no difference at all. ABC is concerned only with the way in which overheads are charged to jobs to derive the full cost.

Criticisms of ABC

Critics of ABC argue that analysis of overheads in order to identify cost drivers is time-consuming and costly, and that the benefit of doing so, in terms of more accurate costing and the potential for cost control, does not justify the cost of carrying out the analysis.

ABC is also criticised for the same reason that full costing generally is criticised: because it does not provide very relevant information for decision making. The point was made in Chapter 4 that full costing tends to use past costs and to ignore opportunity costs. Since past costs are always irrelevant in decision making and opportunity costs can be significant, full costing information is an expensive irrelevance. In contrast, advocates of full costing claim that it *is* relevant, in that it provides a long-run average cost, whereas 'relevant costing', which we considered in Chapter 2, relates only to the specific circumstances of the short term.

Despite the criticisms that are made of full costing (whether 'traditional' or ABC), it is, according to survey evidence, very widely practised.

Real World 5.1 provides some indication of the extent to which ABC is used in practice.

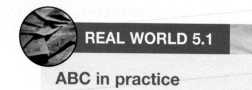

REAL WORLD 5.1

ABC in practice

A survey of large UK businesses in 1999 revealed that, on average, 15 per cent of businesses fully use an ABC approach to dealing with full costing. A further 8 per cent use it partially. The remaining 77 per cent do not use ABC at all. Even so, there was a surprising range in the level of usage of ABC from industry to industry (see Figure 5.2). It is particularly surprising that so few manufacturing businesses use ABC. The survey showed that it tends to be larger businesses that adopt ABC.

Figure 5.2   ABC in practice

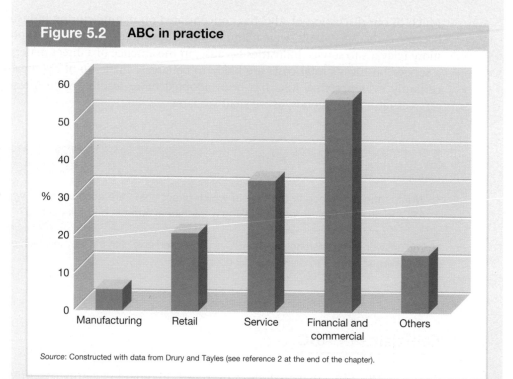

Source: Constructed with data from Drury and Tayles (see reference 2 at the end of the chapter).

There is some evidence of a decrease in the use of ABC over recent years. A different survey of large UK businesses (conducted by Innes, Mitchell and Sinclair) in 1999, replicated a 1994 survey conducted by the same researchers. They found the following:

	1994	*1999*
	%	*%*
Currently using ABC	21.0	17.5
Currently considering using ABC	29.6	20.3
Rejected using ABC after assessing it	13.3	15.3

Thus, it seems that both as to current and potential usage of ABC, it was less popular in 1999 than it had been five years previously.

Source: Innes *et al.* (see reference 3 at the end of the chapter).

Self-assessment question 5.1

Psilis Ltd makes a product in two qualities, called 'Basic' and 'Super'. The business is able to sell these products at a price that gives a standard profit mark-up of 25 per cent of full cost. Management is concerned by the lack of profit.

Full cost for one unit is calculated by charging overheads to each type of product on the basis of direct labour hours. The costs are as follows:

	Basic	Super
	£	£
Direct labour (all £10/hour)	40	60
Direct material	15	20

The total overheads are £1,000,000.

Based on experience over recent years, in the forthcoming year the business expects to make and sell 40,000 Basics and 10,000 Supers.

Recently, the business's management accountant has undertaken an exercise to try to identify cost drivers in an attempt to be able to deal with the overheads on a more precise basis than had been possible before. This exercise has revealed the following analysis of the annual overheads:

Activity (and cost driver)	Cost	Annual number of activities		
	£000	Total	Basic	Super
Number of machine set-ups	280	100	20	80
Number of quality-control inspections	220	2,000	500	1,500
Number of sales orders processed	240	5,000	1,500	3,500
General production (machine hours)	260	500,000	350,000	150,000
Total	1,000			

The management accountant explained the analysis of the £1,000,000 overheads as follows:

- The two products are made in relatively small batches, so that storage of finished stock is negligible. The Supers are made in very small batches because their demand is relatively low. Each time a new batch is produced, the machines have to be reset by skilled staff. Resetting for Basic production occurs about 20 times a year and for Supers about 80 times: about 100 times in total. The cost of employing the machine-setting staff is about £280,000 a year. It is clear that the more set-ups that occur, the higher the total set-up costs; in other words, the number of set-ups is the factor that drives set-up costs.

- All production has to be inspected for quality and this costs about £220,000 a year. The higher specifications of the Supers mean that there is more chance that there will be quality problems. Thus the Supers are inspected in total 1,500 times annually, whereas the Basics only need about 500 inspections. The number of inspections is the factor that drives these costs.

- Sales order processing (dealing with customers' orders, from receiving the original order to despatching the products) costs about £240,000 a year. Despite the larger amount of Basic production, there are only 1,500 sales orders each year because the Basics are sold to wholesalers in relatively large-sized orders. The Supers are sold mainly direct to the public by mail order, usually in very small-sized orders. It is believed that the number of orders drives the costs of processing orders.

→

Self-assessment question 5.1 continued

● The remaining general production overheads, totalling £260,000 a year, are thought to be driven by the number of hours for which the machines operate. The machine time for one unit of the product is somewhat higher for Supers than for Basics.

Required:

(a) Deduce the full cost of each of the two products on the basis used at present and, from these, deduce the current selling price.

(b) Deduce the full cost of each product on an ABC basis, taking account of the management accountant's recent investigations.

(c) What conclusions do you draw? What advice would you offer the management of the business?

Pricing

As we have just seen, full costing can be used as a basis for setting prices for the business's output. We have also seen that it can be criticised in that role. In this section we are going to take a closer look at pricing. We shall begin by considering some theoretical aspects of the subject before going on to look at some more practical issues, particularly the role of management accounting information in pricing decisions.

Economic theory

In most market conditions found in practice, the price charged by a business will determine the number of units sold. This is shown graphically in Figure 5.3.

Figure 5.3 shows the number of units of output that the market would demand at various prices. As price increases, the less willing are people to buy the commodity (call it commodity A). At a relatively low price a unit (P_1), the quantity of units demanded by the market (Q_1) is fairly high. When the price is increased to P_2, the demand decreases to Q_2. The graph shows a linear (straight-line) relationship between the price and demand. In practice, the relationship, though broadly similar, may not be quite so straightforward.

Not all commodities show exactly the same slope of line. Figure 5.4 shows the demand/price relationship for commodity B, a different commodity from the one depicted in Figure 5.3.

Though a rise in price of commodity B, from P_1 to P_2, causes a fall in demand, the fall in demand is much smaller than is the case for commodity A with a similar rise in price. As a result, we say that commodity A has a higher **elasticity of demand** than commodity B. Demand for A reacts much more dramatically (stretches more) to price changes than demand does for B. Elastic demand tends to be associated with commodities that are not essential, perhaps because there is a ready substitute.

It is very helpful for those involved with pricing decisions to have some feel for the elasticity of demand of the commodity that will be the subject of a decision. The sensitivity of the demand to the pricing decision is obviously much greater (and the pricing decision more crucial) with commodities whose demand is elastic than with commodities whose demand is relatively inelastic.

Figure 5.3   Graph of quantity demanded against price for commodity (A)

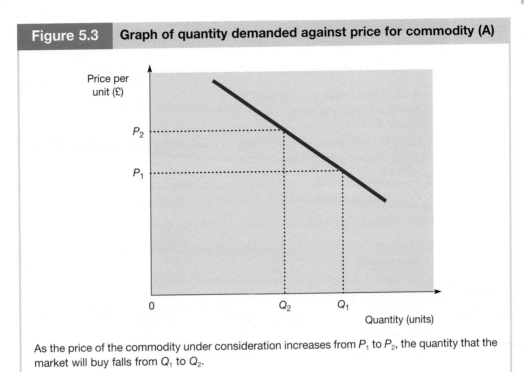

As the price of the commodity under consideration increases from P_1 to P_2, the quantity that the market will buy falls from Q_1 to Q_2.

Figure 5.4   Graph of quantity demanded against price for commodity (B)

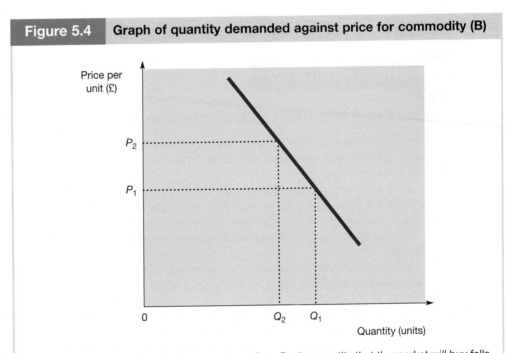

As the price of the commodity increases from P_1 to P_2, the quantity that the market will buy falls from Q_1 to Q_2. This fall in demand is less than was the case for commodity A, which has the greater elasticity of demand.

Activity 5.3

Which would be the more elastic of the following commodities?

● A particular brand of chocolate bar
● Mains electricity supply.

A branded chocolate bar seems likely to have a fairly *elastic* demand. This is for several reasons, including the following:

● Few buyers of the bar would feel that chocolate bars are essentials.
● Other chocolate bars, probably quite similar to the one in question, will be easily available.

Mains electricity probably has a relatively *inelastic* demand. This is because:

● Many users of electricity would find it very difficult to manage without fuel of some description.
● For neither household nor business users of electricity is there an immediate, practical substitute. For some uses of electricity – for example, powering machinery – there is probably no substitute. Even for a purpose such as heating, where there are substitutes such as gas and oil, it may be impractical to switch to the substitute because gas and oil heating appliances are not immediately available and are costly to acquire.

Real World 5.2 provides an example of pricing some well-known elastic-demand products.

REAL WORLD 5.2

Sony and Microsoft in European console price war   **FT**

The battle for control of the European games console market intensified on Wednesday as Sony and Microsoft went head to head with price cuts for their respective Playstation 2 and Xbox consoles.

Sony sought to solidify its leading position in the market by aggressively cutting the price of the Playstation 2 console by 15% in the UK to £169.99 ($260.30) and by up to 17% in continental Europe to between €249 and €259 ($244.10–$253.90).

An hour later, Microsoft responded by slashing the European retail price of the Xbox to €249.99.

In the run up to the lucrative Christmas period, console makers have intensified sales and marketing initiatives, racing to carve out a share of a market estimated to be worth £27bn.

'The games market has a lot of price elasticity – the lower the price, the more people tend to buy consoles. Sony, Microsoft and Nintendo are looking to get their user-base as large as possible, by putting the hardware out at almost cost price. They can then make their money from selling software,' said Peter Reed, analyst at Beeson Gregory.

Making a push on hardware sales now, he noted, will allow them to prepare for games sales in the pre-Christmas period, which can account for more than one third of total yearly sales.

Source: 'Sony and Microsoft in European console price war', FT.com, 28 August 2002.

As we saw in Chapter 1, the objective of most businesses is to enhance the wealth of their owners. Broadly speaking, this will be best achieved by seeking to maximise profits – that is, having the largest possible difference between total costs and total revenues. Thus, prices should be set in a way that is likely to have this effect. To be able to do this, the price decision maker needs to have some insight to the way in which costs and prices relate to volume of output.

Figure 5.5 shows the relationship between cost and volume of output, which we have already met in Chapter 3. The figure shows that the total cost of providing a particular commodity (service X) increases as the quantity of output increases. It is shown here as a straight line. In practice it may be curved, either curving upwards (tending to become closer to the vertical) or flattening out (tending to become closer to the horizontal). The figure assumes that the marginal cost of each unit is constant over the range shown.

Figure 5.5	Graph of total cost against quantity (volume) of output of service X

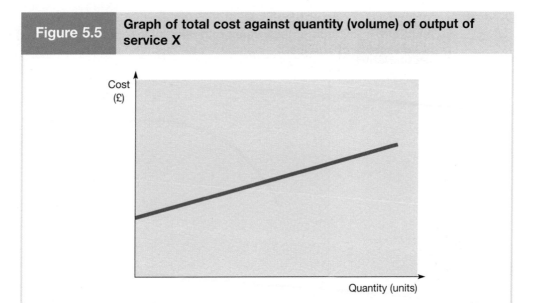

Providing service X will give rise to some costs that are fixed and to some that vary with the level of output.

Activity 5.4

What general effect would tend to cause the total cost line in Figure 5.5 to (a) curve towards the vertical, and (b) curve towards the horizontal? (You may recall that we considered this issue in Chapter 3.)

(a) Curving towards the vertical would mean that the marginal cost (additional cost of making one more) of each successive unit of output would become greater. This would probably imply that increased activity would be causing a shortage of supply of some factor of production, which had the effect of increasing cost prices. This might be caused by a shortage of labour, meaning that overtime payments would need to be made to encourage people to work the hours necessary for increased production. It might also/alternatively be caused by a shortage of raw materials. Perhaps normal supplies were exhausted at lower levels of output and more expensive sources had to be used to expand output.

→

(b) Curving towards the horizontal might be caused by the business being able to exploit the economies of scale at higher levels of output, making the marginal cost of each successive unit of output cheaper. Perhaps higher volumes of output enable division of labour or more mechanisation. Possibly, suppliers of raw materials offer better deals for larger orders.

Figure 5.6 shows the total sales revenue against quantity of service X sold. The total sales revenue increases as the quantity of output increases, but only up to a certain point.

Figure 5.6	**Graph of total sales revenue against quantity (volume) sold of service X**

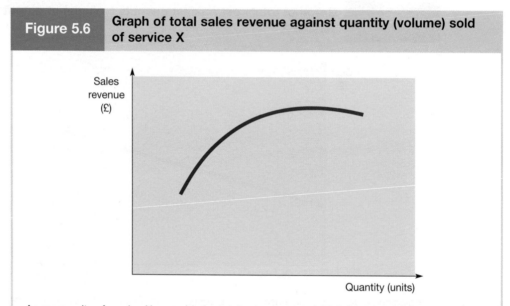

As more units of service X are sold, the total sales revenue initially increases, but at a declining rate. This is because, to persuade people to buy increasing quantities, the price must be reduced. Eventually the price will have to be reduced so much, to encourage additional sales, that the total sales revenue will fall as the number of units sold increases.

Activity 5.5

What assumption does Figure 5.6 make about the price for a unit of service X at which output can be sold as the number of units sold increases?

The graph suggests that, to sell more units, the price must be lowered, meaning that the average price for each unit of output reduces as volume sold increases. As we discussed earlier in this section, this is true of most markets found in practice.

Figure 5.6 implies that there will come a point where, to make increased sales, prices will have to be reduced so much that total sales revenue will not increase; it may even reduce.

In Chapter 3, when we considered break-even analysis, we assumed a steady price per unit over the range that we were considering. Now we are saying that, in practice, it does not work like this. How can these two positions be reconciled? The answer is that, when we dealt with break-even analysis, we were considering only a relatively small range of output, namely from zero sales to the break-even point. It may well be that over a small range, particularly at low levels of output, a constant sales price per unit is a reasonable assumption. That is to say that, to the left of the curve in Figure 5.6, there may be a straight line from zero up to the start of the curve.

There is nothing in break-even analysis that demands that the assumption about steady selling prices is made, but making it does mean that the analysis is very straightforward.

Figure 5.7 combines information about total sales revenue and total cost for service X over a range of output levels.

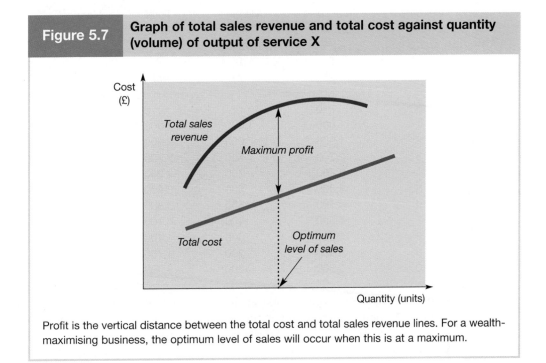

Figure 5.7   **Graph of total sales revenue and total cost against quantity (volume) of output of service X**

Profit is the vertical distance between the total cost and total sales revenue lines. For a wealth-maximising business, the optimum level of sales will occur when this is at a maximum.

The total sales revenue increases, but at a decreasing rate, and the total cost of production increases as the quantity of output increases. The maximum profit is made where the total sales revenue and total cost lines are vertically furthest apart. At the left-hand end of the graph, we are clearly above break-even point because the total sales revenue line has already gone above the total cost line. At the lower levels of volume of sales and output, the total sales revenue line is climbing faster than the total cost line. The business will wish to keep expanding output as long as this continues to be the case, because profit is the vertical distance between the two lines. A point will be reached where the total sales line flattens towards the horizontal to such an extent that further expansion will reduce profit.

The point at which profit is maximised is where the two lines stop diverging, that is, the point at which the two lines are climbing at exactly the same rate. Thus we can say that profit is maximised at the point where:

Marginal sales revenue = Marginal cost of production

that is,

$$
\begin{bmatrix} \text{Increase in total sales} \\ \text{revenue from selling} \\ \text{one more unit} \end{bmatrix} = \begin{bmatrix} \text{Increase in total costs} \\ \text{that will result from} \\ \text{selling one more unit} \end{bmatrix}
$$

To see how this approach can be applied, consider Example 5.3.

Example 5.3

A schedule of predicted total sales revenue and total costs at various levels of provision for service Y is shown in columns (a) and (c) of the table.

Quantity of output	Total sales revenue	Marginal sales revenue	Total cost	Marginal cost	Profit (loss)
	£ (a)	£ (b)	£ (c)	£ (d)	£ (e)
0	0		0		0
1	1,000	1,000	2,300	2,300	(1,300)
2	1,900	900	2,600	300	(700)
3	2,700	800	2,900	300	(200)
4	3,400	700	3,200	300	200
5	4,000	600	3,500	300	500
6	4,500	500	3,800	300	700
7	4,900	400	4,100	300	800
8	5,200	300	4,400	300	800
9	5,400	200	4,700	300	700
10	5,500	100	5,000	300	500

Column (b) is deduced by taking the total sales revenue for one less unit sold from the total sales revenue at the sales level under consideration (column (a)). For example, the marginal sales revenue of the fifth unit of the service sold (£600) is deduced by taking the total sales revenue for four units sold (£3,400) away from the total sales revenue for five units sold (£4,000).

Column (d) is deduced similarly, but using total cost figures from column (c). Column (e) is found by deducting column (c) from column (a).

It can be seen by looking at the profit (loss) column that the maximum profit occurs with an output of seven or eight units (£800). Thus the maximum output should be eight units of the service. This is the point where marginal cost and marginal revenue are equal (at £300).

Activity 5.6

Specialist Ltd makes a very specialised machine that is sold to manufacturing businesses. The business is about to commence production of a new model of machine for which facilities exist to produce a maximum of 10 machines each week. To assist management in a decision on the price to charge for the new machine, two pieces of information have been collected:

● *Market demand*. The business's marketing staff believe that, at a price of £3,000 a machine, the demand would be zero. Each £100 reduction in unit price below £3,000 would generate one additional sale a week. Thus, for example, at a price of £2,800 each, two machines could be sold each week.

● *Manufacturing costs*. Fixed costs associated with manufacture of the machine are estimated at £3,000 a week. Since the work is highly labour-intensive and labour is in short supply, unit variable costs are expected to be progressive. The manufacture of one machine each week is expected to have a variable cost of £1,100, but each additional machine produced will increase the variable cost for the entire output by £100 a machine. For example, if the output were three machines a week, the variable cost for each machine (for all three machines) would be £1,300.

It is the policy of the business always to charge the same price for its entire output of a particular model. What is the most profitable level of output of the new machine?

Output	Unit sales revenue £	Total sales revenue £	Marginal sales revenue £	Unit variable cost £	Total variable cost £	Total cost £	Marginal cost £	Profit (loss) £
0	0	0	0	0	0	3,000	3,000	(3,000)
1	2,900	2,900	2,900	1,100	1,100	4,100	1,100	(1,200)
2	2,800	5,600	2,700	1,200	2,400	5,400	1,300	200
3	2,700	8,100	2,500	1,300	3,900	6,900	1,500	1,200
4	2,600	10,400	2,300	1,400	5,600	8,600	1,700	1,800
5	2,500	12,500	2,100	1,500	7,500	10,500	1,900	2,000
6	2,400	14,400	1,900	1,600	9,600	12,600	2,100	1,800
7	2,300	16,100	1,700	1,700	11,900	14,900	2,300	1,200
8	2,200	17,600	1,500	1,800	14,400	17,400	2,500	200
9	2,100	18,900	1,300	1,900	17,100	20,100	2,700	(1,200)
10	2,000	20,000	1,100	2,000	20,000	23,000	2,900	(3,000)

An output of five machines each week will maximise profit at £2,000 a week.

The additional cost of producing the fifth machine compared with the cost of producing the first four (£1,900) is just below the marginal revenue (the amount by which the total revenue from five machines exceeds that from selling four (£2,100)).

The additional cost of producing the sixth machine compared with the cost of producing the first five (£2,100) is just above the marginal revenue (the amount by which the total revenue from six machines exceeds that from selling five (£1,900)).

Some practical considerations

Despite the analysis in Activity 5.6, in practice the answer of five machines a week may prove not to be the best answer. This might be for one or more of several reasons:

● Demand is notoriously difficult to predict, even assuming no changes in the environment.

● The effect of sales of the new machine on the other of the business's products may mean that the machine cannot be considered in isolation. Five machines a week may be the optimum level of output if sales were being taken from a rival business or a new market were being created, but possibly not in other circumstances.

- Costs are difficult to estimate.
- Since labour is in short supply, the relevant labour cost should probably include an element for opportunity cost.
- The level of sales is calculated on the assumption that short-run profit maximisation is the goal of the business. Unless this is consistent with wealth enhancement in the longer term, it may not be in the business's best interests.

These points highlight some of the weaknesses of the theoretical approaches to pricing, particularly the fact that costs and demands are difficult to predict. It would be wrong, however, to dismiss the theory. The fact that the theory does not work perfectly in practice does not mean that it cannot offer helpful insights to the nature of markets, how profit relates to volume, and the notion of an optimum level of output.

Full cost (cost-plus) pricing

Now that we have considered pricing theory, let us return to the subject of using full cost as the basis for setting prices. We saw in Chapter 4 that one of the reasons why some businesses deduce full costs is to base selling prices on them. There is a lot of logic in this. If a business charges the full cost of its output as a selling price, the business will, in theory, break even, because the sales revenue will exactly cover all of the costs. Charging something above full cost will yield a profit.

If a **full cost (cost-plus) pricing** approach is to be taken, the issue that must be addressed is the level of profit that is required from each unit sold. This must logically be based on the total profit that is required for the period. Normally, businesses seek to enhance their wealth through trading. The extent to which they expect to do this is normally related to the amount of wealth that is invested to promote wealth enhancement. Businesses tend to seek to produce a particular percentage increase in wealth. In other words, businesses seek to generate a target return on capital employed. It seems logical, therefore, that the profit loading on full cost should reflect the business's target profit and that the target should itself be based on a target return on capital employed.

Activity 5.7

A business has just completed a service job whose full cost has been calculated at £112. For the current period, the total costs (direct and indirect) are estimated at £250,000. The profit target for the period is £100,000.
Suggest a selling price for the job.

If the profit is to be earned by jobs in proportion to their full cost, then the profit for each pound of full cost must be £0.40 (that is, £100,000/250,000). Thus, the profit on the job must be:

$$£0.40 \times 112 = £44.80$$

This means that the price for the job must be:

$$£112 + £44.80 = £156.80$$

Other ways could be found for apportioning a share of profit to jobs – for example, direct labour or machine hours. Such bases may be preferred where it is believed that these factors are better representatives of effort and, therefore, profitworthiness. It is clearly a matter of judgement as to how profit is apportioned to units of output.

An obvious problem with cost-plus pricing is that the market may not agree with the price. Put another way, cost-plus pricing takes no account of the market demand function (the relationship between price and quantity demanded, which we considered above). A business may fairly deduce the full cost of some product and then add what might be regarded as a reasonable level of profit, only to find that a rival producer is offering a similar product for a much lower price, or that the market simply will not buy at the cost-plus price.

Most suppliers are not strong enough in the market to dictate pricing. Most are 'price takers' not 'price makers'. They must accept the price offered by the market or they do not sell any of their products. Cost-plus pricing may be appropriate for price makers, but it has less relevance for price takers.

Real World 5.3 illustrates how adopting a cost-plus approach to pricing may lead to a situation where falling demand leads to price rises, which, in turn lead to falling demand.

REAL WORLD 5.3

A vicious circle in the library

Librarians have long complained about the price rises of academic journals and Derek Haan chairman and chief executive of Elsevier Science, which publishes more than 1,600 journals, admits that journal price inflation has been a problem for the industry. He says the problem is due to falling subscription numbers as more readers make photocopies or use interlibrary lending. With fewer subscribers to share the cost of each publication, publishers have to increase prices. To stay within budgets, libraries start cancelling titles, which creates a vicious circle of dwindling subscriber numbers, soaring prices and reduced collections.

Source: Adapted from 'Case Study: Elsevier', FT.com, 19 June 2002.

The cost-plus price is not entirely useless to price takers, however. When contemplating entering a market, knowing the cost-plus price will give useful information. It will tell the price taker whether it can profitably enter the market or not. As has been said already in this chapter, the full cost can be seen as a long-run break-even selling price. If entering a market means that this break-even price, plus an acceptable profit, cannot be achieved, then the business should probably stay out. Having a breakdown of the full cost may put the business in a position to examine where costs might be capable of being cut in order to bring the full cost plus profit within a figure acceptable to the market.

Being a price maker does not always imply that the business dominates a particular market. Many small businesses are, to some extent, price makers. This tends to be where buyers find it difficult to make clear distinctions between the prices offered by various suppliers. An example of this might be a car repair. Though it may be possible to obtain a series of binding estimates for the work from various garages, most people would not normally do so. As a result, garages normally charge cost-plus prices for car repairs.

Real World 5.4 considers the extent to which cost-plus pricing seems to be used in practice.

REAL WORLD 5.4

Cost-plus pricing in practice

The 1999 survey of fairly large UK businesses by Drury and Tayles (see reference 2 at the end of the chapter) revealed that cost-plus pricing is used by 60 per cent of businesses. Of that 60 per cent, not all use it to set the price of all of the business's sales, however. The 60 per cent breaks down as follows:

% of sales accounted for by cost-plus pricing	% of businesses
1 to 20	26
21 to 50	11
51 to 100	23
	60

Thus, for example, 26 per cent of all businesses responding to the survey used a cost-plus approach to pricing for between 1 per cent and 20 per cent of their total sales.

It is difficult to interpret these data to reach a general conclusion, but it is fair to say that cost-plus is an important approach to pricing in the UK.

The 1993 survey by Drury *et al.* (see reference 4 at the end of the chapter) indicated that 39 per cent of respondents used the cost-plus approach to most of their pricing decisions. This might indicate that the cost-plus approach was more popular in 1993 than in 1999, when only 23 per cent of respondents used it for more than 50 per cent of their output.

Relevant/marginal cost pricing

The relevant/marginal cost approach deduces the minimum price for which the business can offer the product for sale. This minimum price will leave the business better off as a result of making the sale than it would have been had it pursued the next best opportunity instead. We considered the more general approach to relevant cost pricing in Chapter 2. In Chapter 3, we looked at the more restricted case of relevant cost pricing: **marginal cost pricing**. Here it is assumed that fixed costs will not be affected by the decision to produce and, therefore, only the variable cost element need be considered.

It would normally be the case that a relevant/marginal cost approach would only be used where there is not the opportunity to sell at a price that will cover the full cost. The business can sell at any price above the marginal cost and still be better off, simply because it happens to find itself in the position that certain costs will be incurred in any case.

Activity 5.8

A commercial aircraft is due to take off in one hour's time with 20 seats unsold. What is the minimum price at which these seats could be sold such that the airline would be no worse off as a result?

The answer is that any price above the additional cost of one more passenger, caused by people occupying the previously unsold seats, would represent an acceptable minimum. If there are no such costs, the minimum price is zero.

This is not to say that the airline will seek to charge the minimum price; it will presumably seek to charge the highest price that the market will bear. The fact that the market will not bear the full cost, plus a profit margin, should not, in principle, be sufficient for the airline to refuse to sell seats.

Relevant/marginal pricing must be regarded as a short-term approach that can be adopted because a business finds itself in a particular position, for example, having spare aircraft seats. Ultimately, if the business is to be profitable, all costs must be covered by sales revenue.

Activity 5.9

When we considered marginal costing in Chapter 3, we identified three problems with its use. Can you remember what these problems are?

The three problems are as follows:

● The possibility that spare capacity will be 'sold off' cheaply when there is another potential customer who will offer a higher price, but by which time the capacity will be fully committed. It is a matter of commercial judgement as to how likely this will be. With reference to Activity 5.8, would an hour before take-off be sufficiently close for the airline to be fairly confident that no 'normal' passenger will come forward to buy a seat?
● The problem that selling the same product but at different prices could lead to a loss of customer goodwill. Would a 'normal' passenger be happy to be told by another passenger that the latter had bought his or her ticket very cheaply, compared with the normal price?
● If the business is going to suffer continually from being unable to sell its full production potential at the 'regular' price, it might be better, in the long run, to reduce capacity and make fixed-cost savings. Using the spare capacity to produce marginal benefits may lead to the business failing to address this issue. Would it be better for the airline to operate smaller aircraft or to have fewer flights, either of these leading to fixed cost savings, than to sell off surplus seats at marginal prices?

Real World 5.5 provides an unusual example where humanitarian issues are the driving force for adopting marginal pricing.

REAL WORLD 5.5

Drug prices in developing countries

In recent years, large pharmaceutical businesses based in the West have been under considerable pressure to provide cheap drugs to developing countries. It has been suggested that life-saving therapeutic drugs should be sold to these countries at a price that is close to their marginal cost. However, two obstacles to such a pricing policy have been identified:

● Firstly, it may lead to customer revolts in the West (the 'loss of customer goodwill' referred to above).
● Secondly, there is a concern that the drugs may not reach their intended patients and could be re-exported to western countries. A major cost of producing a new drug is the research and development costs incurred, and marginal costs of production are usually very low. Thus, a selling price based on marginal cost is likely to be considerably lower than the (full-cost) selling price in the West. This, it is feared, may lead to the cheap drugs provided leaking back into the West. Acquiring drugs at a price near to their marginal cost and reselling them at a figure close to the selling price in the West offers unscrupulous individuals an opportunity to make huge profits.

The above problems are not insurmountable and are not the only problems surrounding this issue, but they do appear to have slowed progress towards a speedier response to a humanitarian crisis.

Source: Based on information from 'Patent nonsense', *Financial Times*, 24 August 2001.

Pricing strategies

Costs and the market-demand function are not the only determinants of price. Businesses often employ pricing strategies that, in the short term, may not maximise profit. They do this in the expectation that they will gain in the long term. An example of such a strategy is **penetration pricing**. Here, the product is sold relatively cheaply in order to sell in quantity and to gain a large share of the market. This would tend to have the effect of dissuading competitors from entering the market. Subsequently, once the business has established itself as the market leader, prices would be raised to more profitable levels. By its nature, penetration pricing would tend to apply to new products.

Price skimming is almost the opposite of penetration pricing. It seeks to exploit the notion that the market can be stratified according to resistance to price. Here a new product is initially priced highly and sold only to those buyers in the stratum that is fairly unconcerned by high prices. Once this stratum of the market is saturated, the price is lowered to attract the next stratum. The price is gradually lowered as each stratum is saturated. This strategy tends only to be able to be employed where there is some significant barrier to entry for other potential suppliers, such as patent protection.

Mobile telephones are an example of a price-skimming strategy.

Recent developments in pricing and cost management

The increasingly competitive environment in which modern businesses operate is leading to greater effort being applied in trying to manage costs. Businesses need to keep costs to a minimum so that they can supply goods and services at a price that customers will be prepared to pay and, at the same time, generate a level of profit necessary to meet the businesses' objectives of enhancing shareholder wealth. We shall now outline some techniques that have recently emerged in an attempt to meet these goals of competitiveness and profitability.

Firstly, we need to appreciate that the total life cycle of a product or service has three phases. These are:

1 The *preproduction phase*. This is the period that precedes production of the product or service for sale. During this phase, research and development – both of the product or service and of the market – is conducted. The product or service is invented/designed and so is the means of production. The phase culminates with acquiring and setting up the necessary production facilities and with advertising and promotion.
2 The *production phase* comes next, being the one in which the product is made and sold or the service is rendered to customers.
3 The *post-production phase* comes last. During this phase, any costs necessary to correct faults that arose with products or services that have been sold (after-sales service) are incurred. There would also be the costs of closing production at the end of the product's or service's life-cycle, such as the cost of decommissioning production facilities. Since after-sales service will tend to arise from as early as the first product or service being sold and, therefore, well before the last one is sold, this phase would typically overlap the manufacturing/service-rendering phase.

The total life cycle is shown in Figure 5.8.

Figure 5.8	The total life-cycle of a product or service

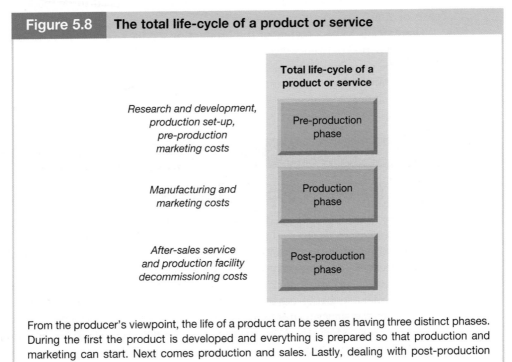

From the producer's viewpoint, the life of a product can be seen as having three distinct phases. During the first the product is developed and everything is prepared so that production and marketing can start. Next comes production and sales. Lastly, dealing with post-production activities is undertaken.

Total life-cycle costing

In some types of business, particularly those engaged in an advanced manufacturing environment, it is estimated that a very high proportion (as much as 80 per cent) of the total costs that will be incurred over the total life of a particular product are either incurred or committed at the pre-production phase. For example, a motor-car manufacturer, when designing, developing and setting up production of a new model, incurs a high proportion of the total costs that will be incurred on that model during the whole of its life. Not only are pre-production costs specifically incurred during this phase, but the need to incur particular costs during the production phase is also established. This is because the design will incorporate features that will lead to particular manufacturing costs. Once the design of the car has been finalised and the manufacturing plant set up, it may be too late to 'design out' a costly feature without incurring another large cost.

Activity 5.10

A decision taken at the design stage could well commit the business to costs after the manufacture of the product has taken place. Can you suggest a potential cost that could be built in at the design stage that will show itself after the manufacture of the product?

After-sales service costs could be incurred as a result of some design fault. Once the manufacturing facilities have been established, it may not be economic to revise the design but merely to deal with the problem through after-sales service procedures.

Total life-cycle costing seeks to focus management's attention on the fact that it is not just during the production phase that attention needs to be paid to cost management. By the start of the production phase it is too late to try to manage a large element of the product's or service's total life-cycle cost. Efforts need to be made to assess the costs of alternative designs.

There needs to be a review of the product or service over its entire life cycle, which could be a period of twenty years or more. Traditional management accounting, however, tends to be concerned with assessing performance over periods of just one year or less.

Real World 5.6 provides some idea of the extent to which total life-cycle costing is used in practice.

REAL WORLD 5.6

Total life-cycle costing in practice

A survey of management accounting practice in the US was conducted in 2003. Nearly 2,000 businesses replied to the survey. These tended to be larger businesses, of which about 40 per cent were manufacturers and about 16 per cent financial services; the remainder were across a range of other industries.

The survey revealed that 22 per cent extensively use a total life-cycle approach to cost control, with a further 37 per cent considering using the technique in the future.

Though the survey relates to the US, in the absence of UK evidence it provides some insight to what is likely also to be practised in the UK and elsewhere in the developed world.

Source: Ernst and Young (see reference 5 at the end of the chapter).

Target costing

With traditional cost-plus pricing, costs are totalled for a product or service and a percentage is added for profit to give a selling price. This, for reasons raised earlier in this chapter, is not a very practical basis on which to price output for many businesses – certainly not those operating in a price-competitive market. The cost-plus price may well be totally unacceptable to the market.

Target costing approaches the problem from the other direction. First, with the help of market research or other means, a unit selling price and sales volume are established. From the unit selling price is taken an amount for profit. This unit profit figure must be such as to be acceptable to meet the business's profit objective. The resulting figure is the target cost. Efforts are then made to establish a way of providing the service or producing the product that will enable the target cost to be met. This may involve revising the design, finding more efficient means of production or requiring suppliers of goods and services to supply more cheaply.

Target costing is seen as a part of a total life-cycle costing approach, in that cost savings are sought at a very early stage in the life cycle, during the pre-production phase.

Real World 5.7 indicates the level of usage of target costing. This shows quite a low level of usage in both the UK and US. In contrast, survey evidence shows that target costing is very widely used by Japanese manufacturing businesses.

REAL WORLD 5.7

Target costing in practice on both sides of the Atlantic

The ACCA survey suggests that target costing is not much used by UK businesses: 22 per cent of respondents never use this approach and only 26 per cent use it often or always.

Source: Drury *et al.* (see reference 4 at the end of the chapter).

The Ernst and Young survey of management accounting practice in the US, conducted in 2003, revealed that 27 per cent use target costing extensively, with a further 41 per cent considering using the technique in the future.

Source: Ernst and Young (see reference 5 at the end of the chapter).

Activity 5.11

Though target costing seems effective and has its enthusiasts, some people feel it has its problems. Can you suggest what these problems might be?

There seem to be three main problem areas:

- It can lead to various conflicts – for example, between the business, its suppliers and its own staff.
- It can cause a great deal of stress for employees who are trying to meet target costs that are sometimes extremely difficult to meet.
- Although, in the end, ways may be found to meet a target cost (through product or service redesign, negotiating lower prices with suppliers and so on), the whole process can be very expensive.

We shall discuss total life-cycle costing and target costing a little more in Chapter 11 when we consider the strategic aspects of management accounting.

Kaizen costing

→ ***Kaizen* costing** is linked to total life-cycle costing and focuses on cost saving during the production phase. Since that is at a relatively late stage in the life cycle (from a cost control point of view), only relatively small cost savings can be made in the production phase. Also, the major production-phase cost savings should already have been made through target costing. The Japanese word *kaizen* implies 'small changes'.

With *kaizen* costing, efforts are made to reduce the unit manufacturing cost of the particular product or service under review, if possible taking it below the unit cost in the previous period. Target percentage reductions can be set. Usually, production workers are encouraged to identify ways of reducing costs. This is something that the 'hands on' experience of those workers may enable them to do. Even though the scope to reduce costs is limited at the production stage, valuable savings can still be made.

Benchmarking

→ **Benchmarking** is an activity – usually a continuing one – where a business, or one of its divisions, seeks to emulate a successful business or division and so achieve a similar level of success. The successful business or division provides a benchmark against which the business can measure its own performance, as well as examples of approaches that can lead to success. Sometimes the benchmark business will help with the activity, but even where no co-operation is given, outside observers can still learn quite a lot about what makes that business successful.

Real Worlds 5.8 and 5.9 outline the use of benchmarking in practice in the UK.

REAL WORLD 5.8

Benchmarking in local government

The Audit Commission is a public body that has a statutory right to investigate public sector organisations and report on the extent to which those organisations provide value for money to the public.

In the context of local government, the Commission sees benchmarking as one way of assessing value for money. It has been doing this since the 1980s, and so while benchmarking may be seen as a recent innovation in the private sector, it has a fairly long history in the public sector.

Since the Commission has legal powers, it has been able to insist that the various local government authorities provide information to enable a comprehensive benchmarking operation to take place. Contrast this with the private sector where benchmarking between businesses is difficult because there is no compulsion. Businesses are reluctant to divulge commercially sensitive information to other businesses with which they may be in competition. Often, the best that can be achieved in the private sector is for businesses to benchmark internally, with one division or department comparing itself with another part of the same business.

REAL WORLD 5.9

Benchmarking on cost of sales and profit margins at New Look

New Look plc is a large womenswear retail chain, with branches in the UK and in Europe. The annual report for 2002/3 describes how the business was able to reduce its cost of sales to sales ratio from 43 per cent to 41 per cent (gross profit margin of 59 per cent). This was achieved by benchmarking against what the business regards as the standard of the better businesses in the industry. This 'world-class standard', the business believes, is a 38 per cent ratio.

Source: New Look Group plc Annual Report 2002/3, p. 6.

Real World 5.10 gives an indication of the extent that benchmarking is used in practice.

REAL WORLD 5.10

Benchmarking in practice

The Ernst and Young survey of management accounting practice in the US, conducted in 2003, revealed that 53 per cent benchmark extensively, with a further 36 per cent considering using the technique in the future.

Source: Ernst and Young (see reference 5 at the end of the chapter).

SUMMARY

The main points of this chapter may be summarised as follows:

Activity based costing is an approach to dealing with overheads (in full costing) that treats all costs as being caused or 'driven' by activities. Advocates argue that it is more relevant to the modern commercial environment than is the traditional approach.

- Identification of the cost drivers can lead to more relevant indirect cost treatment in full costing.
- Critics argue that ABC is time-consuming and expensive to apply – not justified by the possible improvement in the quality of information.

Pricing output

- In theory, profit is maximised where the price is such that:

  Marginal sales revenue = Marginal cost of production

- Elasticity of demand indicates the sensitivity of demand to price changes.

- Full cost (cost-plus) pricing takes the full cost and adds a mark up for profit.
  - it is popular;
  - the market may not accept the price (most businesses are 'price takers');
  - it can provide a useful benchmark.
- Relevant/marginal cost pricing, takes the relevant/marginal cost and adds a mark up for profit.
  - it can be useful in the short term, but in the longer term it may be better to charge a full cost plus price.
- Various pricing strategies can be used, including:
  - penetration pricing;
  - price skimming.

Total life-cycle costing takes account of all of the costs incurred over a product's entire life.

- The life-cycle of a product can be broken down into three phases: pre-production, production and post-production.
- A high proportion of costs is incurred and/or committed during the pre-production phase.
- Target costing attempts to reduce costs so that the market price covers the cost plus an acceptable profit.
- *Kaizen* costing attempts to reduce costs at the production stage.
- Since most costs will have been saved at the pre-production phase and through target costing, only small cost savings are likely to be possible.
- Benchmarking attempts to emulate a successful aspect of, for example, another business or division.

→ Key terms

Activity-based costing (ABC) p. 112	**Penetration pricing** p. 130
Cost driver p. 112	**Price skimming** p. 130
Cost pool p. 113	**Total life-cycle costing** p. 132
Elasticity of demand p. 118	**Target costing** p. 133
Full cost (cost-plus) pricing p. 126	*Kaizen* **costing** p. 134
Marginal cost pricing p. 128	**Benchmarking** p. 134

Further reading

If you would like to explore the topics covered in this chapter in more depth, we recommend the following books:

Management and Cost Accounting, *Drury C.*, 5th edn, Thomson Learning Business Press, 2000, chapters 10, 11 and 23.

Cost Accounting: A managerial emphasis, *Horngren C., Foster G. and Datar S.*, 11th edn, Prentice Hall International, 2002, chapters 5, 12 and 13.

Cost and Management Accounting, *Williamson D.*, Prentice Hall International, 1996, chapters 7, 13 and 20.

Management Accounting, *Atkinson A., Banker R., Kaplan R. and Young S. M.*, 3rd edn, Prentice Hall, 2001, chapters 5, 7 and 9.

References

1 **Activity Based Costing – A review with case studies**, *Innes J. and Mitchell F.*, CIMA Publishing, 1990.

2 **Cost Systems Design and Profitability Analysis in UK Companies**, *Drury C. and Tayles M.*, CIMA Publishing, 2000.

3 'Activity-based costing in the UK's largest companies', *Innes J., Mitchell F. and Sinclair D.*, in **Management Accounting Research**, Vol. 11, No. 3, 2000.

4 **A Survey of Management Accounting Practices in UK Manufacturing Companies**, *Drury C., Braund S., Osborne P. and Tayles M.*, Chartered Association of Certified Accountants, 1993.

5 **2003 Survey of Management Accounting**, *Ernst and Young,* Ernst and Young, 2003.

REVIEW QUESTIONS

Answers to these questions can be found on the students' side of the Companion Website at www.pearsoned.co.uk/atrillmclaney.

5.1 How does activity-based costing differ from the traditional approach? What is the underlying difference in the philosophy of each of them?

5.2 The use of activity-based costing in helping to deduce full costs has been criticised. What has tended to be the basis of this criticism?

5.3 What is meant by elasticity of demand? How does knowledge of the elasticity of demand affect pricing decisions?

5.4 According to economic theory, at what point is profit maximised? Why is it at this point?

EXERCISES

Exercises 5.6 to 5.8 are more advanced than 5.1 to 5.5. Those with a coloured number have answers at the back of the book.

5.1 Woodner Ltd provides a standard service. It is able to provide a maximum of 100 units of this service each week. Experience shows that at a price of £100, no unit of the service would be sold. For every £5 below this price, the business is able to sell 10 more units. For example, at a price of £95, 10 units would be sold, at £90, 20 units would be sold, and so on. The business's fixed costs total £2,500 a week. Variable costs are £20 a unit over the entire range of possible output. The market is such that it is not feasible to charge different prices to different customers.

Required:
What is the most profitable level of output of the service?

5.2 It appears from research evidence that a cost-plus approach influences pricing decisions in practice. What is meant by cost-plus pricing and what are the problems of using this approach?

5.3 Kaplan plc makes a range of suitcases of various sizes and shapes. There are 10 different models of suitcase produced by the business. In order to keep stocks (inventories) of finished suitcases to a minimum, each model is made in a small batch. Each batch is costed as a separate job and the cost for each suitcase deduced by dividing the batch cost by the number of suitcases in the batch.

At present, the business derives the cost of each batch using a traditional job-costing approach. Recently, however, a new management accountant was appointed, who is advocating the use of activity-based costing (ABC) to deduce the cost of the batches. The management accountant claims that ABC leads to much more reliable and relevant costs and that it has other benefits.

Required:
(a) Explain how the business deduces the cost of each suitcase at present.
(b) Discuss the purposes to which the knowledge of the cost for each suitcase, deduced on a traditional basis, can be put and how valid the cost is for the purpose concerned.

(c) Explain how ABC could be applied to costing the suitcases, highlighting the differences between ABC and the traditional approach.

(d) Explain what advantages the new management accountant probably believes ABC to have over the traditional approach.

5.4   Comment critically on the following statements that you have overheard:

(a) 'To maximise profit you need to sell your output at the highest price.'

(b) 'Elasticity of demand deals with the extent to which costs increase as demand increases.'

(c) 'Provided that the price is large enough to cover the marginal cost of production, the sale should be made.'

(d) 'According to economic theory, profit is maximised where total cost equals total revenue.'

(e) 'Price skimming is charging low prices for the output until you have a good share of the market, and then putting up your prices.'

Explain clearly all technical terms.

5.5   Comment critically on the following statements that you have overheard:

(a) 'Direct labour hours are the most appropriate basis to use to charge overheads to jobs in the modern manufacturing environment where people are so important.'

(b) 'Activity-based costing is a means of more accurately accounting for direct labour cost.'

(c) 'Activity-based costing cannot really be applied to the service sector because the "activities" that it seeks to analyse tend to be related to manufacturing.'

(d) 'Kaizen costing is an approach where great efforts are made to reduce the costs of developing a new product and setting up its production processes.'

(e) 'Benchmarking is an approach to job costing where each direct worker keeps a record of the time spent on each job on his or her workbench before it is passed on to the next direct worker or into finished stock (inventory) stores.'

5.6   The GB Company manufactures a variety of electric motors. The business is currently operating at about 70 per cent of capacity and is earning a satisfactory return on investment.

The management of GB has been approached by International Industries (II) with an offer to buy 120,000 units of an electric motor. II manufactures a motor that is almost identical to GB's motor, but a fire at the II plant has shut down its manufacturing operations. II needs the 120,000 motors over the next four months to meet commitments to its regular customers; II is prepared to pay £19 each for the motors, which it will collect from the GB plant.

GB's product cost, based on current planned cost for the motor, is:

	£
Direct materials	5.00
Direct labour (variable)	6.00
Manufacturing overhead	9.00
Total	20.00

Manufacturing overhead is applied to production at the rate of £18.00 a direct labour hour. This overhead rate is made up of the following components:

	£
Variable factory overhead	6.00
Fixed factory overhead – direct	8.00
– allocated	4.00
Applied manufacturing overhead rate	18.00

Additional costs usually incurred in connection with sales of electric motors include sales commissions of 5 per cent and freight expense of £1.00 a unit.

In determining selling prices, GB adds a 40 per cent mark-up to product costs. This provides a suggested selling price of £28 for the motor. The marketing department, however, has set the current selling price at £27.00 to maintain market share. The order would, however, require additional fixed factory overhead of £15,000 a month in the form of supervision and clerical costs. If management accepts the order, 30,000 motors will be manufactured and delivered to II each month for the next four months.

Required:

(a) Prepare a financial evaluation showing the impact of accepting the Industrial Industries order. What is the minimum unit price that the business's management could accept without reducing its operating profit?

(b) State clearly any assumptions contained in the analysis of (a) above and discuss any other organisational or strategic factors that GB should consider.

5.7   Sillycon Ltd is a business engaged in the development of new products in the electronics industry. Subtotals on the spreadsheet of planned overheads reveal:

	Electronics department	Testing department	Service department
Overheads – variable (£000)	1,200	600	700
– fixed (£000)	2,000	500	800
Planned activity: Direct labour hours ('000)	800	600	–

For the purposes of reallocation of service department's overheads, it is agreed that variable overheads vary with the direct labour hours worked in each department. Fixed overheads of the service department are to be reallocated on the basis of maximum practical capacity of the two departments, which is the same for each.

The business has a long-standing practice of marking up full manufacturing costs by between 25 per cent and 35 per cent in order to establish selling prices.

One new product, which is in a final development stage, is hoped to offer some improvement over competitors' products, which are currently marketed at between £110 and £130 each. Product development engineers have determined that the direct material content is £7 a unit. The product will take 4 labour hours in the electronics department and 3 hours in testing. Hourly labour rates are £10 and £6, respectively.

Management estimates that the fixed costs that would be specifically incurred in relation to the product are: supervision £13,000, depreciation of a recently acquired machine £100,000 and advertising £37,000 a year. These fixed costs are included in the table given above.

Market research indicates that the business could expect to obtain and hold about 25 per cent of the market or, optimistically, 30 per cent. The total market is estimated at 20,000 units.

Note: It may be assumed that the existing plan has been prepared to cater for a range of products and no single product decision will cause the business to amend it.

Required:

(a) Prepare a summary of information that would help with the pricing decision. Such information should include marginal cost and full cost implications after allocation of service department overheads.

(b) Explain and elaborate on the information prepared.

5.8   A business manufactures refrigerators for domestic use. There are three models: Lo, Mid and Hi. The models, their quality and their price are aimed at different markets.

Product costs are computed on a blanket overhead-rate basis using a labour-hour method. Prices as a general rule are set based on cost plus 20 per cent. The following information is provided:

	Lo	Mid	Hi
Material cost (£/unit)	25	62.5	105
Direct labour hours (per unit)	$^1/_2$	1	1
Budget production/sales (units)	20,000	1,000	10,000

The budgeted overheads for the business amount to £4,410,000. Direct labour is costed at £8 an hour.

The business is currently facing increasing competition, especially from imported goods. As a result, the selling price of Lo has been reduced to a level that produces very little profit margin. To address this problem, an activity-based costing approach has been suggested. The overheads are examined and these are grouped around main business activities of machining (£2,780,000), logistics (£590,000) and establishment (£1,040,000) costs. It is maintained that these costs could be allocated based respectively on cost drivers of machine hours, material orders and space, to reflect the use of resources in each of these areas. After analysis, the following proportionate statistics are available related to the total volume of products:

	Lo %	Mid %	Hi %
Machine hours	40	15	45
Material orders	47	6	47
Space	42	18	40

Required:
(a) Calculate for each product the full cost and selling price determined by:
   (i) The original costing method.
   (ii) The activity-based costing method.
(b) What are the implications of the two systems of costing in the situation given?
(c) What business/strategic options exist for the business in the light of the new information?

6

Budgeting

OBJECTIVES

When you have completed this chapter, you should be able to:

- Define a budget and show how budgets, strategic objectives and strategic plans are related.

- Explain the budgeting process and the interlinking of the various budgets within the business.

- Indicate the uses of budgeting and construct various budgets, including the cash budget, from relevant data.

- Discuss the criticisms that are made of budgeting.

INTRODUCTION

Budgets are an important tool for management planning and control. In this chapter we consider the role and nature of budgets and we shall also show how budgets are prepared. It is important to recognise that budgets do not exist in a vacuum; they are an integral part of a planning framework that is adopted by well-run businesses. To understand fully the nature of budgets we must, therefore, understand the strategic planning framework within which they are set, a framework that we discussed in Chapter 1. Preparing budgets relies on an understanding of many of the issues relating to the behaviour of costs and full costing, topics that we explored in Chapters 3 and 4 respectively. The chapter begins with a discussion of the budgeting framework and then goes on to consider detailed aspects of the budgeting process.

Budgets, strategic plans and strategic objectives

It is vital that businesses develop plans for the future. Whatever a business is trying to achieve, it is unlikely to come about unless its managers are clear what the future direction of the business is going to be. As we saw in Chapter 1, the development of plans involves five key steps:

1 *Establish mission and objectives*

→ The **mission statement** is a statement of broad intent. See Real World 1.1 (p. 13) for the mission statement of BT, the telecommunications business. Strategic objectives are more specific and quantifiable goals.

2 *Undertake a position analysis*

This is to assess where the business is currently placed relative to where it wants to be, as defined by its objectives.

3 *Identify and assess the strategic options*

Here the business considers the various ways in which it might move from where it is now (identified in step 2) to where in wants to be (identified in step 1).

4 *Select strategic options*

This involves selecting what seems to be the best of the courses of action or strategies (identified in step 3) and formulating a strategic plan. The plan is normally broken down into a series of plans, one for each element of the business. These plans are the

→ budgets. A **budget** is a business plan for the short term – typically one year. It is likely to be expressed mainly in financial terms. Its role is to convert the strategic plans into actionable blueprints for the immediate future. Budgets will define precise targets concerning:

- Cash receipts and payments
- Sales, broken down into amounts and prices for each of the products or services provided by the business
- Detailed stock (inventory) requirements
- Detailed labour requirements
- Specific production requirements.

5 *Perform, review and control*

Here the business pursues the budgets derived in step 4. By comparing the actual outcome with the budgets, managers can see if things are going according to plan or not. Steps would be taken to exercise control where actual performance appears not to be matching the budgets.

Activity 6.1

The approach described in step 3, above, suggests that decision makers will systematically collect information and then carefully evaluate all the options available. Do you think this is what decision makers really do?

In practice, decision makers may not be as rational and capable as implied in the process described. Individuals may find it difficult to handle a wealth of information relating to a wide range of options. To avoid becoming overloaded, they may restrict their range of possible options and/or discard some information. Decision makers may also adopt rather simple approaches to evaluating the mass of information provided. These approaches might not lead to the best decisions being made.

Clearly, the relationship between the mission, strategic objectives, strategic plans and budgets is that the mission, once set, is likely to last for quite a long time – perhaps throughout the life of the business. The objectives are also fairly long-term goals. A series of strategic plans identifies how each objective is to be pursued, and budgets identify how the strategic plan is to be fulfilled.

An analogy might be found in terms of a student enrolling on a course of study. His or her mission might be to have a happy and fulfilling life. A key strategic objective flowing from this mission might be to embark on a career that will be rewarding in various ways. He or she might have identified the particular study course as the most effective way to work towards this objective. Successfully completing the course would then be the strategic plan. In working towards this strategic plan, passing a particular stage of the course might be identified as the target for the forthcoming year. This short-term target is analogous to the budget. Having achieved the 'budget' for the first year, the budget for the second year becomes passing the second stage.

Collecting information on performance and exercising control

However well planned the activities of a business might be, they will come to nothing unless steps are taken to try to achieve them in practice. The process of making planned events actually occur is known as **control**. This is part of step 5 (above).

Control can be defined as compelling events to conform to plan. This definition is valid in any context. For example, when we talk about controlling a motor car, we mean making the car do what we plan that it should do. In a business context, accounting is very useful in the control process. This is because it is possible to state plans in accounting terms (as budgets). Since it is also possible to state *actual* outcomes in the same terms, making comparison between actual and planned outcomes is a relatively easy matter. Where actual outcomes are at variance with budgets, this variance should be highlighted by accounting information. Managers can then take steps to get the business back on track towards the achievement of the budgets. We shall be looking quite closely at the control aspect of budgeting in Chapter 7.

Figure 6.1 shows the planning and control process in diagrammatic form. It should be emphasised that planning (including budgeting) is the responsibility of managers rather than accountants. Though accountants can play a role in the planning process, by supplying relevant information to managers and by contributing to decision making as part of the management team, they should not dominate the process. In practice, it seems that the budgeting aspect of planning is in danger of being dominated by accountants, perhaps because most budgets are expressed in financial terms. However, managers are avoiding their responsibilities if they allow this to happen.

Time horizon of plans and budgets

The setting of strategic plans is typically performed as a major exercise every five years, and budgets are usually set annually. It need not necessarily be the case that strategic plans are set for five years and that budgets are set for one year: it is up to the management of the business concerned. Businesses involved in certain industries – say, information technology – may feel that five years is too long a planning period since new developments can, and do, occur virtually overnight. Such businesses may feel that a planning horizon of two or three years is more feasible. Similarly, a budget need not be set for one year, although this appears to be a widely used time horizon.

Figure 6.1   The planning and control process

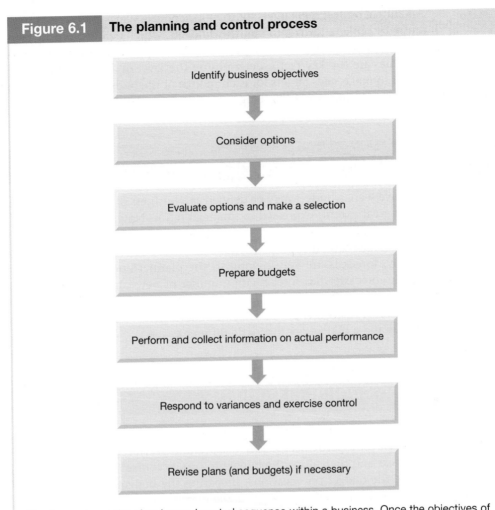

The figure shows the planning and control sequence within a business. Once the objectives of the business have been determined, the various options that can fulfil these objectives must be considered and evaluated in order to derive a strategic plan. The budget is a short-term financial plan for the business that is prepared within the framework of the strategic plan. Control can be exercised through the comparison of budgeted and actual performance. Where a significant divergence emerges, some form of corrective action should be taken. If the budget figures prove to be based on incorrect assumptions about the future, it might be necessary to revise the budget.

Activity 6.2

Can you think of any reason why most businesses prepare detailed budgets for the forthcoming year, rather than for a shorter or longer period?

The reason is probably that a year represents a long enough time for the budget preparation exercise to be worthwhile, yet short enough into the future for detailed plans to be capable of being made. As we shall see later in this chapter, the process of formulating budgets can be a time-consuming exercise, but there are economies of scale – for example, preparing the budget for the next twelve months would not normally take twice as much time and effort as preparing the budget for the next six months.

An annual budget sets targets for the forthcoming year for all aspects of the business. It is usually broken down into monthly budgets, which define monthly targets. Indeed, in many instances, the annual budget will be built up from monthly figures. For example, where sales are the key factor determining the level of activity, the sales staff will be required to make sales targets for each month of the budget period. Other budgets will be set, for each month of the budget period, as we shall explain below.

Budgets and forecasts

As we have seen, a budget may be defined as a business plan for the short term. Budgets are, to a great extent, expressed in financial terms. Note that a budget is a *plan*, not a forecast. To talk of a plan suggests an intention or determination to achieve planned targets; **forecasts** tend to be predictions of the future state of the environment.

Clearly, forecasts are very helpful to the planner/budget-setter. If, for example, a reputable forecaster has forecast the number of new cars to be purchased in the UK during next year, it will be valuable for a manager in a car manufacturing business to obtain and take account of this forecast figure when setting its sales budgets. However, a forecast and a budget are distinctly different.

Periodic and continual budgets

Budgeting can be undertaken on a periodic or a continual basis. A **periodic budget** is prepared for a particular period (usually one year). Managers will agree the budget for the year and then allow the budget to run its course. Although it may be necessary to revise the budget on occasions, preparing the budget is in essence a one-off exercise during a financial year. A **continual budget**, as the name suggests, is continually updated. We have seen that an annual budget will normally be broken down into smaller time intervals (usually monthly periods) to help control the activities of a business. A continual budget will add a new month to replace the month that has just passed, thereby ensuring that, at all times, there will be a budget for a full planning period. Continual budgets are also referred to as **rolling budgets**.

Activity 6.3

What do you think are the advantages and disadvantages of each form of budgeting?

Periodic budgeting will usually take less time and effort to prepare and will therefore be less costly. However, as time passes, the budget period shortens and towards the end of the financial year managers will be working to a very short planning period indeed. Continual budgeting, on the other hand, will ensure that managers always have a full year's budget to help them make decisions. It is claimed that continual budgeting ensures that managers plan throughout the year rather than just once each year. In this way it encourages a forward-looking attitude. However, there is a danger that budgeting will become a mechanical exercise as managers may not have time to step back from their other tasks each month and consider the future carefully. It may be unreasonable to expect managers continually to take this future-oriented perspective.

The interrelationship of various budgets

For a particular business for a particular period, there is more than one budget. Each one will relate to a specific aspect of the business. It is generally considered that the ideal situation is that there should be a separate budget for each person who is in a managerial position, no matter how junior. The contents of all of the individual budgets will be summarised in **master budgets** consisting usually of a budgeted profit and loss account (income statement) and balance sheet. The cash flow statement (in summarised form) is considered by some to be a third master budget.

Figure 6.2 illustrates the interrelationship and interlinking of individual budgets, in this particular case using a manufacturing business as an example.

Figure 6.2	The interrelationship of various budgets

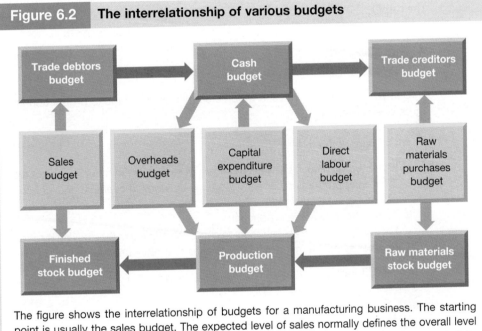

The figure shows the interrelationship of budgets for a manufacturing business. The starting point is usually the sales budget. The expected level of sales normally defines the overall level of activity for the business, and the other budgets will be drawn up in accordance with this. Thus, the sales budget will largely define the finished stock (inventory) requirements, and from this we can define the production requirements and so on.

Starting at the top of Figure 6.2, the sales budget is usually the first budget to be prepared, as this tends to determine the overall level of activity for the forthcoming period. Sales demand is probably the most common factor that limits activity. The level of sales would tend to dictate the finished stock requirement, though it would also be dictated by the policy of the business on finished stockholding. The requirement for finished stock would define the required production levels, which would, in turn, dictate the requirements of the individual production departments or sections. The demands of manufacturing, in conjunction with the business's policy on raw materials stock, define the raw materials stock budget. The purchases budget will be dictated by the materials stock budget which will, in conjunction with the policy of the business on creditor payment, dictate the trade creditors (payables) budget. One of the determinants of the cash budget will be the trade creditors budget; another will be the trade debtors (receivables) budget, which itself derives, through the debtor policy of the business, from the sales budget. Cash will also be affected by overheads and direct labour costs (themselves linked to production) and by capital expenditure. The factors that affect policies on matters such as stockholding and debtor collection and creditor payment periods will be discussed in some detail in Chapter 9.

It may actually prove to be the case that it is not sales demand that limits activities. Assuming that the budgeting process takes the order just described, it might be found in practice that there is some constraint other than sales. For example, the production capacity of the business may be incapable of meeting the necessary levels of output to match the sales budget for one or more months. In this case, it might be reasonable to look at the ways of overcoming the problem. As a last resort, it might be necessary to revise the sales budget to a lower level to enable production to meet the target.

Activity 6.4

Can you think of any ways in which a short-term shortage of production facilities might be overcome?

We thought of the following:

- Higher production in previous months and stockpiling to meet periods of higher demand.
- Increasing production capacity, perhaps by working overtime and/or acquiring (buying or leasing) additional plant.
- Subcontracting some production.
- Encouraging potential customers to change the timing of their buying by offering discounts or other special terms during the months that have been identified as quiet.

You might well have thought of other approaches

There will be the horizontal relationships between budgets, which we have just looked at, but there will usually be vertical ones as well. For example, the sales budget may be broken down into a number of subsidiary budgets, perhaps one for each regional sales manager. The overall sales budget will be a summary of the subsidiary ones. The same may be true of virtually all of the other budgets, most particularly the production budget.

Figure 6.2, which was considered earlier, gives a very simplified outline of the budgetary framework of a typical manufacturing business. We have looked at the interlinking of budgets in the context of a manufacturing business. This is not because such businesses are particularly significant, but purely because they have all of the types of budget that we tend to find in practice. A service supplier, for example, would have a similar set of budgets, but without some or all of those relating to stocks (inventories). All of the issues relating to budgets apply equally well to all types of business.

All of the operating budgets that we have just reviewed have to be consistent with the overall short-term plans laid out in the master budget, that is, the budgeted profit and loss account (income statement) and balance sheet.

The uses of budgets

Budgets are generally regarded as having five areas of usefulness. These are:

1 *Budgets tend to promote forward thinking and the possible identification of short-term problems.* We saw above that a shortage of production capacity might be identified during the budgeting process. Making this discovery in good time could leave a number of means of overcoming the problem open to exploration. If the potential production problem is picked up early enough, all of the suggestions in the answer to Activity 6.4 and, possibly, other ways of overcoming the problem can be explored. Early identification of the potential problem gives managers time for calm and rational consideration of the best way of overcoming it. The best solution to the potential problem may only be feasible if action can be taken well in advance. This would be true of all of the suggestions made in the answer to Activity 6.4.

2 *Budgets can be used to help co-ordination between the various sections of the business.* It is crucially important that the activities of the various departments and sections of the business are linked so that the activities of one are complementary to those of another. For example, the activities of the purchasing/procurement department of a manufacturing business should dovetail with the raw materials needs of the production departments. If this is not the case, production could run out of stock, leading to expensive production stoppages. Possibly, just as undesirable, excessive stocks could be bought, leading to large and unnecessary stockholding costs. We shall see how this co-ordination tends to work in practice later in this chapter.

3 *Budgets can motivate managers to better performance.* Having a stated task can motivate managers and staff in their performance. It is a well-established view that to tell a manager to do his or her best is not very motivating, but to define a required level of achievement is likely to be so. It is felt that managers will be better motivated by being able to relate their particular role in the business to the overall objectives of the business. Since budgets are directly derived from corporate objectives, budgeting makes this possible. It is clearly not possible to allow managers to operate in an unconstrained environment. Having to operate in a way that matches the goals of the business is a price of working in an effective business. We shall consider the role of budgets as motivators in Chapter 7.

4 *Budgets can provide a basis for a system of control.* As mentioned earlier in the chapter, control is concerned with ensuring that events conform to plans. If senior management wishes to control and to monitor the performance of more junior staff, it needs some yardstick against which the performance can be measured and assessed. It is possible to compare current performance with past performance or perhaps with what happens in another business. However, the most logical yardstick is usually planned performance. If there is information available concerning the actual performance for a period, and this can be compared with the planned performance, then a basis for control will have been established. Such a basis will enable the use of **management by exception**, a technique where senior managers can spend most of their time dealing with those staff or activities that have failed to achieve the budget (the exceptions). This means that the senior managers do not have to spend too much time on those that are performing well. It also allows junior managers to exercise self-control. By knowing what is expected of them and what they have actually achieved, they can assess how well they are performing and take steps to correct matters where they are failing to achieve. We shall consider the effect of making plans and being held accountable for their achievement in Chapter 7.

5 *Budgets can provide a system of authorisation* for managers to spend up to a particular limit. A good example of this is where there are certain activities (for example, staff development and research expenditure) that are allocated a fixed amount of funds at the discretion of senior management.

Figure 6.3 shows the benefits of budgets in diagrammatic form.

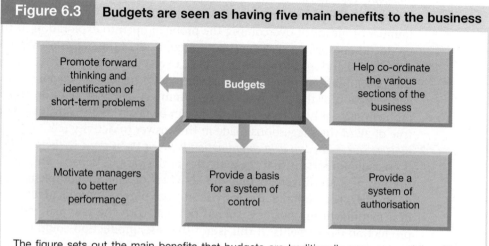

Figure 6.3 **Budgets are seen as having five main benefits to the business**

The figure sets out the main benefits that budgets are traditionally seen as providing. These benefits are discussed in the chapter.

The following three activities pick up issues that relate to some of the uses of budgets.

Activity 6.5

The third on the above list of the uses of budgets (motivation), implies that managers are set stated tasks. Do you think there is a danger that requiring managers to work towards such predetermined targets will stifle their skill, flair and enthusiasm?

If the budgets are set in such a way as to offer challenging yet achievable targets, the manager is still required to show skill, flair and enthusiasm. There is the danger, however, that if targets are badly set (either unreasonably demanding or too easy to achieve), they could be a demotivating force. This could well stifle managers' skill, flair and enthusiasm.

Activity 6.6

The fourth on the above list of the uses of budgets (control), implies that current management performance is compared with some yardstick. What is wrong with comparing actual performance with past performance, or the performance of others, in an effort to exercise control?

There is no automatic reason to believe that what happened in the past, or is happening elsewhere, represents a sensible target for this year in this business. Considering what happened last year, and in other businesses, may help in the formulation of plans, but past events and the performance of others should not automatically be seen as the target.

Activity 6.7

Could the five identified uses of budgets conflict with one another on occasions? For example, can you think of a possible conflict:

(a) between the budget as a motivational device and the budget as a means of control?
(b) between the budget as a means of control and the budget as a system of authorisation?

It is quite possible for the uses identified to be in conflict with one another.

(a) Where the budget is being used as a motivational device, some businesses set the budget targets at a more difficult level than the managers are expected to achieve. This is an attempt to motivate managers to strive to reach their targets. For control purposes, however, the budget becomes less meaningful as a benchmark against which to compare actual performance.
(b) Where a budget is being used as a system of authorisation, managers may be motivated to spend to the limit of their budget, even though this may be wasteful. This may occur where the managers are not allowed to carry over unused funds to the next budget period or if they believe that the budget for the next period will be reduced because not all the funds for the current period were spent. The wasting of resources in this way conflicts with the role of budgets as a means of exercising control.

Conflict between the different uses will mean that managers must decide which particular uses for budgets should be given priority; managers must be prepared, if necessary, to trade off the benefits resulting from one particular use for the benefits of another.

The budget-setting process

Budgeting is such an important area for businesses, and other organisations, that it tends to be approached in a fairly methodical and formal way. This usually involves a number of steps, described below and shown in diagrammatic form in Figure 6.4 (p. 152).

Step 1: Establish who will take responsibility

It is usually seen as crucial that those responsible for the budget-setting process have real authority within the organisation.

Activity 6.8

Why is it crucial that those responsible for the budget-setting process have real authority in the organisation?

One of the crucial aspects of the process is establishing co-ordination between budgets so that the plans of one department match and are complementary to those of other departments. This usually requires compromise where adjustment of initial budgets must be undertaken. This in turn means that someone on the board of directors (or its equivalent) has to be closely involved; only people of this rank are likely to have the necessary moral and, if needed, formal managerial authority to force departmental managers to compromise.

Figure 6.4   Steps in the budget-setting process

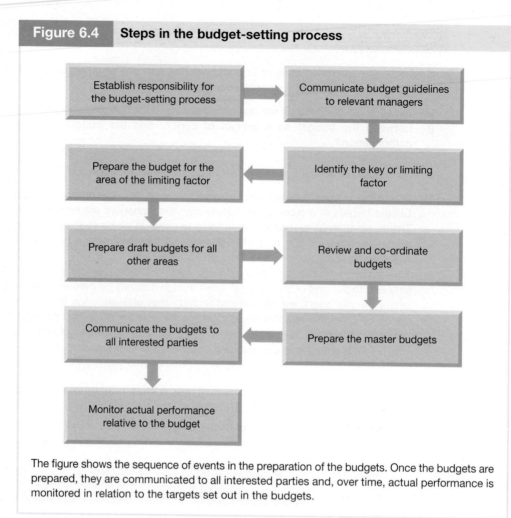

The figure shows the sequence of events in the preparation of the budgets. Once the budgets are prepared, they are communicated to all interested parties and, over time, actual performance is monitored in relation to the targets set out in the budgets.

Quite commonly, a **budget committee** is formed to supervise and take responsibility for the budget-setting process. This committee usually comprises a senior representative of most of the functional areas of the business – marketing, production, personnel and so on. Often, a **budget officer** is appointed to carry out, or to take immediate responsibility for others carrying out, the technical tasks of the committee. Not surprisingly, given their technical expertise in the activity, accountants are often required to take budget officer roles.

Step 2: Communicate budget guidelines to relevant managers

Budgets are intended to be the short-term plans that seek to work towards the achievement of strategic plans and to the overall objectives of the business. It is therefore important that, in drawing up budgets, managers are well aware of what the strategic plans are and how the forthcoming budget period is intended to work towards them. Managers also need to be made well aware of the commercial/economic environment in which they will be operating. It is the responsibility of the budget committee to see that managers have all the necessary information.

Step 3: Identify the key, or limiting, factor

There will always be some aspect of the business that will stop it achieving its object-ives to the maximum extent. This is often a limited ability of the business to sell its products; sometimes, it is some production shortage (such as labour, materials or plant) that is the **limiting factor**, or, linked to these, a shortage of funds. Often, production shortages can be overcome by an increase in funds – for example, more plant can be bought or leased. This is not always a practical solution, because no amount of money will buy certain labour skills or increase the world supply of some raw material.

As has been pointed out earlier in this chapter, it is sometimes possible to ease an initial limiting factor: for example, subcontracting can eliminate a plant capacity problem. This means that some other factor, perhaps sales, will replace the production problem, though at a higher level of output. Ultimately, however, the business will hit a ceiling; some limiting factor will prove impossible to ease.

For entirely practical reasons, it is important that the limiting factor is identified. Ultimately, most, if not all, budgets will be affected by the limiting factor, and so if it can be identified at the outset, all managers can be informed of the restriction early in the process.

Step 4: Prepare the budget for the area of the limiting factor

The limiting factor will determine the overall level of activity for the business. The limiting-factor budget will quite often be the sales budget since the ability to sell is frequently the limiting factor that simply cannot be eased. (When discussing the inter-relationship of budgets earlier in the chapter, we started with the sales budget for this reason.) As we have seen, sales is not always the limiting factor.

Real World 6.1 looks at the methods favoured by businesses of different sizes to determine their sales budgets (see p. 154).

Step 5: Prepare draft budgets for all other areas

The other budgets are prepared, complementing the budget for the area of the limiting factor. In all budget preparation, the computer has become an almost indispensable tool. Much of the work of preparing budgets is repetitive and tedious, yet the resultant budget has to be a reliable representation of the actual plans made. Computers are ideally suited to such tasks and human beings are not. It is often the case that budgets have to be redrafted several times because of some minor alteration, and computers do this without complaint.

There are two broad approaches to setting individual budgets. The *top-down approach* is where the senior management of each budget area originates the budget targets, per-haps discussing them with lower levels of management and, as a result, refining them before the final version is produced. With the *bottom-up approach*, the targets are fed upwards from the lowest level. For example, junior sales managers will be asked to set their own sales targets, which then become incorporated into the budgets of higher levels of management until the overall sales budget emerges.

REAL WORLD 6.1

Sources of the sales budget in practice

Determining the future level of sales can be a difficult problem. In practice, a business may rely on the judgements of sales staff, statistical techniques or market surveys (or some combination of these) to arrive at a sales budget. A 1993 survey of UK manufacturing businesses provides the following insights concerning the use of such techniques and methods.

	All respondents	Small businesses	Large businesses
Number of respondents	281	47	46
	%	%	%
Technique			
Statistical forecasting	31	19	29
Market research	36	13	54
Subjective estimates based on sales staff experience	85	97	80

We can see that the most popular approach by far is the opinion of sales staff. We can also see that there are differences between large and small businesses, particularly concerning the use of market surveys. This evidence is now pretty old, but in the absence of more up-to-date research, it provides some idea of how businesses determine their sales targets.

Source: Drury *et al*. (see reference 1 at the end of the chapter).

Where the bottom-up approach is adopted, it is usually necessary to haggle and negotiate at different levels of authority to achieve agreement. This may be because the plans of some departments do not fit in with those of others or because the targets set by junior managers are not acceptable to their superiors. This approach seems rarely to be found in practice.

Activity 6.9

What are the advantages and disadvantages of each type of budgeting approach?

The bottom-up approach allows greater involvement among managers in the budgeting process and this, in turn, may increase the level of commitment to the targets set. It also allows the business to draw more fully on the local knowledge and expertise of its managers. However, this approach can be time-consuming and may result in some managers setting undemanding targets for themselves in order to have an easy life.

The top-down approach enables senior management to communicate plans to employees and to co-ordinate the activities of the business more easily. It may also help in establishing more demanding targets for managers. However, the level of commitment to the budget may be lower as many of those responsible for achieving the budgets will have been excluded from the budget-setting process.

There will be a brief discussion of the benefits of participation in target setting in Chapter 7.

Step 6: Review and co-ordinate budgets

A business's budget committee must at this stage review the various budgets and satisfy itself that the budgets complement one another. Where there is a lack of co-ordination, steps must be taken to ensure that the budgets mesh. Since this will require that at least one budget must be revised, this activity normally benefits from a diplomatic approach. Ultimately, however, the committee may be forced to assert its authority and insist that alterations are made.

Step 7: Prepare the master budgets

The master budgets are the budgeted profit and loss account (income statement) and budgeted balance sheet (and perhaps a summarised, budgeted cash flow statement). All of the information required to prepare these statements should be available from the individual budgets that have already been prepared. The budget committee usually undertakes the task of preparing the master budgets.

Step 8: Communicate the budgets to all interested parties

The formally agreed budgets are now passed to the individual managers who will be responsible for their implementation. This is, in effect, senior management formally communicating to the other managers the targets that they are expected to achieve.

Step 9: Monitor performance relative to the budget

Much of the budget-setting activity will have been pointless unless each manager's actual performance is compared with planned performance, which is embodied in the budget. This issue is examined in detail in Chapter 7.

Incremental and zero-base budgeting

Traditionally, much budget setting has tended to be on the basis of what happened last year, with some adjustment for any changes in factors that are expected to affect the forthcoming budget period (for example, inflation). This approach is sometimes known as **incremental budgeting**; it is often used for 'discretionary' budgets, such as research and development and staff training, where the **budget holder** (the manager responsible for the budget) is allocated a sum of money to be spent in the area of activity concerned. They are referred to as **discretionary budgets** because the sum allocated is normally at the discretion of senior management. These budgets are very common in local and central government (and in other public bodies), but are also used in commercial businesses to cover certain types of activity.

A feature of the types of activity for which discretionary budgets exist is the lack of a clear relationship between inputs (resources applied) and outputs (benefits). Compare this with, say, a raw materials usage budget in a manufacturing business, where the amount of material used and, therefore, the amount of funds taken by it, is clearly related to the level of production and, ultimately, to sales. It is easy for discretionary budgets to eat up funds with no clear benefit being derived. It is often only proposed increases in these budgets that are closely scrutinised.

→ **Zero-base budgeting (ZBB)** rests on the philosophy that all spending needs to be justified. Thus, when establishing, say, the training budget each year, it is not automatically accepted that training courses should be financed in the future simply because they were undertaken this year. The training budget will start from a zero base and will only be increased above zero if a good case can be made for the scarce resources of the business to be allocated to this form of activity. Top management will need to be convinced that the proposed activities represent 'value for money'.

ZBB encourages managers to adopt a more questioning approach to their areas of responsibility. To justify the allocation of resources, they are often forced to think carefully about the particular activities and the ways in which they are undertaken. This questioning approach should result in a more efficient use of business resources. With an increasing portion of the total costs of most businesses being in areas where the link between outputs and inputs is not always clear, and where commitment of resources is discretionary rather than demonstrably essential to production, ZBB is increasingly relevant.

Activity 6.10

Can you think of any disadvantages of using ZBB? How might any disadvantages be partially overcome?

The principal problems with ZBB are:

- It is time-consuming and therefore expensive to undertake.
- Managers whose sphere of responsibility is subjected to ZBB can feel threatened by it.

The benefits of a ZBB approach can be gained to some extent – perhaps at not too great a cost – by using the approach on a selective basis. For example, a particular budget area could be subjected to ZBB-type scrutiny only every third or fourth year. In any case, if ZBB is used more frequently, there is the danger that managers will use the same arguments each year to justify their activities. The process will simply become a mechanical exercise and the benefits will be lost. For a typical business, some areas are likely to benefit from ZBB more than others. ZBB could, in these circumstances, be applied only to those areas that will benefit from it, and not to the others. The areas that are most likely to benefit from ZBB are discretionary spending ones, such as training, advertising, and research and development.

If senior management is aware of the potentially threatening nature of this form of budgeting, care can be taken to apply ZBB with sensitivity. However, in the quest for value for money, the application of ZBB can result in some tough decisions being made.

The extent to which budgets are utilised

There is recent survey evidence that reveals the extent to which budgeting is used by larger US businesses. It shows that most of them prepare and use budgets (see **Real World 6.2**).

A fairly recent survey of budgeting practice in small and medium-sized enterprises (SMEs) (see **Real World 6.3**) revealed that not all such businesses fully use budgeting. It seems that some smaller businesses prepare budgets only for what they see as key areas. The budget that is most frequently prepared by such businesses is the sales budget, followed by the budgeted profit and loss account and the overheads budget. Perhaps surprisingly, the cash budget is prepared by less than two-thirds of the small businesses surveyed.

REAL WORLD 6.2

Budgeting in practice

A survey of management accounting practice in the US was conducted in 2003. Nearly 2,000 businesses replied to the survey. These tended to be larger businesses, of which about 40 per cent were manufacturers and about 16 per cent financial services; the remainder were across a range of other industries.

The survey revealed that 75 per cent extensively use operational budgeting, with a further 16% considering using the technique in the future.

Though the survey relates to the US, in the absence of UK evidence, it provides some insight to what is likely also to be practice in the UK and elsewhere in the developed world.

Source: Ernst and Young (see reference 2 at the end of the chapter).

REAL WORLD 6.3

Preparation of budgets in SMEs

A study of budgeting practice in small and medium-sized enterprises (SMEs) revealed that the most frequently prepared budget is the sales budget, followed by the budgeted profit and loss account (income statement) and the overheads budget (see Figure 6.5).

Figure 6.5

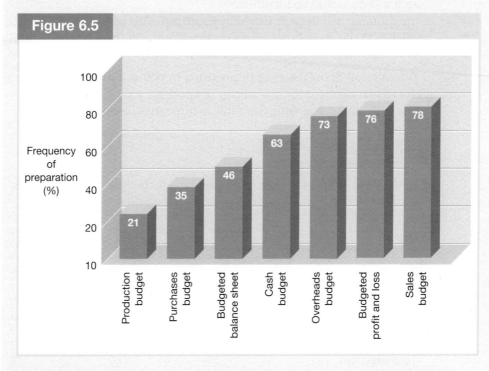

Source: Reproduced from Figure 16 on p. 22 of Chittenden *et al*. (see reference 3 at the end of the chapter). By kind permission of the authors.

Preparing the cash budget

We shall now look in some detail at how the various budgets used by the typical business are prepared, starting with the cash budget and then looking at the others. It is helpful for us to start with the cash budget because:

- it is a key budget; most economic aspects of a business are reflected in cash sooner or later, so that for a typical business the cash budget reflects the whole business more than any other single budget;
- very small, unsophisticated businesses (for example, a corner shop) may feel that full-scale budgeting is not appropriate to their needs, but almost certainly they should prepare a cash budget as a minimum (despite the survey evidence mentioned above).

We shall consider other budgets later in the chapter.

Since budgets are documents that are to be used only internally by a business, their style is a question of management choice and will vary from one business to the next. However, since managers, irrespective of the business, are likely to be using budgets for similar purposes, some consistency of approach can be found. In most businesses the cash budget will probably possess the following features:

1 the budget period would be broken down into sub-periods, typically months;
2 the budget would be in columnar form, with one column for each month;
3 receipts of cash would be identified under various headings and a total for each month's receipts shown;
4 payments of cash would be identified under various headings and a total for each month's payments shown;
5 the surplus of total cash receipts over payments, or of payments over receipts, for each month would be identified;
6 the running cash balance would be identified. This would be achieved by taking the balance at the end of the previous month and adjusting it for the surplus or deficit of receipts over payments for the current month.

Typically, all of the pieces of information in points 3 to 6 in the above list would be useful to management for one reason or another.

The best way to deal with this topic is through an example.

Example 6.1

Vierra Popova Ltd is a wholesale business. The budgeted profit and loss accounts (income statements) for each of the next six months are as follows:

	Jan £000	Feb £000	Mar £000	Apr £000	May £000	June £000
Sales	52	55	55	60	55	53
Cost of goods sold	30	31	31	35	31	32
Salaries and wages	10	10	10	10	10	10
Electricity	5	5	4	3	3	3
Depreciation	3	3	3	3	3	3
Other overheads	2	2	2	2	2	2
Total expenses	50	51	50	53	49	50
Net profit	2	4	5	7	6	3

The business allows all of its customers one month's credit (this means, for example, that cash from January sales will be received in February). Sales during December totalled £60,000.

The business plans to maintain stocks (inventories) at their existing level until some time in March, when they are to be reduced by £5,000. Stocks will remain at this lower level indefinitely. Stock purchases are made on one month's credit. December purchases totalled £30,000. Salaries, wages and 'other overheads' are paid in the month concerned. Electricity is paid quarterly in arrears in March and June. The business plans to buy and pay for a new delivery van in March. This will cost a total of £15,000, but an existing van will be traded in for £4,000 as part of the deal.

The business expects to have £12,000 in cash at the beginning of January.

The cash budget for the six months ending in June will look as follows:

	Jan £000	Feb £000	Mar £000	Apr £000	May £000	June £000
Receipts						
Debtors (note 1)	<u>60</u>	<u>52</u>	<u>55</u>	<u>55</u>	<u>60</u>	<u>55</u>
Payments						
Creditors (note 2)	30	30	31	26	35	31
Salaries and wages	10	10	10	10	10	10
Electricity			14			9
Other overheads	2	2	2	2	2	2
Van purchase	–	–	11	–	–	–
Total payments	<u>42</u>	<u>42</u>	<u>68</u>	<u>38</u>	<u>47</u>	<u>52</u>
Cash surplus	18	10	(13)	17	13	3
Opening balance (note 3)	<u>12</u>	<u>30</u>	<u>40</u>	<u>27</u>	<u>44</u>	<u>57</u>
Closing balance	<u>30</u>	<u>40</u>	<u>27</u>	<u>44</u>	<u>57</u>	<u>60</u>

Notes:

1 The cash receipts from trade debtors (receivables) lag a month behind sales because customers are given a month in which to pay for their purchases. So, December sales will be paid for in January and so on.

2 In most months, the purchases of stock (inventory) will equal the cost of goods sold. This is because the business maintains a constant level of stock. For stock to remain constant at the end of each month, the business must replace exactly the amount that has been used. During March, however, the business plans to reduce its stock by £5,000. This means that stock purchases will be lower than stock usage in that month. The payments for stock purchases lag a month behind purchases because the business expects to be allowed a month to pay for what it buys.

3 Each month's cash balance is the previous month's figure plus the cash surplus (or minus the cash deficit) for the current month. The balance at the start of January is £12,000 according to the information provided earlier.

4 Depreciation does not give rise to a cash payment. In the context of profit measurement (in the profit and loss account), depreciation is a very important aspect. Here, however, we are interested only in cash.

Activity 6.11

Looking at the cash budget of Vierra Popova Ltd, what conclusions do you draw and what possible course of action do you recommend regarding the cash balance over the period concerned?

There appears to be a fairly large cash balance, given the size of the business, and it seems to be increasing. Management might give consideration to putting some of the cash into an income-yielding deposit. Alternatively, it could be used to expand the trading activities of the business by, for example, increasing the investment in non-current (fixed) assets.

Activity 6.12

Vierra Popova Ltd (see Example 6.1) now wishes to prepare its cash budget for the second six months of the year. The budgeted profit and loss accounts (income statements) for each of the second six months are as follows:

	July £000	Aug £000	Sept £000	Oct £000	Nov £000	Dec £000
Sales	57	59	62	57	53	51
Cost of goods sold	32	33	35	32	30	29
Salaries and wages	10	10	10	10	10	10
Electricity	3	3	4	5	6	6
Depreciation	3	3	3	3	3	3
Other overheads	2	2	2	2	2	2
Total expenses	50	51	54	52	51	50
Net profit	7	8	8	5	2	1

The business will continue to allow all of its customers one month's credit.

It plans to increase stocks (inventories) from the 30 June level by £1,000 each month until, and including, September. During the following three months, stock levels will be decreased by £1,000 each month.

Stock purchases, which had been made on one month's credit until the June payment, will, starting with the purchases made in June, be made on two months' credit.

Salaries, wages and 'other overheads' will continue to be paid in the month concerned. Electricity is paid quarterly in arrears in September and December.

At the end of December the business intends to pay off part of a loan. This payment is to be such that it will leave the business with a cash balance of £5,000 with which to start next year.

Required:

Prepare the cash budget for the six months ending in December. (Remember that any information you need that relates to the first six months of the year, including the cash balance that is expected to be brought forward on 1 July, is given in Example 6.1.)

The cash budget for the six months ended 31 December is:

	July £000	Aug £000	Sept £000	Oct £000	Nov £000	Dec £000
Receipts						
Debtors	53	57	59	62	57	53
Payments						
Creditors (note 1)	–	32	33	34	36	31
Salaries and wages	10	10	10	10	10	10
Electricity			10			17
Other overheads	2	2	2	2	2	2
Loan repayment (note 2)	–	–	–	–	–	131
Total payments	12	44	55	46	48	191
Cash surplus	41	13	4	16	9	(138)
Opening balance	60	101	114	118	134	143
Closing balance	101	114	118	134	143	5

Notes:

1 There will be no payment to creditors in July because the June purchases will be made on two months' credit and will therefore be paid in August. The July purchases, which will equal the July cost of sales figure plus the increase in stock made in July, will be paid for in September, and so on.

2 The repayment is simply the amount that will cause the balance at 31 December to be £5,000.

Preparing other budgets

Though each one will have its own particular features, other budgets will tend to follow the same sort of pattern as the cash budget, that is, they will show inflows and outflows during each month and the opening and closing balances in each month.

Example 6.2

To illustrate some of the other budgets, we shall continue to use the example of Vierra Popova Ltd that we considered in Example 6.1, on p. 158. To the information given there, we need to add the fact that the stock balance at 1 January was £30,000.

Show the trade debtors (receivables), trade creditors (payables) and stock (inventory) budgets for the six months.

Solution

Trade debtors (receivables) budget

This would normally show the planned amount owing from credit sales to the business at the beginning and at the end of each month, the planned total sales

Example 6.2 continued

for each month, and the planned total cash receipts from debtors. The layout would be something like the following:

	Jan £000	Feb £000	Mar £000	Apr £000	May £000	June £000
Opening balance	60	52	55	55	60	55
Add Sales	52	55	55	60	55	53
	112	107	110	115	115	108
Less Cash receipts	60	52	55	55	60	55
Closing balance	52	55	55	60	55	53

The opening and closing balances represent the amount that the business plans to be owed (in total) by debtors at the beginning and end of the month, respectively.

Trade creditors (payables) budget

Typically this shows the planned amount owed to suppliers by the business at the beginning and at the end of each month, the planned purchases for each month, and the planned total cash payments to creditors. The layout would be something like the following:

	Jan £000	Feb £000	Mar £000	Apr £000	May £000	June £000
Opening balance	30	30	31	26	35	31
Add Purchases	30	31	26	35	31	32
	60	61	57	61	66	63
Less Cash payment	30	30	31	26	35	31
Closing balance	30	31	26	35	31	32

The opening and closing balances represent the amount planned to be owed (in total) by the business to creditors, at the beginning and end of the month respectively.

Stock (inventory) budget

This would normally show the planned amount of stock to be held by the business at the beginning and at the end of each month, the planned total stock purchases for each month, and the planned total monthly stock usage. The layout would be something like the following:

	Jan £000	Feb £000	Mar £000	Apr £000	May £000	June £000
Opening balance	30	30	30	25	25	25
Add Purchases	30	31	26	35	31	32
	60	61	56	60	56	57
Less Stock used	30	31	31	35	31	32
Closing balance	30	30	25	25	25	25

The opening and closing balances represent the amount of stock, at cost, planned to be held by the business at the beginning and end of the month respectively.

A *raw materials stock (inventory) budget*, for a manufacturing business, would follow a similar pattern, with the 'stock usage' being the cost of the stock put into production. A *finished stock budget* for a manufacturer would also be similar to the above, except that 'stock manufactured' would replace 'purchases'. A manufacturing business would normally prepare both a raw materials stock budget and a finished stock budget.

The stock budget will normally be expressed in financial terms, but may also be expressed in physical terms (for example, kg or metres) for individual stock items.

Note how the trade debtors (receivables), trade creditors (payables) and stock (inventory) budgets in Example 6.2 link to one another, and to the cash budget for the same business in Example 6.1. Note particularly that:

- the rows of purchases figures in both the creditors budget and the stock budget are identical;
- the rows of cash payments figures in both the creditors budget and the cash budget are identical;
- the rows of cash receipts figures in both the debtors budget and the cash budget are identical to the cash budget: the cash receipts row of figures is the same in both. The debtors budget would link to the sales budget in a similar way.

This is how the linking (co-ordination), which was discussed earlier in this chapter, is achieved.

Activity 6.13

Have a go at preparing the trade debtors (receivables) budget for Vierra Popova Ltd for the six months July to December (see Activity 6.12).

The trade debtors budget for the six months ended 31 December is:

	July £000	Aug £000	Sept £000	Oct £000	Nov £000	Dec £000
Opening balance (Note 1)	53	57	59	62	57	53
Add Sales (Note 2)	57	59	62	57	53	51
	110	116	121	119	110	104
Less Cash receipts (Note 3)	53	57	59	62	57	53
Closing balance (Note 4)	57	59	62	57	53	51

Notes:
1 The opening debtors figure is the previous month's sales figure (sales are on one month's credit).
2 The sales are the current month's figure.
3 The cash received each month is equal to the previous month's sales figure.
4 The closing balance is equal to the current month's sales figure.

Note that if we knew three of the four figures each month, we could deduce the fourth.

This budget could, of course, be set out in any manner that would have given the sort of information that management would require in respect of planned levels of debtors and associated transactions.

Activity 6.14

Have a go at preparing the creditors budget for Vierra Popova Ltd for the six months of July to December (see Activity 6.12).

Hint: Remember that the creditors' payment period alters from the June purchases onwards.

The creditors budget for the six months ended 31 December is:

	July £000	Aug £000	Sept £000	Oct £000	Nov £000	Dec £000
Opening balance	32	65	67	70	67	60
Add Purchases	33	34	36	31	29	28
	65	99	103	101	96	88
Less Cash payments	–	32	33	34	36	31
Closing balance	65	67	70	67	60	57

This, again, could be set out in any manner that would have given the sort of information that management would require in respect of planned levels of creditors and associated transactions.

Activity-based budgeting

Activity-based budgeting (ABB) applies the philosophy of activity-based costing (ABC), which we discussed in Chapter 5, to planning and control through budgets. We should recall that ABC recognises that it is activities that cause or 'drive' costs. If the cost-driving activities can be identified, ascertaining the cost of the output of a business can be achieved with greater accuracy. Not only that, but costs become easier to control simply because their cause is known.

It is a central feature of budgeting that those who are responsible for meeting a particular budget (budget holders) should have control over the events that affect performance in their area. Ensuring that this is always the case can be problematical. For example, a decision is made at a senior level to increase the volume of activity for the business. This leads to an increase in the costs of a particular junior manager, that takes those costs above the budgeted level. The junior manager might be held responsible for the cost increase, yet the volume change was beyond that manager's control. In other words, the costs are driven by activities not controlled by the manager who is being held accountable for those costs.

ABB seeks to generate budgets in such a way that the manager who has control over the cost drivers is accountable for the costs that are caused.

Non-financial measures in budgeting

The efficiency of internal operations and customer satisfaction have become of critical importance to businesses striving to survive in an increasingly competitive environment. Non-financial measures have an important role to play in assessing performance in such key areas as customer/supplier delivery times, set-up times, defect levels and customer satisfaction levels.

There is no reason why budgeting need be confined to financial targets and measures. Non-financial measures can also be used as the basis for targets and can be incorporated into the budgeting process and reported alongside the financial targets for the business. **Real World 6.4** gives some idea of the extent of the use of non-financial measures in practice in the UK.

REAL WORLD 6.4

Non-financial measures used in practice

A 1993 survey of UK manufacturing businesses revealed that non-financial measures are widely used by businesses. The following table is taken from this study.

	Extent to which performance is measured					
	Never/rarely		Sometimes		Often/always	
	Smaller businesses %	Larger businesses %	Smaller businesses %	Larger businesses %	Smaller businesses %	Larger businesses %
Customer satisfaction/ product quality	22	2	11	7	67	91
Customer delivery efficiency	16	2	22	7	62	91
Supplier quality/delivery	16	4	32	15	52	81
Throughput times	33	6	24	20	43	74
Set-up times	59	32	19	22	22	46

We can see that customer-based measures are the most widely used form of non-financial performance measures. There are also clear differences between the smaller businesses and larger businesses in the extent to which non-financial measures are used. Though this evidence is now quite old, in the absence of more up-to-date research, it provides some insight to what happens in practice.

Source: Drury et al. (see reference 1 at the end of the chapter).

Budgets and management behaviour

All accounting statements and reports are intended to affect the behaviour of one or another group of people. Budgets are intended to affect the behaviour of managers, for example, to encourage them to work towards the business's objectives and to do this in a co-ordinated manner.

Whether budgets seem to be effective and how they can be made more effective are crucial issues for managers. We shall examine this topic in detail in the next chapter, after we have seen how budgets can be used to help managers to exercise control.

Self-assessment question 6.1

Antonio Ltd has planned production and sales for the next nine months as follows:

	Production units	Sales units
May	350	350
June	400	400
July	500	400
August	600	500
September	600	600
October	700	650
November	750	700
December	750	800
January	750	750

During the period, the business plans to advertise heavily to generate these increases in sales. Payments for advertising of £1,000 and £1,500 will be made in July and October respectively.

The selling price per unit will be £20 throughout the period. Forty per cent of sales are normally made on two months' credit. The other 60 per cent are settled within the month of the sale.

Raw materials will be held in stock for one month before they are taken into production. Purchases of raw materials will be on one month's credit (buy one month, pay the next). The cost of raw materials is £8 per unit of production.

Other direct production expenses, including labour, are £6 per unit of production. These will be paid in the month concerned.

Various production overheads, which during the period to 30 June had run at £1,800 per month, are expected to rise to £2,000 each month from 1 July to 31 October. These are expected to rise again from 1 November to £2,400 per month and to remain at that level for the foreseeable future. These overheads include a steady £400 each month for depreciation. Overheads are planned to be paid 80 per cent in the month of production and 20 per cent in the following month.

To help to meet the planned increased production, a new item of plant will be bought and will be delivered in August. The cost of this item is £6,600; the contract with the supplier will specify that this will be paid in three equal amounts in September, October and November.

Raw materials stock is planned to be 500 units on 1 July. The balance at the bank the same day is planned to be £7,500.

Required:

(a) Draw up the following for the six months ending 31 December:
   (i)   A raw materials budget, showing both physical quantities and financial values.
   (ii) A creditors budget.
   (iii) A cash budget.

(b) The cash budget reveals a potential cash deficiency during October and November. Can you suggest any ways in which a modification of plans could overcome this problem?

Who needs budgets?

Until recently it would have been a heresy to suggest that budgeting was not of central importance to any business. The benefits of budgeting, mentioned earlier in this chapter, have been widely recognised and the vast majority of businesses prepare annual budgets. However, there is increasing concern that, in today's highly dynamic and competitive environment, budgets may actually be harmful to the achievement of business objectives. This has led a small but growing number of businesses to abandon budgets as a tool of planning and control.

Various charges have been levelled against the conventional budgeting process. It is claimed that budgets:

- cannot deal with a fast-changing environment and that they are often out of date before the start of the budget period;
- focus too much management attention on the achievement of short-term financial targets. Instead, managers should focus on the things that create value for the business (for example, innovation, building brand loyalty, responding quickly to competitive threats and so on);
- reinforce a 'command and control' structure that prevents junior managers from exercising autonomy. This may be particularly true where a top-down approach, that allocates budgets to managers, is being used. Where managers feel constrained, attempts to retain and recruit able managers can be difficult;
- take up an enormous amount of management time that could be better used. In practice, budgeting can be a lengthy process that may involve much negotiation, reworking and updating. However, this may add little to the achievement of business objectives;
- are based around business functions (sales, marketing, production and so on). However, to achieve the business's objectives, the focus should be on business processes that cut across functional boundaries and reflect the needs of the customer;
- encourage incremental thinking by employing a 'last year plus x per cent' approach to planning. This can inhibit the development of 'break out' strategies that may be necessary in a fast-changing environment;
- can protect costs rather than lower costs. In some cases, a fixed budget for an activity, such as research and development, is allocated to a manager. If the amount is not spent, the budget may be taken away and, in future periods, the budget for this activity may be either reduced or eliminated. Such a response to unused budget allocations can encourage managers to spend the whole of the budget, irrespective of need, in order to protect the allocations they receive;
- promote 'sharp' practice among managers. In order to meet budget targets, managers may try to negotiate lower sales targets or higher cost allocations than they feel is really necessary. This helps them to build some 'slack' into the budgets and so meeting the budget becomes easier (see reference 4 at the end of the chapter).

Although, some believe that many of the problems identified can be solved by better budgeting systems such as activity-based budgeting and zero-base budgeting, others believe that a more radical solution is required.

Beyond conventional budgeting

In recent years, some businesses have abandoned budgeting, although they still recognise the need for forward planning. No one seriously doubts that there must be appropriate systems in place to steer a business towards its objectives. It is claimed, however, that the systems adopted should reflect a broader, more integrated approach to planning. The new systems that have been implemented are often based around a 'leaner' financial planning process that is more closely linked to other measurement

Figure 6.6	Traditional versus 'beyond budgeting' planning model

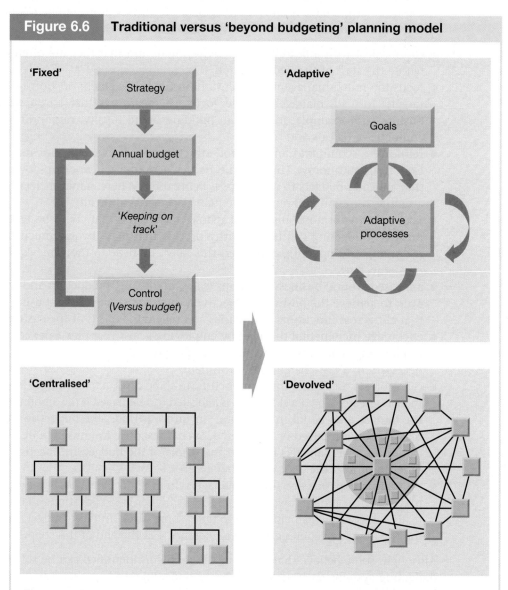

The traditional model is based on the use of fixed targets, which determine the future actions of managers. The 'beyond budgeting' model, on the other hand, is based on the use of stretch targets that can be adapted. The traditional hierarchical management structure is replaced by a network structure.

Source: www.bbrt.org

and reward systems. Emphasis is placed on the use of rolling forecasts, key performance indicators (such as market share, customer satisfaction and innovations) and/or 'scorecards' (like the Balanced Scorecard, which we shall meet in Chapter 11) that identify both monetary and non-monetary targets to be achieved over the long term and short term. These are often very demanding ('stretch') targets, based on benchmarks that have been set by world-class businesses.

The new 'beyond budgeting' model promotes a more decentralised, participative approach to managing the business. It is claimed that the traditional hierarchical management structure, where decision making is concentrated at the higher levels of the hierarchy, encourages a culture of dependency where meeting the budget targets set by senior managers is the key to managerial success. This traditional structure is replaced by a network structure where decision making is devolved to 'front-line' managers. In the new structure a more open, questioning attitude among employees is encouraged. There is a sharing of knowledge and best practice, and protective behaviour by managers is discouraged. In addition, rewards are linked to targets based on improvement in relative performance rather than to meeting the budget. It is claimed that this new approach allows greater adaptability to changing conditions, increases performance and increases motivation among staff.

Figure 6.6 sets out the main differences between the traditional and 'beyond budgeting' planning models.

Real World 6.5 reveals the experience of one business that decided to abandon conventional budgets.

REAL WORLD 6.5

Volvo abandons budgets

Jeremy Hope and Robin Fraser are at the forefront of those who argue that budgeting systems have an adverse effect on the ability of businesses to compete effectively. The following is a short case study of Volvo Cars that they have written.

New steering mechanisms at Volvo Cars

Following losses in 1990–92 and a small profit in 1993, Volvo Cars decided to make a number of important changes, one of which was to adopt a radically different approach to managing the business. But senior managers were quick to realise that such an approach was unlikely to be successful in the longer term unless they tackled the problems of the budgeting and planning process that encouraged the old mindset of compliance and control. As Ole Johannesson, VP finance, explains, 'the budget and long-range planning systems are no longer efficient when the business environment is changing more and more rapidly. Today we need a process that enables us to react not only immediately but even beforehand'. In 1994 there was no budget requested by the Group company, AB Volvo, from operating units for the forthcoming year, 1995. As Johannesson notes, 'we recognised the extent of the cultural change needed. We wanted less and less of order-giving, victims of circumstance, administration, checking, reactive positions, functional ties and hierarchical thinking, and more and more of creating opportunities, communication, development, confidence-building, proactive positions, network ties, and process thinking.' Since that time Volvo Cars has built a highly advanced management model that has helped it face the intense competitive pressures that are endemic to the world car market.

Volvo reckoned that its previous planning, budgeting and control processes absorbed around 20 per cent of total management time. By abandoning these processes and managing in a different way, managers have not only saved significant costs but they now have more time to focus on strategy, action planning and beating the competition. This is a battle not tied to an annual cycle, but is waged continuously month by month and quarter by quarter. Strategy and forecasts are

→

Real World 6.5 continued

reviewed and updated several times a year with four distinct cycles apparent. Each month a 'flash' forecast is prepared covering the next three months; each quarter a two-year rolling forecast is updated; and each year sees a revised four-year and ten-year strategic plan. While targets are broad-brush and comprise a number of key performance indicators, there is more time spent on developing action plans to support them. Monthly reports to the board include financial information (actual month, actual year-to-date, forecast remainder of year, revised forecast for total years, and last year-to-date) and a number of key performance indicators such as market share, order intake, customer satisfaction, product costs, dealer profitability, warranty costs, fault frequency, and total ownership cost (all where possible compared with the competition). Four years after dismantling the budgeting process there is now a strong 'responsibility' and 'no blame' culture at Volvo Cars.

According to Ole Johannesson, 'managers now know that they mustn't come to meetings with problems, but with explanations about what they've done to solve them.' The management accountants now spend more time collecting a whole range of measurement data but, more importantly, they see their role as one of analysing and interpreting the data so that operating managers can take the appropriate action. Indeed the whole emphasis is on 'actions' rather than 'problems'. Volvo has transformed itself into an action-oriented company in which decisions are made by people at the appropriate level to meet changing conditions. This has contributed to Volvo's remarkable turnaround. It now ranks as the sixteenth largest motor vehicle manufacturer in the world, but in terms of profitability it is second only to Ford on profits on sales and assets.

Source: Hope and Fraser (see reference 5 at the end of the chapter), p. 17.

Note: Since this case study was written, Volvo has become part of the Ford Motor Company. It is possible that the success of the business led Ford to acquire Volvo.

It is too early to predict whether or not the trickle of businesses that are now seeking an alternative to budgets will turn into a flood. However, it is clear that in today's highly competitive environment a business must be flexible and responsive to changing conditions. Management systems that in any way hinder these attributes will not survive.

Despite the criticisms made of budgeting, it remains a very widely used technique. Real Worlds 6.3 and 6.4 provide evidence for this. In the next chapter we shall look in some detail at how budgets can be adapted for use as devices for exercising management control.

SUMMARY

The main points of this chapter may be summarised as follows:

A budget is a short-term financial plan.

● Budgets are the short-term means of working towards the business's objectives.
● They are usually prepared for a one-year period with sub-periods of a month.
● There is usually a separate budget for each key area.

Uses of budgets

● Promote forward thinking.
● Help co-ordinate the various aspects of the business.
● Motivate performance.
● Provide the basis of a system of control.
● Provide a system of authorisation.

The budget-setting process

- Establish who will take responsibility.
- Communicate guidelines.
- Identify key factor.
- Prepare budget for key factor area.
- Prepare draft budgets for all other areas.
- Review and co-ordinate.
- Prepare master budgets (profit and loss account (income statement) and balance sheet).
- Communicate the budgets to interested parties.
- Monitor performance relative to budget.

Preparing budgets

- There is no standard style – practicality and usefulness are the key issues.
- They are usually prepared in columnar form, with a column for each month (or similarly short period).
- Each budget must link (co-ordinate) with others.

Criticisms of budgets

- Cannot deal with rapid change.
- Focus on short-term financial targets, rather than value creation.
- Encourage a 'top-down' management style.
- Time-consuming.
- Based around traditional business functions and do not cross boundaries.
- Encourage incremental thinking (last year's figure, plus x per cent).
- Protect rather than lower costs.
- Promote 'sharp' practice among managers.
- Budgeting is very widely practised despite the criticisms.

→ **Key terms**

Further reading

If you would like to explore the topics covered in this chapter in more depth, we recommend the following books:

Management Accounting, *Atkinson A., Banker R., Kaplan R. and Young S. M.*, 3rd edn, Prentice Hall International, 2001, chapter 11.

Management and Cost Accounting, *Drury C.*, 5th edn, Thomson Learning Business Press, 2000, chapter 15.

Cost Accounting: A managerial emphasis, *Horngren C., Foster G. and Datar S.*, 11th edn, Prentice Hall International, 2002, chapter 6.

References

1 **A Survey of Management Accounting Practices in UK Manufacturing Companies**, *Drury C., Braund S., Osborne P. and Tayles M.*, Chartered Association of Certified Accountants, 1993.

2 **2003 Survey of Management Accounting**, *Ernst and Young*, Ernst and Young, 2003.

3 **Financial Management and Working Capital Practices in UK SMEs**, *Chittenden F., Poutziouris P. and Michaelis N.*, Manchester Business School, 1998.

4 **Beyond budgeting**, www.beyondbudgeting.plus.com.

5 'Beyond budgeting', *Hope J. and Fraser R.*, in **Management Accounting**, January 1999.

REVIEW QUESTIONS

Answers to these questions can be found on the students' side of the Companion Website at www.pearsoned.co.uk/atrillmclaney.

6.1   Define a budget. How is a budget different from a forecast?

6.2   What were the five uses of budgets that were identified in the chapter?

6.3   What do budgets have to do with control?

6.4   What is a budget committee? What purpose does it serve?

EXERCISES

Exercises 6.5 to 6.8 are more advanced than 6.1 to 6.4. Those with coloured numbers have answers at the back of the book.

6.1   Daniel Chu Ltd, a new business, will start production on 1 April, but sales will not commence until 1 May. Planned sales for the next nine months are as follows:

	Sales units
May	500
June	600
July	700
August	800
September	900
October	900
November	900
December	800
January	700

The selling price of a unit will be a consistent £100, and all sales will be made on one month's credit. It is planned that sufficient finished goods stock for each month's sales should be available at the end of the previous month.

Raw materials purchases will be such that there will be sufficient raw materials stock available at the end of each month precisely to meet the following month's planned production. This planned policy will operate from the end of April. Purchases of raw materials will be on one month's credit. The cost of raw material is £40 a unit of finished product.

The direct labour cost, which is variable with the level of production, is planned to be £20 a unit of finished production. Production overheads are planned to be £20,000 each month, including £3,000 for depreciation. Non-production overheads are planned to be £11,000 a month, of which £1,000 will be depreciation.

Various non-current (fixed) assets costing £250,000 will be bought and paid for during April.

Except where specified, assume that all payments take place in the same month as the cost is incurred.

The business will raise £300,000 in cash from a share issue in April.

Required:

Draw up the following for the six months ending 30 September:

(a) A finished stock (inventory) budget, showing just physical quantities.

(b) A raw materials stock (inventory) budget showing both physical quantities and financial values.

(c) A trade creditors (payables) budget.

(d) A trade debtors (receivables) budget.

(e) A cash budget.

6.2 You have overheard the following statements:

(a) 'A budget is a forecast of what is expected to happen in a business during the next year.'

(b) 'Monthly budgets must be prepared with a column for each month so that you can see the whole year at a glance, month by month.'

(c) 'Budgets are OK but they stifle all initiative. No manager worth employing would work for a business that seeks to control through budgets.'

(d) 'Activity-based budgeting is an approach that takes account of the planned volume of activity in order to deduce the figures to go into the budget.'

(e) 'Any sensible person would start with the sales budget and build up the other budgets from there.'

Required:

Critically discuss these statements, explaining any technical terms.

6.3 A nursing home, which is linked to a large hospital, has been examining its budgetary control procedures, with particular reference to overhead costs.

The level of activity in the facility is measured by the number of patients treated in the budget period. For the current year, the budget stands at 6,000 patients and this is expected to be met.

For months 1 to 6 of this year (assume 12 months of equal length), 2,700 patients were treated. The actual variable overhead costs incurred during this six-month period are as follows:

Expense	£
Staffing	59,400
Power	27,000
Supplies	54,000
Other	8,100
Total	148,500

The hospital accountant believes that the variable overhead costs will be incurred at the same rate during months 7 to 12 of the year.

Fixed overhead costs are budgeted for the whole year as follows:

Expense	£
Supervision	120,000
Depreciation/financing	187,200
Other	64,800
Total	372,000

Required:

(a) Present an overheads budget for months 7 to 12 of the year. You should show each expense, but should not separate individual months. What is the total overhead cost for each patient that would be incorporated into any statistics?

(b) The home actually treated 3,800 patients during months 7 to 12, the actual variable overheads were £203,300, and the fixed overheads were £190,000. In summary form, examine how well the home exercised control over its overheads.

(c) Interpret your analysis and point out any limitations or assumptions.

6.4   Linpet Ltd is to be incorporated on 1 June. The opening balance sheet of the business will then be as follows:

Assets	£
Cash at bank	60,000
Share capital	
£1 ordinary shares	60,000

During June, the business intends to make payments of £40,000 for a leasehold property, £10,000 for equipment and £6,000 for a motor vehicle. The business will also purchase initial trading stock costing £22,000 on credit.

   The business has produced the following estimates:

(i)   Sales for June will be £8,000 and will increase at the rate of £3,000 a month until September. In October, sales will rise to £22,000 and in subsequent months will be maintained at this figure.

(ii)   The gross profit percentage on goods sold will be 25 per cent.

(iii)   There is a risk that supplies of trading stock will be interrupted towards the end of the accounting year. The business therefore intends to build up its initial level of stock (£22,000) by purchasing £1,000 of stock each month in addition to the monthly purchases necessary to satisfy monthly sales. All purchases of stock (including the initial stock) will be on one month's credit.

(iv)   Sales will be divided equally between cash and credit sales. Credit customers are expected to pay two months after the sale is agreed.

(v)   Wages and salaries will be £900 a month. Other overheads will be £500 a month for the first four months and £650 thereafter. Both types of expense will be payable when incurred.

(vi)   80 per cent of sales will be generated by salespeople, who will receive 5 per cent commission on sales. The commission is payable one month after the sale is agreed.

(vii)   The business intends to purchase further equipment in November for £7,000 cash.

(viii)   Depreciation is to be provided at the rate of 5 per cent a year on freehold property and 20 per cent a year on equipment. (Depreciation has not been included in the overheads mentioned in (v) above.)

Required:

(a)   State why a cash budget is required for a business.

(b)   Prepare a cash budget for Linpet Ltd for the six-month period to 30 November.

6.5   Lewisham Ltd manufactures one product line – the Zenith. Sales of Zeniths over the next few months are planned to be as follows:

1 *Demand*

	Units
July	180,000
August	240,000
September	200,000
October	180,000

Each Zenith sells for £3.

2 *Debtor receipts.*   Debtors are expected to pay as follows:

- 70 per cent during the month of sale
- 28 per cent during the following month.

The remaining debtors are expected to go bad (that is, to be uncollectable).

   Debtors who pay in the month of sale are entitled to deduct a 2 per cent discount from the invoice price.

3 *Finished goods stocks (inventories).* Stocks of finished goods are expected to be 40,000 units at 1 July. The business's policy is that, in future, the stock at the end of each month should equal 20 per cent of the following month's planned sales requirements.

4 *Raw materials stocks (inventories).* Stocks of raw materials are expected to be 40,000 kg on 1 July. The business's policy is that, in future, the stock at the end of each month should equal 50 per cent of the following month's planned production requirements. Each Zenith requires 0.5 kg of the raw material, which costs £1.50/kg. Raw materials purchases are paid in the month after purchase.

5 *Labour and overheads.* The direct labour cost of each Zenith is £0.50. The variable overhead element of each Zenith is £0.30. Fixed overheads, including depreciation of £25,000, total £47,000 a month. All labour and overheads are paid during the month in which they arise.

6 *Cash in hand.* At 1 August the business plans to have a bank balance (in funds) of £20,000.

Required:

Prepare the following budgets:

(a) Finished stock (inventory) budget (expressed in units of Zenith) for each of the three months July, August and September.

(b) Raw materials budget (expressed in kilograms of the raw material) for the two months July and August.

(c) Cash budget for August and September.

6.6 Newtake Records Ltd owns a chain of 14 shops selling cassette tapes and compact discs. At the beginning of June the business had an overdraft of £35,000 and the bank had asked for this to be eliminated by the end of November. As a result, the directors have recently decided to review their plans for the next six months.

The following plans were prepared for the business some months earlier:

	May £000	June £000	July £000	August £000	Sept £000	Oct £000	Nov £000
Sales	180	230	320	250	140	120	110
Purchases	135	180	142	94	75	66	57
Administration expenses	52	55	56	53	48	46	45
Selling expenses	22	24	28	26	21	19	18
Taxation payment				22			
Finance payments	5	5	5	5	5	5	5
Shop refurbishment	–	–	14	18	6	–	–

Notes:

(i) Stock (inventory) held at 1 June was £112,000. The business believes it is preferable to maintain a minimum stock level of £40,000 of goods over the period to 30 November.

(ii) Suppliers allow one month's credit. The first three months' purchases are subject to a contractual agreement, which must be honoured.

(iii) The gross profit margin is 40 per cent.

(iv) All sales income is received in the month of sale. However, 50 per cent of customers pay with a credit card. The charge made by the credit card business to Newtake Records Ltd is 3 per cent of the sales value. These charges are in addition to the selling expenses identified above. The credit card business pays Newtake Records Ltd in the month of sale.

(v) The business has a bank loan, which it is paying off in monthly instalments of £5,000. The interest element represents 20 per cent of each instalment.

(vi) Administration expenses are paid when incurred. This item includes a charge of £15,000 each month in respect of depreciation.

(vii) Selling expenses are payable in the following month.

Required (working to the nearest £1,000):
(a) Prepare a cash budget for the six months ending 30 November which shows the cash balance at the end of each month.
(b) Compute the stock levels at the end of each month for the six months to 30 November.
(c) Prepare a budgeted profit and loss account for the six months period ending 30 November. (A monthly breakdown of profit is *not* required.)
(d) What problems is Newtake Records Ltd likely to face in the next six months? Can you suggest how the business might deal with these problems?

6.7 Prolog Ltd is a small wholesaler of personal computers. It has in recent months been selling 50 machines a month at a price of £2,000 each. These machines cost £1,600 each. A new model has just been launched and this is expected to offer greatly enhanced performance. Its selling price and cost will be the same as for the old model. From the beginning of January, sales are planned to increase at a rate of 20 machines each month until the end of June, when sales will amount to 170 units a month. They are planned to continue at that level thereafter. Operating costs including depreciation of £2,000 a month are planned as follows:

	January	February	March	April	May	June
Operating costs (£000)	6	8	10	12	12	12

Prolog expects to receive no credit for operating costs. Additional shelving for storage will be bought, installed and paid for in April, costing £12,000. Corporation tax of £25,000 is due at the end of March. Prolog anticipates that debtors will amount to two months' sales. To give its customers a good level of service, Prolog plans to hold enough stock at the end of each month to fulfil anticipated demand from customers in the following month. The computer manufacturer, however, grants one month's credit to Prolog. Prolog Ltd's balance sheet appears below.

Balance sheet at 31 December

	£000	£000
Non-current assets		80
Current assets		
Stock	112	
Debtors	200	
Cash	–	
	312	
Current liabilities		
Trade creditors	112	
Taxation	25	
Overdraft	68	
	205	
Net current assets		107
Total assets less current liabilities		187
Equity		
Share capital (25p ordinary shares)		10
Profit and loss account		177
		187

Required:
(a) Prepare a cash budget for Prolog Ltd showing the cash balance or required overdraft for the six months ending 30 June.
(b) State briefly what further information a banker would require from Prolog Ltd before granting additional overdraft facilities for the anticipated expansion of sales.

6.8 Brown and Jeffreys, a West Midlands business, makes one standard product for use in the motor trade. The product, known as the Fuel Miser, for which the business holds the patent, when fitted to the fuel system of production model cars has the effect of reducing petrol consumption.

Part of the production is sold direct to a local car manufacturer, which fits the Fuel Miser as an optional extra to several of its models and the rest of the production is sold through various retail outlets, garages and so on.

Brown and Jeffreys assemble the Fuel Miser, but all three components are manufactured by local engineering businesses. The three components are codenamed A, B and C. One Fuel Miser consists of one of each component.

The planned sales for the first seven months of the forthcoming accounting period, by channels of distribution and in terms of Fuel Miser units, are as follows:

	Jan	Feb	Mar	Apr	May	June	July
Manufacturers	4,000	4,000	4,500	4,500	4,500	4,500	4,500
Retail, and so on	2,000	2,700	3,200	3,000	2,700	2,500	2,400
	6,000	6,700	7,700	7,500	7,200	7,000	6,900

The following further information is available:

(i) There will be a stock of finished units at 1 January of 7,000 Fuel Misers.
(ii) The stocks of raw materials at 1 January will be:
   A   10,000 units
   B   16,500 units
   C   7,200 units
(iii) The selling price of Fuel Misers is to be £10 each to the motor manufacturer and £12 each to retail outlets.
(iv) The maximum production capacity of the business is 7,000 units a month. There is no possibility of increasing this output.
(v) Assembly of each Fuel Miser will take 10 minutes of direct labour. Direct labour is paid at the rate of £7.20 an hour during the month of production.
(vi) The components are each expected to cost the following:
   A   £2.50
   B   £1.30
   C   £0.80
(vii) Indirect costs are to be paid at a regular rate of £32,000 each month.
(viii) The cash at the bank at 1 January will be £2,620.

The business plans to pursue the following policies for as many months as possible and in a manner consistent with the planned sales:

● Finished stocks at the end of each month are to equal the following month's total sales to retail outlets, and half the total of the following month's sales to the motor manufacturer.
● Raw materials at the end of each month are to be sufficient to cover production requirements for the following month. The production for July will be 6,800 units.
● Creditors for raw materials are to be paid during the month following purchase. The creditors payment for January will be £21,250.
● Debtors will pay in the month of sale, in the case of sales to the motor manufacturer, and the month after sale, in the case of retail sales. Retail sales during December were 2,000 units at £12 each.

Required:
Prepare the following budgets in monthly columnar form, both in terms of money and units (where relevant), for the six months of January to June inclusive:

(a) Sales budget.*
(b) Finished stock (inventory) budget (valued at direct cost).[†]
(c) Raw materials stock (inventory) budget.[†]
(d) Production budget (direct costs only).*
(e) Debtors (receivables) budget.[†]
(f) Creditors (payables) budget.[†]
(g) Cash budget.[†]

* The sales and production budgets should merely state each month's sales or production in units and in money terms.
[†] The other budgets should all seek to reconcile the opening balance of stocks, debtors, creditors or cash with the closing balance through movements of the relevant factors over the month.

7

Accounting for control

OBJECTIVES

When you have completed this chapter, you should be able to:

- Discuss the role and limitations of using budgets to help to exercise control.

- Carry out a complete analysis of variances.

- Explain the nature and role of standard costs.

- Discuss possible reasons for key variances and other practical matters surrounding control through budgets.

INTRODUCTION

This chapter deals with the role of budgets in management control. It, therefore, continues some of the themes that we discussed in Chapter 6. We shall consider how a budget can be used in helping to control a business, and we shall see that, by collecting information on actual performance and comparing it with the revised budget, it is possible to identify fairly precisely which activities are in control and which seem to be out of control. The chapter picks up some of the issues relating to the behaviour of costs with changing volumes of activity – topics that we considered in Chapter 3.

Using budgets for control – flexible budgets

In Chapter 6, we saw that budgets can provide a useful basis for exercising control over the business, because control is usually seen as making events conform to a plan. Since the budget represents the plan, making events conform to it is the obvious way to try to control the business. Using budgets in this way is popular in practice.

As we saw in Chapter 6, for most businesses the routine is as shown in Figure 7.1.

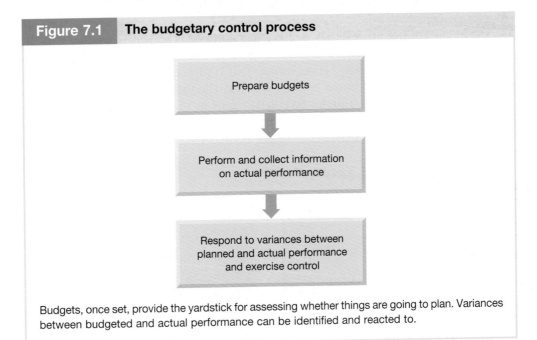

Figure 7.1	**The budgetary control process**

Prepare budgets

Perform and collect information on actual performance

Respond to variances between planned and actual performance and exercise control

Budgets, once set, provide the yardstick for assessing whether things are going to plan. Variances between budgeted and actual performance can be identified and reacted to.

These steps in the control process are fairly easy to understand. The point is that, if plans are drawn up sensibly, we have a basis for exercising control over the business. It also requires us to have the means of measuring actual performance in the same terms as those in which the budget is stated. If they are not in the same terms, comparison will not usually be possible.

Taking steps to exercise control means finding out where and why things did not go according to plan and seeking ways to put things right for the future. One of the reasons why things may have gone wrong is that the plans may, in reality, prove to be unachievable. In this case, if budgets are to be a useful basis for exercising control in the future, it may be necessary to revise the budgets for future periods to bring targets into the realms of achievability.

This last point should not be taken to mean that budget targets can simply be ignored if the going gets tough; rather that they should be adaptable. However, budgets may prove to be totally unrealistic. This could be for a variety of reasons, including unexpected changes in the commercial environment (for example, an unexpected collapse in demand for services of the type that the business provides). In this case, nothing whatsoever will be achieved by pretending that the targets can be met.

By having a system of budgetary control, a position can be established where decision making and responsibility can be delegated to junior management, yet senior management can still retain control. This is because senior managers can use the budgetary control system to ascertain which junior managers are meeting targets and therefore working towards achieving the objectives of the business. (We should remember that budgets are the short-term plans for achieving the business's objectives.) This enables a management-by-exception environment to be created. Here senior management concentrates its energy on areas where things are not going according to plan (the exceptions – it is to be hoped). Junior managers who are performing to budget can be left to get on with their jobs.

Feedback and feedforward controls

The control process that we have just outlined is known as **feedback control**. Its main feature is that steps are taken to get operations back on track as soon as there is a signal that they have gone wrong. This is similar to the thermostatic control that is a feature of most central heating systems. The thermostat senses when the temperature has fallen below a preset level (analogous to the budget), and takes action to correct matters by activating the heating device that restores the required minimum temperature. Figure 7.2 depicts the stages in a feedback control system using budgets.

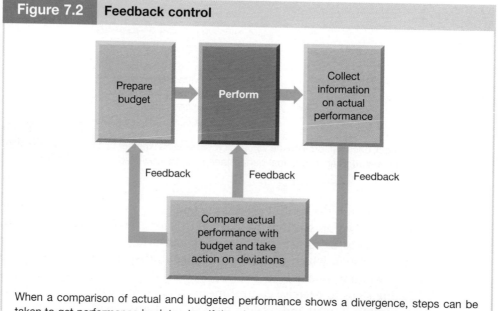

Figure 7.2 **Feedback control**

When a comparison of actual and budgeted performance shows a divergence, steps can be taken to get performance back to plan. If the plan needs revising, this can be done.

There is an alternative type of control, known as **feedforward control**. Here predictions are made as to what can go wrong and steps taken to avoid any undesirable outcome. The preparation of budgets, which we discussed in Chapter 6, provides an example of this type of control. Preparing a particular budget may reveal a problem that will arise unless the business changes its plans. For example, preparing the cash budget may reveal that if the original plans are followed, there will be a negative cash balance for some part of the budget period. By recognising this, the plans could be revised to eliminate the problem.

We have just seen that budgeting embraces both forms of control. Comparing the budget with actual results is a form of feedback control whereas preparing a budget is a form of feedforward control. Generally speaking, the latter form of control is better. Things should not go wrong in the first place when steps are taken to ensure that they do not go wrong. Feedforward controls try to anticipate future problems, whereas feed-back controls simply react to problems that have already occurred. In many situations, however, it is not possible to install feedforward controls.

Comparing the actual performance with the budget

The principal objective of most private sector businesses is to enhance their share-holders' wealth. Since profit is the net increase in wealth as a result of trading, the most important budget target to meet is the profit target. In view of this, we shall begin with that aspect in our consideration of making the comparison between the budget and the actual results. Example 7.1 shows the budgeted and actual profit and loss account (income statement) for Baxter Ltd for the month of May.

Example 7.1

The following are the budgeted and actual profit and loss accounts for Baxter Ltd for the month of May:

	Budget	Actual
Output (production and sales)	1,000 units	900 units
	£	£
Sales	100,000	92,000
Raw materials	(40,000) (40,000 metres)	(36,900) (37,000 metres)
Labour	(20,000) (2,500 hours)	(17,500) (2,150 hours)
Fixed overheads	(20,000)	(20,700)
Operating profit	20,000	16,900

From these figures, it is clear that the budgeted profit was not achieved. As far as May is concerned, this is a matter of history. However, the business (or at least one aspect of it) is out of control. Senior management must discover where things went wrong during May and try to ensure that these mistakes are not repeated in later months. It is not enough to know that, overall, things went wrong. We need to know where and why. The approach taken is to compare the budgeted and actual figures for the various items (sales, raw materials and so on) in the above statement.

Activity 7.1

Can you see any problems in comparing the various items (sales, raw materials and so on) for the budget and the actual performance of Baxter Ltd in order to draw con-clusions as to which aspects were out of control?

The problem is that the actual level of output was not as budgeted. The actual level of output was 10 per cent less than budget. This means that we cannot, for example, say that there was a labour cost saving of £2,500 (that is, £20,000 – £17,500) and conclude that all is well in that area.

Flexing the budget

One practical way to overcome our difficulty is to 'flex' the budget to what it would have been had the planned level of output been 900 units rather than 1,000 units. **Flexing the budget** simply means revising it, assuming a different volume of output.

In the context of control, the budget is usually flexed to reflect the volume that actually occurred, where this is higher or lower than that originally planned. To be able to do this we need to know which items are fixed and which are variable relative to the volume of output. Once we have this knowledge, flexing is a simple operation. We shall assume that sales revenue, material cost and labour cost vary strictly with volume. Fixed overheads, by definition, will not. Whether, in real life, labour cost does vary with the volume of output is not so certain, but it will serve well enough as an assumption for our purposes.

On the basis of our assumptions regarding the behaviour of revenues and costs, the flexed budget would be as follows:

	Flexed budget
Output (production and sales)	900 units
	£
Sales	90,000
Raw materials	(36,000) (36,000 metres)
Labour	(18,000) (2,250 hours)
Fixed overheads	(20,000)
Operating profit	16,000

This is simply the original budget, with the sales, raw materials and labour figures scaled down by 10 per cent (the same factor as the actual output fell short of the budgeted one).

Putting the original budget, the flexed budget and the actual for May together, we obtain the following:

	Original budget	Flexed budget	Actual
Output	1,000 units	900 units	900 units
(production and sales)			
	£	£	£
Sales	100,000	90,000	92,000
Raw materials	(40,000)	(36,000) (36,000 m)	(36,900) (37,000 m)
Labour	(20,000)	(18,000) (2,250 hr)	(17,500) (2,150 hr)
Fixed overheads	(20,000)	(20,000)	(20,700)
Operating profit	20,000	16,000	16,900

Flexible budgets enable us make a more valid comparison between budget (using the flexed figures) and actual. We can now see that there was a genuine labour cost saving, even after allowing for the output shortfall.

Sales volume variance

It may seem as if we are saying that it does not matter if there are volume shortfalls, because we just revise the budget and carry on as if nothing had happened. However, this is not the case, because losing sales means losing profit. The first point we must pick up, therefore, is the loss of profit arising from the loss of sales of 100 units of the product.

Activity 7.2

What will be the loss of profit arising from the sales shortfall, assuming that everything except sales volume was as planned?

The answer is simply the difference between the original and flexed budget profit figures. The only difference between these two profit figures is the volume of sales; everything else was the same. Thus the figure is £4,000 (that is, £20,000 – £16,000).

As we saw in Chapter 3, when we considered the relationship between cost, volume and profit, selling one unit less will result in one less contribution to profit. The contribution is sales revenue for one unit less variable cost. We can see from the original budget that the unit sales revenue is £100 (that is, £100,000/1,000), raw material cost is £40 a unit (that is, £40,000/1,000) and labour cost is £20 a unit (that is, £20,000/1,000). Thus the contribution is £40 a unit (that is, £100 – (£40 + £20)).

If, therefore, 100 units of sales are lost, £4,000 (that is, 100 × £40) of contributions, and therefore profit, are forgone. This would be an alternative means of finding the sales volume variance, instead of taking the difference between the original and flexed budget profit figures; nevertheless once we have produced the flexed budget, it is generally easier simply to compare the two profit figures.

The difference between the original and flexed budget profit figures is called the *sales volume variance*. It is an **adverse variance** because, taken alone, it has the effect of making the actual profit lower than that which was budgeted. A variance that has the effect of increasing profit above that which is budgeted is known as a **favourable variance**. We can therefore say that a **variance** is the effect of that factor (taken alone) on the budgeted profit. When looking at some particular aspect, such as sales volume, we assume that all other factors went according to plan. This is shown in Figure 7.3.

> **Sales volume variance**
> The difference between the profit as shown in the original budget and the profit as shown in the flexed budget for the period.

Figure 7.3	Relationship between the budgeted and actual profit

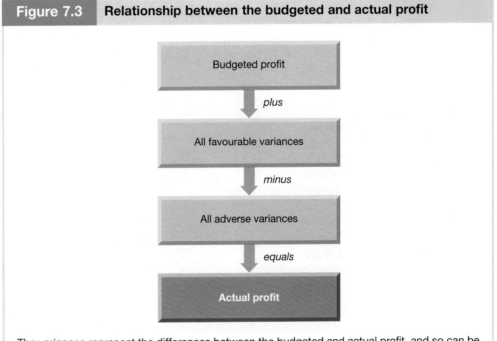

The variances represent the differences between the budgeted and actual profit, and so can be used to reconcile the two profit figures.

Activity 7.3

What else does the senior management of Baxter Ltd need to know about the May sales volume variance?

It needs to know why the volume of sales fell below the budgeted figure. Only by dis-covering this information will management be in a position to try to see that it does not occur again.

Who should be asked about this sales volume variance? The answer would prob-ably be the sales manager. This person should know precisely why the departure from budget has occurred. This is not the same as saying that it was the sales manager's fault. The reason for the problem could easily have been that production was at fault in not having produced the budgeted quantities, meaning that there were not sufficient items to sell. What is not in doubt is that, in the first instance, the sales manager should know the reason for the problem.

The budget and actual figures for Baxter Ltd for June are given in Activity 7.4. They will be used as the basis for a series of activities which you should work through as we look at variance analysis. Note that the business had budgeted for a higher level of output for June than it did for May.

Activity 7.4

	Budget for June	Actual for June
Output (production and sales)	1,100 units	1,150 units
	£	£
Sales	110,000	113,500
Raw materials	(44,000) (44,000 metres)	(46,300) (46,300 metres)
Labour	(22,000) (2,750 hours)	(23,200) (2,960 hours)
Fixed overheads	(20,000)	(19,300)
Operating profit	24,000	24,700

Try flexing the June budget, comparing it with the original June budget, and so find the sales volume variance.

	Flexed budget
Output (production and sales)	1,150 units
	£
Sales	115,000
Raw materials	(46,000) (46,000 metres)
Labour	(23,000) (2,875 hours)
Fixed overheads	(20,000)
Operating profit	26,000

The sales volume variance is £2,000 (favourable) (that is, £26,000 – £24,000). It is favourable since the original budget profit was lower than the flexed budget profit. This is because more sales were actually made than were budgeted.

Having dealt with the sales volume variance, we have picked up the profit difference caused by any variation between the budgeted and the actual volumes of sales. This means that, for the remainder of the analysis of the difference between the actual and budgeted profits, we can ignore the original budget. We can concentrate exclusively on the differences between the figures in the flexed budget and the actual figures.

Sales price variance

Sales price variance
The difference between the actual sales figure for the period and the sales figure as shown in the flexed budget.

Starting with the sales revenue figure, we can see that there is a difference of £2,000 (favourable) between the flexed budget and the actual figures. This can only arise from higher prices being charged than were envisaged in the original budget, because any variance arising from the volume difference has already been 'stripped out' in the flexing process. This price difference is known as the *sales price variance*. Higher sales prices will, all other things being equal, mean more profit. So there is a favourable variance.

Activity 7.5

Using the figures in Activity 7.4, what is the sales price variance for June?

The sales price variance for June is £1,500 (adverse) (that is, £115,000 – £113,500). Actual sales prices, on average, must have been lower than those budgeted. The actual price averaged £98.70 (that is, £113,500/1,150) whereas the budgeted price was £100. Selling output at a lower price than the budgeted one must tend to reduce profit, hence an adverse variance.

We shall now move on to look at the expenses.

Materials variances

Total direct materials variance
The difference between the actual direct materials cost and the direct materials cost according to the flexed budget (budgeted usage for the actual output).

Direct materials usage variance
The difference between the actual quantity of direct materials used and the quantity of direct materials according to the flexed budget (budgeted usage for actual output). This quantity is multiplied by the budgeted direct materials cost for one unit of the direct materials.

In May, there was an overall or *total direct materials variance* of £900 (adverse) (that is, £36,900 – £36,000). It is adverse because the actual material cost was higher than the budgeted one, which has an adverse effect on profit. Who should be held accountable for this variance? The answer depends on whether the difference arises from excess usage of the raw material, in which case it is the production manager, or whether it is a higher-than-budgeted price per metre being paid, in which case it is the responsibility of the buying manager.

Fortunately, we have the means available to go beyond this total variance. We can see from the figures that there was a 1,000 metre excess usage of the raw material (that is, 37,000 metres – 36,000 metres). All other things being equal, this alone would have led to a profit shortfall of £1,000, since clearly the budgeted price per metre is £1. The £1,000 (adverse) variance is known as the *direct materials usage variance*. Normally, this variance would be the responsibility of the production manager.

Activity 7.6

Using the figures in Activity 7.4, what was the direct materials usage variance for June?

The direct materials usage variance for June was £300 (adverse) (that is, (46,300 – 46,000) × £1). It is adverse because more material was used than was budgeted for an output of 1,150 units. Excess usage of material will tend to reduce profit.

Direct materials price variance
The difference between the actual cost of the direct material used and the direct materials cost allowed (actual quantity of material used at the budgeted direct material cost).

The other aspect of direct materials is the *direct materials price variance*. Here we simply take the actual cost of materials used and compare it with the cost that was allowed, given the quantity used. In May the actual cost of direct materials used was £36,900, whereas the allowed cost of the 37,000 metres was £37,000. Thus we have a favourable variance of £100. Paying less than the budgeted price will tend to increase profit, hence a favourable variance.

Activity 7.7

Using the figures in Activity 7.4, what was the direct materials price variance for June?

The direct materials price variance for June was zero (that is, (46,300 – 46,300) × £1).

As we have just seen, the total direct materials variance is the sum of the usage variance and the price variance. This is illustrated in Figure 7.4.

Figure 7.4	**Relationship between the total, usage and price variances of direct materials**

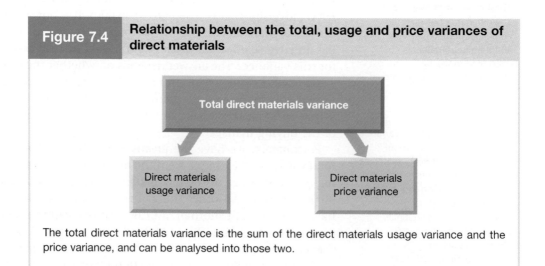

The total direct materials variance is the sum of the direct materials usage variance and the price variance, and can be analysed into those two.

Labour variances

Total direct labour variance
The difference between the actual direct labour cost and the direct labour cost according to the flexed budget (budgeted direct labour hours for the actual output).

Direct labour variances are similar in form to those for raw materials. The *total direct labour variance* for May was £500 (favourable) (that is, £18,000 − £17,500). It is favourable because £500 less was spent on labour than was budgeted for the actual level of output achieved. Again, this information is not particularly helpful, and needs to be analysed further, since the responsibility for the rate of pay lies primarily with the personnel manager, whereas the number of hours taken to complete a particular quantity of output is the responsibility of the production manager.

Direct labour efficiency variance
The difference between the actual direct labour hours worked and the number of direct labour hours according to the flexed budget (budgeted direct labour hours for the actual output). This figure is multiplied by the budgeted direct labour rate for one hour.

The *direct labour efficiency variance* compares the number of hours that would be allowed for the achieved level of production with the actual number of hours. It then costs this difference at the allowed hourly rate. Thus, for May, it was $(2,250 - 2,150) \times £8 = £800$ (favourable). We know that the budgeted hourly rate is £8 because the original budget shows that 2,500 hours were budgeted to cost £20,000. The variance is favourable because fewer hours were used than would have been allowed for the actual level of output. Working more quickly would tend to lead to higher profit.

Activity 7.8

Using the figures in Activity 7.4, what was the direct labour efficiency variance for June?

The direct labour efficiency variance for June was £680 (adverse) (that is, $(2,960 - 2,875) \times £8$). It is adverse because the work took longer than the budget allowed. This would tend to lead to less profit.

Direct labour rate variance
The difference between the actual cost of the direct labour hours worked and the direct labour cost allowed (actual direct labour hours worked at the budgeted labour rate).

The *direct labour rate variance* compares the actual cost of the hours worked with the allowed cost. For 2,150 hours worked in May, the allowed cost would be £17,200 (that is, $2,150 \times £8$). So, the direct labour rate variance is £300 (adverse) (that is, £17,500 − £17,200).

Activity 7.9

Using the figures in Activity 7.4, what was the direct labour rate variance for June?

The direct labour rate variance for June was £480 (favourable) (that is, $(2,960 \times £8)$ − 23,200). It is favourable because a lower rate was paid than the budgeted one. Paying a lower wage rate will tend to increase profit.

Fixed overhead variance

The remaining area is that of overheads. In our example, we have assumed that all of the overheads are fixed. Variable overheads certainly exist in practice, but they have been omitted here simply to restrict the amount of detailed coverage. Variances involving variable overheads are similar in style to labour and material variances.

Fixed overhead spending variance
The difference between the actual fixed overhead cost and the fixed overhead cost according to the flexed (and the original) budget.

The *fixed overhead spending variance* is simply the difference between the flexed (or original – they will be the same) budget and the actual figures. For May, this was £700 (adverse) (that is, £20,700 – £20,000). It is adverse because more overheads cost was actually incurred than was budgeted. This would tend to lead to less profit. In theory, this is the responsibility of whoever controls overheads expenditure. In practice, this tends to be a very slippery area, and one that is notoriously difficult to control.

Activity 7.10

Using the figures in Activity 7.4, what was the fixed overhead spending variance for June?

The fixed overhead spending variance for June was £700 (favourable) (that is, £20,000 – £19,300). It was favourable because less was spent on overheads than was budgeted, tending to increase profit.

We are now in a position to reconcile the original May budgeted profit with the actual profit, as follows:

	£	£
Budgeted profit		20,000
Add **Favourable variances**		
Sales price	2,000	
Direct materials price	100	
Direct labour efficiency	800	2,900
		22,900
Less **Adverse variances**		
Sales volume	4,000	
Direct materials usage	1,000	
Direct labour rate	300	
Fixed overhead spending	700	6,000
Actual profit		16,900

Activity 7.11

Using the figures in Activity 7.4, try reconciling the original profit figure for June with the actual June figure.

	£	£
Budgeted profit		24,000
Add **Favourable variances**		
Sales volume	2,000	
Direct labour rate	480	
Fixed overhead spending	700	
		3,180
		27,180
Less **Adverse variances**		
Sales price	1,500	
Direct materials usage	300	
Direct labour efficiency	680	
		2,480
Actual profit		24,700

Activity 7.12

The following are the budgeted and actual profit and loss accounts (income statements) for Baxter Ltd for the month of July:

	Budget	*Actual*
Output	1,000 units	1,050 units
(production and sales)		
	£	£
Sales	100,000	104,300
Raw materials	(40,000) (40,000 metres)	(41,200) (40,500 metres)
Labour	(20,000) (2,500 hours)	(21,300) (2,600 hours)
Fixed overheads	(20,000)	(19,400)
Operating profit	20,000	22,400

Produce a reconciliation of the budgeted and actual operating profit, going into as much detail as possible with the variance analysis.

The original budget, the flexed budget and the actual are as follows:

	Original budget	*Flexed budget*	*Actual*
Output	1,000 units	1,050 units	1,050 units
(production and sales)			
	£	£	£
Sales	100,000	105,000	104,300
Raw materials	(40,000)	(42,000)	(41,200)
Labour	(20,000)	(21,000)	(21,300)
Fixed overheads	(20,000)	(20,000)	(19,400)
Operating profit	20,000	22,000	22,400

Activity 7.12 continued

Reconciliation of the budgeted and actual operating profits for July

	£	£
Budgeted profit		20,000
Add Favourable variances:		
Sales volume (22,000 − 20,000)	2,000	
Direct materials usage {[(1,050 × 40) − 40,500] × £1}	1,500	
Direct labour efficiency {[(1,050 × 2.50) − 2,600] × £8}	200	
Fixed overhead spending (20,000 − 19,400)	600	4,300
		24,300
Less Adverse variances:		
Sales price (105,000 − 104,300)	700	
Direct materials price [(40,500 × £1) − 41,200]	700	
Direct labour rate [(2,600 × £8) − 21,300]	500	1,900
Actual profit		22,400

→ **Real World 7.1** gives some indication of the extent of use of **variance analysis** in practice.

REAL WORLD 7.1

Accounting for control in practice

A 1993 survey of UK manufacturing businesses showed variance analysis to be very widely used: 76 per cent of all the survey respondents used it, with 83 per cent of larger businesses using it. Interestingly, 11 per cent of businesses had abandoned using variance analysis during the 10 years preceding the date of the survey. Does this imply that there is a significant shift away from its use?

The variances that are widely used, and regarded as important, are those that we have looked at in some detail in this chapter.

Though this survey was conducted some time ago, it represents the most recent such survey and is worth noting.

Source: Taken from information appearing in Drury *et al*. (see reference 1 at the end of the chapter).

Standard quantities and costs

We have already seen that a budget is a business plan for the short term – typically one year – and it is likely to be expressed mainly in financial terms. It is built up from standards. **Standard quantities and costs** (or revenues) are those planned for individual units of input or output. Thus standards are the building blocks of the budget.

We can say about Baxter Ltd's operations that:

● the standard selling price is £100 for one unit of output;
● the standard raw materials cost is £40 for one unit of output;
● the standard raw materials usage is 40 metres for one unit of output;

- the standard raw materials price is £1 a metre (that is, for one unit of input);
- the standard labour cost is £20 for one unit of output;
- the standard labour time is 2.50 hours for one unit of output;
- the standard labour rate is £8 an hour (that is, for one unit of input).

The standards, like the budgets to which they are linked, represent targets and, therefore, yardsticks by which actual performance is measured. They are derived from experience and judgements of what is a reasonable quantity of input (for labour time and materials usage) and from assessments of the market for the product (standard selling price) and the market for the inputs (labour rate and material price). These should be subject to frequent review and, where necessary, revision. It is vital, if they are to be used as part of the control process, that they represent realistic targets.

Calculation of most variances is, in effect, based on standards. For example, the material usage variance is the difference between the standard materials usage for the level of output and the actual usage, costed at the standard materials price.

Standards can have uses other than in the context of budgetary control. Standards provide the business with a database of costs, usages, selling prices and so on, that are known to be broadly realistic. This provides managers with a ready set of information for their decision making and income measurement purposes.

Real World 7.2 provides some information on the use of standard costs in practice.

REAL WORLD 7.2

Standard costing in practice

The Drury, Braund, Osborne and Tayles survey from 1993 showed that the respondent businesses found standard costs important to them for the following purposes:

	Percentage of respondents
Cost control and performance evaluation	72
Valuing stock (inventory) and work in progress	80
Deducing costs for decision-making purposes	62
To help in constructing budgets	69

Thus, standards are seen as very important in the context of the subject of this chapter (cost control and performance evaluation), but they also seem to be widely used for other financial and management accounting purposes.

The conventional wisdom on the level of standards is that they should be demanding but achievable. Thus, if the standard direct labour time for some activity is five minutes, this should be capable of being achieved yet require staff to be working efficiently to achieve it. The survey showed that 44 per cent of respondents deliberately set standards of this type; 46 per cent, however, set standards based on past performance. Perhaps this was because the businesses' managements felt that past performance represents an achievable (obviously) yet demanding level of achievement. Only 5 per cent of respondents set standards at a level that could be achieved if everything went perfectly all of the time. Many people believe that such standards are not helpful because they do not represent a realistic target in a world where things *do* go wrong from time to time.

Standards are formally reviewed annually or more frequently by 91 per cent of the respondent businesses. This would amount to considering whether the existing standards are set at an appropriate level and amending them where necessary.

Source: Drury et al. (see reference 1 at the end of the chapter).

Labour cost standards and the learning-curve effect

Where a particular activity undertaken by direct workers has been unchanged in nature for some time, and the workers are experienced at performing it, normally an established standard labour time will be unchanged over time. Where a new activity is introduced, or new people are involved with performing an existing task, a **learning-curve** effect will normally occur. This is shown in Figure 7.5.

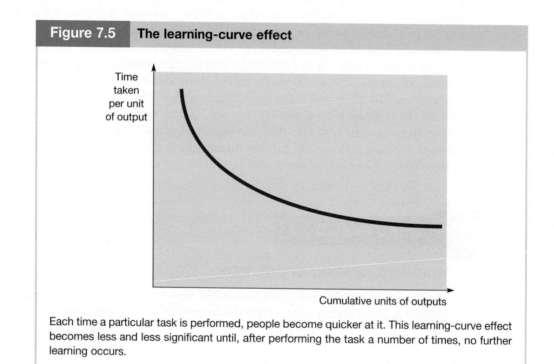

Figure 7.5	The learning-curve effect

Each time a particular task is performed, people become quicker at it. This learning-curve effect becomes less and less significant until, after performing the task a number of times, no further learning occurs.

The first unit of output takes a long time to produce. As experience is gained, the person takes less time to produce each unit of output. The rate of reduction in the time taken will, however, decrease as experience is gained. Thus, for example, the reduction in time taken between the first and second unit produced will be much bigger than the reduction between, say, the ninth and the tenth. Eventually, the rate of reduction in time taken will reduce to zero so that each unit will take as long as the preceding one. At this point, the point where the curve in Figure 7.5 becomes horizontal (the bottom right of the graph), the learning-curve effect will have been eliminated and a steady, long-term standard time for the activity will have been established.

The learning-curve effect seems to have little to do with whether workers are skilled or unskilled; if they are unfamiliar with the task, the learning-curve effect will arise. Practical experience shows that learning curves show remarkable regularity and, therefore, predictability from one activity to the next.

Clearly, the learning-curve effect must be taken into account when setting standards, and when interpreting any adverse labour efficiency variances, where a new process and/or new personnel are involved.

Reasons for adverse variances

A constant possible reason why variances occur is that the standards against which performance is being measured are not reasonable targets. This is certainly not to say that the immediate reaction to an adverse variance should be that the standard is unreasonably harsh. On the other hand, standards that are not achievable are useless.

Activity 7.13

The variances that we have considered are:

- sales volume
- sales price
- direct materials usage
- direct materials price
- direct labour efficiency
- direct labour rate
- fixed overhead spending.

Ignoring the possibility that standards may be unreasonable, jot down any ideas that occur to you as possible practical reasons for adverse variances in each case.

The reasons that we thought of included the following:

Sales volume
- Poor performance by sales personnel.
- Deterioration in market conditions between the setting of the budget and the actual event.
- Lack of stock (inventory) or services to sell as a result of some production problem.

Sales price
- Poor performance by sales personnel.
- Deterioration in market conditions between the setting of the budget and the actual event.

Direct materials usage
- Poor performance by production department staff, leading to high rates of scrap.
- Substandard materials, leading to high rates of scrap.
- Faulty machinery, causing high rates of scrap.

Direct materials price
- Poor performance by the buying department staff.
- Change in market conditions between setting the standard and the actual event.

Labour efficiency
- Poor supervision.
- A low skill grade of worker taking longer to do the work than was envisaged for the correct skill grade.
- Low-grade materials, leading to high levels of scrap and wasted labour time.
- Problems with a customer for whom a service is being rendered.
- Problems with machinery, leading to labour time being wasted.
- Dislocation of materials supply, leading to workers being unable to proceed with production.

Activity 7.13 continued

Labour rate
● Poor performance by the personnel function.
● Using a higher grade of worker than was planned.
● Change in labour market conditions between setting the standard and the actual event.

Fixed overheads
● Poor supervision of overheads.
● General increase in costs of overheads not taken into account in the budget.

Though we have tended to use the example of a manufacturing business to explain variance analysis, this should not be taken to imply that variance analysis is not equally applicable and useful in service sector businesses. It is simply that manufacturing businesses tend to have all of the variances found in practice. Service businesses, for example, may not have material variances.

Non-operating profit variances

There are many areas of business that have a budget but where a failure to meet the budget does not have a direct effect on profit. Frequently, however, it has an indirect effect on profit, and sometimes a profound effect. For example, the cash budget sets out the planned receipts, payments and resultant cash balance for the period. If the person responsible for the cash budget gets things wrong, or is forced to make unplanned expenditures, this could lead to unplanned cash shortages and accompanying costs. These costs might be limited to lost interest on possible investments, which could otherwise have been made, or to the need to pay overdraft interest. If the cash shortage cannot be covered by some form of borrowing, the consequences could be more profound, such as the loss of profits on business that was not able to be undertaken because of the lack of funds.

It is clearly necessary that control be exercised over areas such as cash management as well as over those like production and sales in an attempt to avoid adverse → **non-operating profit variances**.

Investigating variances

It is unreasonable to expect budget targets to be met precisely each month and so variances will usually occur. Whatever the reason for a variance, finding that reason will take time, and time is costly. Small variances are almost inevitable, yet investigating variances can be expensive. Management needs, therefore, to establish a policy concerning which variances to investigate and which to accept. For example, for Baxter Ltd (Example 7.1 on p. 183) the budgeted usage of materials during May was 40,000 metres at a cost of £1 a metre. Suppose that production had been the same as the budgeted quantity of output, but that 40,005 metres of material, costing £1 a metre, had actually been used.

Would this adverse variance of £5 be investigated? Probably not. What, though, if the variance were £50 or £500 or £5,000?

Activity 7.14

What broad approach do you feel should be taken as to whether to spend money investigating a particular variance?

The general approach to this policy must be concerned with cost and benefit. The benefit likely to be gained from knowing why a variance arose needs to be balanced against the cost of obtaining that knowledge. The issue of balancing the benefit of having information with the cost of having it was discussed in Chapter 1.

Unfortunately, as is often the case in practice, both the cost of investigation and the value of the benefit are difficult to assess in advance of the investigation.

Knowing the reason for a variance can have a value only when it might provide management with the means to bring things back under control, enabling future targets to be met. It should be borne in mind here that variances will normally be either zero, or very close to zero. This is to say that achieving targets, give or take small variances, should be normal.

Broadly, we suggest that the following approach seems sensible:

1 Significant *adverse* variances should be investigated because the continuation of the fault that they represent could be very costly. Management must decide what 'significant' means. A certain amount of science, in the form of statistical models, can be brought to bear in making this decision. Ultimately, however, it must be a matter of managerial judgement as to what is significant. Perhaps a variance of 5 per cent from the budgeted figure would be deemed to be significant.

2 Significant *favourable* variances should probably be investigated as well as those that are unfavourable. Though such variances would not cause such immediate management concern as adverse ones, they still represent things not going according to plan. If actual performance is significantly better than target, it may well mean that the target is unrealistically low.

3 Insignificant variances, though not triggering immediate investigation, should be kept under review. For each aspect of operations, the cumulative sum of variances, over a series of control periods, should be zero, with small adverse variances in some periods being compensated for by small favourable ones in others. This should be the case with variances that are caused by chance factors, which will not necessarily repeat themselves.

Where a variance is caused by a more systematic factor, which will repeat itself, the cumulative sum of the periodic variances will not be zero but an increasing figure. Where the increasing figure represents a set of adverse variances it may well be worth investigating the situation, even though the individual variances may be insignificant. Even where the direction of the cumulative total points to favourable variances, investigation may still be considered to be valuable.

To illustrate this last point, let us consider Example 7.2.

Example 7.2

Indisurers Ltd finds that the variances for direct labour efficiency for processing motor insurance claims, since the beginning of the year, are as follows:

	£		£
January	25 (adverse)	July	20 (adverse)
February	15 (favourable)	August	15 (favourable)
March	5 (favourable)	September	23 (adverse)
April	20 (adverse)	October	15 (favourable)
May	22 (adverse)	November	5 (favourable)
June	8 (favourable)	December	26 (adverse)

The average total cost of labour performing this task is about £1,200 a month. Management believes that none of these variances, taken alone, is significant given the labour cost each month. The question is, are they significant when taken together? If we add them together, taking account of the signs, we find that we have a net adverse variance for the year of £73. Of itself this, too, is probably not significant, but we should expect the cumulative total to be close to zero, were the variances random. We might feel that a pattern is developing and, given long enough, a net adverse variance of significant size might build up.

Investigating the labour efficiency might be worth doing. (We should note that 12 periods are probably not enough to reach a statistically sound conclusion on whether the variances are random or not, but it provides an illustration of the point.)

Plotting the cumulative variances, from month to month, as in Figure 7.6, makes it clear what is happening as time proceeds.

Real World 7.3 is taken from the research of Drury, Braund, Osborne and Tayles. The table shows the methods used by respondents to the survey to make the decision on whether to investigate a particular variance.

REAL WORLD 7.3

Methods used to make decisions on investigation of variances

	% 'Often' or 'Always'
Decisions based on managerial judgement	75
Variance exceeds a specific monetary amount	41
Variance exceeds a given percentage of standard	36
Statistical models	3

Source: Reproduced from Drury *et al*. (see reference 1 at the end of the chapter), p. 39, table 5.7.

It is interesting to note the large extent, revealed by this survey, to which decisions on whether to investigate variances are made on the basis of some, presumably subjective, judgement. We might have expected businesses to adopt a more systematic approach. The survey is not very recent, but it probably provides some helpful insights to current practice.

Figure 7.6	The cumulative variances for labour efficiency in motor insurance claim handling at Indisurers Ltd

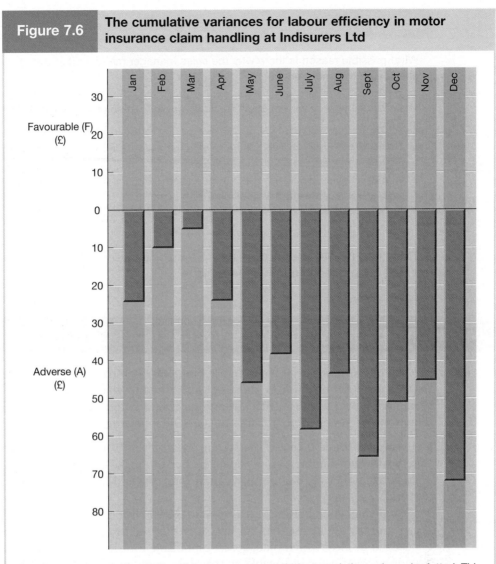

Starting at zero at the beginning of January, each month the cumulative variance is plotted. This is the sum taking account of positive and negative signs. The January figure is £25 (A). The February one is £10 (A) (that is £25 (A) plus £15 (F)) and so on. The graph seems to show an overall trend of adverse variances, but with several favourable variances involved.

Compensating variances

There is superficial appeal in the idea of **compensating variances**. This is trading off linked favourable and adverse variances against each other, without further consideration. For example, a sales manager believes that she could sell more of a particular service if prices were lowered, and that this would feed through to increased net operating profit. This would lead to a favourable sales volume variance, but also to an adverse sales price variance. On the face of it, provided that the former is greater than the latter, all would be well.

Activity 7.15

What possible reason is there why the sales manager mentioned above should not go ahead with the price reduction?

The change in policy will have ramifications for other areas of the business, including the following:

- The need for more provision of the service to be available to sell. Staff and other factors might not be able to supply this increase.
- Increased sales would involve an increased need for finance to pay for increased activity, for example to pay additional staff costs.

Thus 'trading off' variances is not automatically acceptable, without a more far-reaching consultation and revision of plans.

Making budgetary control effective

It is obvious from what we have seen of **budgetary control** that, if it is to be successful, a system, or a set of routines, must be established to enable the potential benefits to be gained. Most businesses that operate successful budgetary control systems tend to share some common factors. These include the following:

1 A serious attitude taken to the system by all levels of management, right from the very top. For example, senior managers need to make clear to junior managers that they take notice of the monthly variance reports and base some of their actions on them.

2 Clear demarcation between areas of managerial responsibility so that accountability can more easily be ascribed for any area that seems to be going out of control. It needs to be clear which manager is responsible for each aspect of the business.

3 Budget targets being reasonable, so that they represent a rigorous yet achievable target. This may be promoted by managers being involved in setting their own targets. It is argued that this can increase the managers' commitment and motivation. We shall consider this in more detail shortly.

4 Established data collection, analysis and dissemination routines, which take the actual results and the budget figures, and calculate and report the variances. This should be part of the business's regular accounting information system, so that the required reports are automatically produced each month.

5 Reports aimed at individual managers, rather than general-purpose documents. This avoids managers having to wade through reams of reports to find the part that is relevant to them.

6 Fairly short reporting periods, typically a month, so that things cannot go too far wrong before they are picked up.

7 Variance reports being produced and disseminated shortly after the end of the relevant reporting period. If it is not until the end of June that a manager is informed that the performance in May was below the budgeted level, it is quite likely that the performance for June will be below target as well. Reports on the performance in May ideally need to emerge in early June.

8 Action being taken to get operations back under control if they are shown to be out of control. The report will not change things by itself. Managers need to take action to try to ensure that the reporting of significant adverse variances leads to action to put things right for the future.

Limitations of the traditional approach to control through variances and standards

Budgetary control, of the type that we have reviewed in this chapter, has obvious appeal and, judging by the wide extent of its use in practice, it has value as well. It is somewhat limited at times, however. Some of its limitations are as follows:

1 Vast areas of most business and commercial activities simply do not have the same direct relationship between inputs and outputs as is the case with, say, level of output and the number of direct labour hours worked. Many of the expenses of a modern business are in areas such as training and advertising, where the expense is discretionary and not linked to the level of output in a direct way.

2 Standards can quickly become out of date as a result of both technological change and price changes. This does not pose insuperable problems, but it does require that the potential problem be systematically addressed. Standards that are unrealistic are, at best, useless. At worst, they could have adverse effects on performance. A personnel manager who knows that it is impossible to meet targets on rates of pay for labour, because of general labour cost rises, may have a reduced incentive to minimise costs.

3 Sometimes factors that are outside the control of the manager concerned can affect the calculation of the variance for which that manager is held accountable. This may have an adverse effect on the assessment of the manager's performance. The situation can often be overcome by a more considered approach to the calculation of the variance, resulting in those factors controllable by the manager being separated from those that are not.

4 In practice, creating clear lines of demarcation between the areas of responsibility of various managers may be difficult. Thus, one of the prerequisites of good budgetary control is lost.

Behavioural aspects of budgetary control

Budgets, perhaps more than any other accounting statement, are prepared with the objective of affecting the attitudes and behaviour of managers. The point was made in Chapter 6 that budgets are intended to motivate managers, and research evidence generally shows this to be true. More specifically, the research shows:

● The existence of budgets generally tends to improve performance.
● Demanding, yet achievable, budget targets tend to motivate better than less demanding targets. It seems that setting the most demanding targets that will be accepted by managers is a very effective way to motivate them.
● Unrealistically demanding targets tend to have an adverse effect on managers' performance.
● The participation of managers in setting their targets tends to improve motivation and performance. This is probably because those managers feel a sense of commitment to the targets and a moral obligation to achieve them.

It has been suggested that allowing managers to set their own targets will lead to slack (that is, easily achievable targets) being introduced. This would make achievement of the target that much easier. On the other hand, in an effort to impress, a manager may select a target that is not really achievable. These points imply that care must be taken in the extent to which managers have unfettered choice of their own targets.

The impact of management style

There has been a great deal of literature published on the way in which managers use information generated by the budgeting system and the impact of its use on the attitudes and behaviour of subordinates. A pioneering study by Hopwood (see reference 2 at the end of the chapter) examined the way in which managers working within a manufacturing environment used budget information to evaluate the performance of subordinates. He argued that three distinct styles of management could be observed. These are:

- *Budget-constrained style.* This management style focuses rigidly on the ability of subordinates to meet the budget. Other factors relating to the performance of subordinates are not given serious consideration even though they might include improving the long-term effectiveness of the area for which the subordinate has responsibility,
- *Profit-conscious style.* This management style uses budget information in a more flexible way and often in conjunction with other data. The main focus is on the ability of each subordinate to improve long-term effectiveness.
- *Non-accounting style.* In this case, budget information plays no significant role in the evaluation of a subordinate's performance.

Activity 7.16

How might a manager respond to budget information that indicates a subordinate has not met the budget targets for the period, assuming the manager adopts:

(a) a budget-constrained style?
(b) a profit-conscious style?
(c) a non-accounting style?

....

(a) A manager adopting a budget-constrained style is likely to take the budget information very seriously. This may result in criticism of the subordinate and, perhaps, some form of punishment.
(b) A manager adopting a profit-conscious style is likely to take a broader view when examining the budget information and so will take other factors into consideration (for example, factors that could not have been anticipated at the time of preparing the budgets), before deciding whether criticism or punishment is justified.
(c) A manager adopting a non-accounting style will regard the failure to meet the budget as being relatively unimportant and so no action may be taken.

Hopwood found that subordinates working for a manager who adopts a budget-constrained style had unfortunate experiences. They suffered higher levels of job-related stress and had poorer working relationships, with both their colleagues and their manager, than those subordinates whose manager adopted one of the other two styles. Hopwood also found that the subordinates of a budget-constrained style of manager were more likely to manipulate the budget figures, or to take other undesirable actions, to ensure the budgets were met.

Reservations about the Hopwood study

Though Hopwood's findings are interesting, subsequent studies have cast doubt on their universal applicability. Later studies confirm that human attitudes and behaviour are complex and can vary according to the particular situation. For example, it has been found that the impact of different management styles on such factors as job-related stress and the manipulation of budget figures seems to vary. The impact is likely to depend on such factors as the level of independence enjoyed by the subordinates and the level of uncertainty associated with the tasks to be undertaken.

It seems that where there is a high level of interdependence between business divisions, subordinate managers are more likely to feel that they have less control over their performance, because the performance of staff in other divisions could be an important influence on the final outcome. In such a situation, rigid application of the budget could be viewed as being unfair and may lead to undesirable behaviour. However, where managers have a high degree of independence, the application of budgets as a measure of performance is likely to be more acceptable. In this case, the managers are likely to feel that the final outcome is much less dependent on the performance of others.

Later studies have also shown that where a subordinate is undertaking a task that has a high degree of uncertainty concerning the outcome (for example, developing a new product for the market), budget targets are unlikely to be an adequate measure of performance. In such a situation, other factors and measures should be taken into account in order to derive a more complete assessment of performance. However, where a task has a low degree of uncertainty concerning the outcome (for example, producing a standard product using standard equipment and an experienced workforce), budget measures may be regarded as more reliable indicators of performance. Thus, it appears that a budget-constrained style is more likely to work where subordinates enjoy a fair amount of independence and where the tasks set have a low level of uncertainty concerning their outcomes.

Failing to meet the budget

The existence of budgets gives senior managers a ready means to assess the performance of their subordinates Where a manager fails to meet a budget, failure must be dealt with carefully by his or her senior manager. A harsh, critical approach may demotivate the manager. Adverse variances may imply that the manager needs some help.

Real World 7.4 gives some indication of the effects of the **behavioural aspects of budgetary control** in practice.

REAL WORLD 7.4

Behavioural aspects of budgetary control in practice

The 1993 survey by Drury, Braund, Osborne and Tayles indicates that there is a large degree of participation in setting budgets by those who will be expected to perform to the budget standard (the budget holders). It also indicates that senior management has greater influence in setting the targets than the budget holders.

Where there is a conflict between the cost estimates submitted by the budget holders and their managers, in 40 per cent of respondent businesses the senior manager's view would prevail without negotiation, but in nearly 60 per cent of cases there would be a reduction, that would be negotiated between the budget holder and the senior manager. The general philosophy of the respondent businesses, regarding budget holders influencing the setting of their own budgets, is:

- 23 per cent of respondents believe that budget holders should not have too much influence since they will seek to obtain easy budgets (build in slack) if they do;
- 69 per cent of respondents take an opposite view.

The general view on how senior managers should judge their subordinates is:

- 46 per cent of respondent businesses think that senior managers should judge junior managers mainly on their ability to achieve the budget;
- 40 per cent think otherwise.

Though this research is not very recent, in the absence of more recent evidence it provides some feel for budget setting in practice.

Source: Drury *et al.* (see reference 1 at the end of the chapter).

Self-assessment question 7.1

Toscanini Ltd makes a standard product, which is budgeted to sell at £4.00 a unit, in a competitive market. It is made by taking a budgeted 0.4 kg of material, budgeted to cost £2.40/kg, and working on it by hand by an employee, paid a budgeted £8.00/hour, for a budgeted 6 minutes. Monthly fixed overheads are budgeted at £4,800. The output for May was budgeted at 4,000 units.

The actual results for May were as follows:

	£
Sales (3,500 units)	13,820
Materials (1,425 kg)	(3,420)
Labour (345 hours)	(2,690)
Fixed overheads	(4,900)
Actual operating profit	2,810

No stocks (inventories) of any description existed at the beginning and end of the month.

Required:

(a) Deduce the budgeted profit for May, and reconcile it with the actual profit in as much detail as the information provided will allow.

(b) State which manager should be held accountable, in the first instance, for each variance calculated.

(c) Assuming that the standards were all well set in terms of labour times and rates and material usage and price, suggest at least one feasible reason for each of the variances that you identified in (a), given what you know about the business's performance for May.

(d) If it were discovered that the actual total world market demand for the business's product was 10 per cent lower than estimated when the May budget was set, explain how and why the variances that you identified in (a) could be revised to provide information that would be potentially more useful.

SUMMARY

The main points of this chapter may be summarised as follows:

Controlling through budgets

- Budgets act as a system of both feedback and feedforward control.
- Budgets can be flexed to match actual volume of output.
- Variance = increase (favourable) or decrease (adverse) in profit, relative to the budgeted profit, as a result of some aspect of the business's activities taken alone.
- Budgeted profit plus all favourable variances less all adverse variances equals actual profit.
- Commonly calculated variances:
  - Sales volume variance = difference between budgeted and actual volume (in units) multiplied by the standard contribution (for one unit).
  - Sales price variance = difference between actual sales revenue and actual volume at the standard sales price.
  - Direct materials usage variance = difference between actual usage and budgeted usage, for the actual volume of output, multiplied by the standard materials cost.
  - Direct materials price variance = difference between the actual materials cost and the actual usage multiplied by the standard materials cost.
  - Direct labour efficiency variance = difference between actual labour time and budgeted time, for the actual volume of output, multiplied by the standard labour rate.
  - Direct labour rate variance = difference between the actual labour cost and the actual labour time multiplied by the standard labour rate.
  - Fixed overhead spending variance = difference between the actual and budgeted spending on fixed overheads.
- Standards = budgeted physical quantities and financial values for one unit of inputs and outputs.
- Standards are useful in providing data for decision making and income measurement.
- There tends to be a learning-curve effect: routine tasks are performed more quickly with experience.
- Significant and/or persistent variances need to be investigated to establish their cause.
- Good budgetary control requires establishing systems and routines to ensure such things as a clear distinction between individual managers' areas of responsibility; prompt; frequent and relevant variance reporting; and senior management commitment.
- Not all activities can usefully be controlled through traditional variance analysis.
- There is a behavioural aspect of control and this should be taken into account by senior managers.

→ Key terms

Feedback control p. 182	**Standard quantities and costs** p. 192
Feedforward control p. 182	**Learning curve** p. 194
Flexing the budget p. 184	**Non-operating profit variances**
Flexible budget p. 184	p. 196
Adverse variance p. 185	**Compensating variances** p. 199
Favourable variance p. 185	**Budgetary control** p. 200
Variance p. 185	**Behavioural aspects of budgetary**
Variance analysis p. 192	**control** p. 203

Further reading

If you would like to explore the topics covered in this chapter in more depth, we recommend the following books:

Management Accounting, *Atkinson A., Banker R., Kaplan R. and Young S. M.*, 3rd edn, Prentice Hall, 2001, chapter 12.

Management and Cost Accounting, *Drury C.*, 5th edn, Thomson Learning Business Press, 2000, chapters 16, 18 and 19.

Cost Accounting: A managerial emphasis, *Horngren C., Foster G. and Datar S.*, 11th edn, Prentice Hall International, 2002, chapters 7 and 8.

Cost and Management Accounting, *Williamson D.*, Prentice Hall International, 1996, chapter 15.

References

1 **A Survey of Managment Accounting Practices in UK Manufacturing Companies**, *Drury C., Braund S., Osborne P. and Tayles M.*, Chartered Association of Certified Accountants, 1993.

2 'An empirical study of the role of accounting data in performance evaluation', *Hopwood A. G.*, **Empirical Research in Accounting**, a supplement to the **Journal of Accounting Research**, 1972, pp. 156–82.

REVIEW QUESTIONS

Answers to these questions can be found on the students' side of the Companion Website at www.pearsoned.co.uk/atrillmclaney.

7.1 Explain what is meant by feedforward control and distinguish it from feedback control.

7.2 What is meant by a variance? What is the point in analysing variances?

7.3 What is the point in flexing the budget in the context of variance analysis? Does flexing imply that differences between budget and actual in the volume of output are ignored in variance analysis?

7.4 Should all variances be investigated to find their cause? Explain your answer.

EXERCISES

Exercises 7.4 to 7.8 are more advanced than 7.1 to 7.3. Those with coloured numbers have answers at the back of the book.

7.1 You have recently overheard the following remarks:

(a) 'A favourable direct labour rate variance can only be caused by staff working more efficiently than budgeted.'
(b) 'Selling more units than budgeted, because the units were sold at less than standard price, automatically leads to a favourable sales volume variance.'
(c) 'Using below-standard materials will tend to lead to adverse materials usage variances but cannot affect labour variances.'
(d) 'Higher-than-budgeted sales could not possibly affect the labour rate variance.'
(e) 'An adverse sales price variance can only arise from selling a product at less than standard price.'

Required:
Critically assess these remarks, explaining any technical terms.

7.2 Pilot Ltd makes a standard product, which is budgeted to sell at £5.00 a unit. It is made by taking a budgeted 0.5 kg of material, budgeted to cost £3.00 a kilogram, and working on it by hand by an employee, paid a budgeted £5.00 an hour, for a budgeted 15 minutes. Monthly fixed overheads are budgeted at £6,000. The output for March was budgeted at 5,000 units.
   The actual results for March were as follows:

	£
Sales (5,400 units)	26,460
Materials (2,830 kg)	(8,770)
Labour (1,300 hours)	(6,885)
Fixed overheads	(6,350)
Actual operating profit	4,455

No stocks existed at the start or end of March.

Required:

(a) Deduce the budgeted profit for March and reconcile it with the actual profit in as much detail as the information provided will allow.

(b) State which manager should be held accountable, in the first instance, for each variance calculated.

7.3 Antonio plc makes product X, the standard costs of which are:

	£
Sales revenue	31
Direct labour (2 hours)	(11)
Direct materials (1 kg)	(10)
Fixed overheads	(3)
Standard profit	7

The budgeted output for March was 1,000 units of product X; the actual output was 1,100 units, which was sold for £34,950. There were no stocks (inventories) at the start or end of March.

The actual production costs were:

	£
Direct labour (2,150 hours)	12,210
Direct materials (1,170 kg)	11,630
Fixed overheads	3,200

Required:

Calculate the variances for March as fully as you are able from the available information, and use them to reconcile the budgeted and actual profit figures.

7.4 You have recently overheard the following remarks:

(a) 'When calculating variances, we in effect ignore differences of volume of output, between original budget and actual, by flexing the budget. If there were a volume difference, it is water under the bridge by the time that the variances come to be calculated.'

(b) 'It is very valuable to calculate variances because they will tell you what went wrong.'

(c) 'All variances should be investigated to find their cause.'

(d) 'Research evidence shows that the more demanding the target, the more motivated the manager.'

(e) 'Most businesses do not have feedforward controls of any type, just feedback controls through budgets.'

Required:

Critically assess these remarks, explaining any technical terms.

7.5 Bradley-Allen Ltd makes one standard product. Its budgeted operating statement for May is as follows:

		£	£
Sales:	800 units		64,000
Direct materials:	Type A	12,000	
	Type B	16,000	
Direct labour:	Skilled	4,000	
	Unskilled	10,000	
Overheads:	(All Fixed)	12,000	
			54,000
Budgeted operating profit			10,000

The standard costs were as follows:

- Direct materials: Type A   £50/kg
                     Type B   £20/m
- Direct labour: Skilled   £10/hour
                     Unskilled £8/hour

During May, the following occurred:

(i)   950 units were sold for a total of £73,000.
(ii) 310 kilos (costing £15,200) of type A material were used in production.
(iii) 920 metres (costing £18,900) of type B material were used in production.
(iv) Skilled workers were paid £4,628 for 445 hours.
(v)   Unskilled workers were paid £11,275 for 1,375 hours.
(vi) Fixed overheads cost £11,960.

There was no stock (inventory) of finished production or of work in progress at either the beginning or end of May.

Required:
(a) Prepare a statement that reconciles the budgeted to the actual profit of the business for May. Your statement should analyse the difference between the two profit figures in as much detail as you are able.
(b) Explain how the statement in (a) might be helpful to managers.

7.6 Mowbray Ltd makes and sells one product, the standard costs of which are as follows:

	£
Direct materials (3 kg at £2.50/kg)	7.50
Direct labour (15 minutes at £9.00/hr)	2.25
Fixed overheads	3.60
	13.35
Selling price	20.00
Standard profit margin	6.65

The monthly production and sales are planned to be 1,200 units.
  The actual results for May were as follows:

	£	
Sales revenue	18,000	
Less Direct materials	(7,400)	(2,800 kg)
Direct labour	(2,300)	(255 hr)
Fixed overheads	(4,100)	
Operating profit	4,200	

There were no stocks at the start or end of May. As a result of poor sales demand during May, the business reduced the price of all sales by 10 per cent.

Required:
Calculate the budgeted profit for May and reconcile it to the actual profit through variances, going into as much detail as is possible from the information available.

7.7 Varne Chemprocessors is a business that specialises in plastics. It uses a standard costing system to monitor and report its purchases and usage of materials. During the most recent month, accounting period six, the purchase and usage of chemical UK194 were as follows:

Purchases/usage:	28,100 litres
Total price:	£51,704

Because of fire risk and the danger to health, no stocks are held by the business.

UK194 is used solely in the manufacture of a product called Varnelyne. The standard cost specification shows that, for the production of 5,000 litres of Varnelyne, 200 litres of UK194 is needed at a total standard cost of £392. During period six, 637,500 litres of Varnelyne were produced.

Required:

(a) Calculate the price and usage variances for UK194 for period six.

(b) The following comment was made by the production manager:

'I knew at the beginning of period six that UK194 would be cheaper than the standard cost specification, so I used rather more of it than normal; this saved £4,900 on other chemicals.'

What changes do you need to make in your analysis for (a) as a result of this comment?

(c) Calculate, for each material below, the cumulative variances and comment briefly on the results.

Variances: periods one to six

Period	UK500		UK800	
	£		£	
1	301	F	298	F
2	251	A	203	F
3	102	F	52	A
4	202	A	98	A
5	153	F	150	A
6	103	A	201	A

where F = cost saving and A = cost overrun.

7.8   Brive plc has the following standards for its only product:

Selling price:	£110/unit
Direct labour:	2 hours at £5.25/hour
Direct material:	3 kg at £14.00/kg
Fixed overheads:	£27.00, based on a budgeted output of 800 units/month

During May, there was an actual output of 850 units and the operating statement for the month was as follows:

	£
Sales	92,930
Direct labour (1,780 hours)	(9,665)
Direct materials (2,410 kg)	(33,258)
Fixed overheads	(21,365)
Operating profit	28,642

There was no stock (inventory) of any description at the beginning and end of May.

Required:

Prepare the original budget and a budget flexed to the actual volume. Use these to compare the budgeted and actual profits of the business for the month, going into as much detail with your analysis as the information given will allow.

8

Making capital investment decisions

OBJECTIVES

When you have completed your study of this chapter you should be able to:

● Explain the nature and importance of investment decision making.

● Identify, use and discuss the qualities of the four main investment appraisal methods used in practice.

● Discuss the strengths and weaknesses of various techniques for dealing with risk in investment appraisal.

● Explain the methods used to review and control capital expenditure projects.

INTRODUCTION

In this chapter we shall look at how businesses can make decisions involving investments in new plant, machinery, buildings and similar non-current assets. The general principles that apply to assessing investments in these types of assets can equally well be applied to investments in the shares of businesses, irrespective of whether the investment is being considered by a business or by a private individual.

Investment decisions require the application of the same principles concerning the identification of relevant costs that we met in Chapters 2 and 3. Failure to identify relevant costs and benefits relating to an investment proposal could lead to bad decisions being made.

We shall consider the research evidence relating to the use of the various appraisal techniques in practice. We shall also consider the problem of risk, which is a major aspect of all decision making. There are various ways in which risk can be incorporated into capital investment appraisal and we shall examine some of the more important of these.

Once a decision has been made to implement a particular capital investment proposal, proper review and control procedures must be in place. We shall, therefore, discuss the ways in which managers can oversee capital investment projects and how control may be exercised throughout the life of the project.

The nature of investment decisions

The essential feature of investment decisions is time. Investment involves making an outlay of something of economic value, usually cash, at one point in time, which is expected to yield economic benefits to the investor at some other point in time. Typically, the outlay precedes the benefits. Also, the outlay is typically one large amount and the benefits arrive as a series of smaller amounts over a fairly protracted period.

Investment decisions tend to be crucial to the business because:

● *Large amounts of resources are often involved.* Many investments made by businesses involve laying out a significant proportion of their total resources (see Real World 8.2 below). If mistakes are made with the decision, the effects on the businesses could be significant, if not catastrophic.

● *It is often difficult and/or expensive to 'bail out' of an investment once it has been undertaken.* It is often the case that investments made by a business are specific to its needs. For example, a hotel business may invest in a new, purpose-designed hotel complex. The specialist nature of this complex will probably lead to it having a rather limited second-hand value to another potential user with different needs. If the business found, after having made the investment, that room occupancy rates were not as buoyant as planned, the only possible course of action might be to close down and sell the complex. This would probably mean that much less could be recouped from the investment than it had originally cost, particularly if the costs of design are included as part of the cost, as logically they should be.

Real World 8.1 gives an illustration of a major investment by a well-known business operating in the UK.

REAL WORLD 8.1

Brittany ferries launches an investment

In the spring of 2004, Brittany Ferries, the cross-channel ferry operator, launched a new ship. The ship had cost the business about £100m. Though Brittany Ferries is a substantial business, this level of expenditure is significant. Clearly, the business believes that acquisition of the new ship will be profitable for it, but how would it have reached this conclusion? Presumably the anticipated future cash flows from passengers and freight operators will have been major inputs to the decision. The ship was specifically designed for Brittany Ferries, so it would be difficult for the business to recoup a large proportion of its £100m, should these projected cash flows not materialise.

Source: Publicity material published by Brittany Ferries.

The issues raised by the Brittany Ferries investment will be the main subject of this chapter.

Real World 8.2 indicates the level of annual investment for a number of randomly selected, well-known UK businesses. It can be seen that the scale of investment varies from one business to another. (It also tends to vary from one year to the next for a particular business.) In nearly all of these businesses the scale of investment is very significant. Real World 8.2 is limited to considering the non-current (fixed) asset investment, but most non-current asset investment also requires a level of current asset investment to support it (additional stock-in-trade (inventories), for example), meaning that the real scale of investment is even greater than indicated.

REAL WORLD 8.2

The scale of investment by UK businesses

Business	Expenditure on additional non-current (fixed) assets as a percentage of:	
	Annual sales	Start of year non-current assets
Associated British Foods plc	10.1	28.6
The Boots Company plc	3.2	7.6
British Airways plc	9.3	7.0
British Sky Broadcasting Group plc	5.0	5.8
BT plc	19.9	17.0
J D Wetherspoon plc	25.1	24.1
Manchester United plc	27.5	20.5
Stagecoach Group plc	6.0	5.4
Tesco plc	8.5	20.1
Vodafone Group plc	79.4	11.8

Source: Annual reports of the businesses concerned for the accounting year ending in 2002.

Activity 8.1

When managers are making decisions involving capital investments, what should the decision seek to achieve?

The answer to this question must be that any decision must be made in the context of the objectives of the business concerned. For a private sector business, this is likely to include increasing the wealth of the shareholders of the business through long-term profitability.

Methods of investment appraisal

Given the importance of investment decisions to the viability of the business, it is essential that investment proposals are all properly screened. Ensuring that the business uses appropriate methods of evaluation is an important part of this screening process.

Research shows that there are basically four methods used in practice by businesses throughout the world to evaluate investment opportunities. They are:

● accounting rate of return (ARR)
● payback period (PP)
● net present value (NPV)
● internal rate of return (IRR).

It is possible to find businesses that use variants of these four methods. It is also possible to find businesses, particularly smaller ones, which do not use any formal appraisal method, but rely more on the 'gut feeling' of their managers. Most businesses, however, seem to use one of the four methods listed above that we shall now review.

We are going to assess the effectiveness of each of these methods and we shall see that only one of them (NPV) is not flawed to some extent. We shall also see how popular these four methods seem to be in practice.

To help us to examine each of the methods, it might be useful to consider how each of them would cope with a particular investment opportunity. Let us consider the following example.

Example 8.1

Billingsgate Battery Company has carried out some research that shows that the business could provide a standard service that it has recently developed.

Provision of the service would require investment in a machine that would cost £100,000, payable immediately. Sales of the service would take place throughout the next five years. At the end of that time, it is estimated that the machine could be sold for £20,000.

Sales of the service would be expected to occur as follows:

	Number of units
Next year	5,000
Second year	10,000
Third year	15,000
Fourth year	15,000
Fifth year	5,000

It is estimated that the new service can be sold for £12 a unit, and that the relevant (variable) costs will total £8 a unit.

To simplify matters, we shall assume that the cash from sales and for the costs of providing the service are paid and received, respectively, at the end of each year. (This is clearly unlikely to be true in real life. Money will have to be paid to employees (for salaries and wages) on a weekly or a monthly basis. Customers will pay within a month or two of buying the service. On the other hand, making the assumption probably does not lead to a serious distortion. It is a simplifying assumption that is often made in real life, and it will make things more straightforward for us now. We should be clear, however, that there is nothing about any of the four approaches that *demands* this assumption to be made.)

Bearing in mind that each unit of the service sold will give rise to a net cash inflow of £4 (that is £12 − £8), the total net cash flows (receipts less payments) for each year will be as follows:

Time		£000
Immediately	Cost of machine	(100)
1 year's time	Net profit before depreciation (£4 × 5,000)	20
2 years' time	Net profit before depreciation (£4 × 10,000)	40
3 years' time	Net profit before depreciation (£4 × 15,000)	60
4 years' time	Net profit before depreciation (£4 × 15,000)	60
5 years' time	Net profit before depreciation (£4 × 5,000)	20
5 years' time	Disposal proceeds from the machine	20

Note that, broadly speaking, the net profit before deducting depreciation (that is, before non-cash items) equals the net amount of cash flowing into the business. Apart from depreciation, all of this business's expenses cause cash to flow out of the business. Sales revenues lead to cash flowing in.

Having set up the example, we shall go on to look at the techniques used to assess investment opportunities and see how they deal with this particular decision.

Accounting rate of return (ARR)

→ The **accounting rate of return (ARR)** method takes the average accounting profit that the investment will generate and expresses it as a percentage of the average investment in the project, as measured in accounting terms. Thus:

$$ARR = \frac{\text{Average annual profit}}{\text{Average investment to earn that profit}} \times 100\%$$

We can see that to calculate the ARR, we need to deduce two pieces of information:

- the annual average profit
- the average investment for the particular project.

In our example, the average profit before depreciation over the five years is £40,000 (that is, £(20 + 40 + 60 + 60 + 20)/5). Assuming straight-line depreciation (that is, equal annual amounts), the annual depreciation charge will be £16,000 (that is, £(100,000 − 20,000)/5). Thus the average annual profit is £24,000 (that is, £40,000 − £16,000).

The average investment over the five years can be calculated as follows:

$$\text{Average investment} = \frac{\text{Cost of machine + Disposal value}}{2}$$

$$= \frac{£100,000 + £20,000}{2}$$

$$= £60,000$$

Thus, the ARR of the investment is:

$$ARR = \frac{£24,000}{£60,000} \times 100\%$$

$$= 40\%$$

To decide whether the 40 per cent return is acceptable, we need to compare this percentage with the minimum required by the business.

Activity 8.2

Chaotic Industries is considering an investment in a fleet of ten delivery vans to take its products to customers. The vans will cost £15,000 each to buy, payable immediately. The annual running costs are expected to total £20,000 for each van (including the driver's salary). The vans are expected to operate successfully for six years, at the end of which period they will all have to be sold, with disposal proceeds expected to be about £3,000 a van. At present, the business uses a commercial carrier for all of its deliveries. It is expected that this carrier will charge a total of £230,000 each year for the next five years to undertake the deliveries.

What is the ARR of buying the vans? (Note that cost savings are as relevant a benefit from an investment as are net cash inflows.)

→

Activity 8.2 continued

The vans will save the business £30,000 a year (that is, £230,000 – (£20,000 × 10)), before depreciation, in total.

Thus, the inflows and outflows will be:

Time		£000
Immediately	Cost of vans	(150)
1 year's time	Net saving before depreciation	30
2 years' time	Net saving before depreciation	30
3 years' time	Net saving before depreciation	30
4 years' time	Net saving before depreciation	30
5 years' time	Net saving before depreciation	30
6 years' time	Net saving before depreciation	30
6 years' time	Disposal proceeds from the vans (10 × 3)	30

The total annual depreciation expense (assuming a straight-line approach) will be £20,000 (that is, (£150,000 – £30,000)/6). Thus, the average annual saving, after depreciation, is £10,000 (that is, £30,000 – £20,000).

The average investment will be:

$$\text{Average investment} = \frac{£150,000 + £30,000}{2}$$

$$= £90,000$$

Thus, the ARR of the investment is:

$$\text{ARR} = \frac{£10,000}{£90,000} \times 100\% = 11.1\%$$

ARR and ROCE

We should note that ARR and the return on capital employed (ROCE) ratio take the same approach to performance measurement, in that they both relate accounting profit to the cost of the assets invested to generate that profit. ROCE is a popular means of assessing the performance of a business, as a whole, *after* it has performed. ARR is an approach that assesses the potential performance of a particular investment, taking the same approach as ROCE, *before* it has performed.

Since private sector businesses are normally seeking to increase the wealth of their owners, ARR may seem to be a sound method of appraising investment opportunities. Profit can be seen as a net increase in wealth over a period, and relating it to the size of investment made to achieve it seems a logical approach.

A user of ARR would require that any investment undertaken by the business would be able to achieve a minimum target ARR. Perhaps the minimum target would be based on the rate that previous investments had actually achieved (as measured by ROCE). Perhaps it would be the industry-average ROCE.

Where there are competing projects that all seem capable of exceeding this minimum rate, the one with the higher or highest ARR would normally be selected.

ARR is said to have a number of advantages as a method of investment appraisal. It was mentioned earlier that ROCE seems a widely used measure of business performance. Shareholders seem to use this ratio to evaluate management performance, and sometimes the financial objective of a business will be expressed in terms of a target ROCE. It therefore seems sensible to use a method of investment appraisal that is consistent with this overall approach to measuring business performance. It also gives the result expressed as a percentage. It seems that some managers feel comfortable with using measures expressed in percentage terms.

Problems with ARR

Activity 8.3

ARR suffers from a very major defect as a means of assessing investment opportunities. Can you reason out what this is? Consider the three competing projects whose cash flows are shown below. All three of these involve investment in a machine that is expected to have no residual value at the end of the five years. Note that all of the projects have the same total net profits over the five years.

Project		A	B	C
Time		£000	£000	£000
Immediately	Cost of machine	(320)	(320)	(320)
1 year's time	Net profit after depreciation	20	10	160
2 years' time	Net profit after depreciation	40	10	10
3 years' time	Net profit after depreciation	60	10	10
4 years' time	Net profit after depreciation	60	10	10
5 years' time	Net profit after depreciation	20	160	10

Hint: The defect is not concerned with the ability of the decision maker to forecast future events, though this too can be a problem. Try to remember what was the essential feature of investment decisions that we identified at the beginning of this chapter.

The problem with ARR is that it almost completely ignores the time factor. In this example, exactly the same ARR would have been computed for each of the three projects.

Since the same total profit over the five years arises in all three of these projects (that is, £200,000) and the average investment in each project is £160,000 (that is, £320,000/2), this means that each case will give rise to the same ARR of 25 per cent (that is, £40,000/ £160,000).

Given a financial objective of increasing the wealth of the business, any rational decision maker faced with a choice between the three projects, set out in Activity 8.3, would strongly prefer Project C. This is because most of the benefits from the investment come in within 12 months of investing the £320,000 to establish the project. Project A would rank second, and Project B would come a poor third in the rankings. Any appraisal technique that is not capable of distinguishing between these three situations is seriously flawed.

Clearly the use of ARR can easily cause poor decisions to be made. We shall look in more detail at the reason for timing being so important later in the chapter.

There are other defects associated with the ARR method. For investment appraisal purposes, it is cash flows rather than accounting profits that are important. Cash is the ultimate measure of the economic wealth generated, because cash is used to acquire resources and for distribution to shareholders. Accounting profit is more appropriate for reporting achievement over the short term. It is a useful measure of productive effort for a relatively short period, such as a year, rather than for a long period.

The ARR method can also create problems when considering competing investments of different size.

Activity 8.4

Sinclair Wholesalers plc is currently considering opening a new sales outlet in Coventry. Two possible sites have been identified for the new outlet. Site A has a capacity of 30,000 sq metres. It will require an average investment of £6m, and will produce an average profit of £600,000 a year. Site B has a capacity of 20,000 sq metres. It will require an average investment of £4m, and will produce an average profit of £500,000 a year.

What is the ARR of each investment opportunity? Which site would you select, and why?

....

The ARR of Site A is £600,000/£6 million = 10 per cent. The ARR of Site B is £500,000/£4 million = 12.5 per cent. Thus, Site B has the higher ARR. However, in terms of the absolute profit generated, Site A is the more attractive. If the ultimate objective is to maximise the wealth of the shareholders of Sinclair Wholesalers plc, it might be better to choose Site A even though the percentage return is lower. It is the absolute size of the return rather than the relative (percentage) size that is important. This is a general problem of using comparative measures, like percentages, when the objective is measured in absolute ones. If businesses were seeking through their investments to generate a percentage rate of return on investment, ARR would be more helpful. The problem is that most businesses seek to achieve increases in their absolute wealth (measured in pounds, euros, dollars and so on), through their investment decisions.

Real World 8.3 illustrates how using percentage measures can lead to confusion.

 REAL WORLD 8.3

Increasing road capacity by sleight of hand

During the 1970s, the Mexican government wanted to increase the capacity of a major four-lane road. It came up with the idea of repainting the lane markings so that there were six narrower lanes occupying the same space as four wider ones had previously done. This increased the capacity of the road by 50 per cent (that is, $(6-4)/4 \times 100$ per cent). A tragic outcome of the narrower lanes was an increase in deaths from road accidents. A year later the Mexican government had the six narrower lanes changed back to the original four wider ones. This reduced the capacity of the road by 33 per cent (that is, $(6-4)/6 \times 100$ per cent). The Mexican government reported that it had increased the capacity of the road by 17 per cent (that is 50 per cent − 33 per cent), despite the fact that its real capacity was identical to that which it had been originally. The confusion arose because each of the two percentages (50 per cent and 33 per cent) is based on different bases (four and six).

Source: Gigerenzer (see reference 1 at the end of the chapter).

Payback period (PP)

→ The **payback period (PP)** method seems to go some way to overcoming the timing problem of ARR, or at least at first glance it does.

It might be useful to consider PP in the context of the Billingsgate Battery example. We should recall that essentially the project's costs and benefits can be summarised as:

Time		£000
Immediately	Cost of machine	(100)
1 year's time	Net profit before depreciation	20
2 years' time	Net profit before depreciation	40
3 years' time	Net profit before depreciation	60
4 years' time	Net profit before depreciation	60
5 years' time	Net profit before depreciation	20
5 years' time	Disposal proceeds	20

Note that all of these figures are amounts of cash to be paid or received (we saw earlier that net profit before depreciation is a rough measure of the cash flows from the project).

The payback period is the length of time it takes for the initial investment to be repaid out of the net cash inflows from the project. In this case, it will be three years before the £100,000 outlay is covered by the inflows, still assuming that the cash flows occur at year ends. The payback period can be derived by calculating the cumulative cash flows as follows:

Time		Net cash flows £000	Cumulative cash flows £000	
Immediately	Cost of machine	(100)	(100)	
1 year's time	Net profit before depreciation	20	(80)	(−100 + 20)
2 years' time	Net profit before depreciation	40	(40)	(−80 + 40)
3 years' time	Net profit before depreciation	60	20	(−40 + 60)
4 years' time	Net profit before depreciation	60	80	(20 + 60)
5 years' time	Net profit before depreciation	20	100	(80 + 20)
5 years' time	Disposal proceeds	20	120	(100 + 20)

We can see that the cumulative cash flows become positive at the end of the third year. Had we assumed that the cash flows arise evenly over the year, the precise payback period would be:

$$2 \text{ years} + (40/60) = 2^2/_3 \text{ years}$$

(where 40 represents the cash flow still required at the beginning of the third year to repay the initial outlay, and 60 is the projected cash flow during the third year). Again we must ask how to decide whether $2^2/_3$ years is acceptable. A manager using PP would need to have a minimum payback period in mind. For example, if Billingsgate Battery had a minimum payback period of three years it would accept the project, but it would not go ahead if its minimum payback period were two years. If two competing projects both met the minimum payback period requirement, the decision maker should select the project with the shorter payback period.

Activity 8.5

What is the payback period of the Chaotic Industries project from Activity 8.2?

→

Activity 8.5 continued

The inflows and outflows are expected to be:

Time		Net cash flows £000	Cumulative net cash flows £000	
Immediately	Cost of vans	(150)	(150)	
1 year's time	Net saving before depreciation	30	(120)	(−150 + 30)
2 years' time	Net saving before depreciation	30	(90)	(−120 + 30)
3 years' time	Net saving before depreciation	30	(60)	(−90 + 30)
4 years' time	Net saving before depreciation	30	(30)	(−60 + 30)
5 years' time	Net saving before depreciation	30	0	(−30 + 30)
6 years' time	Net saving before depreciation	30	30	(0 + 30)
6 years' time	Disposal proceeds from the vans	30	60	(30 + 30)

The payback period here is five years; that is, it is not until the end of the fifth year that the vans will pay for themselves out of the savings that they are expected to generate.

The PP approach has certain advantages. It is quick and easy to calculate, and can be easily understood by managers. The logic of using PP is that projects that can recoup their cost quickly are economically more attractive than those with longer payback periods, that is, PP emphasises liquidity. PP is probably an improvement on ARR in respect of the timing of the cash flows. PP is not, however, the whole answer to the problem.

Problems with PP

Activity 8.6

In what respect, in your opinion, is PP not the whole answer as a means of assessing investment opportunities? Consider the cash flows arising from three competing projects:

Time		Project 1 £000	Project 2 £000	Project 3 £000
Immediately	Cost of machine	(200)	(200)	(200)
1 year's time	Net profit before depreciation	40	10	80
2 years' time	Net profit before depreciation	80	20	100
3 years' time	Net profit before depreciation	80	170	20
4 years' time	Net profit before depreciation	60	20	200
5 years' time	Net profit before depreciation	40	10	500
5 years' time	Disposal proceeds	40	10	20

Hint: Again, the defect is not concerned with the ability of the manager to forecast future events. This is a problem, but it is a problem whatever approach we take.

Any rational manager would prefer Project 3 to either of the other two projects, yet PP sees all three of them as being equally attractive in that they all have a three-year payback period. The method cannot distinguish between those projects that pay back a significant amount early in the three-year payback period and those that do not. Project 3 is by far the best bet because the cash flows come in earlier (most of the cost of the machine has been repaid by the end of the second year) and they are greater in total, yet PP could not identify it as the best.

The cumulative cash flows of each project in Activity 8.6 are set out in Figure 8.1.

Figure 8.1	The cumulative cash flows of each project in Activity 8.6

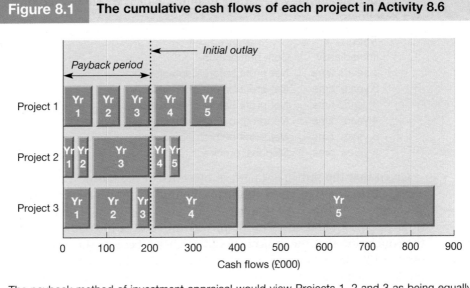

The payback method of investment appraisal would view Projects 1, 2 and 3 as being equally attractive. In doing so, the method completely ignores the fact that Project 3 provides the pay-back cash earlier in the three-year period and goes on to generate large benefits in later years.

Within the payback period, PP ignores the timing of the cash flows. Beyond the payback period, the method totally ignores both the size and the timing of the cash flows. While ignoring cash flows beyond the payback period neatly avoids the practical problems of forecasting cash flows over a long period, it means that crucial information may also be ignored.

The PP approach is often seen as a means of dealing with the problem of risk by favouring projects with a short payback period. However, this is a fairly crude approach to the problem. Also it only looks at the risk that the project will end earlier than expected. This is only one of many risk areas. For example, what about the risk that the demand for the product may be less than expected? There are more systematic approaches to dealing with risk that can be used and we shall look at these later in the chapter.

It seems that PP has the advantage of taking some note of the timing of the costs and benefits from the project. Its key deficiency, however, is that it is not linked to promoting increases in the wealth of the business. PP will tend to recommend under-taking projects that pay for themselves quickly. As we saw earlier, ARR ignores timing to a great extent, but it does take account of all benefits and costs. What we really need to help us to make sensible decisions is a method of appraisal that takes account of all of the costs and benefits of each investment opportunity, but which also makes a logical allowance for the timing of those costs and benefits.

Net present value (NPV)

To make sensible investment decisions, we need a method of appraisal that:

● considers *all* of the costs and benefits of each investment opportunity; and
● makes a logical allowance for the *timing* of those costs and benefits.

The **net present value (NPV)** method provides us with this.

Consider the Billingsgate Battery example, which we should recall can be summarised as follows:

Time		£000
Immediately	Cost of machine	(100)
1 year's time	Net profit before depreciation	20
2 years' time	Net profit before depreciation	40
3 years' time	Net profit before depreciation	60
4 years' time	Net profit before depreciation	60
5 years' time	Net profit before depreciation	20
5 years' time	Disposal proceeds	20

Given that the principal financial objective of the business is to increase wealth, it would be very easy to assess this investment if all of the cash flows were to occur now (all at the same time). All that we should need to do would be to add up the benefits (total £220,000) and compare them with the cost (£100,000). This would lead us to the conclusion that the project should go ahead, because the business would be better off by £120,000. Of course, it is not as easy as this, because time is involved. The cash outflow (payment) will occur immediately if the project is undertaken. The inflows (receipts) will arise at a range of later times.

The time factor arises because normally people do not see £100 paid out now as equivalent in value to £100 receivable in a year's time. If we were to be offered £100 in 12 months' time, provided that we paid £100 now, we should not be prepared to do so, unless we wished to do someone (perhaps a friend or relation) a favour.

Activity 8.7

Why would you see £100 to be received in a year's time as unequal in value to £100 to be paid immediately? (There are basically three reasons.)

The reasons are:

- interest lost
- risk
- effects of inflation.

We shall now take a closer look at these three reasons in turn.

Interest lost

If we are to be deprived for a year of the opportunity to spend our money, we could equally well be deprived of its use by placing it on deposit in a bank or building society. In this case, at the end of the year we could have our money back and have interest as well. Thus, unless the opportunity to invest will offer similar returns, we shall be incurring an *opportunity cost*. An opportunity cost occurs where one course of action, for example making an investment in, say, a computer, deprives us of the opportunity to derive some benefit from an alternative action, for example putting the money in the bank.

From this we can see that any investment opportunity must, if it is to make us wealthiest, do better than the returns that are available from the next best opportunity.

Thus, if Billingsgate Battery Company sees putting the money in the bank on deposit as the alternative to investment in the machine, the return from investing in the machine must be better than that from investing in the bank. If the bank offered a better return, the business would become wealthier by putting the money on deposit.

Risk

Buying a machine to manufacture a product, or to provide a service, to be sold in the market, on the strength of various estimates made in advance of buying the machine, exposes the business to **risk**. Things may not turn out as expected.

Activity 8.8

Can you suggest some areas where things could go other than according to plan in the Billingsgate Battery Company example?

We have come up with the following:

● The machine might not work as well as expected; it might break down, leading to loss of the service.
● Sales of the product or service may not be as buoyant as expected.
● Labour costs may prove to be higher than was expected.
● The sale proceeds of the machine could prove to be less than was estimated.

It is important to remember that the decision as to whether or not to invest in the machine must be taken *before* any of these things are known. It is only after the machine has been purchased that we could discover that the level of sales, which had been estimated before the event, is not going to be achieved. It is not possible to wait until we know for certain whether the market is behaving as we expected before we buy the machine. We can study reports and analyses of the market. We can commission sophisticated market surveys, and these may give us more confidence in the likely outcome. We can advertise strongly and try to expand sales. Ultimately, however, we have to decide whether or not to jump off into the dark and accept the risk if we want the opportunity to make profitable investments.

Normally, people expect to receive greater returns where they perceive risk to be a factor. Examples of this in real life are not difficult to find. One such example is that banks tend to charge higher rates of interest to borrowers whom the bank perceives as more risky. Those who can offer good security for a loan and who can point to a regular source of income tend to be charged fairly low rates of interest.

Going back to Billingsgate Battery Company's investment opportunity, it is not enough to say that we should not advise making the investment unless the returns from it are higher than those from investing in a bank deposit. Clearly we should want returns above the level of bank deposit interest rates, because the logical equivalent to investing in the machine is not putting the money on deposit but making an alternative investment that is risky.

In practice, we tend to expect a higher rate of return from investment projects where the risk is perceived as being higher. How risky a particular project is, and therefore how large this **risk premium** should be, are matters that are difficult to handle. In practice, it is necessary to make some judgement on these questions.

Inflation

If we are to be deprived of £100 for a year, when we come to spend that money it will not buy as many goods and services as it would have done a year earlier. Generally, we shall not be able to buy as many tins of baked beans or loaves of bread or bus tickets as we could have done a year earlier, because of the loss in the purchasing power of money, or **inflation**, that occurs over time. Clearly, the investor needs this loss of purchasing power to be compensated for if the investment is to be made. This is on top of a return that takes account of what could have been gained from an alternative investment of similar risk.

In practice, interest rates observable in the market tend to take inflation into account. Rates that are offered to potential building society and bank depositors include an allowance for the rate of inflation that is expected in the future.

Actions of a logical investor

To summarise these factors, we can say that the logical investor, who is seeking to increase his or her wealth, will only be prepared to make investments that will compensate for the loss of interest and purchasing power of the money invested and for the fact that the returns expected may not materialise (risk). This is usually assessed by seeing whether the proposed investment will yield a return that is greater than the basic rate of interest (which would include an allowance for inflation) plus a risk premium. These three factors (interest lost, risk and inflation) are set out in Figure 8.2.

Naturally, investors need at least the minimum returns before they are prepared to invest. However, it is in terms of the effect on their wealth that they should logically assess an investment. Usually it is the investment with the highest percentage return that will maximise the investor's wealth, but we shall see later in the chapter that this is not always so. For the time being, therefore, we shall concentrate on wealth.

Let us now return to the Billingsgate Battery Company example and assume that instead of making this investment the business could make an alternative investment with similar risk and obtain a return of 20 per cent a year.

We should recall that we have seen that it is not sufficient just to compare the basic cash flow figures for the investment. It would therefore be useful if we could express

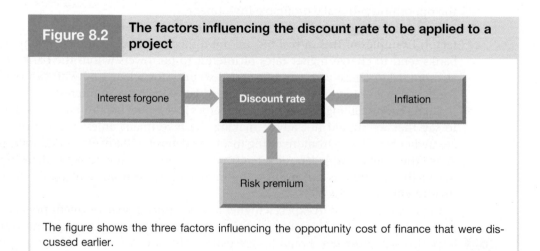

Figure 8.2 **The factors influencing the discount rate to be applied to a project**

The figure shows the three factors influencing the opportunity cost of finance that were discussed earlier.

each of these cash flows in similar terms, so that we could make a direct comparison between the sum of the inflows over time and the immediate £100,000 investment. Fortunately, we can do this.

Activity 8.9

We know that Billingsgate Battery Company could alternatively invest its money at a rate of 20 per cent a year. How much do you judge the present (immediate) value of the expected first year receipt of £20,000 to be? In other words, if instead of having to wait a year for the £20,000, and being deprived of the opportunity to invest it at 20 per cent, you could have some money now, what sum to be received now would you regard as exactly equivalent to getting £20,000, but having to wait a year for it?

We should obviously be happy to accept a lower amount if we could get it immediately than if we had to wait a year. This is because we could invest it at 20% (in the alternative project). Logically, we should be prepared to accept the amount that, with a year's income, will grow to £20,000. If we call this amount PV (for present value) we can say:

$$PV + (PV \times 20\%) = £20,000$$

that is, the amount plus income from investing the amount for the year equals the £20,000.
If we rearrange this equation we find:

$$PV \times (1 + 0.2) = £20,000$$

Note that 0.2 is the same as 20 per cent, but expressed as a decimal.
Further rearranging gives:

$$PV = £20,000/(1 + 0.2)$$
$$PV = £16,667$$

Thus, rational investors who have the opportunity to invest at 20 per cent a year would not mind whether they have £16,667 now or £20,000 in a year's time. In this sense we can say that, given a 20 per cent investment opportunity, the present value of £20,000 to be received in one year's time is £16,667.

If we could derive the present value (PV) of each of the cash flows associated with Billingsgate's machine investment, we could easily make the direct comparison between the cost of making the investment (£100,000) and the various benefits that will derive from it in years 1 to 5. Fortunately we can do precisely this.

We can make a more general statement about the PV of a particular cash flow. It is:

$$\text{PV of the cash flow of year } n = \frac{\text{Actual cash flow of year } n}{(1 + r)^n}$$

where:
n is the year of the cash flow (that is, how many years into the future), and
r is the opportunity investing rate expressed as a decimal (instead of as a percentage).

We have already seen how this works for the £20,000 inflow for year 1. For year 2 the calculation would be:

$$\text{PV of year 2 cash flow (that is, £40,000)} = £40,000/(1 + 0.2)^2$$
$$PV = £40,000/(1.2)^2 = £40,000/1.44 = £27,778$$

Thus the present value of the £40,000 to be received in two years' time is £27,778.

Activity 8.10

See if you can show that an investor would be indifferent to £27,778 receivable now, or £40,000 receivable in two years' time, assuming that there is a 20 per cent investment opportunity.

The reasoning goes like this:

	£
Amount available for immediate investment	27,778
Add Interest for year 1 (20% × 27,778)	5,556
	33,334
Add Interest for year 2 (20% × 33,334)	6,667
	40,001

(The extra £1 is only a rounding error.)

Thus, because the investor can turn £27,778 into £40,000 in two years, these amounts are equivalent. We can say that £27,778 is the present value of £40,000 receivable after two years (given a 20 per cent rate of return).

Now let us deduce the present values of all of the cash flows associated with the Billingsgate machine project and hence the *net present value* of the project as a whole. The relevant cash flows and calculations are as follows:

Time	Cash flow £000	Calculation of PV	PV £000
Immediately (time 0)	(100)	$(100)/(1 + 0.2)^0$	(100.00)
1 year's time	20	$20/(1 + 0.2)^1$	16.67
2 years' time	40	$40/(1 + 0.2)^2$	27.78
3 years' time	60	$60/(1 + 0.2)^3$	34.72
4 years' time	60	$60/(1 + 0.2)^4$	28.94
5 years' time	20	$20/(1 + 0.2)^5$	8.04
5 years' time	20	$20/(1 + 0.2)^5$	8.04
			24.19

(Note that $(1 + 0.2)^0 = 1$)

Once again, we must ask how we can decide whether the machine project is acceptable to the business. In fact, the decision rule is simple. If the NPV is positive we accept the project; if it is negative we reject the project. In this case, the NPV is positive, so we accept the project and buy the machine.

Investing in the machine will make the business £24,190 better off. What the above is saying is that the benefits from investing in this machine are worth a total of £124,190 today. Since the business can 'buy' these benefits for just £100,000, the investment should be made. If, however, the benefits were below £100,000 they would be less than the cost of 'buying' them.

Activity 8.11

What is the *maximum* the Billingsgate Battery Company would be prepared to pay for the machine, given the potential benefits of owning it?

The business would be prepared to pay up to £124,190 since the wealth of the owners of the business would be increased up to this price – though the business would prefer to pay as little as possible.

Using discount tables

Deducing the present values of the various cash flows is a little laborious using the approach that we have just taken. To deduce each PV we took the relevant cash flow and multiplied it by $1/(1 + r)^n$. Fortunately, there is a quicker way. Tables exist that show values of this **discount factor** for a range of values of r and n. Such a table appears at the end of this book in Appendix D. Take a look at it.

Look at the column for 20 per cent and the row for one year. We find that the factor is 0.833. Thus the PV of a cash flow of £1 receivable in one year is £0.833. So a cash flow of £20,000 receivable in one year's time is £16,660 (that is, $0.833 \times £20,000$), the same result as we found doing it in longhand.

Activity 8.12

What is the NPV of the Chaotic Industries project from Activity 8.2, assuming a 15 per cent opportunity cost of finance (discount rate)? You should use the discount table.

Remember that the inflows and outflow are expected to be:

Time		£000
Immediately	Cost of vans	(150)
1 year's time	Net saving before depreciation	30
2 years' time	Net saving before depreciation	30
3 years' time	Net saving before depreciation	30
4 years' time	Net saving before depreciation	30
5 years' time	Net saving before depreciation	30
6 years' time	Net saving before depreciation	30
6 years' time	Disposal proceeds from the vans	30

The calculation of the NPV of the project is as follows:

Time	Cash flows	Discount factor (15% – from the table)	Present value
	£000		£000
Immediately	(150)	1.000	(150.00)
1 year's time	30	0.870	26.10
2 years' time	30	0.756	22.68
3 years' time	30	0.658	19.74
4 years' time	30	0.572	17.16
5 years' time	30	0.497	14.91
6 years' time	30	0.432	12.96
6 years' time	30	0.432	12.96
		Net present value	(23.49)

Activity 8.13

How would you interpret the result in Activity 8.12?

The fact that the project has a negative NPV means that the present values of the benefits from the investment are worth less than the cost of entering into it. Any cost up to £126,510 (the present value of the benefits) would be worth paying, but not £150,000.

The discount tables reveal how the value of £1 diminishes as its receipt goes further into the future. Assuming an opportunity cost of finance of 20 per cent a year, £1 to be received immediately, obviously, has a present value of £1. However, as the time before it is to be received extends, the present value diminishes significantly, as is shown in Figure 8.3.

Figure 8.3	Present value of £1 receivable at various times in the future, assuming an annual financing cost of 20 per cent

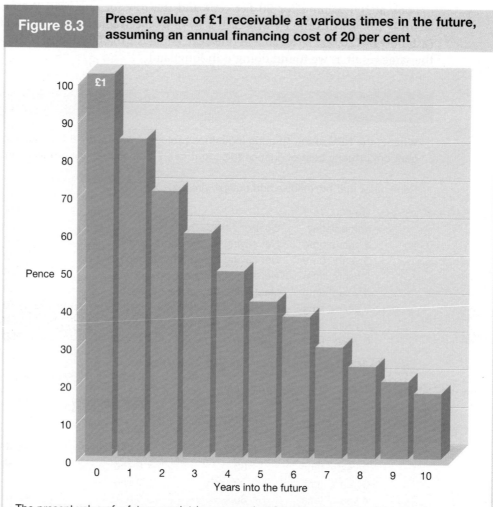

The present value of a future receipt (or payment) of £1 depends on how far in the future it will occur. Those that will occur in the near future will have a larger present value than those whose occurrence is more distant in time.

The discount rate and the cost of capital

We have seen that the appropriate discount rate to use in NPV assessments is the opportunity cost of finance. This is, in effect, the cost to the business of the finance that it will use to finance the investment, should it go ahead. This will normally be the cost of the mixture of funds (shareholders' funds and borrowings) used by the business and is usually known as the cost of capital.

Why NPV is superior to ARR and PP

From what we have seen, NPV seems to be a better method of appraising investment opportunities than either ARR or PP, because it fully takes account of each of the following:

- *The timing of the cash flows.* By discounting the various cash flows associated with each project according to when it is expected to arise, the fact that cash flows do not all occur simultaneously is taken into account by NPV. Associated with this is the fact that by discounting, using the opportunity cost of finance (that is, the return that the next best alternative opportunity would generate), the net benefit after financing costs have been met is identified (as the NPV of the project).
- *The whole of the relevant cash flows.* NPV includes all of the relevant cash flows, irrespective of when they are expected to occur. It treats them differently according to their date of occurrence, but they are all taken into account in the NPV, and they all have an influence on the decision.
- *The objectives of the business.* NPV is the only method of appraisal in which the output of the analysis has a direct bearing on the wealth of the business. (Positive NPVs enhance wealth; negative ones reduce it.) Since most private sector businesses seek to maximise shareholders' wealth, NPV is superior to the methods previously discussed.

We saw earlier that a business should take on all projects with positive NPVs, when their cash flows are discounted at the opportunity cost of finance. Where a choice has to be made among projects, a business should normally select the one with the highest NPV.

Internal rate of return (IRR)

This is the last of the four major methods of investment appraisal that are found in practice. It is quite closely related to the NPV method in that, like NPV, it also involves discounting future cash flows. The **internal rate of return** of a particular investment is the discount rate that, when applied to its future cash flows, will produce an NPV of precisely zero. In essence, it represents the yield from the project.

We should recall that when we discounted the cash flows of the Billingsgate Battery Company machine investment opportunity at 20 per cent, we found that the NPV was a positive figure of £24,190 (see p. 226).

Activity 8.14

What does the NPV of the machine project (that is, £24,190 (positive)) tell us about the rate of return that the investment will yield for the business?

The fact that the NPV is positive when discounting at 20 per cent implies that the rate of return that the project generates is more than 20 per cent. The fact that the NPV is a pretty large figure implies that the actual rate of return is quite a lot above 20 per cent. We should expect increasing the size of the discount rate to reduce NPV, because a higher discount rate gives a lower discounted figure.

It is somewhat laborious to deduce the IRR by hand, since it cannot usually be calculated directly. Thus iteration (trial and error) is the only approach. Fortunately computer spreadsheet packages can deduce the IRR with ease. The package will also use a trial and error approach, but at high speed.

Let us try a higher rate (say, 30 per cent) and see what happens:

Time	Cash flow	Discount factor	PV
	£000	30%	£000
Immediately (time 0)	(100)	1.000	(100.00)
1 year's time	20	0.769	15.38
2 years' time	40	0.592	23.68
3 years' time	60	0.455	27.30
4 years' time	60	0.350	21.00
5 years' time	20	0.269	5.38
5 years' time	20	0.269	5.38
			(1.88)

In increasing the discount rate from 20 per cent to 30 per cent, we have reduced the NPV from £24,190 (positive) to £1,880 (negative). Since the IRR is the discount rate that will give us an NPV of exactly zero, we can conclude that the IRR of Billingsgate Battery Company's machine project is very slightly below 30 per cent. Further trials could lead us to the exact rate, but there is probably not much point, given the likely inaccuracy of the cash flow estimates. It is probably good enough, for practical purposes, to say that the IRR is about 30 per cent.

The relationship between the NPV method discussed earlier and the IRR is shown graphically in Figure 8.4 using the information relating to the Billingsgate Battery Company.

Figure 8.4   The relationship between the NPV and IRR methods

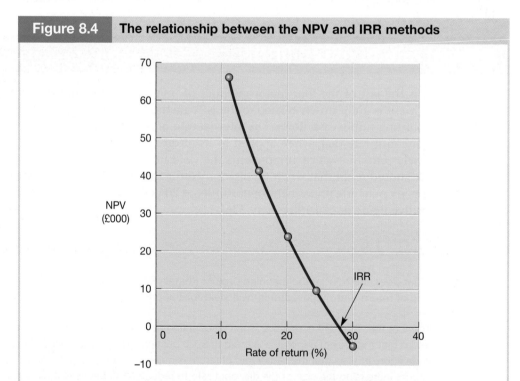

If the discount rate were zero, the NPV would be the sum of the net cash flows. In other words, no account would be taken of the time value of money. However, if we assume increasing discount rates, there is a corresponding decrease in the NPV of the project. When the NPV line crosses the horizontal axis there will be a zero NPV, and the point where it crosses is the IRR.

We can see that, where the discount rate is zero, the NPV will be the sum of the net cash flows. In other words, no account is taken of the time value of money. However, as the discount rate increases there is a corresponding decrease in the NPV of the project. When the NPV line crosses the horizontal axis there will be a zero NPV, and that represents the IRR.

Activity 8.15

What is the internal rate of return of the Chaotic Industries project from Activity 8.2 You should use the discount table at the end of the book.

Hint: Remember that you already know the NPV of this project at 15 per cent.

Since we know (from Activity 8.12) that, at a 15 per cent discount rate, the NPV is a relatively large negative figure, our next trial is using a lower discount rate, say 10 per cent:

Time	Cash flows £000	Discount factor (10% – from the table)	Present value £000
Immediately	(150)	1.000	(150.00)
1 year's time	30	0.909	27.27
2 years' time	30	0.826	24.78
3 years' time	30	0.751	22.53
4 years' time	30	0.683	20.49
5 years' time	30	0.621	18.63
6 years' time	30	0.565	16.95
6 years' time	30	0.565	16.95
		Net present value	(2.40)

We can see that NPV increased by about £21,000 (£23,490 – £2,400) for a 5 per cent drop in the discount rate: that is, about £4,200 for each 1 per cent. We need to know the discount rate for a zero NPV: that is, a fall in the negative NPV of a further £2,400. This logically would be roughly 0.6 per cent (that is, 2,400/4,200). Thus the IRR is close to 9.4 per cent. However, to say that the IRR is about 9 per cent is near enough for most purposes.

Users of the IRR approach should apply the following decision rules:

● For any project to be acceptable, it must meet a minimum IRR requirement. Logically, this minimum should be the opportunity cost of finance.
● Where there are competing projects (for example, the business can choose one of the projects only), the one with the higher or highest IRR would be selected.

IRR has certain attributes in common with NPV. All cash flows are taken into account, and their timing is logically handled.

Problems with IRR

The main disadvantage of IRR is the fact that it does not correctly address the question of wealth generation. It could therefore lead to the wrong decision being made. This is because IRR would, for example always see an IRR of 25 per cent being preferable to one of 20 per cent, assuming an opportunity cost of finance of, say, 15 per cent. Though this may well lead to the project being taken that could most effectively increase wealth, this may not always be the case, because IRR completely ignores the *scale of investment*. With a 15 per cent cost of finance, £15 million invested at 20 per cent (that is, $15 \times (20 - 15\%) = 0.75$) would make us richer than £5 million invested at 25 per cent (that is, $5 \times (25 - 15\%) = 0.50$). IRR does not recognise this. This problem with percentages is another example illustrated by the Mexican road discussed in Real World 8.3. It should be acknowledged that it is not usual for projects to be competing where there is such a large difference in scale. Even though the problem may be rare and so, typically, IRR will give the same signal as NPV, a method (NPV) that is always reliable must be better to use than IRR.

A further problem with the IRR method is that it has difficulty handling projects with unconventional cash flows. In the examples studied so far, each project has a negative cash flow arising at the start of its life and then positive cash flows thereafter. However, in some cases, a project may have both positive and negative cash flows at future points in its life. Such a pattern of cash flows can result in there being more than one IRR, or even no IRR at all.

Some practical points

When undertaking an investment appraisal, there are several practical points that we should bear in mind:

- *Relevant costs.* As with all decision making, we should only take account of cash flows that vary according to the decision in our analysis. Thus, cash flows that will be the same, irrespective of the decision under review, should be ignored. For example, overheads that will be incurred in equal amount whether or not the investment is made, should be ignored despite the fact that the investment could not be made without the infrastructure that the overhead costs create. Similarly, past costs should be ignored as they are not affected by, and do not vary with, the decision.
- *Opportunity costs.* Opportunity costs arising from benefits forgone must be taken into account. Thus, for example, when considering a decision concerning whether or not to continue to use a machine already owned by the business, the realisable value of the machine might be an important opportunity cost.
- *Taxation.* Tax will usually be affected by an investment decision. The profits will be taxed, the capital investment may attract tax relief, and so on. Tax is levied on these at significant rates. This means that, in real life, unless tax is formally taken into account, the wrong decision could easily be made.
- *Cash flows not profit flows.* We have seen that for the NPV, IRR and PP methods, it is cash flows rather than profit flows that are relevant to the evaluation of investment projects. In a problem requiring the application of any of these methods we may be given details of the profits for the investment period, and shall need to adjust these in order to derive the cash flows. Remember, the net profit before depreciation is an approximation to the cash flows for the period, and so we should work back to this figure.

When the figures are expressed in profit rather than cash flow terms, an adjustment for working capital may also be necessary. Some adjustment should be made to take account of changes to working capital. For example, launching a new product may give rise to an increase in the net cash investment made in trade debtors (receivables), stock (inventories) and trade creditors (payables), requiring an immediate outlay of cash. This outlay for additional working capital should be shown in the NPV calculations as part of the initial cost. However, at the end of the life of the project, the additional working capital will be released. The resulting inflow of cash at the end of the life of the project should also be taken into account.

- *Interest payments.* When using discounted cash flow techniques, interest payments should not be taken into account in deriving the cash flows for the period. The discount factor already takes account of the costs of financing, so to take account of interest charges in deriving cash flows for the period would be double counting.
- *Other factors.* Investment decision making must not be viewed as simply a mechanical exercise. The results derived from a particular investment appraisal method will be only one input to the decision-making process. There may be broader issues connected to the decision that have to be taken into account, but which may be difficult or impossible to quantify. The reliability of the forecasts and the validity of the assumptions used in the evaluation will also have a bearing on the final decision.

Activity 8.16

The directors of Manuff (Steel) Ltd are considering closing one of the business's factories. There has been a reduction in the demand for the products made at the factory in recent years, and the directors are not optimistic about the long-term prospects for these products. The factory is situated in an area where unemployment is high.

The factory is leased, and there are still four years of the lease remaining. The directors are uncertain as to whether the factory should be closed immediately or at the end of the period of the lease. Another business has offered to sublease the premises from Manuff Steel Ltd at a rental of £40,000 a year for the remainder of the lease period.

The machinery and equipment at the factory cost £1,500,000, and have a balance sheet value of £400,000. In the event of immediate closure, the machinery and equipment could be sold for £220,000. The working capital at the factory is £420,000, and could be liquidated for that amount immediately, if required. Alternatively, the working capital can be liquidated in full at the end of the lease period. Immediate closure would result in redundancy payments to employees of £180,000.

If the factory continues in operation until the end of the lease period, the following operating profits (losses) are expected:

	Year 1 £000	Year 2 £000	Year 3 £000	Year 4 £000
Operating profit (loss)	160	(40)	30	20

The above figures include a charge of £90,000 a year for depreciation of machinery and equipment. The residual value of the machinery and equipment at the end of the lease period is estimated at £40,000.

Redundancy payments are expected to be £150,000 at the end of the lease period if the factory continues in operation. The business has an annual cost of capital of 12 per cent. Ignore taxation.

Required:
(a) Determine the relevant cash flows arising from a decision to continue operations until the end of the lease period rather than to close immediately.
(b) Calculate the net present value of continuing operations until the end of the lease period, rather than closing immediately.
(c) What other factors might the directors take into account before making a final decision on the timing of the factory closure?
(d) State, with reasons, whether or not the business should continue to operate the factory until the end of the lease period.

→

Activity 8.16 continued

Your answer to this activity should be as follows:

(a)　Relevant cash flows

			Years		
	0	1	2	3	4
	£000	£000	£000	£000	£000
Operating cash flows (Note 1)		250	50	120	110
Sale of machinery (Note 2)	(220)				40
Redundancy costs (Note 3)	180				(150)
Sublease rentals (Note 4)		(40)	(40)	(40)	(40)
Working capital invested (Note 5)	(420)				420
	(460)	210	10	80	380

Notes:

1　Each year's operating cash flow is calculated by adding back the depreciation charge for the year to the operating profit for the year. In the case of the operating loss, the depreciation charge is deducted.

2　In the event of closure, machinery could be sold immediately. Thus an opportunity cost of £220,000 is incurred if operations continue.

3　By continuing operations, there will be a saving in immediate redundancy costs of £180,000. However, redundancy costs of £150,000 will be paid in four years' time.

4　By continuing operations, the opportunity to sublease the factory will be forgone.

5　Immediate closure would mean that working capital could be liquidated. By continuing operations this opportunity is forgone. However, working capital can be liquidated in four years' time.

(b)

Discount rate 12%	1.000	0.893	0.797	0.712	0.636
Present value	(460)	187.5	8.0	57.0	241.7
Net present value	34.2				

(c)　Other factors that may influence the decision include:

● *The overall strategy of the business.* The business may need to set the decision within a broader context. It may be necessary to manufacture the products made at the factory because they are an integral part of the business's product range. The business may wish to avoid redundancies in an area of high unemployment for as long as possible.

● *Flexibility.* A decision to close the factory is probably irreversible. If the factory continues, however, there may be a chance that the prospects for the factory will brighten in the future.

● *Creditworthiness of sublessee.* The business should investigate the creditworthiness of the sublessee. Failure to receive the expected sublease payments would make the closure option far less attractive.

● *Accuracy of forecasts.* The forecasts made by the business should be examined carefully. Inaccuracies in the forecasts or any underlying assumptions may change the expected outcomes.

(d)　The NPV of the decision to continue operations rather than close immediately is positive. Hence, shareholders would be better off if the directors took this course of action. The factory should therefore continue in operation rather than close down. This decision is likely to be welcomed by employees and would allow the business to maintain its flexibility.

Self-assessment question 8.1

Beacon Chemicals plc is considering buying some equipment to produce a chemical named X14. The new equipment's capital cost is estimated at £100,000. If its purchase is approved now, the equipment can be bought and production can commence by the end of this year. £50,000 has already been spent on research and development work. Estimates of revenues and costs arising from the operation of the new equipment appear below:

	Year 1	Year 2	Year 3	Year 4	Year 5
Sales price (£ per litre)	100	120	120	100	80
Sales volume (litres)	800	1,000	1,200	1,000	800
Variable costs (£ per litre)	50	50	40	30	40
Fixed costs (£000)	30	30	30	30	30

If the equipment is bought, sales of some existing products will be lost, and this will result in a loss of contribution of £15,000 a year over its life.

The accountant has informed you that the fixed costs include depreciation of £20,000 a year on the new equipment. They also include an allocation of £10,000 for fixed over-heads. A separate study has indicated that if the new equipment were bought, additional overheads, excluding depreciation, arising from producing the chemical would be £8,000 a year. Production would require additional working capital of £30,000.

For the purposes of your initial calculations ignore taxation.

Required:
(a) Deduce the relevant annual cash flows associated with buying the equipment.
(b) Deduce the payback period.
(c) Calculate the net present value using a discount rate of 8 per cent.

Hint: You should deal with the investment in working capital by treating it as a cash outflow at the start of the project and an inflow at the end.

Investment appraisal in practice

Many surveys have been conducted in the UK into the methods of investment appraisal used in practice. They have tended to show the following features:

- businesses using more than one method to assess each investment decision, increasingly so over time;
- an increased use of the discounting methods (NPV and IRR) over time, with these two becoming the most popular in recent years;
- continued popularity of ARR and PP, despite their theoretical shortcomings and the rise in popularity of the discounting methods;
- a tendency for larger businesses to use the discounting methods and to use more than one method in respect of each decision.

Real World 8.4 shows the results of the most recent (1997) survey conducted of UK businesses regarding their use of investment appraisal methods.

REAL WORLD 8.4

A survey of UK business practice

Method	Percentage of businesses using the method
Net present value	80
Internal rate of return	81
Payback period	70
Accounting rate of return	56
	287

Source: Arnold and Hatzopoulos (see reference 2 at the end of the chapter). Reproduced by kind permission of Blackwell Publishing Ltd.

Activity 8.17

How do you explain the popularity of the PP method, given the theoretical limitations discussed earlier in this chapter?

A number of possible reasons may explain this finding:

- PP is easy to understand and use.
- It can avoid the problems of forecasting far into the future.
- It gives emphasis to the early cash flows when there is greater certainty concerning the accuracy of their predicted value.
- It emphasises the importance of liquidity. Where a business has liquidity problems, a short payback period for a project is likely to appear attractive.

PP can provide a convenient, though rough and ready, assessment of the profitability of a project, in the way that it is used in **Real World 8.5**.

REAL WORLD 8.5

Space to earn

SES Global is the world's largest commercial satellite operator. This means that it rents satellite capacity to broadcasters, governments, telecommunications groups and Internet service providers. It is a risky venture that few are prepared to undertake. As a result, a handful of businesses dominate the market.

Launching a satellite requires a huge initial outlay of capital, but relatively small cash outflows following the launch. Revenues only start to flow once the satellite is in orbit. A satellite launch costs around €250m. The main elements of this cost are the satellite (€120m), the launch vehicle (€80m), insurance (€40m) and ground equipment (€10m).

According to Romain Bausch, president and chief executive of SES Global, it takes three years to build and launch a satellite. However, the average lifetime of a satellite is fifteen years during which time it is generating revenues. The revenues generated are such that the payback period is around four to five years.

Source: Based on information from 'Satellites need space to earn Tim Burt', FT.com, 14 July 2003.

The popularity of PP may suggest a lack of sophistication among managers concerning investment appraisal. This criticism is most often made against managers of smaller business. In fact, the Arnold and Hatzopoulos and other surveys found that smaller businesses were much less likely to use discounted cash flow methods (NPV and IRR) than larger businesses.

IRR may be as popular as NPV, despite IRR's theoretical weaknesses, because it expresses outcomes in percentage terms rather than in absolute terms. This form of expression appears to be more acceptable to managers. This may be because managers are used to using percentage figures as targets (for example, return on capital employed).

The sum of percentage usage for each appraisal method is 287 per cent (see Real World 8.4), which indicates that many businesses use more than one method to appraise investments. Real World 8.4 suggests that most businesses use one of the two discounted cash flow methods.

Generally, survey evidence has shown a strong increase in the rate of usage of both NPV and IRR, in the UK, over the years.

Real World 8.6 shows extracts from the 2002 annual report of a well-known business: Rolls-Royce plc, the builder of engines for aircraft and other purposes.

REAL WORLD 8.6

The use of NPV at Rolls-Royce

In its 2002 annual report, Rolls-Royce said:

> The Group continues to subject all investments to rigorous examination of risks and future cash flows to ensure that they create shareholder value. All major investments require Board approval.
> The Group has a portfolio of projects at different stages of their life cycles. Discounted cash flow analysis of the remaining life of projects is performed on a regular basis.

Source: Rolls-Royce plc Annual Report 2002.

Rolls-Royce makes clear that it uses NPV (the report refers to creating shareholder value and to discounted cash flow, which strongly implies NPV). It is interesting to note that Rolls-Royce not only assesses new projects, but also reassesses existing ones. This must be a sensible commercial approach. Businesses should not continue with existing projects unless those projects have a positive NPV based on future cash flows. Just because a project seemed to have a positive NPV before it started does not mean that this will persist, in the light of changing circumstances. Activity 8.16 (p. 233) considered a decision to close down a project.

Dealing with risk in investment appraisal

We have already considered the fact that risk – the likelihood that what is projected to occur will not actually happen – is an important aspect of financial decision making. It is a particularly important issue in the context of investment decisions, because of:

1 The relatively long timescales involved. There is more time for things to go wrong between the decision being made and the end of the project.
2 The size of the investment. If things go wrong, the impact can be both significant and lasting.

Various approaches to dealing with risk have been proposed. These fall into two categories: assessing the level of risk and reacting to the level of risk. We now consider formal methods of dealing with risk that fall within each category.

Assessing the level of risk

Sensitivity analysis

One popular way of attempting to assess the level of risk is to carry out a **sensitivity analysis** on the proposed project. This involves an examination of the key input values affecting the project to see how changes in each input might influence the viability of the project.

Firstly, the investment is appraised, using the best estimates for each of the input factors (for example, labour cost, material cost, discount rate and so on). Assuming that the NPV is positive, each input value is then examined to see how far the estimated figure could be changed before the project becomes unviable for that reason alone. Let us suppose that the NPV for an investment in a machine to provide a particular service, is a positive value of £50,000. If we were to carry out a sensitivity analysis on this project, we should consider in turn each of the key input factors: cost of the machine, sales volume and price, relevant labour costs, length of the project and the discount rate. We should seek to find the value that each of them could have before the NPV figure would become negative (that is, the value for the factor at which NPV would be zero). The difference between the value for that factor at which the NPV would equal zero and the estimated value represents the margin of safety for that particular input. The process is set out in Figure 8.5.

A computer spreadsheet model of the project can be extremely valuable for this exercise because it then becomes a very simple matter to try various values for the input data and to see the effect of each. As a result of carrying out a sensitivity analysis,

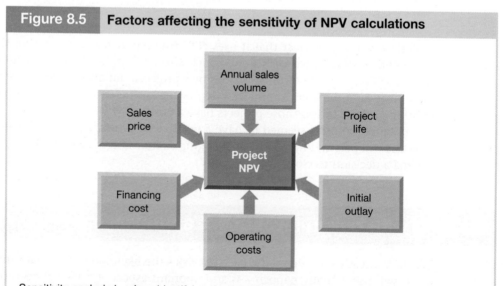

Figure 8.5　Factors affecting the sensitivity of NPV calculations

Sensitivity analysis involves identifying the key factors that affect the project. In the figure, six factors have been identified for the particular project. (In practice, the key factors are likely to vary between projects.) Once identified, each factor will be examined in turn to find the value it should have for the project to have a zero NPV.

the decision maker is able to get a 'feel' for the project, which otherwise might not be possible. The following activity can be undertaken without recourse to a spreadsheet, however.

Activity 8.18

S. Saluja (Property Developers) Ltd intends to bid at an auction, to be held today, for a manor house that has fallen into disrepair. The auctioneer believes that the house will be sold for about £450,000. The business wishes to renovate the property and to divide it into luxury flats, to be sold for £150,000 each. The renovation will be in two stages and will cover a two-year period. Stage 1 will cover the first year of the project. It will cost £500,000 and the six flats completed during this stage are expected to be sold for a total of £900,000 at the end of the first year. Stage 2 will cover the second year of the project. It will cost £300,000 and the three remaining flats are expected to be sold at the end of the second year for a total of £450,000. The cost of renovation is subject to an agreed figure with local builders; however, there is some uncertainty over the remaining input values. The business estimates its cost of capital at 12 per cent a year.

(a) What is the NPV of the proposed project?
(b) Assuming none of the other inputs deviates from the best estimates provided:
   (i)   What auction price would have to be paid for the manor house to cause the project to have a zero NPV?
   (ii) What cost of capital would cause the project to have a zero NPV?
   (iii) What is the sale price of each of the flats that would cause the project to have a zero NPV? (Each flat will be sold for the same price: £150,000.)
(c) Is the level of risk associated with the project high or low? Discuss your findings.

(a) The NPV of the proposed project is as follows:

	Cash flows £	Discount factor 12%	Present value £
Year 1 (£900,000 – £500,000)	400,000	0.893	357,200
Year 2 (£450,000 – £300,000)	150,000	0.797	119,550
Less Initial outlay			(450,000)
Net present value			26,750

(b) (i) To obtain a zero NPV, the auction price would have to be £26,750 higher than the current estimate – that is, a total price of £476,750. This is about 6 per cent above the current estimated price.
   (ii) As there is a positive NPV, the cost of capital that would cause the project to have a zero NPV must be higher than 12 per cent. Let us try 20 per cent.

	Cash flows £	Discount factor 20%	Present value £
Year 1 (£900,000 – £500,000)	400,000	0.833	333,200
Year 2 (£450,000 – £300,000)	150,000	0.694	104,100
Less Initial outlay			(450,000)
Net present value			(12,700)

→

Activity 8.18 continued

The 'break-even' cost of capital lies somewhere between 12 per cent and 20 per cent. Increasing the discount rate by 8 percentage points (from 12 per cent to 20 per cent) causes the NPV to reduce by £39,450 (from £26,750 (positive) to £12,700 (negative)). This means £4,931 (that is £39,450/8) for each 1 percentage point shift in the discount rate. At 12 per cent the NPV is £26,750 (above zero), so a discount rate of 12% + [(26,750/4,931) × 1%] = 17.4 per cent applies.

This approach is, of course, the same as that used when calculating the IRR of the project. In other words, 17.4 per cent is the IRR of the project.

(iii) To obtain a zero NPV, the sale price of each flat must be reduced so that the NPV is reduced by £26,750. In year 1, six flats are sold (in year 2, three flats are sold). The discount factor at the 12 per cent rate for year 1 is 0.893 and for year 2 is 0.797. We can derive the fall in value per flat (Y) to give a zero NPV by using the equation:

$$(6Y \times 0.893) + (3Y \times 0.797) = £26,750$$
$$Y = £3,452$$

The sale price of each flat necessary to obtain a zero NPV is therefore:

$$£150,000 - £3,452 = £146,548$$

This represents a fall in the estimated price of 2.3 per cent.

(c) These calculations indicate that the auction price would have to be about 6 per cent above the estimated price before a zero NPV is obtained. The margin of safety is, therefore, not very high for this factor. The calculations also reveal that the price of the flats would only have to fall by 2.3 per cent from the estimated price before the NPV is reduced to zero. Hence, the margin of safety for this factor is even smaller. However, the cost of capital is less sensitive to changes and there would have to be an increase from 12 per cent to 17.4 per cent before the project produced a zero NPV. It seems from the calculations that the sale price of the flats is the most sensitive factor to consider. A careful re-examination of the market value of the flats seems appropriate before a final decision is made.

There are two major drawbacks with the use of sensitivity analysis:

● It does not give managers clear decision rules concerning acceptance or rejection of the project and so they must rely on their own judgement.
● It is a static form of analysis. Only one input is considered at a time, while the rest are held constant. In practice, however, it is likely that more than one input value will differ from the best estimates provided. Even so it would be possible to deal with changes in various inputs simultaneously, were the project data put onto a spreadsheet model. This approach, where more than one variable is altered at a time, is known as **scenario building**.

Real World 8.7 below shows that it is not only the business that may carry out sensitivity analysis, or scenario building, in order to assess risk. A supplier or a lender may also use these tools to see whether the business is a credit risk.

REAL WORLD 8.7

No fear of flying

Ryanair is a low-cost airline that has enjoyed considerable success over recent years. As part of its expansion programme, the business has ordered 153 Boeing 737–800 aircraft, with an option to purchase a further 125 aircraft, over a period up to 2009. It has been reported that these aircraft cost Ryanair around $32 million each. This represents a huge order for the Boeing Corporation and, of course, a huge risk if the aircraft were built for Ryanair and the business was then unable to pay for them. Around the time of the sale agreement, therefore, Boeing decided to evaluate the future profitability of Ryanair.

Boeing prepared a computer model to test whether changes in key variables such as a fall in passenger demand, changes in currency exchange rates and a rise in aviation fuel prices would damage the profitability of the low-cost airline. Ryanair passed the tests with flying colours: the worst scenario generated was that Ryanair would break even. According to Boeing's sales director for the UK and Ireland, the Ryanair model was probably the most robust that Boeing had encountered.

Source: 'How low can you go?', *Financial Times Magazine*, 21 June 2003, and 'Ryanair: feeding time at the zoo', 11 February 2003, Research report, Goodbody Stockbrokers.

Expected net present value

Another means of assessing risk is through the use of statistical probabilities. It may be possible to identify a range of feasible values for each of the items of input data and to assign a probability of occurrence to each of these values. Using this information, we can derive an **expected net present value (ENPV)**, which is, in effect, a weighted average of the possible outcomes where the probabilities are used as weights. To illustrate this method, let us consider Example 8.2.

Example 8.2

C. Piperis (Properties) Ltd has the opportunity to acquire a lease on a block of flats that has only two years remaining before it expires. The cost of the lease would be £100,000. The occupancy rate of the block of flats is currently around 70 per cent and the flats are let almost exclusively to naval personnel. There is a large naval base located nearby, and there is little other demand for the flats. The occupancy rate of the flats will change in the remaining two years of the lease, depending on the outcome of a defence review. The navy is currently considering three options for the naval base. These are:

- *Option 1*. Increase the size of the base by closing down a base in another region and transferring the personnel to the one located near the flats.
- *Option 2*. Close down the naval base near to the flats and leave only a skeleton staff there for maintenance purposes. The personnel would be moved to a base in another region.
- *Option 3*. Leave the base open but reduce staffing levels by 20 per cent.

Example 8.2 continued

The directors of Piperis have estimated the following net cash flows for each of the two years under each option and the probability of their occurrence:

	£	*Probability*
Option 1	80,000	0.6
Option 2	12,000	0.1
Option 3	40,000	<u>0.3</u>
		<u>1.0</u>

Note that the sum of the probabilities is 1.0 (in other words it is certain that one of the possible options will arise). The business has a cost of capital of 10 per cent.
   Should the business purchase the lease on the block of flats?

Solution

To calculate the expected NPV of the proposed investment, we must first calculate the weighted average of the expected outcomes for each year where the probabilities are used as weights, by multiplying each cash flow by its probability of occurrence. Thus, the expected annual net cash flows will be:

	Cash flows	*Probability*	*Expected cash flows*
	£	£	£
	(a)	*(b)*	*(a × b)*
Option 1	80,000	0.6	48,000
Option 2	12,000	0.1	1,200
Option 3	40,000	0.3	<u>12,000</u>
Expected cash flows in each year			<u>61,200</u>

Having derived the expected annual cash flows, we can now discount these using a rate of 10 per cent to reflect the cost of capital:

Year	*Expected cash flows*	*Discount rate*	*Expected present value*
	£	*10%*	£
1	61,200	0.909	55,631
2	61,200	0.826	<u>50,551</u>
			106,182
Less Initial investment			<u>100,000</u>
Expected NPV			<u>6,182</u>

We can see that the expected NPV is positive. Hence, the wealth of shareholders is expected to increase by purchasing the lease.

   The expected NPV approach has the advantage of producing a single numerical outcome and of having a clear decision rule to apply. If the expected NPV is positive, we should invest; if it is negative, we should not.
   However, the approach produces an average figure that may not be capable of occurring. This point was illustrated in Example 8.2 where the expected NPV does not correspond to any of the stated options.
   Perhaps more importantly, using an average figure can obscure the underlying risk associated with the project. Simply deriving the ENPV, as in Example 8.2, can be

misleading. Without some idea of the individual possible outcomes and their probability of occurring, the decision maker is in the dark. In Example 8.2, were either of Options 2 and 3 to occur, the investment would be adverse (wealth destroying). It is 40 per cent probable that one of these two options will occur, so this is a significant risk. Only should Option 1 arise (60 per cent probable) would investing in the flats represent a good decision. Of course, in advance of making the investment, which option will actually occur is not known. None of this should be taken to mean that the investment in the flats should not be made, simply that the decision maker is better placed to make a judgement where information on the possible outcomes is available. This point is further illustrated by Activity 8.19.

Activity 8.19

Qingdao Manufacturing Ltd is considering two competing projects. Details are as follows:

- Project A has a 0.9 probability of producing a negative NPV of £200,000 and a 0.1 probability of producing a positive NPV of £3.8m.
- Project B has a 0.6 probability of producing a positive NPV of £100,000 and a 0.4 probability of producing a positive NPV of £350,000.

What is the expected net present value of each project?

The expected NPV of Project A is:

$$[(0.1 \times £3.8m) - (0.9 \times £200,000)] = £200,000$$

The expected NPV of Project B is:

$$[(0.6 \times £100,000) + (0.4 \times £350,000)] = £200,000$$

Although the expected NPV of each project in Activity 8.19 is identical, this does not mean that the business will be indifferent about which project to undertake. We can see from the information provided that Project A has a high probability of making a loss whereas Project B is not expected to make a loss under either possible outcome. If we assume that the shareholders dislike risk – which is usually the case – they will prefer the directors to take on Project B as this provides the same level of expected return as Project A but for a lower level of risk.

It can be argued that the problem identified above may not be significant where the business is engaged in several similar projects, as it will be lost in the averaging process. However, in practice, investment projects may be unique events and this argument will not then apply. Also, where the project is large in relation to other projects undertaken, the argument loses its force. There is also the problem that a factor that might cause one project to have an adverse outcome could also have adverse effects on other projects.

Where the expected NPV approach is being used, it is probably a good idea to make known to managers the different possible outcomes and the probability attached to each outcome. By so doing, the managers will be able to gain an insight to the *downside risk* attached to the project. The information relating to each outcome can be presented in the form of a diagram if required. The construction of such a diagram is illustrated in Example 8.3.

Example 8.3

Zeta Computing Services Ltd has recently produced some software for a client organisation. The software has a life of two years and will then become obsolete. The cost of producing the software was £10,000. The client has agreed to pay a licence fee of £8,000 a year for the software if it is used in only one of its two divisions, and £12,000 a year if it is used in both of its divisions. The client may use the software for either one or two years in either division but will definitely use it in at least one division in each of the two years.

Zeta Computing Services believes there is a 0.6 chance that the licence fee received in any one year will be £8,000 and a 0.4 chance that it will be £12,000. There are four possible outcomes attached to this project (where p denotes probability):

- *Outcome 1.* Year 1 cash flow £8,000 ($p = 0.6$) and Year 2 cash flow £8,000 ($p = 0.6$). The probability of both years having cash flows of £8,000 will be:

$$0.6 \times 0.6 = 0.36$$

- *Outcome 2.* Year 1 cash flow £12,000 ($p = 0.4$) and Year 2 cash flow £12,000 ($p = 0.4$). The probability of both years having cash flows of £12,000 will be:

$$0.4 \times 0.4 = 0.16$$

- *Outcome 3.* Year 1 cash flow £12,000 ($p = 0.4$) and Year 2 cash flow £8,000 ($p = 0.6$). The probability of this sequence of cash flows occurring will be:

$$0.4 \times 0.6 = 0.24$$

- *Outcome 4.* Year 1 cash flow £8,000 ($p = 0.6$) and Year 2 cash flow £12,000 ($p = 0.4$). The probability of this sequence of cash flows occurring will be:

$$0.6 \times 0.4 = 0.24$$

The information in Example 8.3 can be displayed in the form of a diagram (Figure 8.6).

The source of probabilities

As we might expect, assigning probabilities to possible outcomes can often be a problem. There may be many possible outcomes arising from a particular investment project, and to identify each outcome and then assign a probability to it may prove to be an impossible task. When assigning probabilities to possible outcomes, either an objective or a subjective approach may be used. **Objective probabilities** are based on information gathered from past experience. Thus, for example, the transport manager of a business operating a fleet of motor vans may be able to provide information concerning the possible life of a new motor van purchased based on the record of similar vans acquired in the past. From the information available, probabilities may be developed for different possible lifespans. However, the past may not always be a reliable guide to the future, particularly during a period of rapid change. In the case of the motor vans, for

| Figure 8.6 | The different possible project outcomes for Example 8.3 |

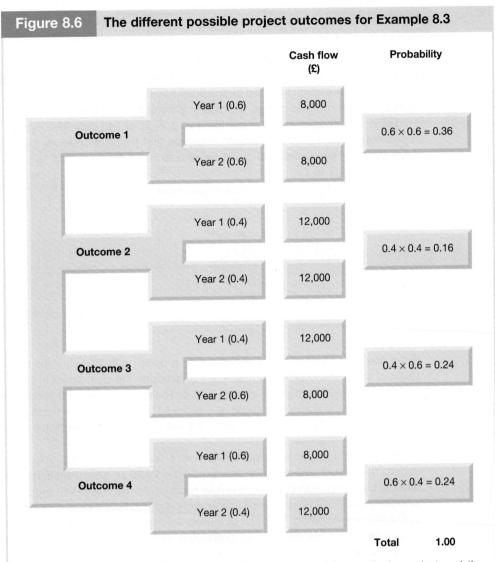

This sets out the different possible outcomes associated with a particular project and the probability of each outcome. The sum of the probabilities attached to each outcome must equal 1.00, in other words it is certain that one of the possible outcomes will occur. For example, outcome 1 would occur where only one division uses the software in each year.

example, changes in design and technology or changes in the purpose for which the vans are being used may undermine the validity of past data.

Subjective probabilities are based on opinion and will be used where past data are either inappropriate or unavailable. The opinions of independent experts may provide a useful basis for developing subjective probabilities, though even these may contain bias, which will affect the reliability of the judgements made.

Despite these problems, we should not be dismissive of the use of probabilities. Assigning probabilities can help to make explicit some of the risks associated with a project and should help decision makers to appreciate the uncertainties that have to be faced.

Activity 8.20

Devonia (Laboratories) Ltd has recently carried out successful clinical trials on a new type of skin cream that has been developed to reduce the effects of ageing. Research and development costs incurred by the business in relation to the new product amount to £160,000. In order to gauge the market potential of the new product, independent market research consultants were hired at a cost of £15,000. The market research report submitted by the consultants indicates that the skin cream is likely to have a product life of four years and could be sold to retail chemists and large department stores at a price of £20 per 100 ml container. For each of the four years of the new product's life, sales demand has been estimated as follows:

Number of 100 ml containers sold	Probability of occurrence
11,000	0.3
14,000	0.6
16,000	0.1

If the business decides to launch the new product, it is possible for production to begin at once. The equipment necessary to produce the skin cream is already owned by the business and originally cost £150,000. At the end of the new product's life, it is estimated that the equipment could be sold for £35,000. If the business decides against launching the new product, the equipment will be sold immediately for £85,000, as it will be of no further use.

The new skin cream will require one hour's labour for each 100 ml container produced. The cost of labour for the new product is £8.00 an hour. Additional workers will have to be recruited to produce the new product. At the end of the product's life, the workers are unlikely to be offered further work with the business and redundancy costs of £10,000 are expected. The cost of the ingredients for each 100 ml container is £6.00. Additional overheads arising from production of the new product are expected to be £15,000 a year.

The new skin cream has attracted the interest of the business's competitors. If the business decides not to produce and sell the skin cream, it can sell the patent rights to a major competitor immediately for £125,000.

Devonia has a cost of capital of 12 per cent. Ignore taxation.

(a) Calculate the expected net present value (ENPV) of the new product.
(b) State, with reasons, whether or not Devonia should launch the new product.

··

Your answer should be as follows:

(a) Expected sales volume per year = $(11,000 \times 0.3) + (14,000 \times 0.6) + (16,000 \times 0.1)$
                                    = 13,300 units

    Expected annual sales revenue = $13,300 \times £20$
                                      = £266,000

    Annual labour   = $13,300 \times £8$
                                      = £106,400

    Annual ingredient costs   = $13,300 \times £6$
                                        = £79,800

Incremental cash flows:

	Years				
	0	1	2	3	4
	£	£	£	£	£
Sale of patent rights	(125.0)				
Sale of equipment	(85.0)				35.0
Sales		266.0	266.0	266.0	266.0
Cost of ingredients		(79.8)	(79.8)	(79.8)	(79.8)
Labour costs		(106.4)	(106.4)	(106.4)	(106.4)
Redundancy					(10.0)
Additional overheads		(15.0)	(15.0)	(15.0)	(15.0)
	(210.0)	64.8	64.8	64.8	89.8
Discount factor (12%)	1.0	0.893	0.797	0.712	0.636
	(210.0)	57.9	51.6	46.1	57.1
ENPV	2.7				

(b) As the ENPV of the project is positive, the wealth of shareholders would be increased by accepting the project. However, the ENPV is very low in relation to the size of the project and careful checking of the key estimates and assumptions would be advisable. A relatively small downward revision of sales or upward revision of costs could make the project ENPV negative.

It would be helpful to derive the NPV for each of the three possible outcomes regarding sales levels. This would enable the decision maker to have a clearer view of the risk involved with the investment.

Reacting to the level of risk

The logical reaction to a risky project is to demand a higher rate of return. Both theory and observable evidence show that there is a relationship between risk and the return required by investors. It was mentioned earlier, for example, that a bank would normally ask for a higher rate of interest on a loan where it perceives the lender to be less likely to be able to repay the amount borrowed.

When evaluating investment projects, it is normal to increase the NPV discount rate in the face of increased risk – that is, to demand a risk premium. The higher the level of risk, therefore, the higher the risk premium that will be demanded. The risk premium is usually added to a 'risk-free' rate of return to derive the total return required. The risk-free rate is normally taken to be equivalent to the rate of return from government loan stock. In practice, a business may divide projects into low-, medium- and high-risk categories and then assign a risk premium to each category. The cash flows from a particular project will then be discounted using a rate based on the risk-free rate plus the appropriate risk premium. This relationship between risk and return is illustrated in Figure 8.7.

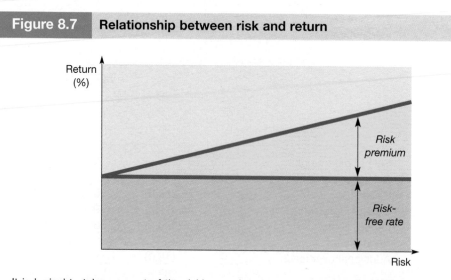

| Figure 8.7 | Relationship between risk and return |

It is logical to take account of the riskiness of projects by changing the discount rate. A risk premium is added to the risk-free rate to derive the appropriate discount rate. A higher return will normally be expected from projects where the risks are higher. Thus, the riskier the project, the higher the risk premium.

The use of a **risk-adjusted discount rate** provides managers with a single value which can be used when making a decision either to accept or to reject a project. Moreover, managers are likely to have an intuitive grasp of the relationship between risk and return and may well feel comfortable with this technique. However, there are practical difficulties with implementing this approach.

Activity 8.21

Can you think of any practical problems with the use of risk-adjusted discount rates?

Subjective judgement is required when assigning an investment project to a particular risk category and then in assigning a risk premium to each category. The choices made will reflect the personal views of the managers responsible and this may differ from the views of the shareholders they represent. The choices made can, nevertheless, make the difference between accepting and rejecting a particular project.

Managing investment projects

So far, we have been concerned with the process of carrying out the necessary calculations that enable managers to select among already identified investment opportunities. This topic is given a great deal of emphasis in the literature on investment appraisal. Though the evaluation of projects is undoubtedly important, we must bear in mind that it is only *part* of the process of investment decision making. There are other important aspects that managers must also consider.

It is possible to see the investment process as a sequence of five stages, each of which managers must consider. The five stages are set out in Figure 8.8 and described below.

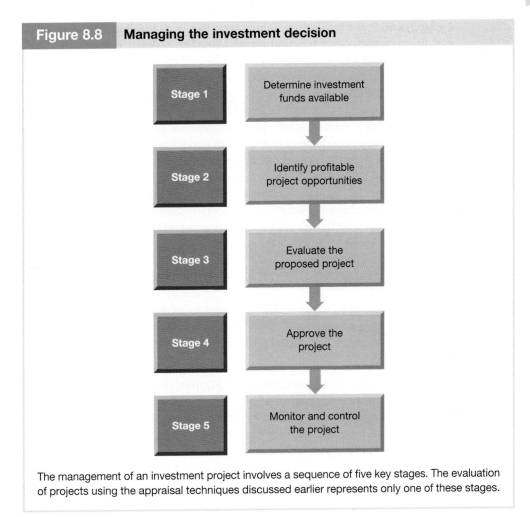

Figure 8.8   Managing the investment decision

Stage 1 — Determine investment funds available

Stage 2 — Identify profitable project opportunities

Stage 3 — Evaluate the proposed project

Stage 4 — Approve the project

Stage 5 — Monitor and control the project

The management of an investment project involves a sequence of five key stages. The evaluation of projects using the appraisal techniques discussed earlier represents only one of these stages.

Stage 1: Determine investment funds available

The amount of funds available for investment may be determined by the external market for funds or by internal management. In practice, it is often the latter that has the greater influence on the amount available. In either case, it may be that the funds will not be sufficient to finance the profitable investment opportunities available. When this occurs, some form of capital rationing has to be undertaken. This means that managers are faced with the task of deciding on the most profitable use of the investment funds available.

Stage 2: Identify profitable project opportunities

A vital part of the investment process is the search for profitable investment opportunities. A business should carry out methodical routines for identifying feasible projects. This may be done through a research and development department or by some other means. Failure to do so will inevitably lead to the business losing its competitive position with respect to product development, production methods or market penetration. To help identify good investment opportunities, some businesses provide financial incentives to staff that have good ideas. The search process will, however, usually involve looking outside the business to identify changes in technology, customer demand, market conditions and so on. Information will need to be gathered and this may take some time, particularly for unusual or non-routine investment opportunities.

It is important that the business's investments should fit in with its strategic plans, a point that we discussed in Chapter 1. The business should seek out investment projects that use its strengths (such as management expertise in a particular activity) to exploit opportunities (such as an expansion of the market). At the same time, investment projects selected should avoid exposing the business's weaknesses (such as a shortage of suitably skilled labour) to threats (such as other businesses poaching skilled staff). The business is likely to be able to generate greater amounts of wealth by investing in particular types of project, rather than in others. It is also possible that the business will be able to generate greater benefits from a particular project than could a different business with different strengths and weaknesses.

Stage 3: Evaluate the proposed project

If management is to agree to the investment of funds in a project, there must be a proper screening of each proposal. For projects of any size, this will involve providing answers to a number of questions, including:

- What are the nature and purpose of the project?
- Does the project align with the overall objectives of the business?
- How much finance is required?
- What other resources (such as expertise, factory space and so on) are required for successful completion of the project?
- How long will the project last and what are its key stages?
- What is the expected pattern of cash flows?
- What are the major problems associated with the project and how can they be overcome?
- What is the NPV/IRR of the project? How does this compare with other opportunities available?
- Have risk and inflation been taken into account in the appraisal process and, if so, what are the results?

It is important to appreciate that the ability and commitment of those responsible for proposing and managing the project will be vital to its success. Hence, when evaluating a new project, those proposing it will be judged by its success. In some cases, senior managers may decide not to support a project that appears profitable on paper if they lack confidence in the ability of key managers to see it through to completion.

Stage 4: Approve the project

Once the managers responsible for investment decision making are satisfied that the project should be undertaken, formal approval can be given. However, a decision on a project may be postponed if senior managers need more information from those proposing the project, or if revisions are required to the proposal. In some cases, the project proposal may be rejected if the project is considered unprofitable or likely to fail. Before rejecting a proposal, however, the implications of not pursuing the project for such areas as market share, staff morale and existing business operations must be carefully considered.

Stage 5: Monitor and control the project

Making a decision to invest in, say, the plant needed to provide a new service does not automatically cause the investment to be made and provision of the service to go smoothly ahead. Managers will need to manage the project actively through to completion. This, in turn, will require further information-gathering exercises.

Management should receive progress reports at regular intervals concerning the project. These reports should provide information relating to the actual cash flows for each stage of the project, which can then be compared against the forecast figures provided when the proposal was submitted for approval. The reasons for significant variations should be ascertained and corrective action taken where possible. Any changes in the expected completion date of the project or any expected variations in future cash flows from budget should be reported immediately; in extreme cases, managers may even abandon the project if circumstances appear to have changed dramatically for the worse. We saw in Real World 8.6 that Rolls-Royce undertakes this kind of reassessment of existing projects. No doubt most other well-managed businesses do this too.

Project management techniques (for example, critical path analysis) should be employed wherever possible and their effectiveness reported to senior management.

→ An important part of the control process is a **post-completion audit** of the project. This is, in essence, a review of the project performance to see if it lived up to expectations and whether any lessons can be learned from the way that the investment process was carried out. In addition to an evaluation of financial costs and benefits, non-financial measures of performance such as the ability to meet deadlines and levels of quality achieved should also be reported. (See Chapter 5 for a discussion of total life-cycle costing, which is based on similar principles.)

The fact that a post-completion audit is an integral part of the management of the project should also encourage those who submit projects to use realistic estimates. Where over-optimistic estimates are used in an attempt to secure project approval, the managers responsible will find themselves accountable at the post-completion audit stage. Such audits, however, can be difficult and time-consuming to carry out, and so the likely benefits must be weighed against the costs involved. Senior management may feel, therefore, that only projects above a certain size should be subject to a post-completion audit.

Real World 8.8 reveals that Tesco and Premier Oil both use post-completion audit approaches to evaluating past investment projects. No doubt most well-managed businesses do the same.

REAL WORLD 8.8

Approaches to investment decisions

In its 2003 annual report, Tesco, the supermarket chain, said:

> The capital investment programme is subject to formalised review procedures requiring key criteria to be met. All major initiatives require business cases to be prepared, normally covering a minimum of five years. Post investment appraisals are also carried out.

In its 2002 annual report, Premier Oil, the oil and gas exploration and production business, said:

> The group has clearly defined procedures for capital expenditure. These include authority levels, commitment records and reporting, annual budget and detailed appraisal and review procedures.

SUMMARY

The main points of this chapter may be summarised as follows:

Accounting rate of return (ARR) = the average accounting profit from the project expressed as a percentage of the average investment.

- Decision rule – projects with an ARR above a defined minimum are acceptable; the greater the ARR, the more attractive the project becomes.
- Conclusions on ARR:
  - It does not relate directly to shareholders' wealth – can lead to illogical decisions.
  - Takes almost no account of the timing of cash flows.
  - Ignores some relevant information and may take account of some irrelevant.
  - Relatively simple to use.
  - Much inferior to NPV.

Payback period (PP) = the length of time that it takes for the cash outflow for the initial investment to be repaid out of resulting cash inflows.

- Decision rule – projects with a PP up to defined maximum period are acceptable; the shorter the PP, the more desirable.
- Conclusions on PP:
  - Does not relate to shareholders' wealth; ignores inflows after the payback date.
  - Takes little account of the timing of cash flows.
  - Ignores much relevant information.
  - Does not always provide clear signals and can be impractical to use.
  - Much inferior to NPV, but it is easy to understand and can offer a liquidity insight, which might be the reason for its widespread use.

Net present value (NPV) = the sum of the discounted values of the cash flows from the investment.

- Money has a time value.
- Decision rule – all positive NPV investments enhance shareholders' wealth; the greater the NPV, the greater the enhancement and the more desirable.
- PV of a cash flow = cash flow $\times 1/(1 + r)^n$, assuming a constant discount rate.
- The act of discounting brings cash flows at different points in time to a common valuation basis (their present value), which enables them to be directly compared.
- Conclusions on NPV:
  - Relates directly to shareholders' wealth objective.
  - Takes account of the timing of cash flows.
  - Takes all relevant information into account.
  - Provides clear signals and practical to use.

Internal rate of return (IRR) = the discount rate that causes a project to have a zero NPV.

- Represents the average percentage return on the investment, taking account of the fact that cash may be flowing into and out of the project at various points in its life.
- Decision rule – projects that have an IRR greater than the cost of capital are acceptable; the greater the IRR, the more attractive the project.
- Usually cannot be calculated directly; a trial and error approach is necessary in most cases.

- Conclusions on IRR:
  - Does not relate directly to shareholders' wealth. Usually gives the same signals as NPV – can mislead where there are competing projects of different scales.
  - Takes account of the timing of cash flows.
  - Takes all relevant information into account.
  - With unconventional cash flows, problems of multiple or no IRR.
  - Inferior to NPV.

Use of appraisal methods in practice

- All four methods are widely used.
- The discounting methods (NPV and IRR) show a strong increase in usage over time.
- Many businesses use more than one method.
- Larger businesses seem to be more sophisticated than smaller ones.

Risk in investment appraisal

- Sensitivity analysis (SA) is an assessment, taking each input factor in turn, of how much each one can vary from estimate before a project is not viable.
  - Provides useful insights to projects.
  - Does not give a clear decision rule, but provides an impression.
  - It can be rather static, but scenario-building solves this problem.
- Expected net present value (ENPV) is the weighted average of the possible outcomes for a project, based on probabilities for each of the inputs:
  - Provides a single value and a clear decision rule.
  - The single ENPV figure can hide the real risk.
  - Useful for the ENPV figure to be supported by information on the range and dispersion of possible outcomes.
  - Probabilities may be subjective (based on opinion) or objective (based on evidence).
- Reacting to the level of risk:
  - Logically, high risk should lead to high returns.
  - Using a risk-adjusted discount rate, where a risk premium is added to the risk-free rate, is a logical response to risk.

Management of the investment project has five stages

- Determine investment funds available – dealing, if necessary, with capital rationing problems.
- Identify profitable project opportunities.
- Evaluate the proposed project.
- Approve the project.
- Monitor and control the project – using a post-completion audit approach.

→ Key terms

Further reading

If you would like to explore the topics covered in this chapter in more depth, we recommend the following books:

Corporate Financial Management, *Arnold G.*, 2nd edn, Financial Times Prentice Hall, 2002, chapters 2, 3 and 4.

Investment Appraisal and Financial Decisions *Lumby S. and Jones C.*, 7th edn, International Thomson Business Press, 2003, chapters 3, 5 and 6.

Business Finance: Theory and practice, *McLaney E.*, 6th edn, Financial Times Prentice Hall, 2003, chapters 4–6.

Corporate Finance and Investment, *Pike R. and Neale B.*, 4th edn, Prentice Hall International, 2002, chapters 5, 6 and 7.

References

1 **Reckoning with Risk**, *Gigerenzer, G.*, Penguin, 2002.
2 'The theory–practice gap in capital budgeting: evidence from the United Kingdom', *Arnold G. C. and Hatzopoulos P. D.*, in **Journal of Business Finance and Accounting**, June/July 2000.

REVIEW QUESTIONS

Answers to these questions can be found on the students' side of the Companion Website at www.pearsoned.co.uk/atrillmclaney.

8.1 Why is the net present value method of investment appraisal considered to be theoretically superior to other methods that are found in practice?

8.2 The payback method has been criticised for not taking the time value of money into account. Could this limitation be overcome? If so, would this method then be preferable to the NPV method?

8.3 Research indicates that the IRR method is a more popular method of investment appraisal than the NPV method. Why might this be?

8.4 Why are cash flows rather than profit flows used in the IRR, NPV and PP methods of investment appraisal?

EXERCISES

Exercise 8.5 to 8.8 are more advanced than 8.1 to 8.4. Those with a coloured number have answers at the back of the book.

8.1 The directors of Mylo Ltd are currently considering two mutually exclusive investment projects. Both projects are concerned with the purchase of new plant. The following data are available for each project:

	Project 1 £	Project 2 £
Cost (immediate outlay)	100,000	60,000
Expected annual net profit (loss):		
Year 1	29,000	18,000
2	(1,000)	(2,000)
3	2,000	4,000
Estimated residual value of the plant	7,000	6,000

The business has an estimated cost of capital of 10 per cent, and uses the straight-line method of depreciation for all non-current (fixed) assets when calculating net profit. Neither project would increase the working capital of the business. The business has sufficient funds to meet all capital expenditure requirements.

Required:

(a) Calculate for each project:
  (i) The net present value.
  (ii) The approximate internal rate of return.
  (iii) The payback period.

(b) State which, if any, of the two investment projects the directors of Mylo Ltd should accept, and why.

(c) State, in general terms, which method of investment appraisal you consider to be most appropriate for evaluating investment projects, and why.

8.2   C. George (Controls) Ltd manufactures a thermostat that can be used in a range of kitchen appliances. The manufacturing process is, at present, semi-automated. The equipment used costs £540,000, and has a written-down (balance sheet) value of £300,000. Demand for the product has been fairly stable, and output has been maintained at 50,000 units a year in recent years.

The following data, based on the current level of output, have been prepared in respect of the product:

	Per unit	
	£	£
Selling price		12.40
Less		
Labour	3.30	
Materials	3.65	
Overheads: Variable	1.58	
Fixed	1.60	
		10.13
Profit		2.27

Although the existing equipment is expected to last for a further four years before it is sold for an estimated £40,000, the business has recently been considering purchasing new equipment that would completely automate much of the production process. The new equipment would cost £670,000 and would have an expected life of four years, at the end of which it would be sold for an estimated £70,000. If the new equipment is purchased, the old equipment could be sold for £150,000 immediately.

The assistant to the business's accountant has prepared a report to help assess the viability of the proposed change, which includes the following data:

	Per unit	
	£	£
Selling price		12.40
Less		
Labour	1.20	
Materials	3.20	
Overheads: Variable	1.40	
Fixed	3.30	
		9.10
Profit		3.30

Depreciation charges will increase by £85,000 a year as a result of purchasing the new machinery; however, other fixed costs are not expected to change.

In the report the assistant wrote:

> The figures shown above that relate to the proposed change are based on the current level of output and take account of a depreciation charge of £150,000 a year in respect of the new equipment. The effect of purchasing the new equipment will be to increase the net profit to sales ratio from 18.3 per cent to 26.6 per cent. In addition, the purchase of the new equipment will enable us to reduce our stock (inventories) level immediately by £130,000.
>   In view of these facts, I recommend purchase of the new equipment.

The business has a cost of capital of 12 per cent.
Ignore taxation.

Required:

(a) Prepare a statement of the incremental cash flows arising from the purchase of the new equipment.

(b) Calculate the net present value of the proposed purchase of new equipment.

(c) State, with reasons, whether the business should purchase the new equipment.

(d) Explain why cash flow forecasts are used rather than profit forecasts to assess the viability of proposed capital expenditure projects.

8.3 The accountant of your business has recently been taken ill through overwork. In his absence his assistant has prepared some calculations of the profitability of a project, which are to be discussed soon at the board meeting of your business. His workings, which are set out below, include some errors of principle. You can assume that the statement below includes no arithmetical errors.

	Year 1 £000	Year 2 £000	Year 3 £000	Year 4 £000	Year 5 £000	Year 6 £000
Sales revenue		450	470	470	470	470
Less Costs						
Materials		126	132	132	132	132
Labour		90	94	94	94	94
Overheads		45	47	47	47	47
Depreciation		120	120	120	120	120
Working capital	180					
Interest on working capital		27	27	27	27	27
Write-off of development costs		30	30	30		
Total costs	180	438	450	450	420	420
Profit/(loss)	(180)	12	20	20	50	50

$$\frac{\text{Total profit (loss)}}{\text{Cost of equipment}} = \frac{(£28,000)}{£600,000} = \text{Return on investment (4.7\%)}$$

You ascertain the following additional information:

- The cost of equipment contains £100,000, being the book value of an old machine. If it were not used for this project it would be scrapped with a zero net realisable value. New equipment costing £500,000 will be purchased on 31 December Year 0. You should assume that all other cash flows occur at the end of the year to which they relate.
- The development costs of £90,000 have already been spent.
- Overheads have been costed at 50 per cent of direct labour, which is the business's normal practice. An independent assessment has suggested that incremental overheads are likely to amount to £30,000 a year.
- The business's cost of capital is 12 per cent.

Ignore taxation in your answer.

Required:
(a) Prepare a corrected statement of the incremental cash flows arising from the project. Where you have altered the assistant's figures you should attach a brief note explaining your alterations.
(b) Calculate:
    (i) The project's payback period.
    (ii) The project's net present value as at 31 December Year 0.
(c) Write a memo to the board advising on the acceptance or rejection of the project.

8.4 Arkwright Mills plc is considering expanding its production of a new yarn, code name X15. The plant is expected to cost £1m and have a life of five years and a nil residual value. It will be bought, paid for and ready for operation on 31 December Year 0. £500,000 has already been spent on development costs of the product, and this has been charged in the profit and loss account (income statement) in the year it was incurred.

The following results are projected for the new yarn:

	Year 1 £m	Year 2 £m	Year 3 £m	Year 4 £m	Year 5 £m
Sales	1.2	1.4	1.4	1.4	1.4
Costs, including depreciation	1.0	1.1	1.1	1.1	1.1
Profit before tax	0.2	0.3	0.3	0.3	0.3

Tax is charged at 50 per cent on annual profits (before tax and after depreciation) and paid one year in arrears. Depreciation of the plant has been calculated on a straight-line basis. Additional working capital of £0.6m will be required at the beginning of the project and released at the end of Year 5. You should assume that all cash flows occur at the end of the year in which they arise.

Required:

(a) Prepare a statement showing the incremental cash flows of the project relevant to a decision concerning whether or not to proceed with the construction of the new plant.

(b) Compute the net present value of the project using a 10 per cent discount rate.

(c) Compute the payback period to the nearest year. Explain the meaning of this term.

8.5   Newton Electronics Ltd has incurred expenditure of £5m over the past three years researching and developing a miniature hearing aid. The hearing aid is now fully developed, and the directors are considering which of three mutually exclusive options should be taken to exploit the potential of the new product. The options are as follows:

1 The business could manufacture the hearing aid itself. This would be a new departure, since the business has so far concentrated on research and development projects. However, the business has manufacturing space available that it currently rents to another business for £100,000 a year. The business would have to purchase plant and equipment costing £9m and invest £3m in working capital immediately for production to begin.

A market research report, for which the business paid £50,000, indicates that the new product has an expected life of five years. Sales of the product during this period are predicted as follows:

	Predicted sales for the year ended 30 November				
	Year 1	Year 2	Year 3	Year 4	Year 5
Number of units ('000)	800	1,400	1,800	1,200	500

The selling price per unit will be £30 in the first year but will fall to £22 in the following three years. In the final year of the product's life, the selling price will fall to £20. Variable production costs are predicted to be £14 a unit, and fixed production costs (including depreciation) will be £2.4m a year. Marketing costs will be £2m a year.

The business intends to depreciate the plant and equipment using the straight-line method and based on an estimated residual value at the end of the five years of £1m. The business has a cost of capital of 10 per cent a year.

2 Newton Electronics Ltd could agree to another business manufacturing and marketing the product under licence. A multinational business, Faraday Electricals plc, has offered to undertake the manufacture and marketing of the product, and in return will make a royalty payment to Newton Electronics Ltd of £5 per unit. It has been estimated that the annual number of sales of the hearing aid will be 10% higher if the multinational business, rather than if Newton Electronics Ltd, manufactures and markets the product.

3 Newton Electronics Ltd could sell the patent rights to Faraday Electricals plc for £24 million, payable in two equal instalments. The first instalment would be payable immediately and the second at the end of two years. This option would give Faraday Electricals plc the exclusive right to manufacture and market the new product.

Ignore taxation.

Assume it is now 30 November Year 0.

Required:
(a) Calculate the net present value of each of the options available to Newton Electronics Ltd.
(b) Identify and discuss any other factors that Newton Electronics Ltd should consider before arriving at a decision.
(c) State what you consider to be the most suitable option, and why.

8.6 Chesterfield Wanderers is a professional football club that has enjoyed considerable success in both national and European competitions in recent years. As a result, the club has accumulated £10m to spend on its further development. The board of directors is currently considering two mutually exclusive options for spending the funds available.

The first option is to acquire another player. The team manager has expressed a keen interest in acquiring Basil ('Bazza') Ramsey, a central defender, who currently plays for a rival club. The rival club has agreed to release the player immediately for £10m if required. A decision to acquire 'Bazza' Ramsey would mean that the existing central defender, Vinnie Smith, could be sold to another club. Chesterfield Wanderers has recently received an offer of £2.2m for this player. This offer is still open but will only be accepted if 'Bazza' Ramsey joins Chesterfield Wanderers. If this does not happen, Vinnie Smith will be expected to stay on with the club until the end of his playing career in five years' time. During this period, Vinnie will receive an annual salary of £400,000 and a loyalty bonus of £200,000 at the end of his five-year period with the club.

Assuming 'Bazza' Ramsey is acquired, the team manager estimates that gate receipts will increase by £2.5m in the first year and £1.3m in each of the four following years. There will also be an increase in advertising and sponsorship revenues of £1.2m for each of the next five years if the player is acquired. At the end of five years, the player can be sold to a club in a lower division and Chesterfield Wanderers will expect to receive £1m as a transfer fee. During his period at the club, 'Bazza' will receive an annual salary of £800,000 and a loyalty bonus of £400,000 after five years.

The second option is for the club to improve its ground facilities. The west stand could be extended and executive boxes could be built for businesses wishing to offer corporate hospitality to clients. These improvements would also cost £10m and would take one year to complete. During this period, the west stand would be closed, resulting in a reduction of gate receipts of £1.8m. However, gate receipts for each of the following four years would be £4.4m higher than current receipts. In five years' time, the club has plans to sell the existing grounds and to move to a new stadium nearby. Improving the ground facilities is not expected to affect the ground's value when it comes to be sold. Payment for the improvements will be made when the work has been completed at the end of the first year.

Whichever option is chosen, the board of directors has decided to take on additional ground staff. The additional wages bill is expected to be £350,000 a year over the next five years.

The club has a cost of capital of 10 per cent. Ignore taxation.

Required:
(a) Calculate the incremental cash flows arising from each of the options available to the club.
(b) Calculate the net present value of each of the options.
(c) On the basis of the calculations made in (b) above, which of the two options would you choose and why?
(d) Discuss the validity of using the net present value method in making investment decisions for a professional football club.

8.7 Simtex Ltd has invested £120,000 to date in developing a new type of shaving foam. The shaving foam is now ready for production and it has been estimated that the new product will sell 160,000 cans a year over the next four years. At the end of four years, the product will be discontinued and replaced by a new product.

The shaving foam is expected to sell at £6 a can and variable costs are estimated at £4 per can. Fixed costs (excluding depreciation) are expected to be £300,000 a year. (This figure includes £130,000 in fixed costs incurred by the existing business that will be apportioned to this new product.)

To manufacture and package the new product, equipment costing £480,000 must be acquired immediately. The estimated value of this equipment in four years' time is £100,000. The business calculates depreciation using the straight-line method, and has an estimated cost of capital of 12 per cent.

Required:
(a) Deduce the net present value of the new product.
(b) Calculate by how much each of the following must change before the new product is no longer profitable:
  (i) the discount rate;
  (ii) the initial outlay on new equipment;
  (iii) the net operating cash flows;
  (iv) the residual value of the equipment.
(c) Should the business produce the new product?

8.8 Kernow Cleaning Services Ltd provides street-cleaning services for local councils in the far south west of England. The work is currently labour intensive and few machines are employed. However, the business has recently been considering the purchase of a fleet of street-cleaning vehicles at a total cost of £540,000. The vehicles have a life of four years and are likely to result in a considerable saving of labour costs. Estimates of the likely labour savings and their probability of occurrence are set out below:

	Estimated savings £	Probability of occurrence
Year 1	80,000	0.3
	160,000	0.5
	200,000	0.2
Year 2	140,000	0.4
	220,000	0.4
	250,000	0.2
Year 3	140,000	0.4
	200,000	0.3
	230,000	0.3
Year 4	100,000	0.3
	170,000	0.6
	200,000	0.1

Estimates for each year are independent of other years. The business has a cost of capital of 10 per cent.

Required:
(a) Calculate the expected net present value (ENPV) of the street-cleaning machines.
(b) Calculate the net present value (NPV) of the worst possible outcome and the probability of its occurrence.

9

Managing working capital

OBJECTIVES

When you have completed this chapter, you should be able to:

- Identify the main elements of working capital.

- Discuss the purpose of working capital and the nature of the working capital cycle.

- Explain the importance of establishing policies for the control of working capital.

- Explain the factors that have to be taken into account when managing each element of working capital.

INTRODUCTION

In this chapter we consider the factors that must be taken into account when managing the working capital of a business. Each element of working capital will be identified, and the major issues surrounding them will be discussed. Working capital represents a significant investment for many businesses and so its proper management and control can be vital. We saw in Chapter 8 that it may be an important aspect of new investment proposals. Budgets, which we explored in Chapter 6, can be useful tools in the management of working capital.

The nature and purpose of working capital

→ **Working capital** is usually defined as current assets less current liabilities.
The major elements of current assets are:

- stocks (inventories)
- trade debtors (receivables)
- cash (in hand and at bank).

The major elements of current liabilities are:

- trade creditors (payables)
- bank overdrafts.

The size and composition of working capital can vary between industries. For some types of business, the investment in working capital can be substantial. For example, a manufacturing business will typically invest heavily in raw material, work in progress and finished goods, and will often sell its goods on credit, thereby generating trade debtors. A retailer, on the other hand, will hold only one form of stock (finished goods), and will usually sell goods for cash. Many service businesses hold no stocks. Most businesses buy goods and/or services on credit, giving rise to trade creditors. Few, if any, businesses operate without a cash balance, though in some cases it is a negative one (bank overdraft).

Working capital represents a net investment in short-term assets. These assets are continually flowing into and out of the business, and are essential for day-to-day operations. The various elements of working capital are interrelated, and can be seen as part of a short-term cycle. For a manufacturing business, the working capital cycle can be depicted as shown in Figure 9.1.

Figure 9.1	The working capital cycle

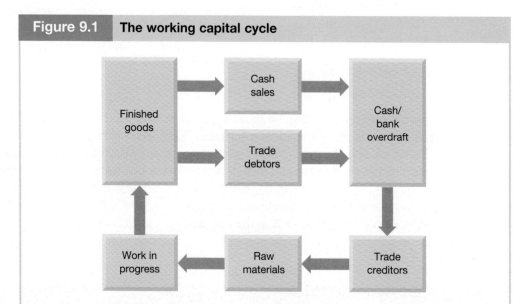

Cash is used to pay trade creditors for raw materials, or raw materials are bought for immediate cash settlement; cash is spent on labour and other aspects that turn raw materials into work in progress and, finally, into finished goods. The finished goods are sold to customers either for cash or on credit. In the case of credit customers, there will be a delay before the cash is received from the sales. Receipt of cash completes the cycle.

For a retailer the situation would be as in Figure 9.1, except that there would be no work in progress and the raw materials and the finished stock would be the same. For a purely service business, the working capital cycle would also be similar to that depicted in Figure 9.1, except that there would be no stock of raw materials and finished goods. There may well be work in progress, as many services, for example a case handled by a firm of solicitors, will take some time to complete and costs will build up before the client is billed for them.

Managing working capital

The management of working capital is an essential part of the business's short-term planning process. It is necessary for management to decide how much of each element should be held. As we shall see later in this chapter, there are costs associated with holding either too much or too little of each element. Management must be aware of these costs, which include opportunity costs, in order to manage effectively. Hence, the potential benefits must be weighed against the likely costs in an attempt to achieve the optimum investment. As with all aspects of management, actions taken should be working towards the business's strategic objectives. The key one in this context is likely to be maximisation of the owners' (shareholders') wealth.

The working capital needs of a particular business are likely to change over time as a result of changes in the business environment. This means that working capital decisions are constantly being made. Managers must try to identify changes in an attempt to ensure that the level of investment in working capital is appropriate.

Activity 9.1

What kind of changes in the commercial environment might lead to a decision to change the level of investment in working capital? Try to identify four possible changes that could affect the working capital needs of a business.

We thought of the following:

● changes in interest rates
● changes in market demand
● changes in the seasons
● changes in the state of the economy.

You may have thought of others.

In addition to changes in the external environment, changes arising within the business could alter the required level of investment in working capital. Examples of such internal changes include using different production methods (resulting, perhaps, in a need to hold less stock) and changes in the level of risk that managers are prepared to take.

The scale of working capital

We might imagine that, compared with the scale of investment in non-current (fixed) assets by the typical business, the amounts involved with working capital are pretty trivial. This would be a false assessment of reality – the scale of the working capital elements for most businesses is vast.

Real World 9.1 gives some impression of the working capital investment for five UK businesses that are either very well known by name, or whose products are everyday commodities for most of us. These businesses were randomly selected, except that each one is high profile and from a different industry. For each business the major balance sheet items are expressed as a percentage of the total investment by the providers of long-term finance.

REAL WORLD 9.1

A summary of the balance sheets of five UK businesses

Business	The Boots Company plc	Go-Ahead Group plc	Rolls-Royce plc	Tesco plc	United Utilities plc
Balance sheet date	31.3.03	28.6.03	31.12.02	22.2.03	31.3.03
	%	%	%	%	%
Non-current assets	74	126	70	126	104
Current assets					
Stock	25	2	27	10	–
Trade debtors	13	23	23	–	3
Other debtors	12	29	33	6	4
Cash and near cash	19	16	17	6	10
	69	70	100	22	17
Current liabilities					
Trade creditors	14	25	11	20	1
Tax and dividends	12	15	9	6	5
Other short-term liabilities	12	55	44	10	12
Overdrafts and short-term loans	5	1	6	12	3
	43	96	70	48	21
Working capital	26	(26)	30	(26)	(4)
Total long-term investment	100	100	100	100	100

The non-current (fixed) assets, current assets and current liabilities are expressed as a percentage of the total net investment (equity plus non-current liabilities) of the business concerned. The businesses were randomly selected, except that they were deliberately taken from different industries. Boots is a major UK health-care manufacturer that operates a chain of high-street retail stores. Go-Ahead is a major passenger transport provider, principally through buses and trains. It runs much of the Central London bus service and owns South Central and Thames Trains. Rolls-Royce builds engines for aircraft and for other purposes. Tesco is one of the major UK supermarkets. United Utilities is a major distributor of electricity and water, particularly in the north west of England.

Source: The table was constructed from information which appeared in the annual reports of the five businesses concerned.

The totals for current assets are pretty large when compared with the total long-term investment. This is particularly true of Boots, Go-Ahead and Rolls-Royce. The amounts vary considerably from one type of business to the next. Rolls-Royce is the only one of the five businesses that is solely a manufacturer. Boots and Tesco are both retailers, though Boots is also a manufacturer. These three are the only ones that hold significant amounts of stock. The other two are service providers. Tesco does not sell on credit and few of United Utilities sales are on credit, so they have little or nothing invested in trade debtors. It is interesting to note that Tesco's trade creditors are much higher than its stock. Since most of these creditors will be suppliers of stock, it means that the business is able, on average, to have the cash from a particular sale in the bank before it needs to pay for the goods concerned.

These types of variation in the amounts and types of working capital elements are typical of other businesses. In the sections that follow, we shall consider each element of working capital separately and how they might be properly managed.

Managing stocks (inventories)

A business may hold stocks for various reasons, the most common of which is to meet the immediate day-to-day requirements of customers and production. However, a business may hold more than is necessary for this purpose if it is believed that future supplies may be interrupted or scarce. Similarly, if the business believes that the cost of stocks will rise in the future, it may decide to stockpile.

For some types of business the stock held may represent a substantial proportion of the total assets held. For example, a car dealership that rents its premises may have nearly all of its total assets in the form of stock. As we have seen, manufacturing businesses' stock levels tend to be higher than in many other types of business. For some types of business, the level of stock held may vary substantially over the year owing to the seasonal nature of the industry. An example of such a business is a greetings card manufacturer. For other businesses, stock levels may remain fairly stable throughout the year.

Where a business holds stock simply to meet the day-to-day requirements of its customers and for production, it will normally seek to minimise the amount of stock held because there are significant costs associated with holding stocks. These include: storage and handling costs, financing costs, the risks of pilferage and obsolescence, and the opportunities forgone in tying up funds in this form of asset. However, a business must also recognise that, if the level of stocks held is too low, there will also be associated costs.

Activity 9.2

What costs might a business incur as a result of holding too low a level of stocks? Try to jot down at least three types of cost.

In answering this activity you may have thought of the following costs:

- loss of sales, from being unable to provide the goods required immediately;
- loss of goodwill from customers, for being unable to satisfy customer demand;
- high transport costs incurred to ensure that stocks are replenished quickly;
- lost production due to shortage of raw materials;
- inefficient production scheduling due to shortages of raw materials;
- purchasing stocks at a higher price than might otherwise have been possible in order to replenish stocks quickly.

Before we go on to deal with the various approaches that can be taken to managing stock, **Real World 9.2** provides an example of how badly things can go wrong if stock is not adequately controlled.

REAL WORLD 9.2

Pallets lost at Brambles

Brambles Industries plc (BI) is an Anglo-Australian industrial services business formed in 2001 when the industrial services subsidiary of GKN plc, the UK engineering business, was merged with the Australian business Brambles Ltd.

BI uses 'pallets' on which it delivers its products to customers. These are returnable by customers so BI holds a stock or 'pool' of pallets. Each pallet costs the business about £10. Unfortunately, BI lost 14 million pallets during the year ended in June 2002 as a result of poor stock control and this led to a significant decline in the business's profits and share price.

At BI's annual general meeting in Sydney, Australia, one of the shareholders was quoted as saying: 'Running a pallet pool is not rocket science. I can teach one of my employees about pallets in 20 minutes.'

Source: Information taken from an article appearing in the *Financial Times*, 27 November 2002.

To try to ensure that the stocks are properly managed, a number of procedures and techniques may be used. These are reviewed below.

Budgeting future demand

One of the best means of a business trying to ensure that there will be stock available to meet future production requirements and sales is to make appropriate plans. These budgets should deal with each product that the business makes and/or sells. It is important that every attempt is made to ensure the budgets' accuracy, as they will determine future ordering and production levels. The budgets may be derived in various ways. They may be developed using statistical techniques such as time series analysis, or they may be based on the judgement of the sales and marketing staff. We considered stock budgets, and their link to sales and production budgets, in Chapter 6.

REAL WORLD 9.3

Dreaming of a bright Christmas

Wal-Mart is the world's largest retailer and has extremely sophisticated stock planning and control systems. Nevertheless, things can still go wrong. During 2002, there was a rise in sales of 12 per cent and a rise in stock levels of 10 per cent. The large rise in stock in relation to the rise in sales was unplanned and was largely due to sales over the Christmas period falling below expectations. This represents poor stock management by Wal-Mart standards. The business, however, expects to get back on track and to ensure that stocks grow by less than half the rate of sales in the future.

Source: Information taken from *Financial Times*, Lex column, 19 February 2003.

Financial ratios

One ratio that can be used to help monitor stock (inventory) levels is the average stock turnover period. This is calculated as follows:

$$\text{Average stock (inventory) turnover period} = \frac{\text{Average stock held}}{\text{Cost of sales}} \times 365$$

This will provide a picture of the average period for which stocks are held, and can be useful as a basis for comparison. It is possible to calculate the stock turnover period for individual product lines as well as for stocks as a whole.

Recording and reordering systems

The management of stocks in a business of any size requires a sound system of recording stock movements. There must be proper procedures for recording stock purchases and sales. Periodic stock checks may be required to ensure that the amount of physical stocks held is consistent with the stock records.

There should also be clear procedures for the reordering of stocks. Authorisation for both the purchase and the issue of stocks should be confined to a few senior staff. This should avoid problems of duplication and lack of co-ordination. To determine the point at which stock should be reordered, information will be required concerning the **lead time** (that is, the time between the placing of an order and the receipt of the goods) and the likely level of demand.

Activity 9.3

An electrical retailer keeps a particular type of light switch in stock. The annual demand for the light switch is 10,400 units, and the lead time for orders is four weeks. Demand for the stock is steady throughout the year. At what level of stock should the business reorder, assuming that it is confident of the information given above?

The average weekly demand for the stock item is 10,400/52 = 200 units. During the time between ordering the stock and receiving it, the stock sold will be 4 × 200 units = 800 units. So the business should reorder no later than when the stock level reaches 800 units, in order to avoid a 'stockout'.

In most businesses, there will be some uncertainty surrounding the above factors and so a buffer or safety stock level may be maintained in case problems occur. The amount of buffer stock to be held is really a matter of judgement. This judgement will depend on:

- the degree of uncertainty concerning the above factors;
- the likely costs of running out of stock; and
- the cost of holding the buffer stock.

REAL WORLD 9.4

Taking on the big boys

The use of technology in stock recording and reordering may be of vital importance to the survival of small businesses that are being threatened by larger rivals. One such example is that of small independent bookshops. Technology can come to their rescue in two ways. First, electronic point-of-sale (EPOS) systems can record books as they are sold and can constantly update stocks held. Thus, books that need to be reordered can be quickly and easily identified. Second, the reordering process can be improved by using web-based technology, which allows books to be ordered in real time. Many large book wholesalers provide free web-based software to their customers for this purpose and try to deliver books ordered during the next working day. This means that a small bookseller, with limited shelf space, may keep only one copy of a particular book, but maintain a range of books that competes with that of a large bookseller.

Source: Information taken from 'Small stores keep up with the big boys', FT.com, 5 February 2003.

Levels of control

Senior managers must make a commitment to the management of stocks (inventories). However, the cost of controlling stocks must be weighed against the potential benefits. It may be possible to have different levels of control according to the nature of the stocks held. The **ABC system of stock control** is based on the idea of selective levels of control.

A business may find that it is possible to divide its stock into three broad categories: A, B and C. Each category will be based on the value of stock held, as is illustrated in Example 9.1.

Example 9.1

Alascan Products plc makes door handles and door fittings. It makes them in brass, in steel and in plastic. The business finds that brass fittings account for 10 per cent of the physical volume of the finished stock that it holds, but these represent 65 per cent of its total value. This is treated as Category A stock. There are sophisticated recording procedures, tight control is exerted over stock movements and there is a high level of security at the stock's location. This is economic because the stock represents a relatively small proportion of the total volume.

The business finds that steel fittings account for 30 per cent of the total volume of finished stock and represent 25 per cent of its total value. This is treated as Category B stock, with a lower level of recording and management control being applied.

The remaining 60 per cent of the volume of stock is plastic fittings, which represent the least valuable items that account for only 10 per cent of the total value of finished stock held. This is treated as Category C stock, so the level of recording and management control would be lower still. Applying to this stock, the level of control that is applied to Category A or even Category B stock would be uneconomic.

Categorising stock in this way seeks to direct management effort to the most important areas, and tries to ensure that the costs of controlling stock are appropriate to its importance.

| Figure 9.2 | ABC method of analysing and controlling stock |

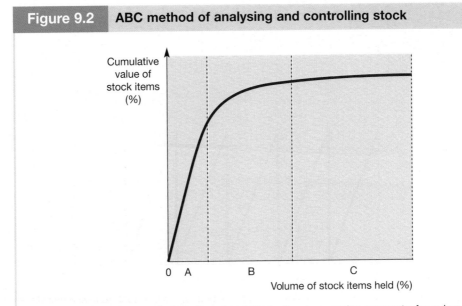

Category A contains stock that, though relatively few in quantity, accounts for a large proportion of the total value. Category B stock consists of those items that are less valuable but more numerous. Category C comprises those stock items that are very numerous but relatively low in value. Different stock control rules would be applied to each category. For example, only Category A stock would attract the more expensive and sophisticated controls.

Figure 9.2 demonstrates the logic of the ABC approach to stock (inventory) control.

Stock (inventory) management models

It is possible to use decision models to help manage stock. The **economic order quantity (EOQ)** model is concerned with answering the question 'How much stock should be ordered?' In its simplest form, the EOQ model assumes that demand is constant, so that stocks will be depleted evenly over time, and replenished just at the point that the stock runs out. These assumptions would lead to a 'saw tooth' pattern to represent stock movements within a business, as shown in Figure 9.3 (see p. 270).

The EOQ model recognises that the key costs associated with stock management are the costs of holding it and the cost of ordering it. The model can be used to calculate the optimum size of a purchase order by taking account of both of these cost elements. The cost of holding stock can be substantial, and so management may try to minimise the average amount of stock held. However, by reducing the level of stock held, and therefore the holding costs, there will be a need to increase the number of orders during the period, and so ordering costs will rise.

Figure 9.4 (see p. 270) shows how, as the level of stock and the size of stock orders increase, the annual costs of placing orders will decrease because fewer orders will be placed. However, the cost of holding stock will increase, as there will be higher average stock levels. The total costs curve, which is based on the sum of holding costs and ordering costs, will fall until the point E, which represents the minimum total cost, is reached. Thereafter, total costs begin to rise. The EOQ model seeks to identify point E at which total costs are minimised. This will represent half of the optimum amount that should be ordered on each occasion. Assuming, as we are doing, that stock is used

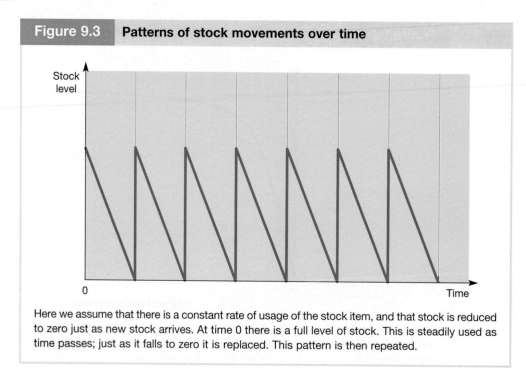

Figure 9.3 **Patterns of stock movements over time**

Here we assume that there is a constant rate of usage of the stock item, and that stock is reduced to zero just as new stock arrives. At time 0 there is a full level of stock. This is steadily used as time passes; just as it falls to zero it is replaced. This pattern is then repeated.

evenly over time and falls to zero before being replaced, the average stock level equals half of the order size.

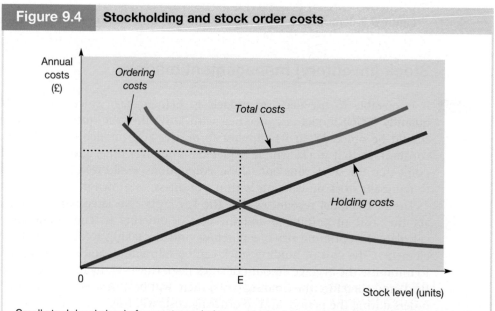

Figure 9.4 **Stockholding and stock order costs**

Small stock levels imply frequent reordering and high annual ordering costs. Small stock levels also imply relatively low stockholding costs. High stock levels imply exactly the opposite. There is, in theory, an optimum order size that will lead to the sum of ordering and stockholding costs (total costs) being at a minimum.

The EOQ model, which can be used to derive the most economic order quantity, is:

$$EOQ = \sqrt{\frac{2DC}{H}}$$

where:

D = the annual demand for the item of stock (expressed in units of the stock)
C = the cost of placing an order
H = the cost of holding one unit of stock for one year.

Activity 9.4

HLA Ltd sells 2,000 bags of cement each year. It has been estimated that the cost of holding one bag of cement for a year is £4. The cost of placing an order for stock is estimated at £250.

   Calculate the EOQ for bags of cement.

Your answer to this activity should be as follows:

$$EOQ = \sqrt{\frac{2 \times 2,000 \times 250}{4}}$$

$$= 500 \text{ units}$$

This will mean that the business will have to order bags of cement four times each year so that sales demand can be met.

Note that the cost of the stock concerned, that is the price paid to the supplier, does not directly impact on the EOQ model. The EOQ model is only concerned with the administrative costs of placing each order and the costs of looking after the stock. Where the business operates an ABC system of stock control, however, more expensive stock items will have greater stockholding costs. So the cost of the stock may have an indirect effect on the economic order size that the model recommends.

The basic EOQ model has a number of limiting assumptions. In particular, it assumes that:

- demand for the product can be predicted with accuracy;
- demand is constant over the period and does not fluctuate through seasonality or for other reasons;
- no 'buffer' stock is required; and
- there are no discounts for bulk purchasing.

However, the model can be developed to accommodate the problems of each of these limiting assumptions. Many businesses use this model (or a development of it) to help in the management of stocks.

Materials requirement planning systems

A **materials requirement planning (MRP) system** takes planned sales demand as its starting point. It then uses a computer package to help schedule the timing of deliveries of bought-in parts and materials to coincide with production requirements. It is a co-ordinated approach that links materials and parts deliveries to the scheduled time of their input to the production process. By ordering only those items that are necessary to ensure the flow of production, stock levels are likely to be reduced. MRP is really a 'top-down' approach to stock management, which recognises that stock ordering decisions cannot be viewed as being independent from production decisions. In recent years, this approach has been extended so as to provide a fully integrated approach to production planning. The approach also takes account of other manufacturing resources such as labour and machine capacity.

Just-in-time stock (inventory) management

In recent years, many businesses have tried to eliminate the need to hold stocks by adopting **'just-in-time' (JIT) stock management**. This approach was first used in the United States defence industry during World War II, but in more recent times it has been widely adopted. It was first used on a wide scale commercially by Japanese manufacturing businesses. The essence of JIT is, as the name suggests, to have supplies delivered to a business just in time for them to be used in the production process or in a sale. By adopting this approach the stockholding costs rest with suppliers rather than with the business itself. On the other hand, a failure by a particular supplier to deliver on time could cause enormous problems and costs for the business. Thus JIT can save cost, but it tends to increase risk.

For JIT to be successful, it is important that the business informs suppliers of its stock requirements in advance, and that suppliers, in their turn, deliver materials of the right quality at the agreed times. Failure to do so could lead to a dislocation of production or supply to customers and could be very costly. Thus a close relationship is required between the business and its suppliers.

Though a business that applies JIT will not have to hold stocks, there may be other costs associated with this approach. As the suppliers will be required to hold stocks for the business, they may try to recoup this additional cost through increased prices. The close relationship necessary between the business and its suppliers may also prevent the business from taking advantage of cheaper sources of supply if they become available.

Many people view JIT as more than simply a stock control system. The philosophy underpinning this approach is concerned with eliminating waste and striving for excellence. There is an expectation that suppliers will always deliver stock on time and that there will be no defects in the items supplied. There is also an expectation that, for manufacturers, the production process will operate at maximum efficiency. This means there will be no production breakdowns and the queuing and storage times of products manufactured will be eliminated, as only that time spent directly on processing the products is seen as adding value. While these expectations may be impossible to achieve, they do help to create a culture that is dedicated to the pursuit of excellence and quality.

Real Worlds 9.5 and **9.6** show how two very well-known businesses operating in the UK (one a retailer, the other a manufacturer) use JIT to advantage.

REAL WORLD 9.5

JIT at Boots

The Boots Company plc, the UK's largest health-care retailer, has recently improved the stock management at its stores. The business is working towards a JIT system where a stock delivery from its central warehouse in Nottingham will be made every day to each retail branch, with nearly all of the stock lines being placed directly onto the sales shelves, not into a branch stock room. The business says that this will bring significant savings of stores staff time and lead to significantly lower levels of stock being held, without any lessening of the service offered to customers. The new system is expected to lead to major economic benefits for the business.

Source: Information taken from The Boots Company plc Annual Report and Accounts for 2003.

REAL WORLD 9.6

JIT at Nissan

Nissan Motors UK Limited, the UK manufacturing arm of the world famous Japanese car business, has a plant in Sunderland in the north east of England. Here it operates a well-developed JIT system. Sommer supplies carpets and soft interior trim from a factory close to the Nissan plant. It makes deliveries to Nissan once every 20 minutes on average, so as to arrive exactly as they are needed in production. This is fairly typical of all of the 200 suppliers of components and materials to the Nissan plant.

Source: Information taken from Partnership Sourcing Best Practice Case Study (www.pslcbi.com/studies/docnissan.hmt).

Managing trade debtors (receivables)

Selling goods or services on credit results in costs being incurred by a business. These costs include credit administration costs, bad debts, and opportunities forgone in using the funds for more profitable purposes. However, these costs must be weighed against the benefits of increased sales resulting from the opportunity for customers to delay payment.

Selling on credit is very widespread, and appears to be the norm outside the retail trade. When a business offers to sell its goods or services on credit, it must have clear policies concerning:

- which customers it is prepared to offer credit to;
- what length of credit it is prepared to offer;
- whether discounts will be offered for prompt payment; and
- what collection policies should be adopted.

In this section we shall consider each of these issues.

Which customers should receive credit?

A business offering credit runs the risk of not receiving payment for goods or services supplied. Thus, care must be taken over the type of customer to whom credit facilities are offered. When considering a proposal from a customer for the supply of goods or services on credit, the business must take a number of factors into account. The following **five Cs of credit** provide a business with a useful checklist.

- *Capital*. The customer must appear to be financially sound before any credit is extended. Where the customer is a business, its financial statements should be examined. Particular regard should be given to the customer's likely future profitability and liquidity.
- *Capacity*. The customer must appear to have the capacity to pay amounts owing. Where possible, the payment record of the customer to date should be examined. If the customer is a business, the type of business operated and the physical resources of the business will be relevant. The value of goods that the customer wishes to buy on credit must be related to the customer's total financial resources.

- *Collateral.* On occasions, it may be necessary to ask for some kind of security for goods supplied on credit. When this occurs, the business must be convinced that the customer is able to offer a satisfactory form of security.
- *Conditions.* The state of the industry in which the customer operates, and the general economic conditions of the particular region or country, may have an important influence on the ability of a customer to pay the amounts outstanding on the due date.
- *Character.* It is important for a business to make some assessment of the customer's character. The willingness to pay will depend on the honesty and integrity of the individual with whom the business is dealing. Where the customer is a limited company this will mean assessing the characters of its directors. The business must feel satisfied that the customer will make every effort to pay any amounts owing.

Once a customer has been considered creditworthy, credit limits for the customer should be established, and procedures should be laid down to ensure that these are adhered to.

Activity 9.5

Assume that you are the credit manager of a business and that a limited company approaches you with a view to buying goods on credit. What sources of information might you decide to use to help assess the financial health of the potential customer?

There are various possibilities. You may have thought of some of the following:

- *Trade references.* Some businesses ask potential customers to supply them with references from other suppliers who have made sales on credit to them. This may be extremely useful, provided that the references supplied are truly representative of the opinions of a customer's suppliers. There is a danger that a potential customer will attempt to be selective when giving details of other suppliers, in order to gain a more favourable impression than is deserved.
- *Bank references.* It is possible to ask the potential customer for a bank reference. Though banks are usually prepared to supply references, the contents of such references are not always very informative. If customers are in financial difficulties, the bank may be unwilling to add to their problems by supplying poor references.
- *Published financial statements.* A limited company is obliged by law to file a copy of its annual financial statements with the Registrar of Companies. These financial statements are available for public inspection and provide a useful source of information.
- *The customer.* You may wish to interview the directors of the customer business and visit its premises in an attempt to gain some impression about the way that the customer conducts its business. Where a significant amount of credit is required, the business may ask the customer for access to internal budgets and other unpublished financial information to help assess the level of risk involved.
- *Credit agencies.* Specialist agencies exist to provide information that can be used to assess the creditworthiness of a potential customer. The information that a credit agency supplies may be gleaned from various sources, including the financial statements of the customer, court judgements and news items relating to the customer from both published and unpublished sources.

Length of credit period

A business must determine what credit terms it is prepared to offer its customers. The length of credit offered to customers can vary significantly between businesses, and may be influenced by such factors as:

- the typical credit terms operating within the industry;
- the degree of competition within the industry;
- the bargaining power of particular customers;
- the risk of non-payment;
- the capacity of the business to offer credit; and
- the marketing strategy of the business.

The last point identified may require some explanation. The marketing strategy of a business may have an important influence on the length of credit allowed. For example, if a business wishes to increase its market share it may decide to be more generous in its credit policy in an attempt to stimulate sales. Potential customers may be attracted by the offer of a longer credit period. However, any such change in policy must take account of the likely costs and benefits arising.

To illustrate this point, consider Example 9.2.

Example 9.2

Torrance Ltd produces a new type of golf putter. The business sells the putter to wholesalers and retailers and has an annual turnover of £600,000. The following data relate to each putter produced.

	£	£
Selling price		40
Variable costs	20	
Fixed cost apportionment	6	26
Net profit		14

The business's cost of capital is estimated at 10 per cent a year.

Torrance Ltd wishes to expand the sales volume of the new putter. It believes that offering a longer credit period can achieve this. The business's average collection period is currently 30 days. It is considering three options in an attempt to increase sales. These are as follows:

	Option		
	1	2	3
Increase in average collection period (days)	10	20	30
Increase in sales (£)	30,000	45,000	50,000

To enable the business to decide on the best option to adopt, it must weigh the benefits of the options against their respective costs. The benefits arising will be represented by the increase in profit from the sale of additional putters. From the cost data supplied we can see that the contribution (that is, selling price (£40) less variable costs (£20)) is £20 a putter, that is, 50 per cent of the selling price. So, whatever increase there may be in sales revenue, the additional contributions will be half of that figure. The fixed costs can be ignored in our calculations, as they will remain the same whichever option is chosen.

Example 9.2 continued

The increase in contribution under each option will therefore be:

	Option		
	1	2	3
50% of the increase in sales revenue (£)	15,000	22,500	25,000

The increase in debtors under each option will be as follows:

	Option		
	1	2	3
	£	£	£
Projected level of debtors			
40 × £630,000/365 (Note 1)	69,041		
50 × £645,000/365		88,356	
60 × £650,000/365			106,849
Less Current level of debtors			
30 × £600,000/365	49,315	49,315	49,315
Increase in debtors	19,726	39,041	57,534

The increase in debtors that results from each option will mean an additional finance cost to the business.

The net increase in the business's profit arising from the projected change is:

	Option		
	1	2	3
	£	£	£
Increase in contribution (see above)	15,000	22,500	25,000
Less Increase in finance cost (Note 2)	1,973	3,904	5,753
Net increase in profits	13,027	18,596	19,247

The calculations show that Option 3 will be the most profitable one.

Notes:
1 If the annual sales total £630,000 and 40 days' credit are allowed (both of which will apply under Option 1), the average amount that will be owed to the business by its customers, at any point during the year, will be the daily sales (that is, £630,000/365) multiplied by the number of days that the customers take to pay (that is, 40).

   Exactly the same logic applies to Options 2 and 3 and to the current level of debtors.
2 The increase in the finance cost for Option 1 will be the increase in debtors (£19,726 × 10%). The equivalent figures for the other options are derived in a similar way.

Example 9.2 illustrates the way in which a business should assess changes in credit terms. However, if there is a risk that, by extending the length of credit, there will be an increase in bad debts, this should also be taken into account in the calculations, as should any additional collection costs that will be incurred.

Real World 9.7 provides some insight to the typical length of credit taken by UK businesses.

Cash discounts

A business may decide to offer a **cash discount** in an attempt to encourage prompt payment from its credit customers. The size of any discount will be an important influence on whether a customer decides to pay promptly.

REAL WORLD 9.7

Length of credit taken by UK businesses

In their annual reports, UK limited companies are legally obliged to disclose the average length of trade credit that they take from their suppliers. For a random sample of 21 Stock Exchange listed UK businesses, the following applied:

Shortest period taken by any business	9 days
Longest period taken by any business	60 days
Mean (simple average) period for all of the businesses	33 days
Median (middle ranking) period of all of the businesses	32 days

Source: Information taken from the 2002 and 2003 annual reports of a random sample of UK Stock Exchange listed businesses.

From the business's viewpoint, the cost of offering discounts must be weighed against the likely benefits in the form of a reduction both in the cost of financing debtors and in the amount of bad debts.

In practice, there is always the danger that a customer may be slow to pay and yet may still take the discount offered. Where the customer is important to the business it may be difficult to insist on full payment.

Self-assessment question 9.1

Williams Wholesalers Ltd at present requires payment from its customers by the end of the month after the month of delivery. On average, customers take 70 days to pay. Sales amount to £4m a year and bad debts to £20,000 a year.

It is planned to offer customers a cash discount of 2 per cent for payment within 30 days. Williams estimates that 50 per cent of customers will accept this facility but that the remaining customers, who tend to be slow payers, will not pay until 80 days after the sale. At present the business has an overdraft facility at an interest rate of 13 per cent a year. If the plan goes ahead, bad debts will be reduced to £10,000 a year and there will be savings in credit administration expenses of £6,000 a year.

Should Williams Wholesalers Ltd offer the new credit terms to customers? You should support your answer with any calculations and explanations that you consider necessary.

Debt factoring and invoice discounting

Trade debts can, in effect, be turned into cash by either factoring them or having sales invoices discounted. These both seem to be fairly popular approaches to managing trade debtors.

Collection policies

A business offering credit must ensure that amounts owing are collected as quickly as possible. An efficient collection policy requires an efficient accounting system. Invoices (bills) must be sent out promptly to customers, as must regular monthly statements. Reminders must also be despatched promptly to customers who are late in paying.

It is almost inevitably the case that a business making significant sales on credit will sometimes be faced with customers who do not pay. When this occurs, there should be agreed procedures for dealing with the situation. However, the cost of any action to be taken against delinquent debtors must be weighed against the likely returns. For example, there is little point in taking legal action against a customer, incurring large legal expenses, if there is evidence that the customer does not have the necessary resources to pay. Where possible, an estimate of the cost of bad debts should be taken into account when setting prices for products or services.

Management can monitor the effectiveness of collection policies in a number of ways. One method is to calculate the **average settlement period for debtors** ratio. This is calculated as follows:

$$\text{Average settlement period for debtors (receivables)} = \frac{\text{Trade debtors}}{\text{Credit sales}} \times 365$$

Though this ratio can be useful, it is important to remember that it produces an *average* figure for the number of days for which debts are outstanding. This average may be badly distorted by a few large customers who are very slow or very fast payers.

A more detailed and informative approach to monitoring debtors may be to produce an **ageing schedule of debtors**. Debts are divided into categories according to the length of time the debt has been outstanding. An ageing schedule can be produced, on a regular basis, to help managers see the pattern of outstanding debts. An example of an ageing schedule is set out in Example 9.3.

Example 9.3

Ageing schedule of debtors at 31 December

Customer	Days outstanding				Total
	1 to 30 days	31 to 60 days	61 to 90 days	More than 90 days	
	£	£	£	£	£
A Ltd	20,000	10,000	–	–	30,000
B Ltd	–	24,000	–	–	24,000
C Ltd	12,000	13,000	14,000	18,000	57,000
Total	32,000	47,000	14,000	18,000	111,000

This shows a business's trade debtor figure at 31 December, which totals £111,000. Each customer's balance is analysed according to how long the debt has been outstanding.

Thus we can see from the schedule that A Ltd has £20,000 outstanding for 30 days or less (that is, arising from sales during December) and £10,000 outstanding for between 31 and 60 days (arising from November sales). This information can be very useful for credit control purposes.

Many accounting software packages now include this ageing schedule as one of the routine reports available to managers. Such packages often have the facility to put customers 'on hold' when they reach their credit limits. Putting a customer on hold means that no further credit sales will be made to that customer until debts arising from past sales have been settled.

Activity 9.6

What kind of corrective action might the managers of a business decide to take if they find that debtors are paying more slowly than anticipated?

Managers might decide to do one or more of the following:

- offer cash discounts to encourage prompt payment;
- inform customers that debts are to be paid more promptly;
- improve the accounting system to ensure that customers are billed more promptly, reminders are sent out promptly and so on; and
- change the eligibility criteria for customers who receive credit.

As a footnote to our consideration of managing debtors, **Real World 9.8** outlines some of the excuses that long-suffering credit managers must listen to when chasing payment for outstanding debt.

REAL WORLD 9.8

It's in the post

Accountants' noses should be growing, if we're to believe a new survey listing the bizarre excuses given by businesses that fail to pay their debts.

'The director's been shot' and 'I'll pay you when God tells me to' are just two of the most outrageous excuses listed in a survey published by the Credit Services Association, the debt collection industry body.

The commercial sector tends to blame financial problems, and excuses such as 'you'll get paid when we do' and 'the finance director is off sick' are common. However, those in the consumer sector apparently feel no shame in citing personal relationship problems as the reason for not paying the bill.

Source: Accountancy, April 2000, p. 18.

Managing cash

Why hold cash?

Most businesses hold a certain amount of cash. The amount of cash held tends to vary considerably between businesses.

Activity 9.7

Why do you think a business may decide to hold at least some of its assets in the form of cash? (*Hint*: There are broadly three reasons.)

They are:

1   To meet day-to-day commitments, a business requires a certain amount of cash. Payments for wages, overhead expenses, goods purchased and so on must be made at the due dates.
2   If future cash flows are uncertain for any reason, it would be prudent to hold a balance of cash. For example, a major customer that owes a large sum to the business may be in financial difficulties. Given this situation, the business can retain its capacity to meet its obligations by holding a cash balance. Similarly, if there is some uncertainty concerning future outlays, a cash balance will be required.
3   A business may decide to hold cash to put itself in a position to exploit profitable opportunities as and when they arise. For example, by holding cash, a business may be able to acquire a competitor business that suddenly becomes available at an attractive price.

How much cash should be held?

Though cash can be held for each of the reasons identified, this may not always be necessary. If a business is able to borrow quickly, the amount of cash it needs to hold can be reduced. Similarly, if the business holds assets that can easily be converted to cash (for example, marketable securities such as shares in Stock Exchange listed businesses or government bonds), the amount of cash held can be reduced.

The decision as to how much cash a particular business should hold is a difficult one. Different businesses will have different views on the subject.

Activity 9.8

What do you think are the major factors that influence how much cash a business will hold? See if you can think of five possible factors.

You may have thought of the following:

● *The nature of the business*. Some businesses such as utilities (for example, water, electricity and gas suppliers) may have cash flows that are both predictable and reasonably certain. This will enable them to hold lower cash balances. For some businesses, cash balances may vary greatly according to the time of year. A seasonal business may accumulate cash during the high season to enable it to meet commitments during the low season.
● *The opportunity cost of holding cash*. Where there are profitable opportunities it may not be wise to hold a large cash balance.
● *The level of inflation*. Holding cash during a period of rising prices will lead to a loss of purchasing power. The higher the level of inflation, the greater will be this loss.
● *The availability of near-liquid assets*. If a business has marketable securities or stocks that may easily be liquidated, the amount of cash held may be reduced.
● *The availability of borrowing*. If a business can borrow easily (and quickly) there is less need to hold cash.
● *The cost of borrowing*. When interest rates are high, the option of borrowing becomes less attractive.
● *Economic conditions*. When the economy is in recession, businesses may prefer to hold cash so that they can be well placed to invest when the economy improves. In addition,

during a recession, businesses may experience difficulties in collecting debts. They may therefore hold higher cash balances than usual in order to meet commitments.
● *Relationships with suppliers*. Too little cash may hinder the ability of the business to pay suppliers promptly. This can lead to a loss of goodwill. It may also lead to discounts being forgone.

Controlling the cash balance

Several models have been developed to help control the cash balance of the business. One such model proposes the use of upper and lower control limits for cash balances and the use of a target cash balance. The model assumes that the business will invest in marketable investments that can easily be liquidated. These investments will be purchased or sold, as necessary, in order to keep the cash balance within the control limits.

The model proposes two upper and two lower control limits (see Figure 9.5). If the business exceeds an *outer* limit, the managers must decide whether or not the cash balance is likely to return to a point within the *inner* control limits set, over the next few days. If this seems likely, then no action is required. If, on the other hand, it does not seem likely, management must change the cash position of the business by either lending or borrowing (or possibly by buying or selling marketable securities).

In Figure 9.5 we can see that the lower outer control limit has been breached for four days. If a four-day period is unacceptable, managers must sell marketable securities to replenish the cash balance.

Figure 9.5	Controlling the cash balance

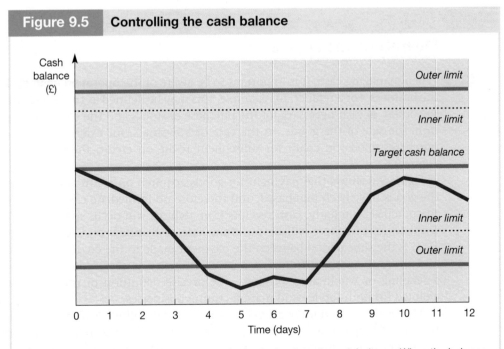

Management sets the upper and lower limits for the business's cash balance. When the balance goes beyond either of these limits, unless it is clear that the balance will return fairly quickly to within the limit, action will need to be taken. If the upper limit is breached, some cash will be placed on deposit or used to buy some marketable securities. If the lower limit is breached, the business will need to borrow some cash or sell some securities.

The model relies heavily on management judgement to determine where the control limits are set and the time period within which breaches of the control limits are acceptable. Past experience may be useful in helping managers decide on these issues. There are other models, however, that do not rely on management judgement. Instead, these use quantitative techniques to determine an optimal cash policy.

Cash budgets and managing cash

To manage cash effectively, it is useful for a business to prepare a cash budget. This is a very important tool for both planning and control purposes. Cash budgets were considered in Chapter 6, and so we shall not consider them again in detail. However, it is worth repeating the point that these statements enable managers to see the expected outcome of planned events on the cash balance. The cash budget will identify periods when cash surpluses and cash deficits are expected.

When a cash surplus is expected to arise, managers must decide on the best use of the surplus funds. When a cash deficit is expected, managers must make adequate provision by borrowing, liquidating assets or rescheduling cash payments or receipts to deal with this. Cash budgets are useful in helping to control the cash held. The actual cash flows can be compared with the budgeted cash flows for the period. If there is a significant divergence between the budgeted cash flows and the actual cash flows, explanations must be sought and corrective action taken where necessary.

Though cash budgets are prepared primarily for internal management purposes, prospective lenders sometimes require them when a loan to a business is being considered.

Operating cash cycle

When managing cash, it is important to be aware of the **operating cash cycle (OCC)** of the business. For a retailer, for example, this may be defined as the time period between the outlay of cash necessary for the purchase of stocks and the ultimate receipt of cash from the sale of the goods. In the case of a business, for example a wholesaler, that purchases goods on credit for subsequent resale on credit, the OCC is as shown in Figure 9.6.

Figure 9.6 shows that payment for goods acquired on credit occurs some time after the goods have been purchased, and therefore no immediate cash outflow arises from the purchase. Similarly, cash receipts from debtors will occur some time after the sale is made, and so there will be no immediate cash inflow as a result of the sale. The OCC is the time period between the payment made to the creditor for goods supplied and the cash received from the debtor. Though Figure 9.6 depicts the position for a retailing or wholesaling business, the precise definition of the OCC can easily be adapted for both service and manufacturing businesses.

The OCC is important because it has a significant influence on the financing requirements of the business: the longer the cycle, the greater the financing requirements of the business and the greater the financial risks. For this reason, a business is likely to want to reduce the OCC to the minimum possible period.

For the type of business mentioned above, which buys and sells on credit, the OCC can be calculated from the financial statements by the use of certain ratios. It is calculated as shown in Figure 9.7.

Figure 9.6 The operating cash cycle

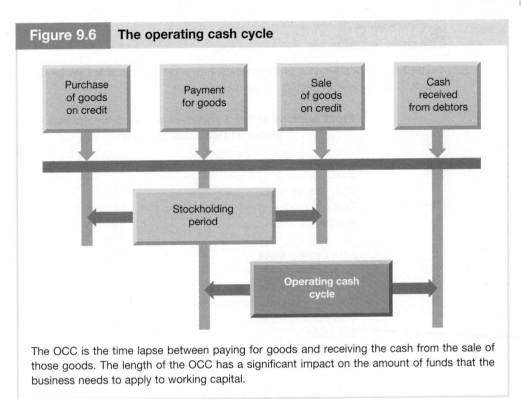

The OCC is the time lapse between paying for goods and receiving the cash from the sale of those goods. The length of the OCC has a significant impact on the amount of funds that the business needs to apply to working capital.

Figure 9.7 Calculating the operating cash cycle

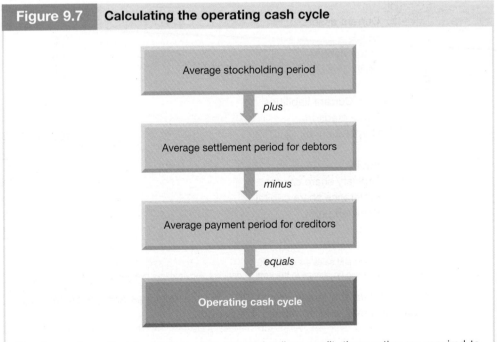

The figure shows that for business that buy and sell on credit, these ratios are required to calculate the OCC.

Activity 9.9

The financial statements of Freezeqwik Ltd, a distributor of frozen foods, are set out below for the year ended 31 December last year.

Profit and loss account (income statement) for the year ended 31 December last year

	£000	£000
Sales		820
Less Cost of sales		
Opening stock	142	
Purchases	<u>568</u>	
	710	
Less Closing stock	<u>166</u>	<u>544</u>
Gross profit		276
Administration expenses	(120)	
Selling and distribution expenses	(95)	
Financial expenses	<u>(32)</u>	<u>(247)</u>
Net profit		29
Corporation tax		<u>(7)</u>
Net profit after tax		<u>22</u>

Balance sheet as at 31 December last year

Non-current assets	£000	£000	£000
Freehold premises at valuation			180
Fixtures and fittings at written-down value			82
Motor vans at written-down value			<u>102</u>
			364
Current assets			
Stock		166	
Trade debtors		264	
Cash		<u>24</u>	
		454	
Less Current liabilities			
Trade creditors	159		
Corporation tax	<u>7</u>	166	<u>288</u>
			652
Equity			
Ordinary share capital			300
Preference share capital			200
Retained profit			<u>152</u>
			<u>652</u>

Notes:
1 All purchases and sales are on credit.
2 There has been no change in the level of debtors and creditors over the year.

Calculate the length of the OCC for the business and go on to suggest how the business may seek to reduce this period.

The OCC may be calculated as follows:

Average stockholding period: *No. of days*

$$\frac{\text{(Opening stock + Closing stock)}/2}{\text{Cost of sales}} \times 365 = \frac{(142 + 166)/2}{544} \times 365 \qquad\qquad 103$$

Average settlement period for debtors:

$$\frac{\text{Trade debtors}}{\text{Credit sales}} \times 365 = \frac{264}{820} \times 365 \qquad\qquad \underline{118}$$

$$221$$

Less

Average settlement period for creditors (payables):

$$\frac{\text{Trade creditors}}{\text{Credit purchases}} \times 365 = \frac{159}{568} \times 365 \qquad\qquad \underline{102}$$

OCC $\underline{119}$

The business can reduce the length of the OCC in a number of ways. The average stock-holding period seems quite long. At present, average stocks held represent more than three months' sales. Lowering the level of stocks held will reduce this. Similarly, the average settlement period for debtors seems long, at nearly four months' sales. Imposing tighter credit control, offering discounts, charging interest on overdue accounts and so on, may reduce this. However, any policy decisions concerning stocks and debtors must take account of current trading conditions.

Extending the period of credit taken to pay suppliers could also reduce the OCC. However, for reasons that will be explained later, this option must be given careful consideration.

Cash transmission

A business will normally wish to benefit from receipts from customers at the earliest opportunity. The benefit is immediate where payment is made in cash. However, when payment is made by cheque, there is normally a delay of three to four working days before the cheque can be cleared through the banking system. The business must therefore wait for this period before it can benefit from the amount paid in. In the case of a business that receives large amounts in the form of cheques, the opportunity cost of this delay can be very significant.

To avoid this delay, a business could require payments to be made in cash. This is not usually very practical, mainly because of the risk of theft and/or the expense of conveying cash securely. Another option is to ask for payment to be made by standing order or direct debit from the customer's bank account. This should ensure that the amount owing is always transferred from the bank account of the customer to the bank account of the business on the day that has been agreed.

It is also possible for funds to be transferred directly to a business's bank account. As a result of developments in computer technology, customers can pay for items by using debit cards, which results in the appropriate account being instantly debited and seller's bank account being instantly credited with the required amount. This method of payment is widely used by large retail businesses, and may well extend to other types of business.

Bank overdrafts

→ **Bank overdrafts** are simply bank current accounts that contain a negative amount of cash. They are a type of bank loan. They can be a useful tool in managing the business's cash flow requirements.

Managing trade creditors (payables)

Trade credit arises from the fact that most businesses buy their goods and service requirements on credit. In effect, suppliers are lending the business money, interest free, on a short-term basis. Trade creditors are the other side of the coin from trade debtors. One business's trade creditor is another one's trade debtor, in respect of a particular transaction. Trade creditors are an important source of finance for most businesses. It has been described as a 'spontaneous' source, as it tends to increase in line with the increase in the level of activity achieved by a business. Trade credit is widely regarded as a 'free' source of finance and, therefore, a good thing for a business to use. There may be real costs associated with taking trade credit, however.

Firstly, customers who take credit may not be as well treated as those who pay immediately. For example, when goods are in short supply, credit customers may receive lower priority when allocating the stock available. In addition, credit customers may be less favoured in terms of delivery dates or the provision of technical support services. Sometimes, the goods or services provided may be more costly if credit is required. However, in most industries trade credit is the norm. As a result, the above costs will not apply except, perhaps, to customers that abuse the credit facilities. A business purchasing supplies on credit may also have to incur additional administration and accounting costs in dealing with the scrutiny and payment of invoices, maintaining and updating creditors' accounts and so on.

REAL WORLD 9.9

Can't pay; won't pay

In some cases, delaying payment to creditors can be a sign of financial distress. One such example occurred in 2001 when Kmart, a large US retailer, suffered a cash crisis. This was largely as a result of one manager ordering $850m worth of stocks, which was later described in an internal report as 'excessive'. To conserve cash, the business implemented Project Slow It Down. This involved systematically delaying or reducing payments to trade creditors. The project also involved denying creditors access to records of the amounts owed by Kmart and giving false reasons as to why they had not been paid on time.

Source: Information taken from 'Kmart's fall is tale of poor governance', *Financial Times*, 29 January 2003.

Where a supplier offers a discount for prompt payment, the business should give careful consideration to the possibility of paying within the discount period. Example 9.4 illustrates the cost of forgoing possible discounts.

Example 9.4

Hassan Ltd takes 70 days to pay for goods from its supplier. To encourage prompt payment, the supplier has offered the business a 2 per cent discount if payment for goods is made within 30 days.

Hassan Ltd is not sure whether it is worth taking the discount offered.

If the discount is taken, payment could be made on the last day of the discount period (that is, the 30th day). However, if the discount is not taken, payment will be made after 70 days. This means that by not taking the discount the business will receive an extra 40 days' (that is, 70 minus 30) credit. The cost of this extra credit to the business will be the 2 per cent discount forgone. If we annualise the cost of this discount forgone, we have:

$$365/40 \times 2\% = 18.3\%*$$

We can see that the annual cost of forgoing the discount is very high, and it may be profitable for the business to pay the supplier within the discount period, even if it means that it will have to borrow to enable it to do so.

* This is an approximate annual rate. For the more mathematically minded, the precise rate is:

$$(((1 + 2/98)^{9.125}) - 1) \times 100\% = 20.2\%$$

The above points are not meant to imply that taking credit is a burden to a business. There are of course real benefits that can accrue. Provided that trade credit is not abused, it can represent a form of interest-free loan. It can be a much more convenient method of paying for goods and services than paying by cash, and during a period of inflation there will be an economic gain by paying later rather than sooner for goods and services purchased. For most businesses, these benefits will exceed the costs involved.

Controlling trade creditors (payables)

To help monitor the level of trade credit taken, management can calculate the **average settlement period for creditors**. This ratio is as follows:

$$\text{Average settlement period} = \frac{\text{Trade creditors}}{\text{Credit purchases}} \times 365$$

Once again this provides an average figure, which could be misleading. A more informative approach would be to produce an ageing schedule for creditors. This would look much the same as the ageing schedule for debtors described earlier.

Since, as was pointed out earlier in this section, one business's trade creditor is another one's trade debtor, the information contained in Real World 9.7 (p. 277) provides some indication of typical lengths of trade credit taken by UK businesses.

Working capital problems of the small business

We saw earlier (**Real World 9.1**, p. 264) that the amounts invested by businesses in working capital are often high in proportion to the total assets employed. It is, therefore, important that these amounts are properly managed. Although this point applies to businesses of all sizes, it may be of particular importance to small businesses. It is often claimed that many small businesses suffer from a lack of capital and, where this is the case, tight control over working capital investment becomes critical. There is evidence, however, that small businesses are not very good at managing their working capital and this has been cited as a major cause of their high failure rate compared with that of large businesses. In this section, we consider the working capital management problems associated with small businesses.

Credit management

Small businesses often lack the resources to manage their trade debtors (receivables) effectively. It is not unusual for a small business to operate without a separate credit control department. This tends to mean that both the expertise and the information required to make sound judgements concerning terms of sale and so on may not be available. A small business may also lack proper debt collection procedures, such as prompt invoicing and sending out regular statements. This will increase the risks of late payment and defaulting debtors.

These risks probably tend to increase where there is an excessive concern for growth. In an attempt to increase sales, small businesses may be too willing to extend credit to customers that are poor credit risks. Whilst this kind of problem can occur in businesses of all sizes, small businesses seem particularly susceptible.

Another problem faced by small businesses is their lack of market power. They will often find themselves in a weak position when negotiating credit terms with larger businesses. Moreover, when a large customer exceeds the terms of credit, the small supplier may feel inhibited from pressing the customer for payment in case future sales are lost.

It seems that small businesses have a much greater proportion of overdue debts than large businesses. **Real World 9.10** refers to evidence of this.

REAL WORLD 9.10

Small businesses wait longer

A survey undertaken by the Credit Management Research Centre (CMRC) during April and June 2003, indicates that small businesses (that is, those with annual sales turnover of less than £5m) are likely to have to wait an average of 60 days for their trade debtors to pay. This contrasts with the average of 32 to 33 days for the large businesses mentioned earlier (see Real World 9.7).

Source: Information taken from 'Small firms still have to wait for their money' by Doug Morrison, *Sunday Telegraph*, 14 September 2003. This article discussed the CMRC research.

The reason for the delay suffered by small businesses probably relates to one of the factors mentioned above, namely the bargaining power of customers. The customers of small businesses may well be larger ones, which can use a threat, perhaps an implied one, of withdrawing custom, to force small businesses to accept later trade debtor settlement.

In the UK, the government has intervened to help deal with this problem and the law now permits small businesses to charge interest on overdue accounts. In addition, large companies are now required to disclose in their published financial statements the payment policy adopted towards suppliers in the hope that this will improve the behaviour of those that delay payments. However, it is unlikely that legislation alone will make a significant improvement. Whilst small businesses may be able to charge interest on overdue accounts, they will often avoid doing so because they fear that large customers would view this as a provocative act. What is really needed to help small businesses is a change in the payment culture.

One way of dealing with the credit management problem is to factor the outstanding debts. Under this kind of arrangement, the factor will take over the sales records of the business and will take responsibility for the prompt collection of debts. However, some businesses are too small to take advantage of this facility. The set-up costs of a factoring arrangement often make businesses with a small turnover (say, £100,000 a year or less) an uneconomic proposition for the factor.

Managing stock (inventory)

A lack of financial management skills within a small business often creates problems in managing stock in an efficient and effective way. The owners of small businesses are not always aware that there are costs involved in holding too much stock and that there are also costs involved in holding too little. These costs, which were discussed earlier, may be very high in certain industries such as manufacturing and wholesaling, where stock accounts for a significant proportion of the total assets held.

It was mentioned earlier in the chapter that the starting point for an effective stock management system is good planning and budgeting systems. In particular, there should be reliable sales forecasts, or budgets, available for stock ordering purposes. However, it seems that not all small businesses prepare these forecasts or budgets. A survey by Chittenden *et al.* (see reference 1 at the end of the chapter) of small and medium-sized businesses indicated that only 78 per cent of those replying prepare a sales budget. Stock management can also benefit from good reporting systems and the application of quantitative techniques (for example, the economic order quantity model) to try to optimise stock levels. However, the same survey found that more than one-third of small businesses rely on manual methods of stock control and the majority do not use stock optimisation techniques.

Managing cash

The management of cash raises similar issues to those relating to the management of stocks. There are costs involved in holding both too much and too little cash. Thus, there is a need for careful planning and monitoring of cash flows over time. The Chittenden survey (see reference 1 at the end of the chapter) found, however, that only 63 per cent of those replying prepared a cash budget. It was also found that cash balances are generally proportionately higher for smaller businesses than for larger ones. More than half of those in the survey held surplus cash balances on a regular basis. Though this may reflect a more conservative approach to liquidity among the owners of smaller businesses, it may suggest a failure to recognise the opportunity costs of cash balances.

Managing credit suppliers

In practice, small businesses often try to cope with the late payment of credit customers by delaying payments to their credit suppliers. We saw earlier in the chapter, however, that this can be an expensive option. Where discounts are forgone, the annual cost of this financing option compares unfavourably with most other forms of short-term financing. Nevertheless, the vast majority of small and medium-sized businesses are unaware of the very high cost of delaying payment, according to the Chittenden survey. (See reference 1 at the end of the chapter.)

SUMMARY

The main points of this chapter may be summarised as follows:

Working capital (WC) = stock + debtors + cash − creditors − bank overdrafts.

- An investment in WC cannot be avoided in practice – typically, large amounts are involved.

Stock-in-trade (inventory)

- Costs of holding stock include:
  - Lost interest.
  - Storage cost.
  - Insurance cost.
  - Obsolescence.
- Costs of not holding sufficient stock include:
  - Loss of sales and customer goodwill.
  - Production dislocation.
  - Loss of flexibility – cannot take advantage of opportunities.
  - Reorder costs – low stock implies more frequent ordering.
- Practical points on stock management include:
  - Identify optimum order size – models can help with this.
  - Set stock reorder levels.
  - Use budgets.
  - Keep reliable stock records.
  - Use accounting ratios (for example, stock turnover period ratio).
  - Establish systems for security of stock and authorisation.
  - Consider just-in-time (JIT) stock management.

Trade debtors (receivables)

- Five Cs of credit:
  - Capital.
  - Capacity.
  - Collateral.
  - Conditions.
  - Character.

- Costs of allowing credit:
  - Lost interest.
  - Lost purchasing power.
  - Costs of assessing customer creditworthiness.
  - Administration cost.
  - Bad debts.
  - Cash discounts (for prompt payment).
- Costs of denying credit:
  - Loss of customer goodwill.
- Practical points on debtor management:
  - Establish a policy.
  - Assess and monitor customer creditworthiness.
  - Establish effective administration of debtors.
  - Establish a policy on bad debts.
  - Consider cash discounts.
  - Use accounting ratios (for example, average settlement period for debtors ratio).
  - Use ageing summaries.

Cash

- Costs of holding cash:
  - Lost interest.
  - Lost purchasing power.
- Costs of holding insufficient cash:
  - Loss of supplier goodwill if unable to meet commitments on time.
  - Loss of opportunities.
  - Inability to claim cash discounts.
  - Costs of borrowing (should an obligation need to be met at short notice).
- Practical points on cash management:
  - Establish a policy.
  - Plan cash flows.
  - Make judicious use of bank overdraft finance – it can be cheap and flexible.
  - Use short-term cash surpluses profitably.
  - Bank frequently.
  - Operating cash cycle (for a retailer) = length of time from buying stock to receiving cash from debtors less creditors' payment period (in days).
  - Transmit cash promptly.
- An objective of WC management is to limit the length of the OCC, subject to any risks that this may cause.

Trade creditors (payables)

- Costs of taking credit:
  - Higher price than purchases for immediate cash settlement.
  - Administrative costs.
  - Restrictions imposed by seller.
- Costs of not taking credit:
  - Lost interest-free borrowing.
  - Lost purchasing power.
  - Inconvenience – paying at the time of purchase can be inconvenient.
- Practical points on creditor management:
  - Establish a policy.
  - Exploit free credit as far as possible.
  - Use accounting ratios (for example, average settlement period ratio).

● Working capital and the small business:
  – Small businesses often lack the skills and resources to manage working capital effectively.
  – Small businesses often suffer from large businessses delaying payments for goods supplied.
  – Changes in the law designed to help small businesses have had limited success.

→ **Key terms**

Working capital   p. 262
Lead time   p. 267
ABC system of stock control   p. 268
Economic order quantity (EOQ)
   p. 269
Materials requirement planning (MRP) system   p. 271
Just-in-time (JIT) stock management
   p. 272

Five Cs of credit   p. 273
Cash discount   p. 276
Average settlement period for debtors
   p. 278
Ageing schedule of debtors   p. 278
Operating cash cycle (OCC)   p. 282
Bank overdrafts   p. 286
Average settlement period for creditors   p. 287

Further reading

If you would like to explore the topics covered in this chapter in more depth, we recommend the following books:

Corporate Financial Management, *Arnold G.*, 2nd edn, Financial Times Prentice Hall, 1998, chapter 13.

Business Finance: Theory and practice, *McLaney E.*, 6th edn, Financial Times Prentice Hall, 2003, chapter 13.

Corporate Finance and Investment, *Pike R. and Neale B.*, 4th edn, Prentice Hall International, 2002, chapters 14 and 15.

Financial Management and Decision Making, *Samuels J., Wilkes F. and Brayshaw R.*, International Thomson Business Press, 1999, chapter 18.

Reference

1 **Financial Management and Working Capital Practices in UK SMEs**, *Chittenden F., Poutziouris P. and Michaelis N.*, Manchester Business School, 1998.

REVIEW QUESTIONS

Answers to these questions can be found on the students' side of the Companion Website at www.pearsoned.co.uk/atrillmclaney.

9.1 Tariq is the credit manager of Heltex plc. He is concerned that the pattern of monthly sales receipts shows that credit collection is poor compared with budget. Heltex's sales director believes that Tariq is to blame for this situation, but Tariq insists that he is not. Why might Tariq not be to blame for the deterioration in the credit collection period?

9.2 How might each of the following affect the level of stocks (inventories) held by a business?
- An increase in the number of production bottlenecks experienced by the business.
- A rise in the level of interest rates.
- A decision to offer customers a narrower range of products in the future.
- A switch of suppliers from an overseas business to a local business.
- A deterioration in the quality and reliability of bought-in components.

9.3 What are the reasons for holding stocks (inventories)? Are these reasons different from the reasons for holding cash?

9.4 Identify the costs of holding:
(a) too little cash, and
(b) too much cash.

EXERCISES

Exercises 9.4 to 9.8 are more advanced than 9.1 to 9.3. Those with a coloured number have answers at the back of the book.

9.1 Hercules Wholesalers Ltd has been particularly concerned with its liquidity position in recent months. The most recent profit and loss account (income statement) and balance sheet of the business are as follows:

Profit and loss account (income statement) for the year ended 31 December last year

	£000	£000
Sales		452
Less Cost of sales		
Opening stock	125	
Add Purchases	341	
	466	
Less Closing stock	143	323
Gross profit		129
Expenses		132
Net loss for the period		(3)

Balance sheet as at 31 December last year

	£000	£000	£000
Non-current assets			
Freehold premises at valuation			280
Fixtures and fittings at cost less depreciation			25
Motor vehicles at cost less depreciation			52
			357
Current assets			
Stock		143	
Debtors		163	
		306	
Less **Current liabilities**			
Trade creditors	145		
Bank overdraft	140	285	21
			378
Less **Non-current liabilities**			
Loans			120
			258
Equity			
Ordinary share capital			100
Retained profit			158
			258

The debtors and creditors were maintained at a constant level throughout the year.

Required:
(a) Calculate the operating cash cycle for Hercules Wholesalers Ltd based on the information above. (Assume a 360-day year.)
(b) State what steps may be taken to improve the operating cash cycle of the business.

9.2 International Electric plc at present offers its customers 30 days' credit. Half the customers, by value, pay on time. The other half takes an average of 70 days to pay. The business is considering offering a cash discount of 2 per cent to its customers for payment within 30 days.

The credit controller anticipates that half of the customers who now take an average of 70 days to pay (that is, a quarter of all customers) will pay in 30 days. The other half (the final quarter) will still take an average of 70 days to pay. The scheme will also reduce bad debts by £300,000 a year.

Annual sales of £365m are made evenly throughout the year. At present the business has a large overdraft (£60m) with its bank at 12 per cent a year.

Required:
(a) Calculate the approximate equivalent annual percentage cost of a discount of 2 per cent, which reduces the time taken by debtors to pay from 70 days to 30 days. (*Hint*: This part can be answered without reference to the narrative above.)
(b) Calculate debtors outstanding under both the old and new schemes.
(c) How much will the scheme cost the business in discounts?
(d) Should the business go ahead with the scheme? State what other factors, if any, should be taken into account.
(e) Outline the controls and procedures that a business should adopt to manage the level of its debtors.

9.3 The managing director of Sparkrite Ltd, a trading business, has just received summary sets of financial statements for last year and this year:

Sparkrite Ltd
Profit and loss accounts (income statement) for years
ended 30 September last year and this year

	Last year		This year	
	£000	£000	£000	£000
Sales		1,800		1,920
Less Cost of sales				
Opening stock	160		200	
Purchases	1,120		1,175	
	1,280		1,375	
Less Closing stock	200		250	
		1,080		1,125
Gross profit		720		795
Less Expenses		680		750
Net profit		40		45

Balance sheets as at 30 September last year and this year

	Last year		This year	
	£000	£000	£000	£000
Non-current assets		950		930
Current assets				
Stock	200		250	
Debtors	375		480	
Bank	4		2	
	579		732	
Less Current liabilities	195		225	
		384		507
		1,334		1,437
Equity				
Fully paid £1 ordinary shares		825		883
Reserves		509		554
		1,334		1,437

The finance director has expressed concern at the increase in stock and debtors levels.

Required:
(a) Show, by using the data given, how you would calculate ratios that could be used to measure stock and debtor levels during last year and this year.
(b) Discuss the ways in which the management of Sparkrite Ltd could exercise control over:
    (i) stock levels;
    (ii) debtor levels.

9.4 Your superior, the general manager of Plastics Manufacturers Limited, has recently been talking to the chief buyer of Plastic Toys Limited, which manufactures a wide range of toys for young children. At present, Plastic Toys is considering changing its supplier of plastic granules and has offered to buy its entire requirement of 2,000 kg a month from you at the going market rate, provided that you will grant it three months' credit on its purchases. The following information is available:

1 Plastic granules sell for £10 a kg, variable costs are £7 a kg, and fixed costs £2 a kg.
2 Your own business is financially strong, and has sales of £15 million a year. For the foreseeable future it will have surplus capacity, and it is actively looking for new outlets.

3 Extracts from Plastic Toys' financial statements:

Year	1	2	3
	£000	£000	£000
Sales	800	980	640
Profit before interest and tax	100	110	(150)
Capital employed	600	650	575

Year	1	2	3
	£000	£000	£000
Current assets			
Stocks	200	220	320
Debtors	140	160	160
	340	380	480
Current liabilities			
Creditors	180	190	220
Overdraft	100	150	310
	280	340	530
Net current assets	60	40	(50)

Required:

(a) Write some short notes suggesting sources of information that you would use to assess the creditworthiness of potential customers who are unknown to you. You should critically evaluate each source of information.

(b) Describe the accounting controls that you would use to monitor the level of your business's trade debtors.

(c) Advise your general manager on the acceptability of the proposal. You should give your reasons and do any calculations you consider necessary. (*Hint*: To answer this question you must weigh the costs of administration and cash discounts against the savings in bad debts and interest charges.)

9.5 Mayo Computers Ltd has an annual turnover of £20m before taking into account bad debts of £0.1m. All sales made by the business are on credit, and, at present, credit terms are negotiable by the customer. On average, the settlement period for trade debtors is 60 days. Trade debtors are financed by an overdraft bearing a 14 per cent a year interest rate. The business is currently reviewing its credit policies to see whether more efficient and profitable methods could be employed. Only one proposal has so far been put forward concerning the management of trade credit.

The credit control department has proposed that customers should be given a $2^1/_2$ per cent discount if they pay within 30 days. For those who do not pay within this period, a maximum of 50 days' credit should be given. The credit department believes that 60 per cent of customers will take advantage of the discount by paying at the end of the discount period, and the remainder will pay at the end of 50 days. The credit department believes that bad debts can be effectively eliminated by adopting the above policies and by employing stricter credit investigation procedures, which will cost an additional £20,000 a year. The credit department is confident that these new policies will not result in any reduction in sales.

Required:

Calculate the net annual cost (savings) to the business of abandoning its existing credit policies and adopting the proposals of the credit control department. (*Hint*: To answer this question you must weigh the costs of administration and cash discounts against the savings in bad debts and interest charges.)

9.6 Boswell Enterprises Ltd is reviewing its trade credit policy. The business, which sells all of its goods on credit, has estimated that sales for the forthcoming year will be £3m under the existing policy. Thirty per cent of trade debtors are expected to pay one month after being invoiced and 70 per cent are expected to pay two months after being invoiced. These estimates are in line with previous years' figures.

At present, no cash discounts are offered to customers. However, to encourage prompt payment, the business is considering giving a $2^1/_2$ per cent cash discount to debtors who pay in one month or less. Given this incentive, the business expects 60 per cent of trade debtors to pay one month after being invoiced and 40 per cent of debtors to pay two months after being invoiced. The business believes that the introduction of a cash discount policy will prove attractive to some customers and will lead to a 5 per cent increase in total sales.

Irrespective of the trade credit policy adopted, the gross profit margin of the business will be 20 per cent for the forthcoming year and three months' stock will be held. Fixed monthly expenses of £15,000 and variable expenses (excluding discounts), equivalent to 10 per cent of sales, will be incurred and will be paid one month in arrears. Trade creditors will be paid in arrears and will be equal to two months' cost of sales. The business will hold a fixed cash balance of £140,000 throughout the year, whichever trade credit policy is adopted. No dividends will be proposed or paid during the year. Ignore taxation.

Required:
(a) Calculate the investment in working capital at the end of the forthcoming year under:
  ● The existing policy
  ● The proposed policy.
(b) Calculate the expected net profit for the forthcoming year under:
  ● The existing policy
  ● The proposed policy.
(c) Advise the business as to whether it should implement the proposed policy.

(*Hint*: The investment in working capital will be made up of stock, debtors and cash, *less* trade creditors and any unpaid expenses at the year end.)

9.7 Delphi plc has recently decided to enter the expanding market for minidisc players. The business will manufacture the players and sell them to small TV and hi-fi specialists, medium-sized music stores and large retail chain stores. The new product will be launched next February and predicted sales for the product from each customer group for February and the expected rate of growth for subsequent months are as follows:

Customer type	February sales (£000)	Monthly compound sales growth (%)	Credit sales (months)
TV and hi-fi specialists	20	4	1
Music stores	30	6	2
Retail chain stores	40	8	3

The business is concerned about the financing implications of launching the new product, as it is already experiencing liquidity problems. In addition, it is concerned that the credit control department will find it difficult to cope. This is a new market for the business and there are likely to be many new customers who will have to be investigated for creditworthiness.

Workings should be in £000 and calculations made to one decimal point only.

Required:
(a) Prepare an ageing schedule of the monthly debtors' balance relating to the new product for each of the first four months of the new product's life, and comment on the results. The schedule should analyse the debts outstanding according to customer type. It should also indicate, for each customer type, the relevant percentage outstanding in relation to the total amount outstanding for each month.
(b) Identify and discuss the factors that should be taken into account when evaluating the creditworthiness of the new business customers.

9.8 Goliath plc is a retail business operating in Ireland. The most recent financial statements of the business are as follows:

Profit and loss account (income statement) for the year to 31 May

	£000	£000
Sales		2,400.0
Less Cost of sales		
Opening stock	550.0	
Add Purchases	1,450.0	
	2,000.0	
Less Closing stock	560.0	1,440.0
Gross profit		960.0
Administration expenses	(300.0)	
Selling expenses	(436.0)	
Interest payable	(40.0)	(776.0)
Net profit before taxation		184.0
Less Corporation tax (25%)		46.0
Net profit after taxation		138.0

Balance sheet as at 31 May

	£000	£000	£000
Non-current assets			
Machinery and equipment at cost		424.4	
Less Accumulated depreciation		140.8	283.6
Motor vehicles at cost		308.4	
Less Accumulated depreciation		135.6	172.8
			456.4
Current assets			
Stock at cost		560.0	
Trade debtors		565.0	
Cash at bank		36.4	
		1,161.4	
Current liabilities			
Trade creditors	(451.0)		
Corporation tax due	(46.0)	(497.0)	664.4
			1,120.8
Non-current liabilities			
Loan capital			(400.0)
			720.8
Equity			
£1 ordinary shares			200.0
Retained profit			520.8
			720.8

All sales and purchases are made on credit.

The business is considering whether to grant extended credit facilities to its customers. It has been estimated that increasing the settlement period for debtors by a further 20 days will increase the turnover of the business by 10 per cent. However, stocks will have to be increased by 15 per cent to cope with the increased demand. It is estimated that purchases will have to rise to £1,668,000 during the next year as a result of these changes. To finance the increase in stocks and debtors, the business will increase the settlement period taken for suppliers by 15 days and utilise a loan facility bearing a 10 per cent rate of interest for the remaining balance.

If the policy is implemented, bad debts are likely to increase by £120,000 and administration costs will rise by 15 per cent.

Required:
(a) Calculate the increase or decrease to each of the following that will occur in the forthcoming year if the proposed policy is implemented:
  (i) operating cash cycle (based on year-end figures)
  (ii) net investment in stock, debtors and creditors
  (iii) net profit after taxation.
(b) Should the business implement the proposed policy? Give reasons for your conclusion.

10

Measuring and controlling divisional performance

OBJECTIVES

When you have completed this chapter, you should be able to:

- Explain the potential advantages and disadvantages for a business of adopting a divisional structure.

- Identify the major methods of measuring the performance of operating divisions and divisional managers and discuss the issues surrounding these measures.

- Explain the problems of determining transfer prices between divisions and outline the methods used in practice.

INTRODUCTION

Although small businesses can be managed as a single unit, most businesses are divided into a number of operating units, or divisions. It is generally believed that a business will work more effectively towards its strategic objectives if it is managed as a set of relatively small units or divisions. Naturally managers, both of individual divisions and those to whom those divisional managers are responsible, will be very interested in the performance of each division. This raises the question of how best to assess divisional performance.

In some cases, an operating division will provide products or services to other divisions within the same business. When this occurs, the problem of measuring divisional performance can be more difficult, because the price at which goods are transferred to the 'buying' divisions will have an important influence on key performance measures such as sales and profits.

In this chapter we shall address these two issues of divisional performance measurement and transfer pricing. In doing this, we shall be picking up some of the points made in earlier chapters, particularly Chapters 3 and 8.

Why do businesses divisionalise?

Modern businesses are often extremely complex organisations. Many large businesses, for example, supply a wide range of products and services. Many have operating units located throughout the world and have an extended management hierarchy. Where business operations are complex, it is not really feasible for those at the top of the management hierarchy to know everything that is going on within the various operating units. It is, therefore, impractical for senior managers to take all the decisions necessary for running these units in such a way that will enable the business as a whole to meet its strategic objectives. As a result, it is usually sensible to devolve some decisions to those further down the hierarchy.

→ To achieve this, larger businesses tend to be split into a number of operating **divisions**. These divisions are usually organised according to:

● the services provided or the products made; and/or
● the geographical location.

The managers of these divisions are then given discretion over various aspects of divisional operations. The extent of the discretion allowed to divisional managers will vary from one business to the next.

In practice, divisions tend to fall into two broad classes:

→ ● **Profit centres.** The divisional manager of a profit centre will have responsibility for production and sales performance and can therefore decide on such matters as pricing, marketing, volume of output, sources of supply and sales mix. Divisional managers will each be assigned particular non-current (fixed) assets and working capital by central management and will be expected to generate profits from the effective use of those assets. Any additional capital expenditure relating to the division would have to be agreed by central management.

→ ● **Investment centres.** The divisional manager of an investment centre has discretion over capital expenditure and working capital decisions as well as production and sales performance. It is, in many respects, a business within a business. Thus, an investment centre is a profit centre with added authority to make investment decisions.

In both types of division, profit is measured and the divisional manager is held accountable for divisional performance. In practice, it appears that central management is more prepared to allow discretion over production and sales decisions than over capital expenditure decisions. Thus profit centres are more common than investment centres.

The organisation chart for a business that is divisionalised by business activity is shown in Figure 10.1. This hypothetical business has three operating divisions – brick manufacturing, engineering and food processing – with a director in charge of each division. We can see that the divisional directors will report to the managing director of the business. The organisation structure set out contrasts with that of a business organised as a single unit. The latter type of business would have a marketing director, finance director, production director and so on reporting to the managing director. Within a highly divisionalised structure, however, these functional specialists would be employed within each of the operating divisions and so would report to the director of that division.

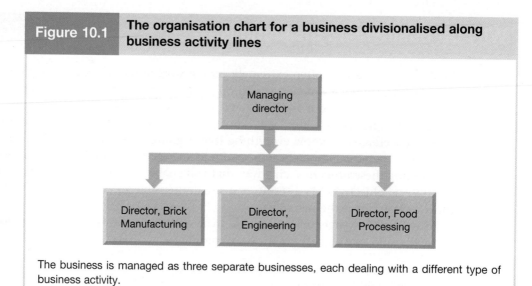

Figure 10.1　**The organisation chart for a business divisionalised along business activity lines**

The business is managed as three separate businesses, each dealing with a different type of business activity.

There are several advantages claimed for dividing business operations into divisions and for allowing divisional managers a measure of autonomy.

Activity 10.1

Try to identify and briefly explain the various reasons why businesses may division-alise. (We have already touched on some of the reasons why businesses operate on divisional lines.)

The following reasons occurred to us:

- *Market information*. Divisional managers will gather an enormous amount of information concerning customers, markets, sources of supply and so on, which may be difficult and costly to transmit to central management. In some cases, they might find it impossible to pass on to management at head office all of the knowledge and experience gathered. Furthermore, as divisional managers are 'in the front line' they can often use this information to best advantage.
- *Management motivation*. Divisional managers are likely to have a greater commitment to their work if they feel they have a significant influence over divisional decisions. Research evidence suggests that participation in decision making encourages a sense of responsibility towards seeing those decisions through. There is a danger that divisional managers will simply 'turn off' if decisions concerning the division are made by central management and then imposed on them.
- *Management development*. Allowing divisional managers a degree of autonomy should help in their development. They will become exposed to marketing, production, financial problems and so on. This should help them to gain valuable specialist skills. In addition, the opportunity to run a division more or less as a separate business should develop their ability to think in strategic terms. This can be of great benefit to the business when it is looking for successors to the current generation of senior managers.

- *Specialist knowledge*. Where a business offers a wide range of products and services, it would be difficult for central management to have the expertise to make operating decisions concerning each product and service. It is more practical to give divisional managers, with the detailed knowledge of the products and services, responsibility for such matters.
- *Allowing a strategic role for central managers*. If central managers were given responsibility for the day-to-day operations of each division, they could become bogged down with making a huge number of relatively small decisions. Even if they were capable of making better operating decisions than the divisional managers, this is unlikely to be the best use of their time. Managers operating at the centre of the business should develop a strategic role. They must look to the future to identify the opportunities and threats facing the business and make appropriate plans. By taking a broader view of the business and plotting a course to be followed, senior managers will be making the most valuable use of their time.
- *Timely decisions*. If information concerning a local division has to be gathered, shaped into a report and then passed up the hierarchy before a decision is made, it is unlikely that the business will be able to act quickly when dealing with changing conditions or emerging issues. In a highly competitive or turbulent environment, the speed of response to market changes can be critical. Divisional managers can usually formulate a response much more quickly than central managers.

Real World 10.1 provides an example of a business in which decision making has become highly devolved.

REAL WORLD 10.1

Showing enterprise

Enterprise is the largest car rental business in the US and is expanding its operations into the UK, Germany and Ireland. It has a fleet of 500,000 cars, valued at around $8bn, which is managed by a network of 5,000 offices and 50,000 employees. An important market for the business is renting replacement cars for people involved in an accident or breakdown and for people whose car is being serviced. It is not an easy market to serve as day-to-day demand is difficult to predict and, often, customers are feeling anxious or distressed. Furthermore, the requirements of insurance companies and garage repair businesses often have to be considered.

To deal with this type of market, decision making has become highly devolved and offices within the network enjoy considerable autonomy. With this high degree of autonomy, however, comes responsibility. Each office is regarded as a profit centre and those who manage an office are accountable for profits (or losses) made. To help managers to monitor performance, the head office issues more than 5,000 financial statements each month. This allows the manager of each office within the network to have frequent feedback on costs, profits and customer satisfaction ratings relating to the office.

Senior management views Enterprise as a confederation of small businesses and the role of head office is that of a 'switching station' for the best ideas.

Source: Based on information from 'Enterprise drives home the service ethic', *Financial Times*, 2 June 2003.

Activity 10.2

Can you think of any problems that might arise when a business is organised into divisions?

A number of problems may arise as a result of adopting a divisionalised structure. These include:

- *Goal conflict*. It is possible that the goals of the operating division will be inconsistent with those either of the business as a whole or of other divisions of the business. For example, an operating division of a business may be unable to sell computer equipment to a particular overseas government because another operating division within the business is selling military equipment to a hostile government. The overall profits of the business, however, may be increased if the military equipment sales ceased in order to allow a new market to develop for the computing equipment sold by the other division.
- *Risk avoidance*. Where managers of a division are faced with a large project, which involves a high level of risk, they may decide against the project even though the potential returns are high. The reason for this may be the consequences of failure for their job security and remuneration. However, the business's shareholders may prefer to take the risks involved because they view the project as just one of a number of projects undertaken by the business. Whilst each particular project will have its risks, there is an expectation by investors that, overall, the expected returns will outweigh the risks involved. Divisional managers may be unable to take such a detached view, as they may not have a diversified portfolio of projects within the division to help reduce the effect of things going badly wrong.
- *Management 'perks'*. By allowing divisional managers autonomy, there is a danger that they will award themselves substantial perquisites or 'perks'. These perks may include such things as a generous expense allowance, first-class travel and a chauffeur. These additional benefits may mean that divisional managers receive a far better remuneration package than the market requires for their services. The obvious way to avoid this is to monitor divisional managers' behaviour. The costs of monitoring, however, may outweigh any benefits arising from identifying and reducing these perks.
- *Increasing costs*. Additional costs may be borne by the business as a result of organising into divisions. For example, each division may have its own market research department, which may duplicate the efforts of market research departments in other divisions. By organising into smaller operating units, the business may also be unable to take advantage of its size in order to reduce costs. For example, it may be unable to negotiate quantity discounts with suppliers, as each division will be deciding on which supplier it uses and will only be purchasing quantities that are appropriate for its needs.
- *Competition*. Divisions within the same business offering similar or substitute products may find themselves in competition with one another. Where this competition is intense, prices may be reduced which may, in turn, have the effect of reducing profits of the business as a whole. For this reason, divisionalisation often works best where the different divisions do not offer closely related products or services.

It is clear from the above that divisionalisation is not without its problems. Although these problems may not be capable of being eliminated, it may be possible to reduce their severity. Thus, an important task of central management is to devise a divisional framework that reaps the benefits of divisional autonomy and yet minimises the problems that divisionalisation brings.

Activity 10.3

Assume that you are the chief executive of a divisionalised business. How might you try to reduce the effects of some of the problems identified above?

The problems of goal conflict and competition may be dealt with by regulating the behaviour of divisional managers. They should be prevented from making decisions that result in an increase in profits for their particular division, but which reduce the profits of the business as a whole. Though such a policy would cut across the autonomy of divisional managers, it is important for them to appreciate that they are not operating completely independent units and that divisional managers also have responsibilities towards the business as a whole.

The problem of risk avoidance by management is a complex one that may be difficult to deal with in practice. It might be possible, however, to encourage divisional managers to take on more risk if the rewards offered reflect the higher levels of risk involved. Both intuition and theory tell us that individuals will often be prepared to take on greater risk provided that they receive compensation in the form of higher rewards.

If things start to go wrong, it may also be possible for the business, through the use of budget variance reports, to distinguish between those variances that are outside the control of the divisional manager and those that are within the manager's control. Divisional managers would then be accountable only for the variances within their control. It is not always easy, however, to obtain unbiased information for preparing budgets from divisional managers when they know that such information will be used to evaluate their performance.

Management 'perks' may be controlled, to some extent, by observing the behaviour and actions of divisional managers. Many 'perks', such as luxury cars, chauffeurs and large offices, are quite visible. Central management should be alert to any signs that divisional managers are rewarding themselves in this way.

Duplication of effort in certain areas can be extremely costly. For this reason, some businesses prefer particular functions, such as administration, accounting, research and development and marketing, to be undertaken by central staff rather than at the divisional level. Again, this means that divisional managers will have to sacrifice some autonomy for the sake of the performance of the business overall.

The way in which divisional managers are assessed and rewarded is important both to the managers themselves and to the business as a whole. In practice, targets are often set for managers and they are usually assessed and rewarded according to their ability to meet these targets. Thus, financial bonuses and increased promotional opportunities may be dependent on achieving particular targets. Unless these targets are carefully established, there is a risk that what managers are working towards will not be in the best interests of the business as a whole. **Real World 10.2** shows how one business aligns the factors that are critical to its success with the way in which managers are rewarded.

We can see that divisionalisation poses a major challenge for central management. Somehow, it must encourage management discretion at the divisional level whilst trying to ensure that the divisional objectives are consistent with the overall strategic objectives of the business as a whole. This requires sound judgement, as there are really no techniques or models that can be applied to solve this problem. For the management accountant of a divisionalised business there are also major challenges. One such

REAL WORLD 10.2

Is everybody happy?

Enterprise (see **Real World 10.1**) is a car rental business that is committed to high standards of service to its customers. To monitor performance it has developed an Enterprise service quality index (ESQI) that measures customer satisfaction. Experience has shown that those customers who express themselves to be 'completely satisfied' with the service provided are three times more likely to come back. Thus, the index is seen as a key indicator of future growth and success. To demonstrate to staff how seriously the ESQI is taken by the business, no manager can be promoted from a network office where the ESQI score is below average, no matter how impressive the financial performance of that office may be.

According to Andy Taylor, chairman and chief executive, rising ESQI scores give him greater confidence about the future than Enterprise's strong cash flow or increase in market share: 'ESQI doesn't mean we can ignore other things but it will keep us on track.'

Source: Based on information from 'Enterprise drives home the work ethic', *Financial Times*, 2 June 2003.

challenge is to provide valid and reliable measures of performance relating to both the division and the divisional managers. It is to this challenge that we now turn.

Divisional performance measurement

Businesses operate with the primary objective of increasing shareholders' wealth, which on a short-term basis translates into making a profit. It is not surprising, therefore, that profits and profitability are of central importance in **divisional performance measurement** of both the divisional managers and the operating divisions. There are, however, various measures of profit that we can use for evaluation purposes. Consider the following divisional profit statement:

Household Appliances Divisional Profit Statement for last year

	£000
Sales	980
Less Variable expenses	490
Contribution	490
Less Controllable divisional fixed expenses	130
Controllable profit	360
Less Non-controllable divisional fixed expenses	150
Divisional profit before central management expenses	210
Less Apportioned central management expenses	80
Divisional net profit (loss)	130

The words 'controllable' and 'non-controllable' in this profit statement refer to the ability of the divisional manager to exert influence over them. A fixed expense that is authorised by a senior manager at head office will not be under the control of the divisional manager, despite the fact that the expense may relate to the division. An expense that arises directly from a decision taken by the divisional manager, on the other hand, is controllable at divisional level.

This profit statement reveals that there are four measures of performance that could be used to assess the division. When deciding on the appropriate measure, it is important to be clear about the purpose for which it is to be used. The *contribution* represents the difference between the total sales of the division and the variable expenses incurred. We considered this measure at length in Chapter 3. There we saw that it can be a useful measure for gaining an insight into the relationship between costs, output and profit.

Activity 10.4

Assume that you are the chief executive of a divisionalised business. Would you use contribution as a primary measure of divisional performance?

This measure has its drawbacks for this purpose. The most important drawback is that it only takes account of variable expenses and ignores any fixed expenses incurred. This means that not all aspects of operating performance are considered.

Activity 10.5

Assume now that you are a divisional manager. What might you be encouraged to do if the contribution were used to assess your performance?

As variable expenses are taken into account in this measure and fixed expenses are ignored, it would be tempting to arrange things so that fixed expenses rather than variable expenses are incurred wherever possible. In this way, the contribution will be maximised. For example, you may decide, as divisional manager, to employ less casual labour and to use machines to do the work instead (even though this may be a more expensive option).

The *controllable profit* takes account of all expenses that are within the control of divisional managers in arriving at a measure of performance. Many view this as the best measure of performance for divisional managers, as they will be in a position to determine the level of expenses incurred. However, in practice, it may be difficult to categorise costs as being either **controllable costs** or **non-controllable costs**. Some expenses may be capable of being influenced by divisional managers, yet not be entirely under their control.

Depreciation can be one example of such an expense. The divisional manager may be required to purchase a particular type of computer hardware so that the information systems of the division are compatible with the systems used throughout the business. The manager may, however, have some discretion over how often the computer hardware is replaced, as well as over the purchase of particular hardware models that perform beyond the requirement standards needed for the business. By exercising this discretion, the depreciation charge for the year will be different from the one that would arise if the manager stuck to the minimum standards laid down by central management.

The *divisional profit before central management expenses* takes account of all divisional expenses (controllable and non-controllable) that are incurred by the division. This provides us with a measure of how the division contributes to the overall profits of the business.

Activity 10.6

Which of the measures so far discussed is most useful for evaluating the performance of:

● Divisional managers, and
● Divisions?

It can be argued that the performance of divisional managers should be judged on the basis of those things that are within their control. Hence, the controllable profit would be the most appropriate measure to use. The contribution measure does not take account of all the expenses that are controllable by divisional managers, whilst the divisional profit before central management expenses takes account of some expenses that are not under the control of divisional managers. The latter measure, however, may be appropriate for evaluating the performance of the division, as it deducts all divisional expenses from the divisional revenues earned. It is a fairly comprehensive measure of divisional achievement.

Divisional net profit is derived after deducting a proportion of the central management expenses incurred for the period. The expenses apportioned to each division will presumably represent what central management believes to be a fair share of the total central management expenses incurred. In practice, the way that these apportionments are made between divisions can be extremely contentious. Some divisional managers may be convinced that they have been apportioned an unfair share of central management expenses. They may also believe that the divisions are being loaded with expenses over which they have little control and that the divisional net profit figure derived will not truly represent the achievements of the division. These are often compelling arguments for not apportioning central management expenses to the various divisions.

Activity 10.7

Can you think of any arguments for apportioning central management expenses to divisions?

The business as a whole will only make a profit after all central management expenses have been covered. Apportioning these expenses to the divisions should help make divisional managers more aware of this fact. In addition, central management may wish to compare the results of the division with the results of similar businesses in the same industry that are operating as independent entities. By apportioning expenses such as research and development costs and administration expenses to the divisions, a more valid basis for comparison is provided. Independent businesses will have to bear these kinds of expenses before arriving at *their* profit for the period. The effect of apportioning central management expenses may also help to impose an element of control over these costs. Divisional managers may put pressure on central managers to keep apportioned expenses low so as to minimise the adverse effect on divisional profits.

Return on investment

→ **Return on investment (ROI)** is a popular method of assessing the profitability of divisions. The ratio is calculated in the following way:

$$ROI = \frac{\text{Divisional profit}}{\text{Divisional investment (assets employed)}} \times 100\%$$

When defining divisional profit for this ratio, the purpose for which the ratio is to be used must be considered. For evaluating the performance of a divisional manager, the controllable profit is likely to be the most appropriate, whereas for evaluating the performance of a division, the divisional profit is likely to be more appropriate. The reasons for this have already been discussed above. Various definitions can be used for divisional investment. The total assets (non-current (fixed) assets plus current assets) or the net assets (non-current assets plus current assets less current liabilities) figure may be used. In addition, non-current assets may be shown at their historic cost or their historic cost less accumulated depreciation or on some other basis, such as current replacement cost.

It is important that, whichever definitions of divisional profit and investment are used, there is absolute consistency. It is not helpful to try to compare the ROIs of two different divisions, using one set of definitions for one division and another set for the other division.

The ROI ratio can be broken down into two main elements. These are:

$$ROI = \frac{\text{Divisional profit}}{\text{Sales}} \times \frac{\text{Sales}}{\text{Divisional investment}}$$

This separation into the two main elements is useful, because it shows that ROI is determined by both the profit margin on each £ of sales and the ability to generate a high level of sales in relation to the investment base.

Activity 10.8

The following data relate to the performance and position of two operating divisions that sell similar products:

	Kuala Lumpur Division £000	Singapore Division £000
Sales	300	750
Divisional profit	30	25
Divisional investment	600	500

What observations can you make about the performance of each division?

Firstly, the ROIs for both divisions are identical at 5 per cent a year.

The information shows, however, that the divisions appear to be pursuing different strategies. The profit margins for the Kuala Lumpur and Singapore Divisions are 10 per cent (30/300) and 3.3 per cent (25/750) respectively. The sales to divisional investment ratios for the Kuala Lumpur and Singapore Divisions are 50 per cent (300/600) and 150 per cent (750/500) respectively. Thus, we can see that the Kuala Lumpur Division prefers to sell goods at a higher profit margin than the Singapore Division and this results in a lower sales turnover in relation to assets employed.

ROI is a measure of *profitability*, as it relates profits to the size of the investment made in the division. This relative measure allows comparisons between divisions of different sizes. However, ROI has its drawbacks. Where it is used as the primary measure of performance for divisional managers, there is a danger that it will lead to behaviour that is not really consistent with the interests of the business overall.

Activity 10.9

Russell Francis plc has two divisions, both selling similar products but operating in different geographical areas. The Wessex Division reported a £200,000 controllable profit from a divisional investment of £1m and the Sussex Division a £150,000 controllable profit from a divisional investment of £500,000.

The divisional manager of each division has the opportunity to invest £200,000 in the development of a new product line that will boost divisional profit by £50,000. The finance cost for each division is 16 per cent a year.

Which operating division do you think has been the more successful? How might each divisional manager react to the new opportunity?

Although the Wessex Division has achieved a higher profit in absolute terms, it has a lower ROI than the Sussex Division. The ROI for Wessex is 20 per cent a year (£200,000/£1,000,000) compared with 30 per cent (£150,000/£500,000) for the Sussex Division. Using ROI as the measure of performance, the Sussex Division is therefore the better performing division.

The ROI from the new investment is 25 per cent a year (£50,000/£200,000). Thus, by taking on this investment, the divisional manager of Wessex will increase the ROI of the division, which currently stands at 20 per cent a year. However, the divisional manager of Sussex will reduce the ROI of the division by taking this opportunity as its ROI is below the overall ROI of 30 per cent a year for the division.

If ROI is used as the primary measure of divisional performance, the divisional manager of Sussex may decline the opportunity for fear that a decline in divisional ROI will reflect poorly on performance. However, the returns from the opportunity are 25 per cent a year, which comfortably exceed the cost of finance of 16 per cent a year. So failure to exploit the opportunity will mean the profit potential of the division is not fully realised.

This is an example of the problems that can arise as a result of using a comparative measure like percentages. Real World 8.3 (p. 218) provides an example of how percentage measurements can mislead.

A further disincentive to invest can result where the divisional investment in assets is measured in terms of the original cost less any accumulated depreciation to date (that is, net book value or written-down value). Where depreciation is being charged each year, the net book value of the divisional investment will be reduced. Provided that profits stay at the same level, this means that ROI will start to climb.

To illustrate this point, assume the following profits and investment for a division:

Year	Divisional profit £	Divisional investment £	ROI at net book value %
1	30,000	200,000	15.0
2	30,000	180,000	16.7
3	30,000	160,000	18.8
4	30,000	140,000	21.4

The investment is an item of equipment that cost £200,000 at the beginning of Year 1. It is being depreciated at the rate of 10 per cent of cost each year.

We can see that the ROI increases over time simply because the investment base is shrinking. We saw above that divisional managers may be discouraged from investing in further assets where the ROI is below the existing ROI for the division. In this example, the divisional manager may increase the 'hurdle rate' for new investments each year in line with the rise in ROI. This would make new investments increasingly more difficult to accept, even though the need for new investment is likely to increase as the existing assets become fully depreciated.

Activity 10.10

How might the problem caused by ROI being boosted simply through a reduction in the investment base be dealt with?

....

One way around the problem would be to keep the investment in assets at original cost and not to deduct depreciation for purposes of calculating ROI. However, non-current (fixed) assets normally lose their productive capacity over time, and this fact should really be recognised. Another way around the problem is to use some measure of current market value, such as replacement cost, for the investment in assets. However, there may be problems in establishing current values for some assets.

Residual income

The weaknesses of the ROI method, particularly the fact that it ignores the cost of financing the division, have led to a search for a more appropriate measure of divisional performance. **Residual income (RI)** has been advocated by many as being more acceptable. RI is the amount of income or profit generated by a division, which is in excess of the minimum acceptable level of income. If we assume that the objective of the business is to maximise shareholder wealth, the minimum acceptable level of income to be generated is the amount necessary to cover the cost of capital.

RI is calculated by taking the divisional profit figure and then deducting an imputed interest charge for the capital invested. A simple illustration should make the process clear. Let us assume that a division produced a profit of £100,000 and there was a divisional investment of £600,000 with a cost of financing this investment of 15 per cent a year. The residual income would be as follows:

	£
Divisional profit	100,000
Less Charge for capital invested	
(15% × £600,000)	90,000
Residual income	10,000

A positive RI (shown above) means that the division is generating returns in excess of the minimum requirements of the business. The higher these excess returns, the better the performance of the division.

Activity 10.11

Are there any similarities between the ROI and RI methods discussed above and the methods of investment appraisal dealt with in Chapter 8?

The RI method is similar to the NPV method in many respects. We should recall that, with NPV, a project is accepted where the returns (discounted cash flows) exceed the amount invested. The returns are discounted using the cost of capital. The higher the NPV, the greater the wealth generated for shareholders. The ROI is similar in some respects to the IRR method. The IRR method derives a percentage rate of return which is then compared with a 'hurdle rate' to see whether the return is acceptable.

Activity 10.12

Simonson Pharmaceuticals plc operates the Helena Beauty Care Division, which has reported the following results for last year:

Divisional investment	£2,000,000
Divisional profit	£300,000

The division has the opportunity to invest in a new product. This will require an additional investment in non-current (fixed) assets of £400,000 and is expected to generate additional profits of £50,000 a year. This business has a cost of capital of 12 per cent a year.
   Have a go at calculating the residual income of the division for last year.
   Do you believe that the division should produce the new product or not?
   How do you think that the divisional manager might react to the new product opportunity if ROI were used as the means of evaluating performance?

The residual income for last year is:

	£
Divisional profit	300,000
Less Charge for capital invested	
(12% × £2,000,000)	240,000
Residual income	60,000

The residual income expected from the new product is:

	£
Additional divisional profit	50,000
Less Charge for additional capital	
(12% × £400,000)	48,000
Residual income	2,000

The residual income is positive and, therefore, it would be worthwhile to produce the new product.

   The ROI of the division for last year was 15 per cent a year (that is, £300,000/£2m). However, the new product is only expected to produce an ROI of 12.5 per cent a year (that is, £50,000/£400,000). The effect of producing the new product will be to reduce the overall ROI of the division (assuming similar results from the existing activities next year). The divisional manager may, therefore, reject the new investment opportunity, despite the fact that acceptance would enhance the shareholders' wealth. The new product would cover all of the costs, including the cost of financing the investment.

Real World 10.3 provides information on how a very well known retailer, Marks and Spencer, approaches divisional performance measurement.

REAL WORLD 10.3

RI at M&S

Marks and Spencer plc assesses divisional performance using the residual income approach. In deriving the RI, the business's cost of capital of 10 per cent a year is used to calculate the capital charge. In deriving divisional profit, divisions are charged a notional rent for the use of premises, even where the business owns the freehold. This is to make a more valid comparison between divisions. The capital charge must be based on the assets used by the divisions, excluding premises. The notional rent covers the use of the premises.

Source: Based an information taken from Marks and Spencer plc Annual Reports 2000 and 2001.

Divisional performance measures and long-term performance

A problem of both ROI and RI is that divisional managers may focus on short-term divisional performance at the expense of the longer term. There is a danger that investment opportunities will be rejected because they reduce short-term ROI and RI, even though over the longer term they have a positive NPV.

Let us assume that there is an investment opportunity for a division that will require an initial investment of £90,000 and will produce the following operating cash flows (net profit before depreciation) over the next five years:

Year	£
1	18,000
2	18,000
3	25,000
4	50,000
5	60,000

Assuming a cost of capital of 16 per cent a year, the NPV of the project will be:

Year	Cash flows £	Discount rate 16%	Present value £
1	18,000	0.862	15,516
2	18,000	0.743	13,374
3	25,000	0.641	16,025
4	50,000	0.552	27,600
5	60,000	0.476	28,560
			101,075
Less Initial investment			90,000
Net present value			11,075

This indicates that the NPV is positive and, therefore, it would be in the shareholders' interests to undertake the project.

To calculate ROI and RI, we need to derive the divisional profit for each year (that is, deduct a charge for depreciation from the operating cash flows shown above).

Assuming that depreciation is charged equally over the life of the assets acquired and there is no residual value for the assets, the annual depreciation charge will be £18,000 (that is, £90,000/5).

After deducting an annual depreciation charge, the divisional profit for each year will be as follows:

Year	£
1	–
2	–
3	7,000
4	32,000
5	42,000

Activity 10.13

Calculate the project ROI and RI for each of the five years of the project's life. (Base the ROI calculation on the cost of the assets concerned.)

The ROI for the project will be as follows:

Year	£	ROI %
1	–	–
2	–	–
3	7,000/90,000	7.8
4	32,000/90,000	35.6
5	42,000/90,000	46.7

The RI will be as follows:

Year	Divisional profit £	Capital charge £	RI £
1	–	14,400*	(14,400)
2	–	14,400	(14,400)
3	7,000	14,400	(7,400)
4	32,000	14,400	17,600
5	42,000	14,400	27,600
			9,000

* 16% × £90,000

Activity 10.14

What do you deduce from the calculations resulting from the previous activity?

We can see that, in the early years, the ROI and RI calculations do not produce good results, though the situation is reversed in later years. For the first two years the ROI is zero and for the first three years the RI is negative. Divisional managers may, therefore, be discouraged from making investments if they feel that central management would view the results in the early years unfavourably. Given the results of the NPV analysis, this means that the managers would not be acting in the shareholders' best interests in rejecting the proposal. Note, however, that the RI of the project overall is positive and so provides a result that is consistent with the NPV result.

Various approaches have been proposed in an attempt to avoid the kind of problem described above. It has been suggested, for example, that for the purpose of calculating divisional ROI and RI, the assets employed in the project should not be included in the divisional investment base until the project is generating good returns.

Further measurement issues

Interpreting divisional performance requires that we have some basis for comparison. There are various bases that can be used:

- *Other divisions within the business.* Comparing the ROI or RI of different divisions within the same business may not be very useful where the divisions operate in different industries. Different types of industries have different levels of risk and this in turn produces different expectations concerning acceptable levels of return.
- *Previous performance of the division.* It is possible to compare current performance with previous performance to see whether there has been any improvement or deterioration. However, it is often necessary to compare performance against some external standard in order to bring to light operating inefficiencies within the division. Also, the economic environment in previous periods may be different from the current environment and so may invalidate comparisons of this nature.
- *Similar businesses within the same industry.* The ROI or RI of other divisions or independent entities operating within the same industry may provide a useful basis for comparison. However, there are often problems associated with this basis.

Activity 10.15

What problems are we likely to come across, in practice, when seeking to compare the performance of a division within a business with an independent business or similar division of another business?

We may encounter a number of problems such as:

- *Problems of obtaining the information we require.* This is particularly true for a division within another business. This information may not be available to those outside the business.
- *Differences in accounting policies.* Different approaches to such matters as depreciation methods and stock (inventory) valuation methods may result in different measures of profit.
- *Differences in asset structure.* The different age of non-current (fixed) assets employed, the decision to rent rather than buy particular assets and so on may result in differences in the measures derived.

One final basis for comparison is:

- *Budgeted performance.* This should be a good basis for comparison because achievement of the budget should lead the division, and the business as a whole, towards its strategic objectives. In setting the budget, performances elsewhere in the business, previous levels of performance by the division and the performance of competitors, may well be considered. Ultimately, however, it is against what the division has planned for that its actual performance should be assessed.

We have seen that a single measure of performance cannot really capture all the various aspects of divisional performance. Moreover, it tends to be the case that 'the things that count are the things that get counted'. This is to say that importance is given to matters that can be measured in figures and reported, irrespective of their real significance. Thus, by focusing on a single measure, there is a risk that managerial actions and behaviour will become distorted. Managers may become more concerned with the particular measure of performance used (and, perhaps, with manipulating its outcome) than with the underlying economic reality, which the measure tries to portray. This could, as we have seen, lead to decisions being made that run counter to the interests of the owners of the business.

It may, therefore, be useful to use a variety of different measures of performance. These might cover both financial and non-financial aspects of performance and be concerned with both short-term and long-term achievement. Examples of other aspects of the division that may be usefully assessed are:

- *Research and development (R&D) expenditure*. An assessment of the level of investment in R&D and the benefits derived over the longer term can be illuminating. If a single measure of performance were used to assess divisional performance, such as ROI or RI, it would be possible to improve these measures in the short term simply by cutting back on this type of expenditure. However, this may be to the detriment of the longer-term profitability of the division.
- *Staff training and morale*. It is widely recognised that, for most businesses, the employees are the most valuable assets. It is, therefore, useful to know how the divisional managers are cultivating this resource. Once again, it is possible to improve ROI and RI in the short term by reducing the level of investment in the human assets of the business. Staff morale as revealed by staff turnover and the number of complaints and disputes arising may also help in assessing the management of the division.
- *Product/service quality*. In a competitive environment, the quality of the products and services offered can be of vital importance to long-term survival. Maintaining and improving quality, however, may require high levels of investment in equipment with strict tolerance levels, automated inspection methods and staff training.
- *Environmental and social concerns*. In highly industrialised societies, there is increasing pressure on businesses to acknowledge their responsibility towards the environment and to assess the impact of their activities on the communities in which they are based. An assessment of the policies adopted by the division on such matters as pollution, wildlife protection and employment policies for minorities can be carried out to see whether it is being a good 'corporate citizen'.
- *Productivity*. The efficiency of the division in producing its output and the level of production achieved may be extremely valuable to central management.

Activity 10.16

Runne & Co. is a large firm of solicitors that has a property conveyancing division specialising in assisting clients with the purchase and sale of private houses.

How might the productivity of this division be assessed? Can you think of four possible measures of productivity for this division?

Possible measures might include some of the following:

- Total number of conveyances undertaken by the division.
- Total fees generated by the conveyancing division.
- Average time taken to complete conveyances of property.
- Gross income generated per member of conveyancing staff.
- Net income generated per member of conveyancing staff.

Real World 10.4 shows how Ford Europe uses non-financial measures to provide a clearer picture of performance to investors.

REAL WORLD 10.4

Non-financial measures at Ford

Ford Motor Company is the world's second biggest car maker. In 2003 it implemented changes to its accounting methods for divisional reporting. These changes were expected to benefit the car maker's US division at the expense of its other international operations. Although the calculation of the business's overall profit remains unaffected by the changes, some expenses, previously charged to the US operation, are to be reallocated to other operating divisions.

One result of this change is that the reported profit of Ford Europe is expected to be lower.

However, non-financial measures, which are unaffected by the changes, have been employed to illustrate Ford Europe's success to investors. These measures show increasing sales, growing market share, improved quality and busier factories.

Source: Adapted from 'Ford to shake up accounting methods', *Financial Times*, 9 April 2003.

Self-assessment question 10.1

Andromeda International plc has two operating divisions, the managers of which are given considerable autonomy. In order to assess the performance of divisional managers, the central management uses ROI. For the purposes of this measure the assets employed include both non current (fixed) and current assets. The business has a cost of capital of 15 per cent a year and uses the straight-line method of depreciation for external reporting purposes.

Extracts from the budgets, for each of the two divisions for next year are as follows:

	Jupiter division £000	Mars division £000
Net profit	260	50
Non-current assets at cost	940	1,200
Current assets	390	180

Since the budgets were prepared, two investment opportunities have been brought to the attention of the relevant divisional managers. These are as follows:

(i) Central management would like to see the productivity of the Mars division improve. To help achieve this, they have informed the divisional manager that equipment costing £300,000 can be purchased. This will have a life of five years and will lead to operating savings of £90,000 each year.

(ii) A new product can be sold by the Jupiter division. This will increase sales by £250,000 each year over the next five years. It will be necessary to increase marketing costs by £60,000 a year and stocks (inventories) held will increase by £90,000. The contribution to sales ratio for the new product will be 30 per cent.

→

Self-assessment question 10.1 continued

Required:

(a) Calculate the expected ROI for each division assuming:
   (i) the investment opportunities are not taken up.
   (ii) the investment opportunities are taken up.

(b) Comment on the results obtained in (a) and state how the divisional managers and central managers might view the investment opportunities.

(c) Discuss the implications of using net book value (that is, after accumulated depreciation) rather than gross book value (that is, before accumulated depreciation) as a basis for valuing non-current assets when calculating ROI.

Real World 10.5 gives some indication of the approaches taken to divisional performance measurement in practice.

REAL WORLD 10.5

Divisional performance measurement in practice

The 1993 survey of manufacturing businesses by Drury, Braund, Osborne and Tayles found that 85 per cent of respondents were divisionalised. The majority of these (78 per cent of respondents) based their divisions on the nature of their products, that is, divisions specialised in particular products or types of product.

The survey also found that businesses seem to use more than one method of measuring divisional performance with various approaches being used as follows:

	% of respondents
Target ROI	55
Target RI	20
Target profit before a finance charge on assets used	61
A target cash flow figure	43
Ability to stay within the budget	57

This evidence is now quite old, but in the absence of a more recent survey it provides us with some feeling for what happens in practice. There is no reason to believe that current practice is dramatically different from what applied in 1993.

Source: Drury *et al.* (see reference 1 at the end of the chapter).

Transfer pricing

In some cases, one division will sell goods or services to another division within the same business. For example, a brick manufacturing division of a business may sell its products to another division within the same business, which is a house-builder. The price at which such transfers between divisions are made can be an important issue. Setting appropriate prices for such inter-divisional trading is known as **transfer pricing**. To the division that is providing the goods or service, transfers represent part, or possibly all, of its output. If the performance of the division is to be measured in any useful way, the division should be credited with 'sales revenues' for these goods or services transferred. Failure to credit the supplying division in this way would mean that it would have to bear the expenses of creating the goods or service, but get no credit for it. By the same token, the receiving ('buying') division needs to be charged with the expense of using the goods or service supplied by the other division, if its performance is to be measured in any meaningful way.

Where inter-divisional transfers represent a large part of the total sales or purchases of a division, 'transfer pricing' is a very important issue. Small changes in the transfer price of goods or services can result in large changes in profits for the division concerned. As divisional managers are often assessed according to the profits generated by their division, setting transfer prices may be a sensitive issue between divisional managers.

Whilst the transfer prices agreed will affect the profits of individual divisions, the profits of the business as a whole should not normally be affected. An increase in the transfer price of goods or services will lead to an increase in the profits of the selling division, which is normally cancelled out by the decrease in profits of the buying division. However, transfer prices between divisions can indirectly lead to a loss of profits to the business as a whole. The level at which the transfer price for a particular good or service is set could lead divisional managers to make decisions which are in the interests of their division but which are not in the interests of the business as a whole. An example of this is a division buying a particular product or service from a supplier outside the business, because the supplier's price is cheaper than the established internal transfer price. In such a situation, the profits of the business as a whole may well be adversely affected.

Activity 10.17

What should transfer-pricing policies seek to achieve?

(*Hint*: When considering this question, remember what the business as a whole is trying to achieve and why businesses seek to achieve it through divisionalisation.)

Transfer pricing seeks to achieve the following:

- *The independence of divisions*. By allowing divisional managers to set their own transfer prices and by allowing other divisions to decide whether or not to trade at the prices quoted, the autonomy of individual divisions is encouraged. This, in turn, should help motivate divisional managers.
- *The assessment of divisional performance*. Inter-divisional sales will contribute to total revenues for a division, which in turn influence divisional profit. Setting an appropriate transfer price can, therefore, be important in deriving a valid measure of divisional profit for evaluation purposes. They should be of value in helping to establish incentives for, and promoting accountability of, divisional managers.
- *Promoting the optimisation of profits for the business*. Transfer prices may seek to optimise profits for the business as a whole. For example, a division may be prevented from quoting a transfer price for goods that will make buying divisions seek cheaper sources of supply from outside the business.
- *Allocating divisional resources*. Transfer prices will be important in determining the level of output for particular goods and services. The level of return from inter-divisional sales can be important in deciding on the level of sales and investment relating to a particular product or group of products.
- *Tax minimisation*. Where a business has operations in various countries, it may be beneficial to set transfer prices such that the bulk of profits are reported in divisions where the host country has low corporation tax rates. However, tax laws operating in many countries will seek to prevent this kind of profit manipulation.

Real World 10.6 gives an example of a business using transfer prices to the disadvantage of both the tax authorities and some investors.

REAL WORLD 10.6

Pouring oil on troubled waters

Sidanco is a large Russian oil company that has been accused of hiding more than $2.5 billion in revenues from both the Russian tax authorities and outside shareholders in subsidiary businesses. It is claimed that this was achieved by a complex transfer-pricing mechanism, resulting in the parent business paying its subsidiary businesses less than the market rate for oil purchased. Lawyers acting on behalf of aggrieved shareholders in the subsidiary businesses claim that in 2000, three subsidiaries supplied oil to Sidanco at a quarter, or less than a quarter, of the selling price to other parties.

Source: Based on information from 'Investors chase BP for compensation', *Financial Times*, 17 February 2003.

Activity 10.18

Is there a conflict between any of the transfer-pricing objectives identified in the solution to Activity 10.17 above? If so, can a single transfer price help achieve all these objectives?

It is quite possible for there to be a conflict between the objectives identified. As a result, a single transfer price is unlikely to be able to achieve all the stated objectives. For example, in order to optimise the profits for the business as a whole it may be necessary to determine transfer prices centrally, which would undermine the autonomy of divisions. In addition, a centrally imposed transfer price may result in inter-divisional sales at artificially low prices which would disadvantage particular divisions and might result in reported profit figures in both the buying and selling divisions becoming invalid measures of productivity.

Transfer pricing policies

There are various approaches to setting a transfer price for goods and services between divisions. In this section we shall explore some of the major approaches. Before going on to do this, however, it is probably worth identifying the principle that the best transfer price is one based closely on the **opportunity cost** of the good or service concerned. This opportunity cost represents the best alternative forgone.

Market prices

Market prices are the prices that exist in the 'outside' market (that is, outside the business whose divisions are involved in the transfer). Intuition may tell us that market prices should be the appropriate method of setting transfer prices. Using this approach, the transfer price is an objective, verifiable amount that has some real economic credibility. Where there is a competitive and active market for the products, the market price will represent the 'opportunity cost' of goods and services. For the selling division it is the revenue lost by selling to another division rather than to an outside customer. For the buying division, it is the best purchase price available.

However, the market price may not always be appropriate.

Activity 10.19

Wolf Industries plc has an operating division that produces microwave ovens. The ovens are normally sold to retailers for £120. The division is currently producing 3,000 ovens a month (which uses only about 50 per cent of the division's manufacturing capacity). The ovens have the following cost structure:

	Cost for one oven £
Variable cost	70
Fixed cost apportionment	20
	90

Another division of the business has offered to buy 2,000 ovens for £75 each. How would you respond to such an offer if you were manager of the division making micro-wave ovens?

Since the division is operating below capacity, basing the transfer price on market prices may lead to lost sales. Other divisions within the business may prefer to buy from outside sources rather than from the selling division and this loss of sales will not be made good by sales to outside customers. We saw in Chapter 3 that businesses may base selling prices on the variable cost of the goods or services, rather than on the market price, where there is a short-term problem of excess capacity. Provided that the selling price exceeds the variable cost of the goods, a contribution will be made towards the profits of the business. This principle can equally be applied to divisions of businesses. Thus, in such circumstances, a selling price somewhere between the variable cost of the product (£70) and the market price (£120) may be the best price for divisional transfers.

Another point to consider when making inter-divisional transfers is that the selling division may make savings owing to the fact that selling and distribution costs may be lower. In such a situation, part of these savings may be passed on to the buying division in the form of lower prices. Thus, some adjustment may be made to the market price of the goods being transferred.

In some cases, the transfer price may be set above the market price of the product or service. **Real World 10.7** below provides such an example.

REAL WORLD 10.7

Flat beer

Scottish and Newcastle is a leading brewer that also owns a chain of pubs. The brewing business sells beer to the pubs at a transfer price above the market price. However, the business intends to sell off the pubs and to focus exclusively on brewing. This means that future beer sales will be to outside businesses and will therefore be sold at market prices rather than at above-market prices. This change is expected to result in a reduction in brewing profits of £12m.

Source: Based on information from 'Scottish and Newcastle', Lex column, *Financial Times*, 2 July 2003.

Activity 10.20

Apart from the problems, which we have just considered, of trying to base inter-divisional transfer prices on external market prices, there is another, perhaps more fundamental, problem with market prices. What is it?

This problem is that there is often not an external market in existence. It simply may not be possible for the potential 'buying' division to identify external suppliers and a price for the particular good or service required. Still more likely is that there would be no potential external customer for the 'selling' division's output. It may be so specific to the needs of its fellow division that the division represents the only market there is.

Variable cost of goods or services

We saw above, in the context of market prices, that a **variable cost** approach is appropriate when the division is operating below capacity. This is because, in these particular circumstances, the opportunity cost to the supplying division is not the market price. It will not have to give up selling in the market to enable it to supply its fellow division, since there is a capacity to do both. In these circumstances, the opportunity cost is equal to the variable cost of producing the good or service. However, this represents an absolute minimum transfer price and a figure above the variable cost is required for a contribution to be made towards fixed costs and profit. Where the division is operating at full capacity and external customers are prepared to pay above the variable cost of the goods, a variable-cost internal transfer price would mean that inter-divisional sales are less profitable than sales to external customers. Managers of the selling division would therefore have no incentive to agree transfer prices on this basis (even though the business as a whole may benefit). If central management imposed this pricing method, divisional autonomy would be undermined.

Full cost of goods or services

Transfers can be made at **full cost**. In such circumstances no profit will be made on the transactions and this can hinder an evaluation of divisional performance. It will also be more difficult when making resource allocation decisions within the division concerning such matters as level of output, product mix and investment levels, as profit cannot be used as a measure of efficiency.

It is possible to add a mark-up to the full cost of the goods or services in order to derive a profit figure. However, the amount of the mark-up must be justified in some way or it will become a contentious issue between buying and selling divisions. A cost-based approach (with or without the use of a mark-up) does not provide any real incentive for divisional managers to keep costs down, since they can pass the costs on to the buying division. This will result in selling divisions transferring their operating inefficiences to buying divisions. Where the mark-up is a percentage of cost, the selling division's profit will be higher if it incurs higher costs. However, where buying divisions have the ability to go to outside suppliers, pressure can be exerted on the selling divisions to control their costs.

Though use of the full cost approach is found in practice (see **Real World 10.8**), it is not an approach that is particularly logical, since it is not linked to the opportunity cost approach.

Negotiated prices

It is possible to adopt an approach that allows the divisional managers to arrive at **negotiated prices** for inter-divisional transfers. However, this can lead to serious disputes, and where divisional managers are unable to agree a price, central management will be required to arbitrate. This can be a time-consuming process and may deflect central management from its more strategic role. Furthermore, divisional managers may resent the decisions made by central managers and see these as undermining the autonomy of their divisions.

Negotiated transfer prices probably work best where there is an external market for the goods supplied by the buying and selling divisions and where divisional managers are free to accept or reject offers made by other divisions. Under such circumstances, the negotiated price is likely to be closely related to the external market price of the products. In other circumstances, the negotiated prices may be artificial and misleading. For example, where a division sells the whole of its output to another division, the selling division is likely to be in a weak bargaining position and the transfer price agreed may not provide a valid measure of divisional performance. Negotiated prices are likely to be influenced by the negotiating skills of managers. This can be a problem where the outcome is largely determined by this factor.

Figure 10.2 summarises the various approaches to transfer pricing.

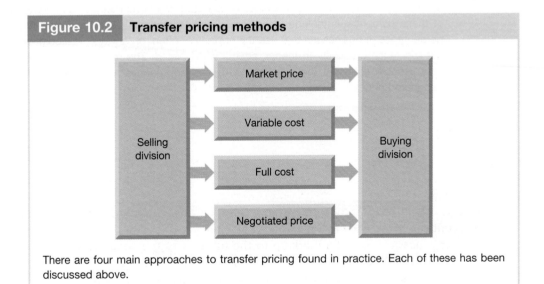

Figure 10.2   Transfer pricing methods

There are four main approaches to transfer pricing found in practice. Each of these has been discussed above.

Real World 10.8 provides detail about the use of transfer pricing in UK manufacturing businesses. This survey evidence is now quite old, but there is no more recent evidence of UK practice. **Real World 10.9**, however, is much more recent but is concerned with practice in the US.

REAL WORLD 10.8

Transfer pricing in practice

The 1993 survey by Drury, Braund, Osborne and Tayles gives some indication of the importance of inter-divisional transfers in practice as follows:

Internal transfers as a proportion of total external sales	% of divisionalised respondents
Under 5%	36
5% to 19%	36
20% to 49%	16
Over 50%	12

Thus transfer pricing is an important issue for a very significant proportion of larger businesses.

The approaches to setting transfer prices were discovered to be as follows:

Approach used	% of divisionalised respondents	
Variable cost	37	(2)
Full cost	42	(22)
Variable cost plus a profit mark-up	30	(11)
Full cost plus a profit mark-up	52	(27)
Market price	52	(33)
Negotiated price	70	(30)
Other methods	9	(1)

It is clear from the table that businesses use more than one method, on average. Some of these percentages include 'used rarely' and 'sometimes'. The bracketed figures are percentages of businesses that use the approach 'often' or 'always'. Full cost, which has not too much credibility in theory, seems widely used. The more theoretically respectable variable cost and the market-price-based approaches also seem popular, as do negotiated prices.

Source: Drury *et al.* (see reference 1 at the end of the chapter).

REAL WORLD 10.9

Transfer pricing in practice in the US

A survey of management accounting practice in the US was conducted in 2003. Nearly 2,000 businesses replied to the survey. These tended to be larger businesses, of which about 40 per cent were manufacturers and about 16 per cent financial services; the remainder were across a range of other industries.

The survey revealed that 58 per cent extensively use internal transfer pricing, with a further 22 per cent considering using the technique in the future.

Source: Ernst and Young (see reference 2 at the end of the chapter).

The difference in the sample (various businesses in the US, but only manufacturers in the UK) makes comparison between these two surveys difficult. Both make it clear that transfer pricing is an important issue on both sides of the Atlantic and, no doubt, generally in the developed world.

Transfer pricing and service industries

There is absolutely no reason why the item being transferred inter-divisionally need be a physical object. (See Activity 10.16 for an example of a division supplying a service to the outside world.) Most businesses transfer services from one department to another, even where the ultimate product sold to the outside world is a physical object. For example, the personnel department of a business may be treated as a separate division and charge other divisions for its services. Thus transfer pricing is important to service providers, just as it is important to manufacturers. Also, the subject of a transfer price can easily be a service, even where the business does not provide services to the outside world.

SUMMARY

The main points of this chapter may be summarised as follows:

Divisionalisation
- Many large businesses operate through relatively independent divisions.
- The basis of divisionalisation is usually:
  - Specialism of product or service.
  - Geographical.
- Divisions are typically either:
  - Profit centres, which have responsibility for most aspects except investment.
  - Investment centres, which have responsibility for most aspects including investment.
- Benefits of divisionalisation are said to include:
  - Better access to market information.
  - Motivating middle and junior managers.
  - Developing managers through experience.
  - Better use of specialised knowledge.
  - Allowing senior managers to deal with strategic issues.
  - Enabling timely decision making.
- Problems of divisionalisation are said to include:
  - Goal conflict between divisions.
  - Excessive avoidance of risky courses of action.
  - Excessive management 'perks'.
  - Costly duplication of facilities and other losses of economies of scale.
  - Divisions may compete with each other to the detriment of the business as a whole.

Divisional performance measurement
- Divisions are probably best assessed using the profit after taking account of controllable expenses (controllable profit).

- Return on investment (ROI) = (divisional profit/divisional investment) × 100%
  - Resembles the return on capital employed ratio, which seems to be widely used.
  - Can be broken down into a profit margin and an asset turnover element.
  - Problems of definition of the divisional profit and investment – need to be consistent.
  - Is a comparative (percentage) measure that can mislead.
  - Can lead to the rejection of beneficial activities because they lower the ROI despite generating wealth.
  - Tends to focus on the short term.
- Residual income (RI) = divisional profit less a capital charge (investment × cost of capital)
  - Relates to wealth generated.
  - An absolute measure (£s), not a percentage.
  - Tends to focus on the short term.
- RI is generally considered a better performance indicator than ROI.
- The RI or ROI for a particular division can be compared with that for:
  - Other divisions of the same business.
  - Previous performance of the same division.
  - Performance of businesses in the same industry as the division.
  - Budgeted performance – probably the best basis of comparison.
- Other possible divisional performance indicators include:
  - Research and development expenditure.
  - Staff training and morale.
  - Product/service quality.
  - Environmental and social concerns.
  - Productivity.

Transfer pricing = setting prices for transfers ('sales' and 'purchases') between divisions of the same business

- An important issue because transfer prices (TPs) have a direct effect on divisional profit and therefore on ROI and RI.
- Transfer pricing has the following objectives:
  - Promoting divisional independence, by allowing divisions to act as if they are independent businesses.
  - Providing a basis for measuring the effectiveness of divisions through, for example ROI and RI.
  - Promoting the objectives of the business as a whole.
  - Allocating resources provided for individual divisions.
  - Minimising tax charges by moving profits to low-tax countries.
- Best TPs are based on the opportunity cost for both divisions.
- In practice, the following are found:
  - Market prices – usually best because they tend to represent the opportunity cost, but a market may not exist in practice.
  - Variable cost – will represent the opportunity cost to a supplying division with spare capacity.
  - Full cost, usually plus a profit loading – rarely reflects the opportunity cost and tends to pass on inefficiencies.
  - Negotiated prices, enable the divisions to act as independent businesses but can be unfair.

→ **Key terms**

Divisions   p. 301
Profit centre   p. 301
Investment centre   p. 301
Divisional performance
  measurement   p. 306
Controllable costs   p. 307
Non-controllable costs   p. 307
Return on investment (ROI)   p. 309

Residual income (RI)   p. 311
Transfer pricing   p. 318
Opportunity cost   p. 320
Market prices   p. 320
Variable cost   p. 322
Full cost   p. 322
Negotiated prices   p. 323

Further reading

If you would like to explore the topics covered in this chapter in more depth, we recommend the following books:

Accounting for Management Decisions, *Arnold J. and Turley S.*, 3rd edn, Prentice Hall, 1996, chapter 18.

Management and Cost Accounting, *Drury C.*, Thomson Learning Business Press, 5th edn, 2000, chapters 20 and 21.

Cost and Management Accounting, *Williamson D.*, Prentice Hall, 1996, chapters 18 and 19.

Cost Accounting, *Horngren C., Foster, G. and Datar S.*, 11th edn, Prentice Hall International, 2002, chapter 22.

References

1 **A Survey of Management Accounting Practices in UK Manufacturing Companies**, *Drury C., Braund S., Osborne, P.* and *Tayles M.*, Chartered Association of Certified Accountants, 1993.

2 **2003 Survey of Management Accounting**, *Ernst and Young*, Ernst and Young, 2003.

REVIEW QUESTIONS

Answers to these questions can be found on the students' side of the Companion Website at **www.pearsoned.co.uk/atrillmclaney**.

10.1 Research shows that, in practice in the UK, ROI is a much more popular method of assessing divisional performance than RI. However, the literature suggests that RI is conceptually superior to ROI.

Can you explain this apparent paradox?

10.2 J. Westcott Supplies Ltd has an operating division which produces a single product. In addition to the conventional RI and ROI measures, central management wishes to use other methods of measuring performance and productivity to help assess the division.

Identify four possible measures (financial or non-financial) that central management may decide to use.

10.3 Jerry and Co. is a large computer consultancy firm which has a division specialising in robotics. Can you identify three *non-financial measures* that might be used to help assess the performance of this division?

10.4 A UK survey of decentralised businesses revealed that negotiated prices are the most popular form of transfer pricing method.

Is this approach necessarily the best approach in theory? Why?

EXERCISES

Exercises 10.4 to 10.8 are more advanced than 10.1 to 10.3. Those with a coloured number have answers at the back of the book.

10.1 In divisionalised organisations, complete autonomy of action is impossible when a substantial level of inter-divisional transfers take place.

Required:
(a) In this context, what is meant by 'divisionalised organisation' and 'autonomy of action'?
(b) Is this autonomy good? Why?
(c) Are there any dangers from permitting autonomy of action and in what ways do inter-divisional transfers make complete autonomy impossible?

10.2 Measures are required to assess the performance of divisions and of divisional managers. Three financial measures are:
● contribution;
● controllable profit; and
● return on investment (ROI).

Required:
(a) For each of the above measures show:
   ● the way in which each measure is calculated;
   ● for what purpose they are most suitably applied; and
   ● by providing examples, how the exclusive focus on each single measure may be undesirable.

(b) Suggest three different non-financial measures of performance that may be appropriate to an operating division and consider how such measures, in general, offer improvements when used in conjunction with financial measures.

10.3 You have recently taken a management post in a large divisionalised business. A substantial proportion of the business of, your division is undertaken through inter-divisional transfers.

Required:

(a) What are the objectives of a system of transfer pricing?
(b) Describe the use of, and problems associated with, transfer prices based on variable cost and full cost.
(c) Where an external market exists, to what extent is market price an improvement on cost?

10.4 The following information applies to the planned operations of Division A of ABC Corporation for next year:

		£
Sales	(100,000 units at £12)	1,200,000
Variable costs	(100,000 units at £8)	800,000
Fixed costs (including depreciation)		250,000
Division A investment (at original cost)		500,000

The minimum desired rate of return on investment is the cost of capital of 20 per cent a year.

The business is highly profit-conscious and delegates a considerable level of autonomy to divisional managers. As part of a procedure to review planned operations of Division A, a meeting has been convened to consider two options:

Option I

Division A may sell a further 20,000 units at £11 to customers outside ABC Corporation. Variable costs per unit will be the same as budgeted, but to enable capacity to increase by 20,000 units, one extra piece of equipment will be required costing £80,000. The equipment will have a four-year life and the business depreciates assets on a straight-line basis. No extra cash fixed costs will occur.

Option II

Included in the current plan of operations of Division A is the sale of 20,000 units to Division B also within ABC Corporation. A competitor of Division A, from outside ABC Corporation, has offered to supply Division B at £10 per unit. Division A intends to adopt a strategy of matching the price quoted from outside ABC Corporation to retain the order.

Required:

(a) Calculate Division A's residual income based on:
   (i)   the original planned operation
   (ii) Option I only added to the original plan
   (iii) Option II only added to the original plan
   and briefly interpret the results of the options as they affect Division A.
(b) Assess the implications for Division A, Division B and the ABC Corporation as a whole of Option II, bearing in mind that if Division A does not compete on price, it will lose the 20,000 units order from Division B. Make any recommendations you consider appropriate.

10.5 The following information applies to the budgeted operations of the Goodman division of the Telling Company.

		£
Sales	(50,000 units at £8)	400,000
Variable costs	(50,000 units at £6)	300,000
Contribution		100,000
Fixed costs		75,000
Divisional profit		25,000
Divisional investment		150,000

The minimum desired return on investment is the cost of capital of 20 per cent a year.

Required:

(a) (i) Calculate the divisional expected ROI (return on investment).
    (ii) Calculate the division's expected RI (residual income).
    (iii) Comment on the results of (i) and (ii).

(b) The manager has the opportunity to sell 10,000 units at £7.50. Variable cost per unit would be the same as budgeted, but fixed costs would increase by £5,000. Additional investment of £20,000 would also be required. If the manager accepted this opportunity, by how much and in what direction would the residual income change?

(c) Goodman expects to sell 10,000 units of its budgeted volume of 50,000 units to Sharp, another division of the Telling Company. An outside business has promised to supply the 10,000 units to Sharp at £7.20. If Goodman does not meet the £7.20 price, Sharp will buy from the outside business. Goodman will not save any fixed costs if the work goes outside, but variable costs will be avoided.

    (i) Show the effect on the total profit of the Telling Company if Goodman meets the £7.20 price.

    (ii) Show the effect on the total profit of the Telling Company if Goodman does not meet the price and the work goes outside.

10.6 Glasnost plc is a large business organised on divisional lines. Two typical divisions are East and West. They are engaged in broadly similar activities and, therefore, central management compares their results in order to make judgements on managerial performance. Both divisions are regarded as investment centres.

    A summary of last year's financial results of the two divisions is as follows:

	West		East	
	£000	£000	£000	£000
Capital employed		2,500		500
Sales		1,000		400
Manufacturing cost:				
Direct	300		212	
Indirect	220		48	
Selling and distribution cost	180	700	40	300
Divisional profit		300		100
Apportionment of uncontrollable central				
overhead costs		50		20
Net profit		250		80

At the beginning of last year, West division incurred substantial expenditure on automated production lines and new equipment. East has quite old plant. Approximately 50 per cent of the sales of East are internal transfers to other divisions within the business. These transfers are based on an unadjusted prevailing market price. The inter-divisional transfers of West are minimal.

Management of the business focuses on return on investment as a major performance indicator. The required minimum rate of return is the business's cost of capital of 10 per cent a year.

Required:

(a) Compute any ratios (or other measures) that you consider will help in an assessment of the costs and performance of the two divisions.

(b) Comment on this performance, making reference to any matters that give cause for concern when comparing the divisions or in divisional performance generally.

10.7 The University of Devonport consists of six faculties and an administration unit. Under the university's management philosophy, each faculty is treated, as far as is reasonable, as an independent entity. Each faculty is responsible for its own budget and financial decision making.

A new course in the Faculty of Geography (FG) requires some input from a member of staff of the Faculty of Modern Languages (FML).

The two faculties are in dispute about the 'price' that FG should pay FML for each hour of the staff member's time. FML argues that the hourly rate should be £97.

This is based on the FML budget for this year, which in broad outline is as follows:

	£000
Academic staff salaries 45 staff	1,062
Faculty overheads (nearly all fixed costs)	903
	1,965

Each academic is expected to teach on average for 15 hours a week for 33 weeks a year.

FML wishes to charge FG an hourly rate, which will cover the appropriate proportion of the member of staff's salary plus a 'fair' share of the overheads plus 10 for a small surplus.

FG is refusing to pay this rate. One of FG's arguments is that it should not have to bear any other cost than the appropriate share of the salary. FG also argues that it could find a lecturer who works at the nearby University of Tavistock and is prepared to do the work for £25 an hour, as an additional, spare-time activity.

FML argues that it has deliberately staffed itself at a level which will enable it to cover FG's requirements and that the price must therefore cover the costs.

The university's Vice-Chancellor (its most senior manager) has been asked to resolve the dispute. You are the university's finance manager.

Required:

Make notes in preparation for a meeting with the Vice-Chancellor, where you will discuss the problem with her. The Vice-Chancellor is an historian by background and is not familiar with financial matters. Your notes will therefore need to be expressed in language that an intelligent layperson can understand.

Your notes should deal both with the objectives of effective transfer prices and with the specifics of this case. You should raise any issues which seem to you might be relevant.

10.8 AB Ltd operates retail stores throughout the country. The business is divisionalised. Included in its business are Divisions A and B. The work of these divisions is supported by a centralised and automated warehouse that replenishes stock (inventory) using computer-based systems.

For many years this organisation, which gives considerable autonomy to divisional managers, has emphasised return on investment (ROI) as a composite performance measure. This is calculated after apportionment of all actual costs and assets of the business and 'its appropriate service facilities', which includes the costs and assets of the warehouse.

The following information is available for last year:

	Division A		Division B	
	Actual	Budget	Actual	Budget
	£m	£m	£m	£m
Sales	30.0	50.0	110.0	96.0
Assets employed	20.0		48.0	
Operating profit	4.3		14.7	

These actual figures do not include the apportioned costs or assets of the automated warehouse shared by the two divisions. The data available for the warehouse facility for last year are:

	Warehouse Actual £m	Budget £m
Despatches (that is, sales)	140.0	146.0
Assets employed at book value	8.0	8.0
Operating costs:		
Depreciation	1.6	1.6
Other fixed costs	1.1	0.9
Variable storage costs	0.6	0.5
Variable handling costs	1.3	1.1
Total operating costs	4.6	4.1

When the warehouse investment was authorised it was agreed that the assets employed and the actual expenses were to be apportioned between the divisions concerned in the proportions originally agreed (50 per cent each). However, it was also pointed out that in the future the situation could be redesigned and there was no need for one single basis to apply. For example, it would be possible to use the information that space occupied by stocks (inventories) of the two divisions is now A 40 per cent and B 60 per cent.

Required:

(a) (i)   Calculate the actual return on investment (ROI) for Divisions A and B after incorporating the warehouse assets and actual costs apportioned on an equal basis as originally agreed.

   (ii) What basis of apportionment of assets and actual costs would the manager of Division A argue for, in order to maximise the reported ROI of the division? How would you anticipate that the manager of Division B might react?

(b) It has been pointed out that a combination of bases of apportionment may be used instead of just one, such as the space occupied by stocks (A 40 per cent, B 60 per cent) or the level of actual or budgeted sales and so on. If you were given the freedom to revise the calculation, what bases of apportionment would you recommend in the circumstances? Discuss your approach and recalculate the ROI of Division A on your recommended basis.

Work to two places of decimals only.

11

Strategic management accounting

OBJECTIVES

When you have completed this chapter, you should be able to:

- Discuss the nature and role of strategic management accounting.

- Explain how management accounting information can help a business gain a better understanding of its competitors and customers.

- Describe the techniques available for gaining competitive advantage through cost leadership.

- Explain how the Balanced Scorecard can help monitor and measure progress towards the achievement of strategic objectives.

- Explain the role of shareholder value analysis and economic value added in strategic financial decision making.

INTRODUCTION

Businesses are increasingly being managed along strategic lines. By this we mean that strategies adopted by a business are increasingly providing the basis for both long-term and short-term decisions. If management accounting is to help guide decision making within a strategic framework, the reports provided and techniques used must align closely with the framework that has been put in place. Conventional management accounting has been criticised, however, for failing to address fully the strategic aspects of managing a business. This criticism does not mean that the management accounting techniques discussed so far are obsolete, but it does mean that the subject must continue to develop if it is to retain a high degree of relevance for decision makers.

Strategic management accounting (SMA) is still a fairly new topic and there is no generally agreed set of concepts and techniques that can help us define precisely what is meant by this term. Nevertheless, some key features of this new topic can →

be identified and new accounting techniques, which are seen as useful for strategic decision making, have emerged.

We shall begin the chapter by discussing the nature of strategic management accounting and then go on to look at some of the techniques and methods of analysis that fall within its scope. In this chapter we shall draw on the understanding of topics covered in many of the preceding chapters of the book, particularly Chapters 1, 5, 7, 8 and 10.

What is strategic management accounting?

Strategic management accounting is concerned with providing information that will support the strategic plans and decisions made within a business. We saw in Chapter 1 that strategic planning involves five steps:

1 Establishing the mission and objectives of a business.
2 Undertaking a position analysis (such as a SWOT – strengths, weaknesses, opportunities, threats – analysis) to establish how the business is placed in relation to its environment.
3 Identifying and assessing the possible strategic options that will lead the business from its present position (identified in step 2) to the achievement of its objectives (identified in step 1).
4 Selecting the most appropriate strategic options (from those identified in step 3) and formulating long- and short-term plans to pursue them.
5 Reviewing business performance and exercising control by comparing actual performance against planned performance (identified in step 4).

To some extent, conventional management accounting already supports this strategic process. We have seen in Chapter 6, for example, how budgets can be used to compare actual performance with earlier planned performance. We have also seen in Chapter 8 the role of investment appraisal techniques in evaluating long-term plans. Nevertheless, there is scope for further development. It can be argued that if management accounting is to fully support the strategic planning process, it must develop in three broad areas:

● *It must become more outward looking.* There is general agreement that the conventional approach to management accounting does not give enough consideration to external factors affecting the business. These factors, however, are vitally important to strategic planning and decision making. We need, for example, to understand the environment within which the business operates when we are undertaking a position analysis or when we are formulating plans for the future. Management accounting can play a useful role here by providing information relating to the environment, such as the performance of the business's competitors and the key features of its customers.
● *There must be greater concern for developing and implementing methods through which a business can outperform the competition.* In a competitive environment, a business must be able to gain an advantage over its rivals, so that it can survive and prosper over the longer term. Competitive advantage can be gained in various ways and one important way is through cost leadership: that is, the ability to produce products or services at a lower cost than that of other businesses. Although conventional management accounting provides a number of cost determination and control techniques to help a business operate more efficiently, these techniques are not always enough.

Rather than seeking simply to count and manage the costs incurred, costs and cost structures may need to be transformed. Thus, management accounting has a role to play in helping to shape the costs of the business to fit the strategic objectives.

● *There must be a concern for monitoring the strategies of the business and for bringing these strategies to a successful conclusion.* This means that management accounting should place greater emphasis on long-term planning issues and on developing a comprehensive range of performance measures to ensure that the objectives of the business are being met. The objectives of a business are often couched in both financial and non-financial terms and so the measures developed must reflect this fact.

Let us now turn our attention to the ways in which management accounting can help in each of the three areas identified.

Accounting for external factors

If a business is to thrive, it needs to have a good understanding of the environment within which it operates. In particular, it should have a good understanding of the threat posed by its competitors and the benefits obtained from its customers. There is a strong case for reporting certain information, relating to competitors and customers, frequently and routinely to managers. By so doing, managers can respond more quickly to any changes in the environment that may occur. However, few businesses appear to do this at present. In this section we consider some of the techniques and measures that may help managers gain a better understanding of these two important groups.

Competitor profitability analysis

The ability of a business to meet its objectives depends on its ability to compete effectively. An important tool in the commercial struggle with competitors is knowledge of the competitors' costs and profits. Such knowledge can, for example, enable a particular business to make an informed assessment of what effect a decision to reduce its own sales prices would have on its competitors. Would a 10 per cent reduction in selling price be matched by competitors, or would it force them out of the market? If the competitors cannot match the price reduction, would they be able to continue to supply, given the likely sales volume reduction that they would suffer? A business would normally know what effect a price reduction would have on its own ability to compete, but the effect of such a reduction on its competitors is often not analysed.

Gaining information about competitors is not always easy as businesses are reluctant to release information that may damage their competitive position. Nevertheless, there are sources of information that can be used to gain an insight to the costs and profits of competitors. In the UK, all limited companies are legally obliged to provide information about their business in an annual report that is available to the public. Similar provisions relate to limited companies in most countries in the world. This information tends, however, to be of limited value in **competitor profitability analysis**. One important reason for this is that the competitor may not be the whole business, but just a part of it, such as an operating division. Though large businesses operating as limited companies must publish some information about the sales and profit relating to their various operating segments, this is often not enough to enable a full picture of the competitor to be built up. Nonetheless, a competitor's annual report will usually offer some useful information.

A business should, of course, have detailed knowledge of its own costs and profits, so it may well be able to make informed estimates of what these are likely to be for the competitor. Any differences may be able to be identified and taken into account. For example, if a business knows that the competitor's approach is more capital intensive than its own, it may be able to estimate how this would make the competitor's costs different from its own.

It may be possible to gain other information. This could be from:

- press coverage of the competitor's business;
- talking to customers who trade both with the business and with the competitor;
- talking to suppliers to both the business and its competitor;
- physical observation;
- industry reports; and
- government statistics on such matters as the total size of the market.

There is a wide range of potential sources of information about competitors. All of these sources will provide clues that can be pieced together in an attempt to build up as full a picture as possible of each significant competitor. Figure 11.1 shows some of the likely sources of information.

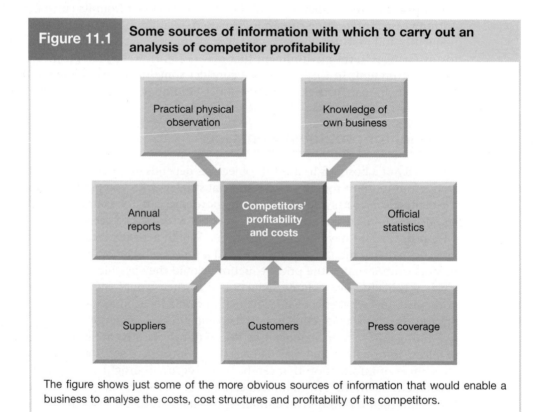

Figure 11.1 **Some sources of information with which to carry out an analysis of competitor profitability**

The figure shows just some of the more obvious sources of information that would enable a business to analyse the costs, cost structures and profitability of its competitors.

Of particular value to a business is knowledge of its competitors' cost structures in terms of the extent to which costs are fixed and variable. This would enable a business to make some estimate of the effect on the competitors' profit of an increase or decrease in sales volume. This might, in turn, enable a business to assess how well placed each competitor might be to react to a change in sales volume and/or sales price. For example, a competitor with a high level of fixed costs (high operating gearing) and, consequently, a low margin of safety may not be able to withstand a downturn in sales volume as comfortably as another business with lower operating gearing.

Competitor profiling

If a business has one or two major competitors, a more detailed investigation may be useful. In addition to information relating to sales, costs and profits, a profile of each major competitor may be built up that covers areas such as:

- objectives and strategies;
- resources, including financial, technological and human resources;
- products and/or services offered or being developed; and
- alliances and joint ventures with other businesses that affect market power.

This is like carrying out a SWOT analysis for each competitor. Information sources such as those mentioned earlier can help provide insights here. Business information agencies may also provide information, at a price, relating to each area.

It may be argued that **competitor profiling** such as this goes beyond the realms of accounting. However, it was argued in Chapter 1 that the boundaries of management accounting are not clearly defined. Moreover, this kind of information gathering and reporting is often best done by the management accounting function within a business.

Of course, a business can never know everything about its competitors, and there must be a practical limit on how much it is worth spending to gain more information. As ever, it is a question of balancing the potential benefits of having information against the costs involved in obtaining it.

Real World 11.1 provides an example of how one business came to realise that it had to pay more attention to the competition.

REAL WORLD 11.1

Angling for recovery

House of Hardy is a world-famous manufacturer of fishing rods and tackle. It enjoys an unrivalled reputation for its products and has a highly skilled workforce. In recent years, however, it has experienced problems, which have been partly caused by global competition. The business is trying to recover and, in analysing its past mistakes, has recognised that it has been rather too complacent in its approach to competitors. As part of its recovery plan it is now paying much more attention to what they are doing. It is now analysing the products offered by competitors and reviewing its own pricing policies in an attempt to compete more effectively.

Source: Based on information from 'How Hardy lost the lure of heritage', FT.com, 1 December 2003.

Customer profitability analysis

A business will seek to attract and retain customers who provide it with profitable sales orders. It is, therefore, worth knowing whether a particular customer, or type of customer, is, or is likely to be, profitable to the business. **Customer profitability analysis (CPA)** assesses the profitability of the business, customer by customer, or type of customer by type of customer.

A CPA is essentially an abbreviated 'profit and loss account' for each customer and/or type of customer, for a period. It compares the total revenues for that period with the associated costs for each customer or type of customer. These costs will obviously include the basic cost of creating or buying in the goods or services supplied to the customer. This cost will already be available from the business's product cost records, perhaps derived using an activity-based costing (ABC) approach. Total customer costs will also include selling and distribution costs. These will encompass such things as the cost to the business of:

- Handling orders from the customer. This encompasses the costs involved with receiving the order and activities relating to it to the point where the goods are despatched, or the service rendered, including the costs of raising invoices and other accounting work.
- Visiting the customer by the business's sales staff. Many businesses have a member of staff visit customers, perhaps to take orders, but often to keep the customer up to date with the latest developments in the business's products.
- Delivering goods to the customer, using either a delivery service provided by another business, or the business's own transport. Naturally, the distance travelled and the bulkiness and fragility of the goods will have an effect on this cost.
- Stockholding costs. Some customers may require a particular level of stock to be held by the business. For example, a customer operating a 'just-in-time' raw material stock policy will tend, in effect, to put pressure on the supplier to hold stock.
- Credit costs. The business will have to finance any credit allowed to its customers. This could vary from customer to customer, depending on how promptly they pay.

A customer who places lots of small orders, necessitating numerous deliveries to a distant location, who receives many visits from sales staff, who requires the business to hold large stocks and who pays slowly is likely to be much less profitable, for the same total sales revenue, than other, less demanding customers. Figure 11.2 shows some of the factors that could be considered in a CPA.

It seems that where CPA is applied in practice, businesses use an ABC approach. Activities, such as handling sales orders, drive costs. The extent to which a particular customer drives order-handling costs is likely to be in proportion to the number of orders placed, irrespective of the size of the order. This is likely to be similar for other customer-related costs.

CPA enables management to know which customers generate profit for the business and which do not.

Activity 11.1

Amal plc carried out a CPA and discovered that a number of its customers are unprofitable to the business. These tended to be those who placed a number of small orders. How might Amal plc react to the information provided by the CPA?

We thought of the following:

- Increase prices to the customers concerned.
- Impose a minimum order size: that is, refuse to accept orders below a particular value.
- Increase prices, but allow discounts for larger orders.

Figure 11.2   **Factors in a customer profitability analysis**

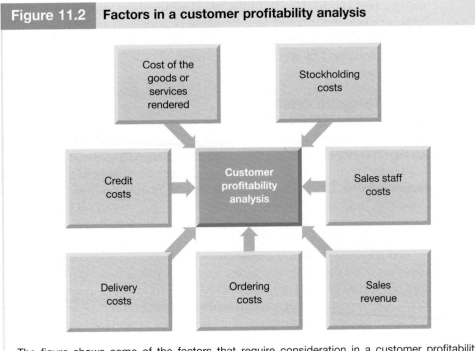

The figure shows some of the factors that require consideration in a customer profitability analysis.

Real World 11.2 provides some impression of the extent to which customer profitability is assessed in practice.

REAL WORLD 11.2

CPA in practice

A survey of 176 fairly large UK businesses, conducted during 1999, revealed that 76 per cent of respondents analyse the profitability of trading with customers. Nearly two-thirds of those who do this update the analysis monthly and nearly all do so annually or even more frequently than annually.

Source: Drury and Tayles (see reference 1 at the end of the chapter).

Competitive advantage through cost leadership

Many businesses try to compete on price: that is, they try to provide goods or services at prices that compare favourably with those of their competitors. To do this successfully over time, they must compete on costs: lower prices can only be sustained by lower costs. A strategic commitment to competitive pricing should, therefore, be accompanied by a strategic commitment to managing the cost base.

In Chapter 5 we saw that, to actively manage costs, new forms of costing have been devised. Some of these new costing techniques reflect a concern for long-term cost management and so fall within the broad scope of strategic management accounting. Total life-cycle costing and target costing provide two examples. In this section, we shall briefly review these two forms of costing and then go on to consider other ways in which costs may be strategically managed.

Total life-cycle costing

We saw in Chapter 5 that total life-cycle costing draws management's attention to the fact that it is not only during the production phase that costs are incurred. Costs begin to accumulate at earlier phases, such as design, development and setting up the production process. (For some businesses, such as pharmaceutical businesses, these early-phase costs may represent a high proportion of the total costs incurred.) Furthermore, costs continue to accumulate after production, such as those relating to distribution and after-sales service.

Total life-cycle costing is concerned with tracking and reporting all costs relating to a product from the beginning to the end of its life. If the revenues generated over the life-cycle of the product are also tracked, we can assess its profitability. Conventional accounting reports do not attempt to do this and so it is may be difficult for managers to know whether the decision to launch a new a product generated profits or losses.

Target costing

Target costing is a market-based approach to managing costs. We saw in Chapter 5 that the starting point is to set the target price of a product on the basis of market research, which may include an analysis of competitors' prices. The target price, less the required profit from the product, will be the target cost of the product. Target costing places demands on managers because the target cost is usually lower than the current full cost of the product. To achieve the target cost, a systematic approach to cost reduction is often required. All aspects of the key manufacturing processes, including raw material purchasing, design, development and production, may have to be reviewed in order to identify cost savings. Such a fundamental review of key processes can often reap long-term benefits.

Value chain analysis

Another approach that seeks to manage costs, and which recognises the total life-cycle concept, is **value chain analysis**. The value chain is the linking sequence of activities, through the three phases of the product life-cycle (see Figure 5.8, p. 131) from research and development to after-sales activities. In a wealth-seeking business, the objective for the product is that it should create value for the business and its owners. Each link in the value chain represents a particular activity. All of the activities will lead to a cost. Ideally, each link should add value to the product, making the product more valuable to the customer. Any links in the chain that fail to add value should be examined very critically. The objective of this examination is to assess whether the particular link could be eliminated completely or, at least, have its cost reduced.

An example of a typical non-value-added activity is inspection of the completed product or service by a quality controller. This activity does not add value to the product or service, yet it adds cost. This inspection cost might well be capable of being reduced, or even completely eliminated. The introduction of a 'quality' culture in the business could lead to all output being reliable and not needing to be inspected. This is a development that many modern businesses have achieved.

An example of a value-added activity would be the rendering of a service to a customer for which the customer is prepared to pay more than it cost. **Real World 11.3** gives some indication of the extent to which value chain analysis is used in practice.

REAL WORLD 11.3

Value chain analysis in practice

The Ernst and Young survey of management accounting practice in the US, conducted in 2003, revealed that 27 per cent of managers extensively use value chain analysis, with a further 47 per cent considering using the technique in the future.

Source: Ernst and Young (see reference 2 at the end of the chapter).

Real World 11.4 reveals how the elimination of non-value-creating activities may lead to a transformation in the nature of the business.

REAL WORLD 11.4

Driving in a different direction

In the US, the big three car makers, General Motor, Ford and Chrysler, have suffered from intense competition for market share. They have responded by re-examining all aspects of their business in order to save costs and to eliminate non-value-creating activities. They have standardised components across vehicle platforms and brands and have stream-lined their purchasing systems so that they deal with fewer suppliers. In the future, they are expected to collaborate strongly with key suppliers over the engineering aspects of cars to explore whether further costs may be saved. It is predicted that this will lead to greater pressure for suppliers to assume responsibility for engineering. This part of the car makers' task will be passed down the 'value chain' so that, ultimately, car makers may simply market and design cars.

Source: Based on information from 'Parts companies feel knock-on effect', FT.com, 4 March 2003.

An alternative vision of cost management

Although the techniques described above are being used and are seen as useful by many businesses, some believe that they fail to provide the key to successful strategic cost management. It has been suggested that undue emphasis on techniques, such as total life-cycle costing and target costing, is misplaced and what is really needed is for businesses to develop ways of learning and adapting to their changing environment. To manage costs successfully, businesses should continually review them in the face of new threats and pressures rather than relying on particular techniques to provide solutions.

Hopwood (see reference 3 at the end of the chapter) suggests that to transform costs over time so that they fit the strategic objectives, businesses do not need very sophisticated techniques or highly bureaucratic systems. Rather, they need to change the ways in which costs are viewed and dealt with by staff. He suggests that the following broad principles should be adopted.

1 Spread the responsibility

Employees throughout the business should share responsibility for managing costs. Design experts, development engineers, warehouse managers, sales managers and so on, should all contribute towards managing costs and should see this as part of their job. To enable these employees to contribute fully, they should be provided with a basic understanding of costing ideas such as fixed and variable costs, relevant costs and so on. This will give them the basic tools required to evaluate options and to have a dialogue with the accountants.

As cost consciousness permeates the business and non-accounting employees become more involved in costing issues, the role of the accountants will change. They will often facilitate rather than initiate cost management proposals and will become part of multi-skilled teams engaged in creatively managing costs.

2 Spread the word

Throughout the business, costs and cost management should become everyday topics for discussion. Managers should seize every opportunity to raise these topics with employees, as talking about costs can often lead to ideas being developed and action being taken to manage costs.

3 Think local

Emphasis should be placed on managing costs within specific sites and settings. Managers of departments, product lines or local offices are more likely to become engaged in managing costs if they are allowed to take initiatives in areas over which they have control. Local managers tend to have local knowledge not possessed by managers at head office. They are more likely to be able to spot cost saving opportunities than are their more senior colleagues. Business-wide initiatives for cost management, which have been developed by senior management, are unlikely to have the same beneficial effect.

4 Benchmark continually

There should be regular, as well as special-purpose, reporting of cost information for benchmarking purposes. The costs of competitors may provide a useful basis for comparison, as we saw earlier. In addition, costs that may be expected as a result of moving to new technology or work patterns may be helpful.

5 Focus on managing rather than reducing costs

Conventional management accounting tends to focus on cost reduction, which is, essentially, a short-term perspective on costs. Strategic cost management, however, means that in some situations, costs should be increased rather than reduced.

Real World 11.5 gives an example of how local managers, who are not accountants, can identify potential cost savings and not resent their implementation.

REAL WORLD 11.5

Costing problem? Call a doctor.

A fairly recent research study contrasts the difference in approach to cost management in UK and Finnish hospitals.

In the UK, cost management is seen as the domain of financial staff. This can lead to problems as financial systems that have been introduced to manage costs have led to more complex organisational structures. In addition there is often an emphasis on cost savings, which can lead to conflict between financial staff and medical staff. The latter often resent cost cuts being imposed on them by the financial staff.

In contrast, medical staff in Finnish hospitals share responsibility for cost management. Doctors and other medical professionals recognise the need to use resources in an efficient way and are committed to ensuring that resources are not wasted. Rather than fighting cost-cutting initiatives from financial staff, they see both medical knowledge and cost awareness as being necessary to successful medical practice.

Source: Based on information in 'Costs count in the strategic agenda', A. Hopwood, FT.com, 13 August 2002.

Activity 11.2

Under what kind of circumstances might it be a good idea to increase costs?

This may include situations that could lead to:

● additional revenues being generated
● lower costs being incurred over the longer term
● lower costs being incurred in other areas of the business.

Hopwood argues that the above principles, when used in conjunction with overall financial controls, provide the best way to strategically manage costs.

Accounting for strategy

In this section we shall consider ways in which management accounting can help mangers to set strategic objectives and to measure the extent to which strategic object- ives have been met. We begin by considering the way a change in strategy may be assessed and we shall see that the approach used is an adaptation of a technique that we met earlier in the book. Following this, we go on to consider new measures and frameworks that have been suggested for use within a strategic context.

Assessing strategic change

One way in which management accounting can play a useful part in a strategic approach to management is in analysing the effects of a change in strategy, so that the success of the change can be assessed. The analysis undertaken can follow the same broad principles as variance analysis, which we met in Chapter 7. It would, in effect, be a comparison of the performance after the change of strategy with that for the period immediately preceding it. The following example provides an illustration of the process.

Example 11.1

Cosyco is a business that makes ceramic patio heaters. It uses only one raw material to make them. The market for the heaters is now quite competitive, with all of the competitors providing a very similar product at roughly the same price. The managers of Cosyco have been looking for a way to generate more profit. One strategy considered was to reduce prices in an attempt to gain a greater market share, but this was rejected on the grounds that the increased sales would probably not be sufficient to compensate for the reduced selling prices. Finally, it was decided to pursue a policy of 'product differentiation': that is, to make a better quality, more attractive heater. This would require the use of a more expensive raw material, which would need to be used in greater quantities than in the present heater. It was believed that the change of strategy would enable the business to charge a higher price for each heater sold and to sell more of them. The strategic change was effective from 1 January Year 5.

A summary of Cosyco's trading for Year 4, the last year of the old strategy, and Year 5, the first year of the new strategy, is as follows:

Year	Year 4	Year 5
1 Number of heaters made and sold	5,000	6,000
2 Selling price per heater	£40	£45
3 Total sales (line 1 × line 2)	£200,000	£270,000
4 Direct materials (DM) used per heater	0.500 kg	0.533 kg
5 DM cost per kg	£15	£16
6 Total DM cost (line 1 × line 4 × line 5)	£37,500	£51,200

The income statements for the two years are, therefore, as follows:

Year	Year 4	Year 5
	£	£
Sales	200,000	270,000
DM	37,500	51,200
Contribution	162,500	218,800

It is known that other manufacturing costs are fixed and have not been affected by the change in strategy.

Assuming that the increase in contribution of £56,300 (that is, £218,800 – £162,500) is all caused by the strategic change, it might be useful to Cosyco's management to know in more detail how the additional contribution arose.

The contribution change (£56,300 increase) can be analysed into three aspects:

- The *growth aspect*, which assesses the extent to which the increased sales alone affected the contribution. Here we ignore the effects of price differences, both the selling and materials purchase price, and the effect of using more materials. We are, therefore, looking at the equivalent of the *sales volume variance* that we met in Chapter 7.
- The *price aspect*, which arises from the differences both in the selling price and the increased price of the DM. Here we ignore the effect of growth and usage and just concentrate on the effect of price difference. This is equivalent to the *sales price variance* and the *raw material price variance*.
- The *usage (or productivity) aspect*, which arises from the use of larger amounts of DM for each heater produced. This is, of course, the equivalent of the *DM usage*

variance. Here we ignore the effects of growth and price differences and concentrate only on usage differences.

We can now carry out the analysis of Cosyco's change in strategy.

Growth aspect

- Revenue growth is the effect of the growth in revenues arising from the volume growth: (units sold in Year 5 less units sold in Year 4) × Year 4 selling price per unit

$$= (6,000 - 5,000) \times £40 = £40,000 \text{ (F)}$$

(it is 'favourable' because it represents a contribution increase arising from the change in strategy).

- Cost of growth is the effect on costs of the sales volume growth: (usage of DM for Year 5, based on usage of DM per heater that applied in Year 4, less usage of DM in Year 4) × price of DM in Year 4

$$= [(6,000 \times 0.5) - (5,000 \times 0.5)] \times £15 = £7,500 \text{ (A)}$$

(it is 'adverse' because it represents a contribution decrease arising from the change in strategy).

		£
Summary of growth aspect	Revenue growth	40,000 (F)
	Cost growth	7,500 (A)
		32,500 (F)

Price aspect

- Revenue price is the effect of the increase in revenues arising from the price rise: (selling price per unit in Year 5 less selling price per unit in Year 4) × Year 5 sales volume

$$= (£45 - £40) \times 6,000 = £30,000 \text{ (F)}$$

- Cost price increase effect on costs: (cost per kg of DM in Year 5 less cost per kg of DM in Year 4) × usage of DM for Year 5, based on usage of DM per heater that applied in Year 4

$$= (£16 - £15) \times (6,000 \times 0.5) = £3,000 \text{ (A)}.$$

		£
Summary of price aspect	Revenue price	30,000 (F)
	Cost price	3,000 (A)
		27,000 (F)

Usage (or productivity) aspect

DM usage effect on costs: (actual usage of DM in Year 5 less usage of DM for Year 5, based on usage of DM per heater that applied in Year 4) × Year 5 price per kg of DM

$$= [3,200 - (6,000 \times 0.5)] \times £16 = £3,200 \text{ (A)}$$

Summary of usage aspect	DM usage	£3,200 (A)
		£
Overall summary	Growth aspect	32,500 (F)
	Price aspect	27,000 (F)
	Usage aspect	3,200 (A)
		56,300 (F)

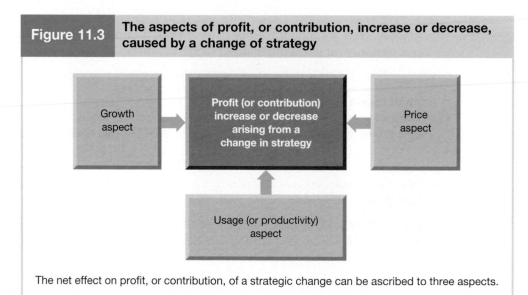

Figure 11.3 The aspects of profit, or contribution, increase or decrease, caused by a change of strategy

The net effect on profit, or contribution, of a strategic change can be ascribed to three aspects.

Figure 11.3 shows the aspects that are caused by a change of strategy.

Activity 11.3

Try to explain briefly, on the basis of the analysis in Example 11.1, why Cosyco's contribution was greater in Year 5 than it had been in Year 4.

We can say that, of the £56,300 additional contribution generated by the change in strategy, £32,500 arose from sales volume growth alone and £27,000 from the higher prices charged, after allowing for the higher cost of the better quality DM. These growth and price benefits were offset to the extent of £3,200 by increased costs arising from a higher usage of DM.

Monitoring and measuring progress towards strategic objectives

Having set out the strategic objectives of a business, progress towards these objectives must be monitored. This means that there must be appropriate measures by which progress can be assessed. Financial measures have long held sway as the most important measures for a business. They provide us with a valuable means of summarising and evaluating business achievement and there is no real doubt about the continued importance of financial measures in this role.

In recent years, however, there has been increasing recognition that financial measures alone will not provide managers with sufficient information to manage a business effectively. Non-financial measures must also be used to gain a deeper understanding of the business and to achieve the objectives of the business, including the financial objectives.

Financial measures portray various aspects of business achievement (for example, sales, profits, return on capital employed and so on) that can help managers determine whether the business is increasing the wealth of its owners. These measures are vitally important but, in an increasingly competitive environment, managers also need to understand what drives the creation of wealth. These **value drivers** may be such things as employee satisfaction, customer loyalty and the level of product innovation. Often they do not lend themselves to financial measurement, although non-financial measures may provide some means of assessment.

Activity 11.4

How might we measure:

(a) employee satisfaction?
(b) customer loyalty?
(c) the level of product innovation?

....

(a) Employee satisfaction may be measured through the use of an employee survey. This could examine attitudes towards various aspects of the job, the degree of autonomy that is permitted, the level of recognition and reward received, the level of participation in decision making, the degree of support received in carrying out tasks, and so on. Less direct measures of satisfaction may include employee turnover rates and employee productivity. However, other factors may have a significant influence on these measures.

(b) Customer loyalty may be measured through the proportion of total sales generated from existing customers, the number of repeat sales made to customers, the percentage of customers renewing subscriptions or other contracts, and so on.

(c) The level of product innovation may be measured through the number of innovations during a period compared to those of competitors, the percentage of sales attributable to recent product innovations, the number of innovations that are brought successfully to market and so on.

Real World 11.6 gives an example of a very well-known international business that focuses a lot of attention on non-financial measures.

REAL WORLD 11.6

Non-financial measures at Pepsi

Pepsi-Cola attaches considerable importance to non-financial measures when assessing the success of the business. This is reflected in the fact that managers' bonuses are linked to meeting targets based on non-financial measures, as well as more conventional financial measures. The non-financial measures include:

● market-oriented measures, based on quality, customer attitudes and market share (known as marketplace P and L); and
● employee motivation, based on regular surveys.

Source: Based on information from 'The marketing route to value', *Financial Times*, 14 October 2002.

Financial measures are normally 'lag' indicators, in that they tell us about outcomes. In other words, they measure the consequences arising from management decisions that were made earlier. Non-financial measures can also be used as lag indicators, of course. However, they can also be used as 'lead' indicators by focusing on those things that drive performance. It is argued that if we measure changes in these value drivers, we may be able to predict changes in future financial performance. For example, a business may find from experience that a 10 per cent fall in levels of product innovation during one period will lead to a 20 per cent fall in sales over the next three periods. In this case, the levels of product innovation can be regarded as a lead indicator that can alert managers to a future decline in sales unless corrective action is taken. Thus, by using this lead indicator, managers can identify key changes at an early stage and can respond quickly.

The Balanced Scorecard

One of the most impressive attempts to integrate the use of financial and non-financial measures has been the **Balanced Scorecard**, developed by Robert Kaplan and David Norton (see reference 4 at the end of the chapter). The Balanced Scorecard is both a management system and a measurement system. In essence, it provides a framework that translates the aims and objectives of a business into a series of key performance measures and targets. This framework is intended to make the strategy of the business more coherent by tightly linking it to particular targets and initiatives. As a result, managers should be able to see more clearly whether the objectives that have been set have actually been achieved.

The Balanced Scorecard approach involves setting objectives and developing appropriate measures and targets in four main areas:

1 *Financial.* This area will specify the financial returns required by shareholders and may involve the use of financial measures such as return on capital employed, net profit margin, percentage sales growth and so on.

2 *Customer.* This area will specify the kind of customer and/or markets the business wishes to service and will establish appropriate measures such as customer satisfaction, new customer growth levels and so on.

3 *Internal business process.* This area will specify those business processes (for example, innovation, types of operation and after-sales service) that are important to the success of the business and will establish appropriate measures such as percentage of sales from new products, time to market for new products, product cycle times, and speed of response to customer complaints.

4 *Learning and growth.* This area will specify the kind of people, the systems and the procedures that are necessary to deliver long-term business growth. This area is often the most difficult for the development of appropriate measures. However, examples of measures may include employee motivation, employee skills profiles, information systems capabilities and so on.

These four areas are shown in Figure 11.4.

The Balanced Scorecard approach does not prescribe the particular objectives, measures or targets that a business should adopt; this is a matter for the individual business to decide upon. There are differences between businesses in terms of technology employed, organisational structure, management philosophy and business

| Figure 11.4 | The Balanced Scorecard – for translating a strategy into operational processes |

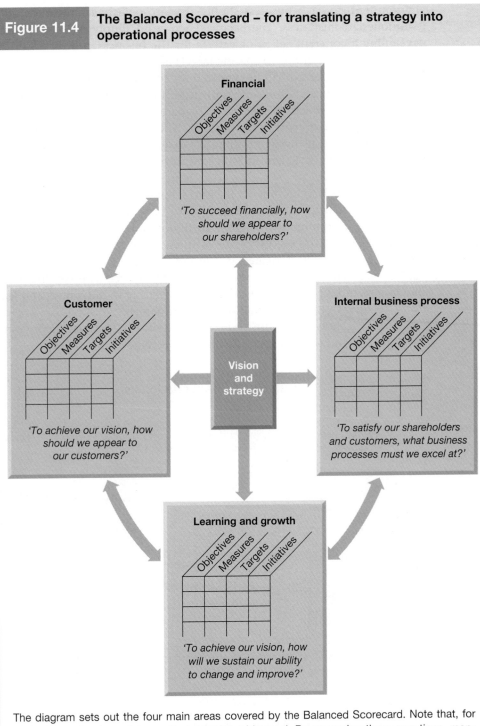

The diagram sets out the four main areas covered by the Balanced Scorecard. Note that, for each area, a fundamental question must be addressed. By answering these questions, managers should be able to develop the key objectives of the business. Once this has been done, suitable measures and targets can be developed that are relevant to those objectives. Finally, appropriate management initiatives will be developed to achieve the targets set.

Source: The Balanced Scorecard (see reference 4 at the end of the chapter).

environment, so each business should develop objectives and measures that reflect its unique circumstances. The Balanced Scorecard simply sets out the framework for developing a coherent set of objectives for the business and for ensuring that these objectives are then linked to specific targets and initiatives.

A Balanced Scorecard will be prepared for the business as a whole (or in the case of large, diverse businesses, for each strategic business unit). However, having prepared an overall scorecard, it is then possible to prepare a Balanced Scorecard for each sub-unit, such as a department, within the business. Thus, the Balanced Scorecard approach can cascade down the business and can result in a pyramid of Balanced Scorecards that are linked to the 'master' Balanced Scorecard through an alignment of the objectives and measures employed.

Though a very large number of measures, both financial and non-financial, exist and so could be used in a Balanced Scorecard, only a handful of measures should be employed. A maximum of 20 measures will normally be sufficient to enable the factors that are critical to the success of the business to be captured. (If a business has come up with more than 20 measures, it is usually because the managers have not thought hard enough about what the key measures really are.) The key measures developed should be a mix of lagging indicators (those relating to outcomes) and lead indicators (those relating to the things that drive performance).

Figure 11.5 shows the cause and effect relationship between the investment in staff development and the business's financial objectives.

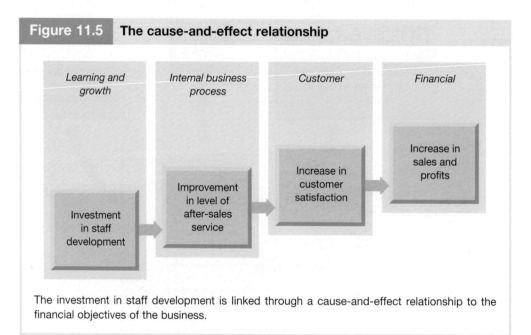

Figure 11.5　**The cause-and-effect relationship**

The investment in staff development is linked through a cause-and-effect relationship to the financial objectives of the business.

Although the Balanced Scorecard employs measures across a wide range of business activity, it does not seek to dilute the importance of financial measures and objectives. In fact, the opposite is true. Kaplan and Norton (see reference 4 at the end of the chapter) emphasise the point that a Balanced Scorecard must reflect a concern for the financial objectives of the business and so measures and objectives in the other three areas that have been identified must ultimately be related back to the financial objectives. There must be a clear cause-and-effect relationship. So, for example, an investment in staff development (in the learning and growth area) may lead to improved levels of after-sales service (internal business process area), which, in turn, may lead to higher levels of customer satisfaction (customer area) and, ultimately, higher sales and profits (financial area).

Activity 11.5

Do you think this is a rather hard-nosed approach to dealing with staff development? Should staff development always have to be justified in terms of the financial results achieved?

This approach may seem rather hard-nosed. However, Kaplan and Norton argue that unless this kind of link between staff development and increased financial returns can be demonstrated, managers are likely to become cynical about the benefits of staff development and so the result may be that there will be no investment in staff.

You may wonder why this framework is referred to as a *Balanced* Scorecard. According to Kaplan and Norton there are various reasons. Firstly, it is because it aims to strike a balance between *external* measures relating to customers and shareholders, and internal measures relating to *internal* business process and learning and growth. Secondly, it aims to strike a balance between the measures that portray *outcomes* (lag indicators) and measures that help *predict future performance* (lead indicators). Finally, the framework aims to strike a balance between *hard* financial measures and *soft* non-financial measures.

Real World 11.7 shows how the Balanced Scorecard is used by one very well-known UK business.

REAL WORLD 11.7

The Balanced Scorecard at Tesco

Tesco plc, the major supermarket chain, said in its 2003 annual report:

> The Steering Wheel is the term used to describe our balanced scorecard approach, which we believe is the best way to achieve results for our shareholders. It sets out a broad range of targets under quadrant headings of customers, operations, people and finance. This allows the business to be operated and monitored on a balanced basis with due regard for all stakeholders. The Board undertakes a formal review of progress on a quarterly basis and any resulting actions considered appropriate are communicated throughout the business.

Source: Tesco plc, Annual Report 2003, p. 8.

As a footnote to our consideration of the Balanced Scorecard, **Real World 11.8** provides an interesting analogy with aeroplane pilots limiting themselves to just one control device.

(UN)REAL WORLD 11.8

Fear of flying

Kaplan and Norton invite you to imagine the following conversation between you and the pilot of a jet aeroplane in which you are flying:

Q: I'm surprised to see you operating the plane with only a single instrument. What does it measure?

A: Airspeed. I'm really working on airspeed this flight.

Q: That's good. Airspeed certainly seems important. But what about altitude? Wouldn't an altimeter be helpful?

A: I worked on altitude for the last few flights and I've gotten pretty good on it. Now I have to concentrate on proper airspeed.

Q: But I notice you don't even have a fuel gauge. Wouldn't that be useful?

A: You're right; fuel is significant, but I can't concentrate on doing too many things well at the same time. So on this flight I'm focusing on airspeed. Once I get to be excellent at airspeed, as well as altitude, I intend to concentrate on fuel consumption on the next set of flights.

The point they are trying to make (apart from warning you against flying with a pilot like this!) is that to fly an aeroplane, which is a complex activity, a wide range of navigation instruments is required. A business, however, can be even more complex to manage than an aeroplane and so a wide range of measures, both financial and non-financial, is necessary. Reliance on financial measures is not enough and so the Balanced Scorecard aims to provide managers with a more complete navigation system.

Source: Kaplan and Norton (see reference 4 at the end of the chapter).

Financial measures of performance

Traditional measures of financial performance have been subject to much criticism in recent years and new measures have been advocated to guide and to assess strategic management decisions. In this section we shall consider two new measures, both of which are based on the idea of increasing shareholder value. Before examining each method, we shall first consider why increasing shareholder value is regarded as the ultimate financial objective of a business.

The quest for shareholder value

For some years, shareholder value has been a 'hot' issue among managers. Many leading businesses now claim that the quest for shareholder value is the driving force behind their strategic and operational decisions. As a starting point, we shall consider what is meant by the term 'shareholder value' and in the sections that follow we shall look at two of the main approaches to measuring shareholder value.

Let us start by considering what the term 'shareholder value' means. In simple terms, it is about putting the needs of shareholders at the heart of management decisions. It is argued that shareholders invest in a business with a view to maximising their financial returns in relation to the risks that they are prepared to take. As managers are appointed by the shareholders to act on their behalf, management decisions and actions should therefore reflect a concern for maximising shareholder returns. Though the business may have other 'stakeholder' groups, such as employees, customers and suppliers, it is the shareholders that should be seen as the most important group.

This, of course, is not a new idea. As we discussed in Chapter 1, maximising shareholder returns is assumed to be the key objective of a business. However, not everyone accepts this idea. Some believe that a balance must be struck between the competing claims of the various stakeholders. A debate concerning the merits of each viewpoint is beyond the scope of this book; however, it is worth pointing out that, in recent years, the business environment has radically changed.

In the past, shareholders have been accused of being too passive and of accepting too readily the profits and dividends that managers have delivered. However, this has changed. Shareholders are now much more assertive, and, as owners of the business, are in a position to insist that their needs are given priority. Since the 1980s we have witnessed the deregulation and globalisation of business, as well as enormous changes in technology. The effect has been to create a much more competitive world. This has meant not only competition for products and services but also competition for funds. Businesses must now compete more strongly for shareholder funds and so must offer competitive rates of return.

Thus, self-interest may be the most powerful reason for managers to commit themselves to maximising shareholder returns. If they do not do this, there is a real risk that shareholders will either replace them with managers who will, or shareholders will allow the business to be taken over by another business, which has managers who are dedicated to maximising shareholder returns.

How can shareholder value be created?

Creating shareholder value involves a four-stage process. The first stage is to set objectives for the business that recognise the central importance of maximising shareholder returns. This will set a clear direction for the business. The second stage is to establish an appropriate means of measuring the returns, or value, that have been generated for shareholders. For reasons that we shall discuss later, the traditional methods of measuring returns to shareholders are inadequate for this purpose. The third stage is to manage the business in such a manner as to ensure that shareholder returns are maximised. This means setting demanding targets and then achieving them through the best possible use of resources, the use of incentive systems and the embedding of a shareholder value culture throughout the business. The final stage is to measure the shareholder returns over a period of time to see whether the objectives have actually been achieved.

Figure 11.6 (p. 354) shows the shareholder value creation process.

The need for new forms of measurement

Given a commitment to maximise shareholder returns, we must select an appropriate measure that will help us assess the returns to shareholders over time. It is argued that the traditional methods for measuring shareholder returns are seriously flawed and so should not be used for this purpose.

Figure 11.6	The four-stage process for creating shareholder value

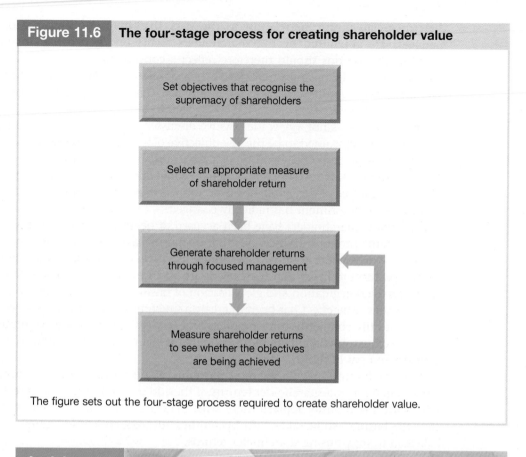

The figure sets out the four-stage process required to create shareholder value.

What are the traditional methods of measuring shareholder returns?

The traditional approach is to use accounting profit or some ratio that is based on accounting profit, such as return on shareholders' funds or earnings per share.

There are broadly four problems with using accounting profit, or a ratio based on profit, to assess shareholder returns. These are:

- *Profit is measured over a relatively short period of time* (usually one year). However, when we talk about maximising shareholder returns, we are concerned with maximising returns over the *long term*. It has been suggested that using profit as the key measure will run the risk that managers will take decisions that improve performance in the short term, but which may have an adverse effect on long-term performance. For example, profits may be increased in the short term by cutting back on staff training and research expenditure. However, this type of expenditure may be vital to long-term survival.
- *Risk is ignored.* A fundamental principle in finance is that there is a clear relationship between the level of returns achieved and the level of risk that must be taken to achieve those returns. The higher the level of returns required, the higher the level of risk that must be taken to achieve the returns. A management strategy that produces an increase in profits can reduce shareholder value if the increase in profits achieved is not commensurate with the increase in the level of risk. Thus, profit alone is not enough.

● *Accounting profit does not take account of all of the costs of the capital invested by the business*. The conventional approach to measuring profit will deduct the cost of loan capital (that is, interest charges) in arriving at net profit, but there is no similar deduction for the cost of shareholder funds. (Any dividends payable, which is part of the return to shareholders, is deducted after arriving at the net profit figure.) Critics of the conventional approach point out that a business will not make a profit, in an economic sense, unless it covers the cost of all capital invested, including shareholder funds. Unless this done, the business will operate at a loss and so shareholder value will be reduced.

● *Accounting profit reported by a business can vary according to the particular policies that have been adopted*. These can vary from one business to another. Some businesses adopt a very conservative approach, which would be reflected in particular accounting policies such as the immediate writing-off of intangible assets (for example, research and development and goodwill), the use of the reducing-balance method of depreciation (which means high depreciation charges in the early years), and so on. Businesses that do not adopt conservative accounting policies would report higher profits in the early years of owning depreciating assets. The writing-off of intangible assets over a long time period (or perhaps, not writing off intangible assets at all), the use of the straight-line method of depreciation and so on will have this effect. In addition, there may be some businesses that adopt particular accounting policies or carry out particular transactions in a way that paints a picture of financial health that is in line with what those who prepared the financial statements would like shareholders and other users to see, rather than what is a true and fair view of financial performance and position. This practice is referred to as 'creative accounting' and has been a major problem for accounting rule makers and for society generally.

Real World 11.9 provides some examples of creative accounting methods that have recently been found in practice.

REAL WORLD 11.9

Dirty laundry: how companies fudge the numbers

The ways in which managers can manipulate the financial statements are many and varied. The methods below have come to light in the recent wave of accounting scandals that have been reported in the US and UK.

Hollow swaps: telecoms businesses sell useless fibre optic capacity to each other in order to generate revenues on their income statements.

Channel stuffing: a business floods the market with more products than its distributors can sell, artificially boosting its sales. An international condom maker shifted £60m in excess stock on to trade customers. Also known as 'trade loading'.

Round tripping: also known as 'in-and-out trading'. Used to notorious effect by Enron. Two or more traders buy and sell energy among themselves for the same price and at the same time. Inflates trading volumes and makes participants appear to be doing more business than they really are.

Pre-despatching: goods such as carpets are marked as 'sold' as soon as an order is placed. This inflates sales and profits.

Off-balance-sheet activities: businesses use special-purpose entities and other devices such as leasing to push assets and liabilities off their balance sheets.

Net present value (NPV) analysis

To summarise the points made above, we can say that, in order to measure changes in shareholder value, what we really need is a measure that will consider the long term, take account of risk and the cost of shareholders' funds and will not be affected by accounting policy choices. Fortunately, we have a measure that can, in theory, do just this.

Net present value analysis was discussed in Chapter 8. We saw that if we want to know the net present value (NPV) of an asset (whether this is a physical asset such as a machine or a financial asset such as a share in a business) we must discount the future cash flows generated by the asset over its life. Thus:

$$\text{NPV} = \frac{C_1}{(1+r)^1} + \frac{C_2}{(1+r)^2} + \frac{C_3}{(1+r)^3} + \frac{C_n}{(1+r)^n}$$

where:

C_1, C_2, C_3 and C_n = cash flows after one year, two years, three years and n years, respectively

r = the required rate of return.

Shareholders have a required rate of return and managers must strive to generate long-term cash flows for shares (in the form of dividends or proceeds from the sale of the shares) that meet this rate of return. A negative present value will indicate that the cash flows generated do not meet the minimum required rate of return. If a business is to create value for its shareholders, it must generate cash flows that exceed the required returns of shareholders. This means that the cash flows generated must produce a positive present value.

The NPV method fulfils the criteria that we mentioned earlier because:

- It considers the long term. The returns from an investment, such as shares, are considered over the whole of its life.
- It takes account of the cost of capital and risk. Future cash flows are discounted using the required rates of returns from investors (that is, both long-term lenders and shareholders). Moreover, this required rate of return will reflect the level of risk associated with the investment. The higher the level of risk, the higher the required level of return.
- It is not sensitive to the choice of accounting policies. Cash rather than profit is used in the calculations and is a more objective measure of return.

Extending NPV analysis: shareholder value analysis

We know from our earlier study of NPV that, when evaluating an investment project, shareholder wealth will be maximised if we maximise the net present value of the cash flows generated from the project. Leading on from this, the business as a whole can be viewed as simply a portfolio of investment projects and so to maximise the wealth of shareholders the same principles should apply. **Shareholder value analysis (SVA)** is founded on this basic idea.

The SVA approach involves evaluating strategic decisions according to their ability to maximise value, or wealth, for shareholders. To undertake this evaluation, conventional measures are discarded and replaced by discounted cash flows. We have seen that the net present value of a project represents the value of that particular project. Given that the business can be viewed as a portfolio of projects, the value of the business as a whole can, therefore, be viewed as the net present value of the cash flows generated by the business as a whole. SVA seeks to measure the discounted cash flows of the business as a whole and then seeks to identify that part which is available to the shareholders.

Activity 11.7

If the net present value of future cash flows generated by the business represents the value of the business as a whole, how can we derive that part of the value of the business that is available to shareholders?

....

A business will normally be financed by a combination of loan capital and ordinary shareholders' funds. Thus holders of loan capital will also have a claim on the total value of the business. That part of the total business value that is available to ordinary shareholders can therefore be derived by deducting from the total value of the business (total NPV) the market value of any loans outstanding. Hence:

  Shareholder value = Total business value – Market value of outstanding loans

---

Measuring free cash flows

→ The cash flows used to measure total business value are the **free cash flows**. These are the cash flows generated by the business that are available to ordinary shareholders and long-term lenders. In other words, they are equivalent to the net cash flows from operations after deducting tax paid and cash for additional investment. These free cash flows can be deduced from information contained within the profit and loss account (income statement) and balance sheet of a business.

It is probably worth going through a simple example to illustrate how the free cash flows are calculated in practice.

Example 11.2

Sagittarius plc generated sales of £220m during the year and has an operating profit margin of 25 per cent of sales. Depreciation charges for the year were £8.0m and the cash tax rate for the year was 20 per cent of operating profit. During the year £11.3m was invested in additional working capital and £15.2m was invested in additional non-current (fixed) assets. A further £8.0m was invested in the replacement of existing non-current assets.

The free cash flows are calculated as follows:

	£m	£m
Sales		220.0
Operating profit (25% × £220m)		55.0
Add Depreciation charge		8.0
Operating cash flows		63.0
Less Cash tax (20% × £55m)		11.0
Operating cash flows after tax		52.0
Less Additional working capital	11.3	
Additional non-current assets	15.2	
Replacement non-current assets	8.0	34.5
Free cash flows		17.5

→

Example 11.2 continued

We can see that to derive the operating cash flows, the depreciation charge is added back to the operating profit figure. We can also see that the cost of replacement of existing non-current assets is deducted from the operating cash flows to deduce the free cash flows. When we are trying to predict future free cash flows, one way of arriving at an approximate figure for the cost of replacing existing assets is to assume that the depreciation charge for the year is equivalent to the replacement charge for non-current (fixed) assets. This would mean that the two adjustments mentioned cancel each other out. In other words, the calculation above could be shortened to:

	£m	£m
Sales		220.0
Operating profit (25% × £220m)		55.0
Less Cash tax (20% × £55m)		11.0
		44.0
Less Additional working capital	11.3	
Additional non-current assets	15.2	26.5
Free cash flows		17.5

This shortened approach leads us to identify the key variables in determining free cash flows as being:

- Sales
- Operating profit margin
- Tax rate
- Additional investment in working capital
- Additional investment in non-current (fixed) assets.

These are value drivers of the business that reflect key business decisions. These decisions convert into free cash flows and finally into shareholder value. Any actions that management can take to:

- boost sales; and/or
- increase the operating profit margin; and/or
- reduce the effective tax rate; and/or
- reduce the investment in working capital; and/or
- reduce the investment in non-current assets

will have the effect of increasing shareholders' wealth.

Figure 11.7 shows the process of measuring free cash flows.

The free cash flows should be projected over the life of the business. However, this is usually a difficult task. To overcome the problem, it is helpful to divide the future cash flows into two elements:

- a planning period over which cash flows can be projected with a reasonable level of accuracy;
- a terminal calculation to represent the cash flows occurring beyond the planning horizon.

It is a good idea to try to make the planning period as long as possible, because the discounting process ensures that values in the distant future are given little weight. As

Figure 11.7   Measuring free cash flows

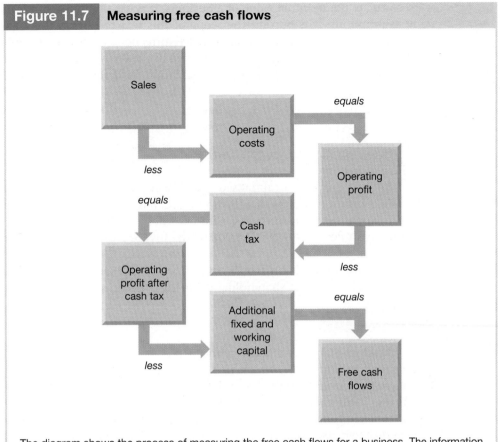

The diagram shows the process of measuring the free cash flows for a business. The information required can be gleaned from the profit and loss account and balance sheet of a business.

you can imagine, the terminal value of a business can be extremely difficult to forecast with accuracy and so the less weight given to the figure the better.

Activity 11.8

Libra plc has an estimated terminal value of £100m. What is the present value of this figure assuming a discount rate of 12 per cent and a planning horizon of:

(a) 5 years?
(b) 10 years?
(c) 15 years?

(You may find it helpful to refer to the discount tables that are in Appendix D at the back of the book.)

The answer is:

(a) £100m × 0.567 = £56.7m
(b) £100m × 0.322 = £32.2m
(c) £100m × 0.183 = £18.3m

We can see that there is a dramatic difference in the present value of the terminal calculation between the three time horizons, given a 12 per cent discount rate.

To calculate the terminal value of a business, it is usually necessary to make simplifying assumptions. It is beyond the scope of this text to discuss this topic in detail. However, one common assumption is that returns beyond the planning horizon will remain constant (perhaps at the level achieved in the last year of the planning period). Using the formula for a perpetuity, the calculation for determining the terminal value (TV) will be:

$$TV = C_1/r$$

where:
C_1 = the free cash flows in the following year
r = the required rate of return of investors.

This formula provides a capitalised value for future cash flows. Thus if an investor receives a constant cash flow of £100 a year and has a required rate of return of 10 per cent, the capitalised value of these cash flows will be £100/0.1 = £1,000. In other words the future cash flows are worth £1,000 to the investor when invested at the required rate of return.

At this point, it is probably worth going through an example to illustrate the way in which we might calculate shareholder value for a business.

Example 11.3

The directors of United Pharmaceuticals plc are considering the purchase of all the shares in Bortex plc, which produces vitamins and health foods. Bortex plc has a strong presence in the UK and it is expected that the directors will reject any bids that value the shares of the business at less than £11 per share.

Bortex plc generated sales for the most recent year end of £3,000m. Extracts from the business's balance sheet at the end of the most recent year are as follows:

	£m
Capital and reserves	
Share capital £1 ordinary shares	400
Reserves	380
	780
Non-current (long-term liabilities)	
Loan capital	120

Forecasts that have been prepared by the Business Planning Department of Bortex plc are as follows:

● Sales will grow at 10 per cent a year for the next five years.
● The operating profit margin is currently 15 per cent and is likely to be maintained at this rate in the future.
● The cash tax rate is 25 per cent.
● Replacement non-current (fixed) asset investment (RNCAI) will be in line with the annual depreciation charge each year.
● Additional non-current (fixed) asset investment (ANCAI) for each year over the next five years will be 10 per cent of sales growth.
● Additional working capital investment (AWCI) for each year over the next five years will be 5 per cent of sales growth.

After five years, the business's sales will stabilise at their Year 5 level. The business has a cost of capital of 10 per cent and the loan capital figure in the balance sheet reflects its current market value.

The free cash flow calculation will be as follows:

	Year 1 £m	Year 2 £m	Year 3 £m	Year 4 £m	Year 5 £m	After Year 5 £m
Sales	3,300.0	3,630.0	3,993.0	4,392.3	4,831.5	4,831.5
Operating profit (15%)	495.0	544.5	599.0	658.8	724.7	724.7
Less Cash tax (25%)	(123.8)	(136.1)	(149.8)	(164.7)	(181.2)	(181.2)
Operating profit after cash tax	371.2	408.4	449.2	494.1	543.5	543.5
Less						
ANCAI*	(30.0)	(33.0)	(36.3)	(39.9)	(43.9)	–
AWCI†	(15.0)	(16.5)	(18.2)	(20.0)	(22.0)	–
Free cash flows	326.2	358.9	394.7	434.2	477.6	543.5

Notes:
* The additional non-current (fixed) asset investment is 10 per cent of sales growth. In the first year, sales growth is £300m (that is, £3,300m – £3,000m). Thus, the investment will be 10% × £300m = £30m. Similar calculations are carried out for the following years.
† The additional working capital investment is 5 per cent of sales growth. In the first year the investment will be 5% × £300m = £15m. Similar calculations are carried out in following years.

Having derived the free cash flows (FCF), the total business value can be calculated as follows:

Year	FCF £m	Discount rate 10%	Present value £m
1	326.2	0.909	296.5
2	358.9	0.826	296.5
3	394.7	0.751	296.4
4	434.2	0.683	296.6
5	477.6	0.621	296.6
Terminal value: 543.5/0.10	5,435.0	0.621	3,375.1
Total business value			4,857.7

Activity 11.9

What is the shareholder value figure for the business in Example 11.3?
Would the sale of the shares at £11 per share add value for the shareholders of Bortex plc?

Shareholder value will be the total business value less the market value of the loan capital. Hence, shareholder value is:

$$£4,857.7m – £120m = £4,737.7m$$

The proceeds from the sale of the shares to United Pharmaceuticals would yield:

$$400m × £11 = £4,400.0m$$

Thus, from the point of view of the shareholders of Bortex plc, the sale of the business, at the share price mentioned, would not increase shareholder value.

Managing the business with SVA

We saw earlier that the adoption of SVA indicates a commitment to managing the business in such a way as to maximise shareholder returns. Those who support this approach argue that SVA can be a powerful tool for strategic planning. For example, SVA can be extremely useful when considering major shifts of direction such as:

● acquiring new businesses
● selling existing businesses
● developing new products or markets
● reorganising or restructuring the business,

because it takes account of all the elements that determine shareholder value.

Figure 11.8 shows how shareholder value is derived.

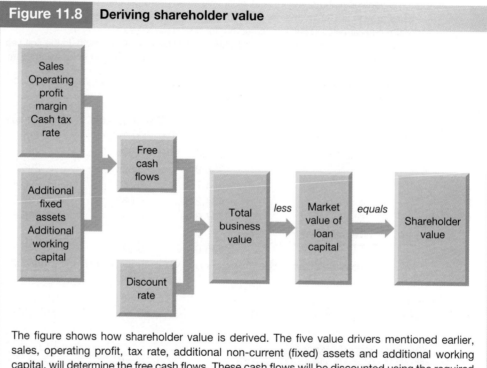

| Figure 11.8 | Deriving shareholder value |

The figure shows how shareholder value is derived. The five value drivers mentioned earlier, sales, operating profit, tax rate, additional non-current (fixed) assets and additional working capital, will determine the free cash flows. These cash flows will be discounted using the required rate of return from investors to determine the total value of the business. If we deduct the market value of any loan capital from this figure, we are left with a measure of shareholder value.

To illustrate this point let us suppose that a business develops a new product that is quite different from those within its existing range of products and appeals to a quite different market. Profit forecasts may indicate that the product is likely to be profitable and so a decision to launch the product may be made. However, this decision may increase the level of risk for the business and, if so, investors will demand higher levels of return. In addition, there may have to be a significant investment in additional non-current (fixed) assets and working capital in order to undertake the venture. When these factors are taken into account, using the type of analysis shown above, it may be found that the present value of the venture is negative. In other words, shareholder value will be destroyed.

SVA is also useful in focusing attention on the value drivers that create shareholder wealth. For example, we saw earlier that the key variables in determining free cash flows were:

- sales
- operating profit margin
- cash tax rate
- additional investment in working capital
- additional investment in non-current (fixed) assets.

In order to improve free cash flows and, in turn, shareholder value, management targets can be set for improving performance in relation to each value driver and responsibility assigned for achieving these targets.

Activity 11.10

Can you suggest what might be the practical problems of adopting an SVA approach?

Two practical problems spring to mind:

1 Forecasting future cash flows lies at the heart of this approach. In practice, forecasting can be difficult and simplifying assumptions will usually have to be made.
2 SVA requires more comprehensive information (for example, information concerning the value drivers) than the traditional measures discussed earlier.

You may have thought of other problems.

The implications of SVA

It is worth emphasising that supporters of SVA believe that this measure should replace the traditional accounting measures of value creation such as profit, earnings per share and return on ordinary shareholders' funds. Thus, only if shareholder value increases over time can we say that there has been an increase in shareholder wealth. Any change over time can be measured by comparing shareholder value at the beginning and the end of a particular period.

We can see that SVA is really a radical departure from the conventional approach to managing a business. It will require different performance indicators, different financial reporting systems and different management incentive methods. It may also require a change of culture within the business to accommodate the shareholder value philosophy. Not all employees may be focused on the need to maximise shareholder wealth.

If SVA is implemented, it can provide the basis of targets for managers to work towards, on a day-to-day basis, which should promote maximisation of shareholder value.

Economic value added (EVA®)

Economic value added (EVA®) has been developed and trademarked by a US management consultancy firm, Stern Stewart. However, EVA® is based on the idea of economic profit, which has been around for many years. The measure reflects the point made earlier that, for a business to be profitable in an economic sense, it must generate returns that exceed the required returns of investors. It is not enough simply to make an accounting profit, because this measure does not take full account of the returns required by investors.

EVA® indicates whether or not the returns generated exceed the required returns by investors. The formula is as follows:

$$EVA^® = NOPAT - (R \times C)$$

where:
NOPAT = net operating profit after tax
R = required returns of investors
C = capital invested (that is, the net assets of the business).

Activity 11.11

Does this measure seem familiar to you? Where have we discussed a similar measure to this earlier in the text?

This measure is based on the same idea as the residual income measure that we discussed when considering ways of assessing divisional performance (see Chapter 10).

Only when EVA® is positive can we say that the business is increasing shareholder wealth. To maximise shareholder wealth, managers must increase EVA® by as much as possible.

Activity 11.12

Can you suggest what managers might do in order to increase EVA®?
(*Hint*: Use the formula shown above as your starting point.)

The formula suggests that in order to increase EVA® managers may try to:

- Increase NOPAT. This may be done either by reducing expenses or by increasing sales.
- Use capital invested more efficiently. This means selling off any assets that are not generating adequate returns and investing in assets that are generating a satisfactory NOPAT.
- Reduce the required rates of return for investors. This may be achieved by changing the capital structure in favour of loan capital (which tends to be cheaper to service than share capital). However, this strategy can create problems.

Real World 11.10 shows economic value added measures for six well-known US businesses.

EVA® relies on conventional financial statements (profit and loss account (income statment) and balance sheet) to measure the wealth created for shareholders. However, the NOPAT and capital figures shown on these statements are used only as a starting point. They have to be adjusted because of the problems and limitations of conventional measures. According to Stern Stewart, the major problem is that profit and capital are

REAL WORLD 11.10

Measuring EVA®

Each year, Stern Stewart measures the economic value added (or destroyed) by large US businesses and publishes this information on its website. Below are the EVA® measures for six well-known businesses for 2002:

	EVA® $m
Microsoft Corporation	2,201
Wal-Mart Stores	2,928
IBM	(8,032)
Exxon Mobil	(2,175)
Coca-Cola Co.	2,496
Dell Computer Corporation	360

We can see that, in two cases, there is a significant loss of shareholder value for the year. It is interesting to note that, for both of these businesses, the net operating profit after tax expressed as a percentage of average capital employed for the year is positive (3.7 per cent for IBM and 6.6 per cent for Exxon Mobil). Based on this information alone, it may therefore appear that these two businesses created value for their shareholders. However, when EVA® is used, a large loss of economic value is revealed. This apparent anomaly can be explained by the fact that EVA® also takes account of the required rates of return from investors, and, therefore risk.

Source: www.eva.com. Copyright © Stern Stewart and Co.

understated because of the conservative bias in accounting measurement. Profit is understated as a result of judgemental write-offs (such as goodwill written off or research and development expenditure written off) and as a result of excessive provisions being created (such as a provision for doubtful debts). Capital is understated because assets are reported at their original cost (less amounts written off), which can produce figures considerably below current market values. In addition, certain assets, such as internally generated goodwill and brand names, are omitted from the financial statements because no external transactions have occurred.

Stern Stewart has identified more than 100 adjustments that could be made to the conventional financial statements in order to eliminate the conservative bias. However, it is believed that, in practice, only a handful of adjustments will usually have to be made to the accounting figures of any particular business. Unless an adjustment is going to have a significant effect on the calculation of EVA® it is really not worth making. The adjustments made should reflect the nature of the particular business. Each business is unique and so must customise the calculation of EVA® to its particular circumstances. (This aspect of EVA® can be seen as either indicating flexibility or as being open to manipulation depending on whether or not you support this measure.)

The most common adjustments that have to be made are:

● *Research and development (R&D) costs and market costs*. These costs should be written off over the period that they benefit. In practice, however, they are often written off in the period in which they are incurred. This means that any amounts written off immediately should be added back to the assets on the balance sheet, thereby increasing invested capital, and then written off over time.

- *Goodwill*. In theory, goodwill should receive the same treatment as R&D and marketing costs. However, Stern Stewart suggests leaving goodwill on the balance sheet. One argument in favour of this treatment is that goodwill is really a 'catch-all' that includes intangible items such as brand names and reputation that have infinite lives. Thus any amounts written off should be added back to assets.

- *Restructuring costs*. This item can be viewed as an investment in the future rather than an expense to be written off. Supporters of EVA® argue that, by restructuring, the business is better placed to meet future challenges, and so any amounts incurred should be added back to assets.

- *Marketable investments*. Investments in shares and loan capital are not included as part of the capital invested in the business. This is because the income from marketable investments is not included in the calculation of operating profit. (Income from this source will be added in the profit and loss account (income statement) *after* operating profit has been calculated.)

Let us now consider a simple example to show how EVA® may be calculated.

Example 11.4

Scorpio plc was established two years ago and has produced the following balance sheet and profit and loss account at the end of the second year of trading.

Balance sheet as at the end of the second year

	£m	£m	£m
Non-current (fixed) assets			
Goodwill		24.0	
Plant and equipment		56.0	
Motor vehicles		12.4	
Marketable investments		6.6	99.0
Current assets			
Stock		34.5	
Debtors		29.3	
Cash		2.1	
		65.9	
Current liabilities			
Trade creditors	29.4		
Taxation	1.8	31.2	34.7
			133.7
Non-current liabilities			
Loan capital			50.0
			83.7
Equity			
Share capital			60.0
Reserves			23.7
			83.7

Profit and loss account for the second year

	£m	£m
Sales		148.6
Cost of sales		76.2
Gross profit		72.4
Wages	24.5	
Depreciation of plant and equipment	8.8	
Goodwill written off	4.0	
Marketing costs	22.5	
Provision for doubtful debts	4.5	64.3
Operating profit		8.1
Income from investments		0.4
		8.5
Interest payable		0.5
Ordinary profit before taxation		8.0
Restructuring costs		2.0
Profit before taxation		6.0
Corporation tax		1.8
Profit after taxation		4.2

Discussions with the finance director reveal the following:

1 Goodwill was purchased during the first year of trading when another business was acquired. The goodwill cost £32.0m and this amount is being written off over an eight-year period (starting in the first year of the business).

2 Marketing costs relate to the launch of a new product. The benefits of the marketing campaign are expected to last for a three-year period (including this most recent year).

3 The provision for doubtful debts was created this year and the amount of the provision is very high. A more realistic figure for the provision would be £2.0m.

4 Restructuring costs were incurred as a result of a collapse in a particular product market. By restructuring the business, benefits are expected to flow for an infinite period.

5 The business has a 10 per cent required rate of return for investors.

The first step in calculating EVA® is to adjust the net operating profit after tax to take account of the various points revealed from the discussion with the finance director. The revised figure is calculated as follows:

NOPAT adjustment

	£m	£m
Operating profit		8.1
Less Corporation tax		1.8
		6.3
EVA® adjustments (to be added back to profit)		
Goodwill*	4.0	
Marketing costs ($^2/_3 \times 22.5$)†	15.0	
Excess doubtful debts provision	2.5	21.5
Adjusted NOPAT		27.8

→

Example 11.4 continued

The next step is to adjust the net assets (as represented by capital and reserves and loan capital) to take account of the points revealed.

Adjusted net assets (or capital invested)

	£m	£m
Net assets per balance sheet		133.7
Add		
Goodwill adjustment*	8.0	
Marketing costs†	15.0	
Provision for doubtful debts	2.5	
Restructuring costs‡	2.0	27.5
		161.2
Less		
Marketable investments§		6.6
Adjusted net assets		154.6

* The goodwill adjustment takes account of the fact that there was a £4.0m write-off in years 1 and 2.

† The marketing costs represent two years' benefits added back ($^2/_3 \times$ £22.5m).

‡ The restructuring costs are added back to the net assets as they provide benefits over an infinite period. (Note that they were not added back to the operating profit, as these costs were deducted *after* arriving at operating profit in the profit and loss account.)

§ The marketable investments do not form part of the operating assets of the business and the income from these investments is not part of the operating income.

Activity 11.13

Can you work out the EVA® for the second year of the business in Example 11.4?

EVA® can be calculated as follows:

$$\text{EVA}^® = \text{NOPAT} - (R \times C)$$
$$= \text{£27.8m} - (10\% \times \text{£154.6m})$$
$$= \text{£12.3m (to one decimal place)}$$

Thus, we can see that the business increased shareholder wealth during the year.

The main advantage of this measure is the discipline to which managers are subjected as a result of the charge for capital that has been invested. Before any increase in shareholder wealth can be recognised, an appropriate deduction is made for the use of business resources. Thus EVA® encourages managers to use these resources efficiently. Where managers are focused simply on increasing profits, there is a danger that the resources used to achieve any increase in profits will not be taken into proper account.

Real World 11.11 provides an example of the use of EVA® by a well-known German business in an attempt to generate shareholder value.

REAL WORLD 11.11

VW changes gear

Following a change in top management, the German car maker VW has begun to focus more attention on controlling its capital spending. In particular, research and development expenditure is seen as a key area to be contained. The size of the problem is partly illustrated by the fact that the first-half-year results for 2003 showed that the cash flow from auto operations was €1bn less than needed to cover the €3.9bn of investment and research and development expenditure. In the drive to contain capital spending, performance measures such as return on sales are being abandoned in favour of performance measures that focus on the profitable use of capital. One effect of this change is that bonuses of managers are to be linked to EVA® to encourage them to reduce their capital requirements.

Source: Based on information from 'VW signals passing of the age of engineers', FT.com, 7 September 2003.

EVA® and SVA

Although at first glance it may appear that EVA® and SVA are worlds apart, this is not the case. In fact EVA® and SVA are very closely related and, in theory at least, should produce the same figure for shareholder value. The way in which shareholder value is calculated using SVA has already been described. The EVA® approach to calculating shareholder value adds the capital invested to the present value of future EVA® flows and then deducts the market value of any loan capital. Figure 11.9 illustrates the two approaches to determining shareholder value.

Figure 11.9   Two approaches to determining shareholder value

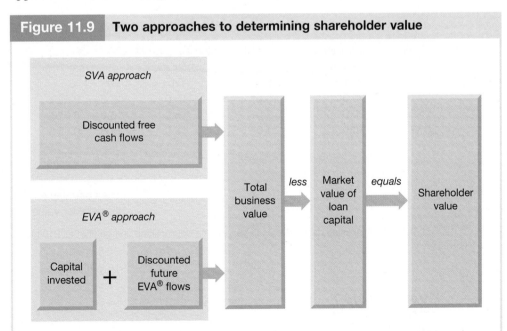

The figure shows how EVA® and SVA can both provide a measure of shareholder value. Total business value can be derived either by discounting the free cash flows over time or by discounting the EVA® flows over time and adding the capital invested. Whichever approach is used, the market value of loan capital must then be deducted to derive shareholder value.

Let us go through a simple example to illustrate the point that the two measurement approaches should provide broadly the same value.

Example 11.5

Leo Ltd has just been formed and has been financed by a £20m issue of share capital and a £10m issue of loan capital. The proceeds of the issue have been invested in non-current (fixed) assets with a life of three years and during this period the non-current assets will depreciate by £10m per year. The operating profit after tax is expected to be £15m each year. There will be no replacement of non-current assets during the three-year period and no investment in working capital. At the end of the three years, the business will be wound up and the non-current (fixed) assets will have no residual value. The required rate of return by investors is 10 per cent.

The SVA approach to determining shareholder value will be as follows:

Year	FCF £m	Discount rate 10%	Present value £m
1	25.0*	0.909	22.7
2	25.0	0.826	20.7
3	25.0	0.751	18.8
	Total business value		62.2
	Less Loan capital		10.0
	Shareholder value		52.2

* The free cash flows will be the operating profit after tax *plus* the depreciation charge (that is, £15m + £10m). There are no replacement non-current (fixed) assets, in this case, against which the depreciation charge can be netted off. It must therefore be added back.

The EVA® approach to determining shareholder value will be as follows:

Year	Opening capital invested (C) £m	Capital charge (10% × C) £m	Operating profit after tax £m	EVA® £m	Discount rate 10%	Present value of EVA® £m
1	30.0*	3.0	15.0	12.0	0.909	10.9
2	20.0	2.0	15.0	13.0	0.826	10.7
3	10.0	1.0	15.0	14.0	0.751	10.5
						32.1
					Opening capital	30.0
						62.1
					Less Loan capital	10.0
					Shareholder value	52.1

* The capital invested decreases each year by the depreciation charge (that is, £10m).

EVA® or SVA?

Although EVA® and SVA are both consistent with the idea of maximising shareholder wealth and, in theory, should produce the same decisions and results, the supporters of EVA® claim that this measure has a number of practical advantages over SVA. One such advantage is that EVA® sits more comfortably with the conventional financial reporting systems and financial reports. There is no need to develop entirely new systems to implement EVA® as it can be calculated by making a few adjustments to the conventional profit and loss accounts and balance sheets.

It is also claimed that EVA® is more useful as a basis for rewarding managers. Both EVA® and SVA support the idea that management rewards should be linked to increases in shareholder value. This should ensure that the interests of managers are closely aligned to the interests of shareholders. Under the SVA approach, management rewards will be determined on the basis of the contribution made to the generation of long-term cash flows. However, there are practical problems in using SVA for this purpose.

Activity 11.14

Can you think of any practical problems that may arise when using SVA calculations to reward managers?

The SVA approach measures changes in shareholder value by reference to predicted changes in future cash flows and it is unwise to pay managers on the basis of predicted rather than actual achievements. If the predictions are optimistic, the effect will be that the business rewards optimism rather than real achievement. There is also a risk that unscrupulous managers will manipulate predicted future cash flows in order to increase their rewards.

Under EVA®, managers can receive bonuses based on actual achievement during a particular period. However, if management rewards are linked to a single period, there is a danger that managers will place undue attention on increases during this period rather than over the long term. Any reward system must encourage a long-term perspective and Stern Stewart has tried to develop a system, based on EVA®, that does this. It is worth noting that Stern Stewart believes that bonuses, calculated as a percentage of EVA®, should form a very large part of the total remuneration package for managers. Thus, the higher the EVA® figure, the higher the rewards to managers – with no upper limits. The view held is that EVA® should make managers wealthy provided it makes shareholders extremely wealthy!

Real World 11.12 gives some indication of the extent of the usage of value-based management (broadly, SVA and EVA®) in the US.

REAL WORLD 11.12

The extent of the use of value-based management in practice

The Ernst and Young survey of management accounting practice in the US, conducted in 2003, revealed that 52 per cent of managers use value-based management, with a further 40 per cent considering using this approach in the future.

Source: Ernst and Young (see reference 2 at the end of the chapter).

Self-assessment question 11.1

You have recently heard a fellow student talking about strategic management accounting as follows:

'Assessing strategic change is concerned with undertaking a SWOT analysis and then making plans to change strategy.'

'Customer profitability analysis is about finding out which of your customers are the more profitable businesses and trying to encourage the ones that are more profitable to place orders. This is to avoid having customers that go bankrupt.'

'Shareholder value analysis (SVA) tries to give shareholders their returns in the form that they like. Some shareholders prefer dividends and others prefer profits to be ploughed back. EVA® stands for 'equity value analysis' and is an alternative name for SVA.'

'The "Balanced Scorecard" is the American name for what people in the UK call a "balance sheet".'

Required:

Critically comment on the student's statements, explaining any technical terms.

SUMMARY

The main points in this chapter may be summarised as follows:

Strategic management accounting

- Concerned with providing information to support strategic plans and decisions.
- More outward looking, more concerned with outperforming the competition and more concerned with monitoring progress towards strategic objectives than conventional management accounting.

Accounting for external factors

- Competitor profitability analysis examining cost structures and profitability of competitors.
- Competitor profiling tries to build up a more complete picture of each major competitor.
- Customer profitability analysis assesses the profitability of each customer or type of customer.

Competitive advantage through cost leadership

- Total life-cycle accounting is concerned with tracking and reporting all costs relating to a product from the beginning to the end of its life.
- By reporting revenues over the same period, we can determine the profitability of the product.
- Target costing is a market-based approach to managing costs.
- It attempts to reduce costs so that the market price covers the cost plus an acceptable profit.
- Value chain analysis involves analysing the various activities in the product life cycle.
- It distinguishes between activities that add value and those that do not; it may be possible to save costs by eliminating or reducing the cost of the non-value-adding ones.

- Costs may be managed without using sophisticated techniques if:
  - There is a shared responsibility for managing costs.
  - Discussion of costs becomes an everyday activity.
  - Costs are managed locally.
  - Benchmarking is used at regular intervals.
  - The focus is on managing rather than reducing costs.

Accounting for strategy

- Assessment of strategic change can be done using a technique similar to variance analysis.
- Balanced Scorecard is a management tool that attempts to integrate financial and non-financial measures to give a balanced approach to pursuit of key performance indicators.
- Four areas: financial, customer, internal business process, and learning and growth.
- Encourages a balanced approach to managing the business.
- Seems to be used effectively in practice.
- Increasing shareholder value is seen as the key objective of most businesses.
- Two approaches used to measure shareholder value are shareholder value analysis (SVA) and economic value added (EVA®).
- Shareholder value analysis (SVA) is based on the concept of net present value analysis.
- It identifies key value drivers for generating shareholder value.
- Economic value added is a means of measuring whether the returns generated by the business exceed the required returns of investors.
- $$EVA^{®} = NOPAT - (R \times C)$$

where:
NOPAT = net operating profit after tax
R = required returns from investors
C = capital invested (that is, the net assets of the business).

→ Key terms

Competitor profitability analysis p. 335
Competitor profiling p. 337
Customer profitability analysis (CPA) p. 337
Value chain analysis p. 340

Value drivers p. 347
Balanced Scorecard p. 348
Shareholder value analysis p. 356
Free cash flows p. 357
Economic value added (EVA®) p. 363

Further reading

If you would like to explore topics covered in this chapter in more depth, we recommend the following books:

Management and Cost Accounting, *Drury C.*, 5th edn, Thomson Learning Business Press, 2000, chapter 23.

Management and Cost Accounting, *Horngren C., Bhimani A., Datar S. and Foster G.*, 2nd edn, Prentice Hall International, 2002, chapter 22.

The Balanced Scorecard, *Kaplan R. and Norton D.*, Harvard Business School Press, 1996.

The Dynamics of Shareholder Value, *Mills R.*, Mars Business Associates, 1998.

The EVA Challenge, *Stern J. and Shelly J.*, John Wiley, 2001.

References

1 **Cost Systems Design and Profitability Analysis in UK Companies**, *Drury C. and Tayles M.*, CIMA Publishing, 2000.

2 **2003 Survey of Management Accounting**, *Ernst and Young*, Ernst and Young, 2003.

3 'Costs count in the strategic agenda', *Hopwood A.*, FT.com, 13 August 2002.

4 **The Balanced Scorecard**, *Kaplan R. and Norton D.*, Harvard Business School Press, 1996.

REVIEW QUESTIONS

Answers to these questions can be found on the students' side of the Companion Website at www.pearsoned.co.uk/atrillmclaney.

11.1 What is the objective of assessment of strategic change and broadly how is this achieved?

11.2 Both customer A and customer B buy 1,000 units of your business's service each year, paying the same price per unit. Why might your business regard customer A as a desirable customer, but not customer B?

11.3 What is the principle on which shareholder value analysis is based?

11.4 What are the four main areas on which the Balanced Scorecard is based?

EXERCISES

Questions 11.4 to 11.8 are more advanced than 11.1 to 11.3. Those with a coloured number have answers at the back of the book.

11.1 Aires plc was recently formed and issued 80 million £0.50 shares at par and loan capital of £24m. The business used the proceeds from the capital issues to purchase the remaining lease on some commercial properties that are rented out to small businesses. The lease will expire in four years' time and during that period the operating profits are expected to be £12m each year. At the end of the three years, the business will be wound up and the lease will have no residual value.

The required rate of return by investors is 12 per cent.

Required:

Calculate the expected shareholder value generated by the business over the four years, using:
(a) the SVA approach
(b) the EVA® approach.

11.2 You have recently heard someone making the following statement about competitor profitability analysis (CPA).

> CPA is an assessment of how profitable competitors are, that is carried out in an attempt to establish a benchmark by which one's own business's success can be measured. Usually most of the information for this can be found in the competitors' annual report and financial statements. Usually competitors are willing to provide information about their financial results so that any gaps in the CPA can be filled in.

Required:

Comment on this statement.

11.3 Sharma plc makes one standard product for which it charges the same basic price of £20 a unit, though discounts are allowed to certain customers. The business is in the process of carrying out a profitability analysis of all of its customers during the financial year just ended.

Information about Lopez Ltd, one of Sharma's customers, is as follows:

Discount on sales price	5%
Number of products sold	40,000 units

Manufacturing cost	£12
Number of sales orders	22
Number of deliveries	22
Distance travelled to deliver	120 miles
Number of sales visits from Sharma's staff	30

Sharma uses an activity-based approach to ascribing costs to customers, as follows:

Cost pool	*Cost driver*	*Rate*
Order handling	Number of orders	£75 an order
Delivery costs	Miles travelled	£1.50 a mile
Customer sales visits	Number of visits	£230 a visit

Lopez Ltd usually takes two months' credit, of which the cost to Sharma is estimated at 2 per cent per month.

Required:
Calculate the net profit that Sharma plc derived from sales to Lopez Ltd during last year.

11.4 Vitality Ltd imports bottles of French spring water that it markets to shops in the UK. The market is very price competitive. The directors believed that a change in marketing strategy would be beneficial. They felt that if the selling price to the shops were lowered, a greater sales volume would be able to be achieved.

In the expectation of additional sales volume, the business was able to negotiate a lower price with the French bottler for all of its purchases. The increased sales volume did not increase the business's fixed costs. The change in marketing strategy took place on 1 January Year 3.

Vitality Ltd's water sales results for Year 2 and Year 3 can be summarised as follows:

	Year 2	*Year 3*
1 Number of bottles bought and sold	100,000	123,000
2 Selling price per bottle	£0.50	£0.40
3 Total sales (line 1 × line 2)	£50,000	£49,200
4 Cost price per bottle	£0.30	£0.28
5 Total cost of bottles (line 1 × line 4)	£30,000	£34,440

Required:
(a) Calculate the change in contribution caused by the change in strategy.
(b) Analyse the figure calculated in (a) into the growth aspect, the price aspect and the usage (productivity) aspect.
(c) Briefly explain and comment on how successful the change in strategy was and why.

11.5 Virgo plc is considering introducing a system of EVA® and wants its managers to focus on the longer term rather than simply focus on the year-to-year EVA® results. The business is seeking your advice as to how a management bonus system could be arranged so as to ensure the longer term is taken into account. The business is also unclear as to how much of the managers' pay should be paid in the form of a bonus and when such bonuses should be paid. Finally, the business is unclear as to where the balance between individual performance and corporate performance should be struck within any bonus system.

The Finance Director has recently produced figures that show that if Virgo plc had used EVA® over the past three years, the results would have been as follows:

2000	£25m (profit)
2001	£20m (loss)
2002	£10m (profit)

Required:
Set out your recommendations for a suitable bonus system for the divisional managers of the business.

11.6 Leo plc is considering entering a new market. A new product has been developed at a cost of £5m and is now ready for production. The market is growing and estimates from the finance department concerning future sales of the new product are as follows:

Year	Sales £m
1	30
2	36
3	40
4	48
5	60

After Year 5, sales are expected to stabilise at the Year 5 level.
You are informed that:

● The operating profit margin from sales in the new market is likely to be a constant 20 per cent of sales.
● The cash tax rate is 25 per cent of operating profit.
● Replacement non-current (fixed) asset investment (RNCAI) will be in line with the annual depreciation charge each year.
● Additional non-current (fixed) asset investment (ANCAI) over the next five years will be 15 per cent of sales growth.
● Additional working capital investment (AWCI) for each year over the next five years will be 10 per cent of sales growth.

The business has a cost of capital of 12 per cent. The new market is considered to be no more risky than the markets in which the business already has a presence.

Required:
Using an SVA approach, indicate the effect of entering the new market on shareholder value. (Workings should be to one decimal place.)

11.7 Pisces plc produced the following balance sheet and profit and loss account at the end of the third year of trading:

Balance sheet as at the end of the third year

	£m	£m
Non-current assets		
Goodwill	40.0	
Machinery and equipment	80.0	
Motor vans	18.6	
Marketable investments	9.0	147.6
Current assets		
Stock (inventory)	45.8	
Debtors (receivables)	64.6	
Cash	1.0	
	111.4	
Current liabilities		
Trade creditors (payables)	62.5	
		48.9
		196.5
Non-current liabilities		
Loan capital		80.0
		116.5
Equity		
Share capital		80.0
Reserves		36.5
		116.5

Profit and loss account for the third year

	£m	£m
Sales		231.5
Cost of sales		(143.2)
Gross profit		88.3
Wages	(33.5)	
Depreciation of machinery and equipment	(14.8)	
Goodwill written off	(10.0)	
Research and development costs	(40.0)	
Provision for doubtful debts	(10.5)	(108.8)
Operating loss		(20.5)
Income from investments		0.6
		(19.9)
Interest payable		(0.8)
Ordinary loss before taxation		(20.7)
Restructuring costs		(6.0)
Profit before taxation		(26.7)
Corporation tax		–
Loss after tax		(26.7)

An analysis of the underlying records reveals the following:

1 Goodwill was purchased during the first year of trading when an existing business was acquired. The goodwill cost £70.0m and this amount is being written off over a seven-year period (starting in the first year of the business).

2 R&D costs relate to the development of a new product in the previous year. These costs are written off over a two-year period (starting last year). However, this is a prudent approach and the benefits are expected to last for 16 years.

3 The provision for doubtful debts was created this year and the amount of the provision is very high. A more realistic figure for the provision would be £4.0m.

4 Restructuring costs were incurred at the beginning of the year and are expected to provide benefits for an infinite period.

5 The business has an 8 per cent required rate of return for investors.

Required:
Calculate the EVA® for the business for the third year of trading.

11.8 Aquarius plc has estimated the following free cash flows for its five-year planning period:

Year	Free cash flows
	£m
1	35
2	38
3	45
4	49
5	53

Required:
How might it be possible to check the accuracy of these figures? What internal and external sources of information might be used to see whether the figures are realistic?

Appendix A
Glossary of key terms

ABC system of stock control   A method of applying different levels of stock control, based on the value of each category of stock. *p. 268*

Accounting   The process of identifying, measuring and communicating information to permit informed judgements and decisions by users of the information. *p. 2*

Accounting information system   The system used within a business to identify, record, analyse and report accounting information. *p. 9*

Accounting rate of return (ARR)   The average profit from an investment, expressed as a percentage of the average investment made. *p. 215*

Activity-based budgeting (ABB)   A system of budgeting based on the philosophy of activity-based costing (ABC). *p. 164*

Activity-based costing (ABC)   A technique for more accurately relating overheads to specific production or provision of a service. It is based on acceptance of the fact that overheads do not just occur but are caused by activities, such as holding products in stores, which 'drive' the costs. *p. 112*

Adverse variance   A difference between planned and actual performance, where the difference will cause the actual profit to be lower than the budgeted one. *p. 185*

Ageing schedule of debtors   A report analysing debtors into categories, depending on the length of time outstanding. *p. 278*

Average settlement period for creditors   The average time taken for a business to pay its creditors. *p. 287*

Average settlement period for debtors   The average time taken for debtors to pay the amounts owing to a business. *p. 278*

Average stock turnover period   The average period for which stocks are held by a business. *p. 267*

Balanced Scorecard   A framework for translating the aims and objectives of a business into a series of key performance measures and targets. *p. 348*

Bank overdraft   A flexible form of borrowing which allows an individual or business to have a negative bank current account balance. *p. 286*

Batch costing   A technique for identifying full cost, where the production of many types of goods and services, particularly goods, involves producing a batch of identical or nearly identical units of output, but where each batch is distinctly different from other batches. *p. 99*

Behavioural aspects of budgetary control   The effect on people's attitudes and behaviour of the various aspects of using budgets as the basis of exercising control over performance. *p. 203*

Benchmarking   Identifying a successful business, or part of a business, and measuring the effectiveness of one's own business by comparison with this standard. *p. 134*

Break-even analysis   The activity of deducing the break-even point of some activity through analysing costs and revenues. *p. 48*

Break-even chart   A graphical representation of the costs and revenues of some activity, at various levels, which enables the break-even point to be identified. *p. 49*

Break-even point (BEP)   A level of activity where revenue will exactly equal total cost, so there is neither profit nor loss. *p. 49*

Budget   A financial plan for the short term, typically one year. *p. 143*

Budget committee   A group of managers formed to supervise and take responsibility for the budget-setting process. *p. 152*

Budget holder   An individual responsible for a particular budget. *p. 155*

Budget officer   An individual, often an accountant, appointed to carry out, or take immediate responsibility for having carried out, the tasks of the budget committee. *p. 152*

Budgetary control   Using the budget as a yardstick against which the effectiveness of actual performance may be assessed. *p. 200*

Cash discount   A reduction in the amount due for goods or services sold on credit in return for prompt payment. *p. 276*

Committed cost   A cost which has not yet been incurred, but which must, under some existing contract or obligation, be incurred. *p. 32*

Common costs   Costs that relate to more than one business segment. *p. 79*

Comparability   The requirement that items, which are basically the same, should be treated in the same manner for measurement and reporting purposes. Lack of comparability will limit the usefulness of accounting information. *p. 6*

Compensating variances   The situation that exists when two variances, both caused by the same factor, one adverse and the other favourable, are of equal size and, therefore, cancel out. *p. 199*

Competitor profiling   A detailed profile of a business competitor, which is developed by gathering information about its objectives, strategies, resources and products. *p. 337*

Competitor profitability analysis   An assessment of the costs and cost structure of rival businesses with the objective of putting the business in a position to assess how individual competitors might react to strategic moves by the business. *p. 335*

Continual (or rolling) budget   A budgeting system that continually updates budgets so that there is always a budget for a full planning period. *p. 146*

Contribution (per unit)   Sales revenue per unit less variable costs per unit. *p. 53*

Control   Compelling events to conform to plan. *p. 144*

Controllable cost   A cost that is the responsibility of a specific manager. *p. 307*

Cost The amount of resources, usually measured in monetary terms, sacrificed to achieve a particular objective. *p. 27*

Cost allocation Dividing costs between cost centres according to the amount of cost which has been incurred in them. *p. 92*

Cost apportionment Dividing costs between cost centres according to the amount of cost that is seen as being fair. *p. 92*

Cost behaviour The manner in which costs alter with changes in the level of activity. *p. 81*

Cost centre Some area, object, person or activity for which costs are separately collected. *p. 90*

Cost driver An activity that causes costs. *p. 112*

Cost-plus pricing An approach to pricing output that is based on full cost plus a percentage profit loading. *p. 100*

Cost pool The sum of the overhead costs that are seen as being caused by the same cost driver. *p. 113*

Cost unit The objective for which the cost is being deduced, usually a product or service. *p. 82*

Customer profitability analysis (CPA) An assessment of the profitability to the business of individual customers, or types of customer. *p. 337*

Direct costs Costs that can be identified with specific cost units, to the extent that the effect of the cost can be measured in respect of each particular unit of output. *p. 78*

Discount factor The rate applied to future cash flows to derive the present value of those cash flows. *p. 227*

Discretionary budget A budget based on a sum allocated at the discretion of top management. *p. 155*

Divisional performance measurement The activity of assessing the effectiveness of individual departments or sections of a business. *p. 306*

Divisions Sections or departments through which large businesses are organised and managed. *p. 301*

Economic order quantity (EOQ) The quantity of stocks that should be purchased in order to minimise total stock costs. *p. 269*

Economic value added (EVA®) A measure of economic, as opposed to accounting, profit. It is said to be more useful than accounting profit as a measure of business performance because it overcomes some weaknesses of accounting in this context. *p. 363*

Economies of scale Cost savings per unit that result from undertaking a large volume of activities; they are due to factors such as division and specialisation of labour *p. 58*

Elasticity of demand The manner in which the level of demand alters with changes in price. *p. 118*

Expected net present value (ENPV) A weighted average of the possible present value outcomes, where the probabilities associated with each outcome are used as weights. *p. 241*

Favourable variance   A difference between planned and actual performance where the difference will cause the actual profit to be higher than the budgeted one. *p. 185*

Feedback control   A control device where actual performance is compared with planned and where action is taken to deal with future divergences between these. *p. 182*

Feedforward control   A control device where forecast future performance is compared with planned performance and where action is taken to deal with divergences between these. *p. 182*

Financial accounting   The measuring and reporting of accounting information for external users (those users other than the managers of the business). *p. 11*

Five Cs of credit   A checklist of factors to be taken into account when assessing the creditworthiness of a customer. *p. 273*

Fixed cost   A cost that stays the same when changes occur to the volume of activity. *p. 44*

Flexible budget   A budget that is adjusted to reflect the actual level of output achieved. *p. 184*

Flex (the budget)   Revising the budget to what it would have been had the planned level of output been different. *p. 184*

Forecast   A prediction of future outcomes or of the future state of the environment. *p. 146*

Free cash flows   The cash flows generated by the business that are available to the ordinary shareholders and long-term lenders. This is the net cash flow from operating activities, less tax and funds laid out on additional non-current assets. *p. 357*

Full cost   The total amount of resources, usually measured in monetary terms, sacrificed to achieve a particular objective. *pp. 77, 322*

Full cost (cost-plus) pricing   Pricing output on the basis of its full cost, normally with a loading for profit. *p. 126*

Full costing   Deducing the total direct and indirect (overhead) costs of pursuing some activity or objective. *p. 77*

Historic cost   What an asset cost when it was originally acquired. *p. 27*

Incremental budgeting   Constructing budgets on the basis of what happened in the previous period, with some adjustment for expected changes in the forthcoming budget period. *p. 155*

Indirect costs (or overheads)   All costs except direct costs: that is, those which cannot be directly measured in respect of each particular unit of output. *p. 79*

Inflation   The increase in money prices causing erosion of the value of goods or services. *p. 224*

Internal rate of return (IRR)   The discount rate for a project that will have the effect of producing a zero NPV. *p. 229*

Investment centre   Some area, object, person or activity in which management is responsible and accountable for all, or most, investment decisions. *p. 301*

Irrelevant cost   A cost that is not relevant to a particular decision. *p. 28*

Job costing   A technique for identifying the full cost per unit of output, where that output is not similar to other units of output. *p. 79*

Just-in-time (JIT) stock management   A system of stock management that aims to have supplies delivered to production just in time for their required use. *p. 272*

***Kaizen* costing**   An approach to cost control where an attempt is made to control costs by trying continually to make cost savings, often only small ones, from one time period to the next. *p. 134*

Lead time   The time lag between placing an order for goods or services and their delivery. *p. 267*

Learning curve   The tendency for people to carry out tasks more quickly as they become more experienced in doing so. *p. 194*

Limiting factor   Some aspect of the business (for example, lack of sales demand) that will prevent it achieving its objectives to the maximum extent. *p. 153*

Management accounting   The measuring and reporting of accounting information for the managers of a business. *p. 11*

Management by exception   A system of control, based on a comparison of planned and actual performance, that allows managers to focus on areas of poor performance rather than dealing with areas where performance is satisfactory. *p. 149*

Margin of safety   The extent to which the planned level of output or sales lies above the break-even point. *p. 54*

Marginal analysis   The activity of decision making through analysing variable costs and revenues, ignoring fixed costs. *p. 61*

Marginal cost   The addition to total cost that will be incurred by making/providing one more unit of output. *p. 61*

Marginal cost pricing   Pricing output on the basis of its marginal cost, normally with a loading for profit. *p. 128*

Market prices (as transfer prices)   Using a price set by the market outside the business as a suitable price for internal, inter-divisional transfers. *p. 320*

Master budget   A summary of the individual budgets, usually consisting of a budgeted profit and loss account (income statement), a budgeted balance sheet and a budgeted cash flow statement. *p. 147*

Materiality   The requirement that material information should be disclosed to users of financial reports. *p. 7*

Materials requirement planning (MRP) system   A computer-based system of stock control that schedules the timing of deliveries of bought-in parts and materials to coincide with production requirements to meet demand. *p. 271*

Mission statement   A brief statement setting out the aims of the business. *p. 143*

Negotiated prices   Transfer prices that are derived as a result of negotiation between managers of the divisions concerned, possibly with the involvement of the business's central management as well. *p. 323*

Net present value (NPV)   A method of investment appraisal based on the present value of all relevant cash flows associated with the project. *p. 221*

Non-controllable cost   A cost for which a specific manager is not held responsible. *p. 307*

Non-operating profit variances   Differences between budgeted and actual performance which do not lead directly to differences between budgeted and actual operating profit. *p. 196*

Objective probabilities   Probabilities based on information gathered from past experience. *p. 244*

Operating cash cycle (OCC)   The period between the outlay of cash to purchase supplies and the ultimate receipt of cash from the sale of goods. *p. 282*

Operating gearing   The relationship between the total fixed and the total variable costs for some activity. *p. 54*

Opportunity cost   The cost incurred when one course of action prevents an opportunity to derive some benefit from another course of action. *pp. 27, 320*

Outlay cost   A cost that involves the spending of money or some other transfer of assets. *p. 28*

Outsourcing   Subcontracting activities to (sourcing goods or services from) outside organisation. *p. 65*

Overhead (or indirect cost)   Any cost except a direct cost; a cost that cannot be directly measured in respect of each particular unit of output. *p. 79*

Overhead absorption (recovery) rate   The rate at which overheads are charged to cost units (jobs), usually in a job costing system. *p. 83*

Past cost   A cost that has been incurred in the past. *p. 28*

Payback period (PP)   The time taken for the initial investment in a project to be repaid from the net cash inflows of the project. *p. 219*

Penetration pricing   Setting prices at a level low enough to encourage wide market acceptance of a product or service. *p. 130*

Periodic budget   A budget developed on a one-off basis to cover a particular planning period. *p. 146*

Position analysis   A step in the strategic planning process in which the business assesses its present position in the light of the commercial and economic environment in which it operates. *p. 14*

Post-completion audit   A review of the performance of an investment project to see whether actual performance matched planned performance and whether any lessons can be drawn from the way in which the investment was carried out. *p. 251*

Price skimming   Setting prices at a high level to make the maximum profit from the product or service before the price is lowered to attract the next segment of the market. *p. 130*

Process costing   A technique for deriving the full cost per unit of output, where the units of output are exactly similar or it is reasonable to treat them as being so. *p. 78*

Product cost centre   Some area, object, person or activity for which costs are separately collected, in which cost units have costs added. *p. 91*

Profit centre   Some area, object, person or activity for which its revenues and expenses are compared to derive a profit figure, for which the manager is held accountable. *p. 301*

Profit–volume (PV) chart   A graphical representation of the contributions (revenues less variable costs) of some activity, at various levels, which enables the break-even point, and the profit at various activity levels, to be identified. *p. 57*

Relevance   The ability of accounting information to influence decisions. Relevance is regarded as a key characteristic of useful accounting information. *p. 6*

Relevant cost   A cost that is relevant to a particular decision. *p. 27*

Relevant range   The range of volume of activities that a particular business is expected to operate. *p. 59*

Reliability   The requirement that accounting should be free from material error or bias. Reliability is regarded as a key characteristic of useful accounting information. *p. 6*

Residual income (RI)   A divisional performance measure. The operating profit of a division, less an interest charge based on the business's investment in the division. *p. 311*

Return on investment (ROI)   A divisional performance measure. The operating profit of a division expressed as a percentage of the business's investment in the division. *p. 309*

Risk   The extent and likelihood that what is estimated to occur will not actually occur. *p. 223*

Risk-adjusted discount rate   A discount rate applied to investment projects that is increased (decreased) in the face of increased (decreased) risk. *p. 248*

Risk premium   An extra amount of return required from an investment, owing to a perceived level of risk. The greater the perceived risk, the larger the required risk premium. *p. 223*

Rolling (or continual) budget   A budgeting system which continually updates budgets so that there is always a budget for a full planning period. *p. 146*

Scenario building   Creating a model of a business decision, usually on a computer spreadsheet, enabling the decision maker to look at the effect of different assumptions on the decision outcome. *p. 240*

Semi-fixed (semi-variable) cost   A cost that has an element of both fixed and variable cost. *p. 47*

Sensitivity analysis   An examination of the key variables affecting a project, to see how changes in each input might influence the outcome. *p. 238*

Service cost centre   Some area, object, person or activity for which costs are collected separately, in which cost units do not have cost added, because service cost centres only render services to product cost services and to other service cost centres. *p. 91*

Shareholder value analysis (SVA)   Method of measuring and managing business value based on the long-term cash flows generated. *p. 356*

Standard quantities and costs   Planned quantities and costs (or revenues) for individual units of input or output. Standards are the building blocks used to produce the budget. *p. 192*

Stepped fixed cost   A fixed cost that does not remain fixed over all levels of output but which changes in steps as a threshold level of output is reached. *p. 46*

Strategic management   The process of setting a course to achieve the business's objectives, taking account of the commercial and economic environment in which the business operates. *p. 13*

Subjective probabilities   Probabilities based on opinion rather than past data. *p. 245*

Sunk cost   A cost that has been incurred in the past; the same as a past cost. *p. 32*

SWOT analysis   A framework in which many businesses set a position analysis. Here the business lists its strengths, weaknesses, opportunities and threats. *p. 14*

Target costing   Where the business starts with the projected selling price and from it deduces the target cost per unit which must be met to enable the company to meet its profit objectives. *p. 133*

Total cost   The sum of the variable and fixed costs of pursuing some activity. *p. 81*

Total life-cycle costing   Paying attention to all of the costs that will be incurred during the entire life of a product or service. *p. 132*

Transfer pricing   The activity of setting prices at which products or services will be transferred from one division of the business to another division of the same business. *p. 318*

Understandability   The requirement that accounting information should be understood by those for whom the information is primarily compiled. Lack of understandability will limit the usefulness of accounting information. *p. 6*

Value chain analysis   Analysing each activity undertaken by a business to identify any that do not add value to the output of goods or services. *p. 340*

Value drivers   The factors that are seen in shareholder value analysis as being key in generating shareholder value. *p. 347*

Variable cost   A cost that varies according to the volume of activity. *pp. 44, 322*

Variance   The financial effect, usually on the budgeted profit, of the particular factor under consideration being more or less than budgeted. *p. 185*

Variance analysis   Carrying out calculations to find the area of the business's operations that has caused the budgets not to have been met. *p. 192*

Working capital   Current assets less current liabilities. *p. 262*

Zero-base budgeting (ZBB)   An approach to budgeting, based on the philosophy that all spending needs to be justified annually and that each budget should start as a clean sheet. *p. 156*

Appendix B

Solutions to self-assessment questions

Chapter 2

2.1 JB Limited

(a)

	£	
Material M1		
1,200 @ £5.50	6,600	The original cost is irrelevant since any stock (inventory) used will need to be replaced
Material P2		
800 @ £2.00 (that is, £3.60 – £1.60)	1,600	The best alternative use of this material is as a substitute for P4 – an effective opportunity cost of £2.00/kg
Part no. 678		
400 @ £50	20,000	
Labour		
Skilled 2,000 @ £6	12,000	The effective cost is £6/hour
Unskilled 2,000 @ £5	10,000	
Overheads	3,200	It is only the additional cost which is relevant, the method of apportioning total overheads is not relevant
Total relevant cost	53,400	
Potential revenue		
400 @ £150	60,000	

Clearly, on the basis of the information available it would be beneficial for the business to undertake the contract.

(b) There is an almost infinite number of possible answers to this part of the question, including:

- If material P2 had not been in stock, it may be that it would not be possible to buy it in and still leave the contract as a beneficial one. In this case the business may be unhappy about accepting a price under the particular conditions that apply, which could not be accepted under other conditions.
- Will the replacement for the skilled worker be able to do the normal work of that person to the necessary standard?
- Is JB Limited confident that the additional unskilled employee can be made redundant at the end of this contract without cost to itself?

Chapter 3

3.1 Khan Ltd

(a) The break-even point if only the Alpha service were rendered would be:

$$\frac{\text{Fixed costs}}{\text{Sales revenue per unit} - \text{Variable cost per unit}} = \frac{£40,000}{£30 - £(15 + 6)} = 4,445 \text{ units (a year)}$$

(Strictly it is 4,444.44 but 4,445 is the smallest number of units of the service that must be rendered to avoid a loss.)

(b)

	Alpha £/unit	Beta £/unit	Gamma £/unit
Selling price	30	39	20
Variable materials	(15)	(18)	(10)
Variable production costs	(6)	(10)	(5)
Contribution	9	11	5
Staff time (hr/unit)	2	3	1
Contribution/staff hour	£4.50	£3.67	£5.00
Order of priority	2nd	3rd	1st

(c)

	Hours		Contribution £
Render:			
5,000 Gamma using	5,000	generating (that is, 5,000 × £5 =)	25,000
2,500 Alpha using	5,000	generating (that is, 2,500 × £9 =)	22,500
	10,000		47,500
		Less Fixed costs	40,000
		Profit	7,500

Leaving a demand for 500 units of Alpha and 2,000 units of Beta unsatisfied.

Chapter 4

4.1 Hector and Co. Ltd

Job costing basis

			£
Materials:	Metal wire	1,000 × 2 × £2.20*	4,400
	Fabric	1,000 × 0.5 × £1.00*	500
Labour:	Skilled	1,000 × (10/60) × £7.50	1,250
	Unskilled	1,000 × (5/60) × £5.00	417
Overheads		1,000 × (15/60) × (50,000/12,500)	1,000
Total cost			7,567
Add Profit loading		12.5% thereof	946
Total tender price			8,513

* In the traditional approach to full costing, historic costs of materials tend to be used. It would not necessarily have been incorrect to used the 'relevant' (opportunity) costs here.

Minimum contract price (relevant cost basis)

			£
Materials:	Metal wire	1,000 × 2 × £2.50 (replacement cost)	5,000
	Fabric	1,000 × 0.5 × £0.40 (scrap value)	200
Labour:	Skilled	(there is no effective cost of skilled staff)	–
	Unskilled	1,000 × 5/60 × £5.00	417
Minimum tender price			5,617

The difference between the two prices is partly that the relevant costing approach tends to look to the future, partly that it considers opportunity costs, and partly that the job-costing basis total has a profit loading.

Chapter 5

5.1   Psilis Ltd

(a) Full cost (present basis)

	Basic		Super	
	£		£	
Direct labour (all £10/hour)	40.00	(4 hours)	60.00	(6 hours)
Direct material	15.00		20.00	
Overheads	18.20	(£4.55* × 4)	27.30	(£4.55* × 6)
	73.20		107.30	

* Total direct labour hours worked = (40,000 × 4) + (10,000 × 6) = 220,000 hours. Overhead recovery rate = £1,000,000/220,000 = £4.55 per direct labour hour.

Thus the selling prices are currently:

Basic: £73.20 + 25% = £91.50
Super: £107.30 + 25% = £134.13

(b) Full cost (activity basis)
Here, the cost of each cost-driving activity is apportioned between total production of the two products.

Activity	Cost £000	Basis of apportionment	Basic £000		Super £000	
Machine set-ups	280	Number of set-ups	56	(20/100)	224	(80/100)
Quality inspection	220	Number of inspections	55	(500/2,000)	165	(1,500/2,000)
Sales order processing	240	Number of orders processed	72	(1,500/5,000)	168	(3,500/5,000)
General production	260	Machine hours	182	(350/500)	78	(150/500)
Total	1,000		365		635	

The overheads per unit are:

$$\text{Basic:} \quad \frac{£365,000}{40,000} = £9.13$$

$$\text{Super:} \quad \frac{£635,000}{10,000} = £63.50$$

Thus, on an activity basis the full costs are as follows:

	Basic £		Super £	
Direct labour (all £10/hour)	40.00	(4 hours)	60.00	(6 hours)
Direct material	15.00		20.00	
Overheads	9.13		63.50	
Full cost	64.13		143.50	
Current selling price	£91.50		£134.13	

(c) It seems that the Supers are being sold for less than they cost to produce. If the price cannot be increased, there is a very strong case for abandoning this product. At the same time, the Basics are very profitable to the extent that it may be worth considering lowering the price to attract more sales revenue.

The fact that the overhead costs can be related to activities and, more specifically, to products does not mean that abandoning Super production would lead to immediate overhead cost savings. For example, it may not be possible or desirable to dismiss machine-setting staff overnight. It would certainly rarely be possible to release factory space occupied by machine setters and make immediate cost savings. Nevertheless, in the medium term these costs can be avoided and it may be sensible to do so.

Chapter 6

6.1 **Antonio Ltd**

(a) (i) Raw materials stock (inventory) budget for the six months ending 31 December (physical quantities):

	July units	Aug units	Sept units	Oct units	Nov units	Dec units
Opening stock						
(Current month's production)	500	600	600	700	750	750
Purchases						
(Balance figure)	600	600	700	750	750	750
	1,100	1,200	1,300	1,450	1,500	1,500
Less Issues to production						
(From question)	500	600	600	700	750	750
Closing stock						
(Next month's production)	600	600	700	750	750	750

Raw materials' stock (inventory) budget for the six months ending 31 December (in financial terms), that is, the physical quantities × £8:

	July £	Aug £	Sept £	Oct £	Nov £	Dec £
Opening stock	4,000	4,800	4,800	5,600	6,000	6,000
Purchases	4,800	4,800	5,600	6,000	6,000	6,000
	8,800	9,600	10,400	11,600	12,000	12,000
Less Issues to production	4,000	4,800	4,800	5,600	6,000	6,000
Closing stock	4,800	4,800	5,600	6,000	6,000	6,000

(ii) Trade creditors (payables) budget for the six months ending 31 December:

	July £	Aug £	Sept £	Oct £	Nov £	Dec £
Opening balance (Current month's payment)	4,000	4,800	4,800	5,600	6,000	6,000
Purchases (From raw materials stock budget)	4,800	4,800	5,600	6,000	6,000	6,000
	8,800	9,600	10,400	11,600	12,000	12,000
Less Payments	4,000	4,800	4,800	5,600	6,000	6,000
Closing balance (Next month's payment)	4,800	4,800	5,600	6,000	6,000	6,000

(iii) Cash budget for the six months ending 31 December:

	July £	Aug £	Sept £	Oct £	Nov £	Dec £
Inflows						
Receipts:						
Trade debtors (40% of sales of two months previous)	2,800	3,200	3,200	4,000	4,800	5,200
Cash sales (60% of current month's sales)	4,800	6,000	7,200	7,800	8,400	9,600
Total inflows	7,600	9,200	10,400	11,800	13,200	14,800
Outflows						
Creditors (from creditors budget)	(4,000)	(4,800)	(4,800)	(5,600)	(6,000)	(6,000)
Direct costs	(3,000)	(3,600)	(3,600)	(4,200)	(4,500)	(4,500)
Advertising	(1,000)	–	–	(1,500)	–	–
Overheads: 80%	(1,280)	(1,280)	(1,280)	(1,280)	(1,600)	(1,600)
20%	(280)	(320)	(320)	(320)	(320)	(400)
New plant			(2,200)	(2,200)	(2,200)	
Total outflows	(9,560)	(10,000)	(12,200)	(15,100)	(14,620)	(12,500)
Net inflows (outflows)	(1,960)	(800)	(1,800)	(3,300)	(1,420)	2,300
Balance c/f	5,540	4,740	2,940	(360)	(1,780)	520

The balances carried forward are deduced by deducting the deficit (net outflows) for the month from (or adding the surplus for the month to) the previous month's balance.

Note how budgets are linked; in this case the stock budget to the creditors budget and the creditors budget to the cash budget.

(b) The following are possible means of relieving the cash shortages revealed by the budget:

- Make a higher proportion of sales on a cash basis.
- Collect the money from debtors (receivables) more promptly, for example during the month following the sale.
- Hold lower stocks, both of raw materials and of finished goods.
- Increase the creditor payment period.
- Delay the payments for advertising.
- Obtain more credit for the overhead costs; at present only 20 per cent are on credit.
- Delay the payments for the new plant.

Chapter 7

7.1   Toscanini Ltd

(a) and (b)

	Budget			Actual	
	Original	Flexed			
Output (units) (prod'n and sales)	4,000	3,500		3,500	
	£	£		£	
Sales	16,000	14,000		13,820	
Raw materials	(3,840)	(3,360)	(1,400 kg)	(3,420)	(1,425 kg)
Labour	(3,200)	(2,800)	(350 hr)	(2,690)	(345 hr)
Fixed overheads	(4,800)	(4,800)		(4,900)	
Operating profit	4,160	3,040		2,810	

	£		Manager accountable
Sales volume variance (4,160 – 3,040)	(1,120)	(A)	Sales
Sales price variance (14,000 – 13,820)	(180)	(A)	Sales
Materials price variance (1,425 × 2.40) – 3,420	0	–	
Materials usage variance [(3,500 × 0.4) – 1,425] × £2.40	(60)	(A)	Production
Labour rate variance (345 × £8) – 2,690	70	(F)	Personnel
Labour efficiency variance [(3,500 × 0.10) – 345] × £8	40	(F)	Production
Fixed overhead spending (4,800 – 4,900)	(100)	(A)	Various depending on the nature of the overheads
Total net variances	(1,350)	(A)	
Budgeted profit	4,160		
Less Total net variance	1,350		
Actual profit	2,810		

(c) Feasible explanations include the following:

- Sales volume — Unanticipated fall in world demand would account for $400 \times £2.24 = £896$ of this variance (£2.24 is the budgeted contribution per unit). Ineffective marketing probably caused the remainder, though a lack of availability of stock to sell may be a reason.
- Sales price — Ineffective selling seems the only logical reason.
- Materials usage — Inefficient usage of material, perhaps because of poor performance by labour or substandard materials.
- Labour rate — Less overtime worked or lower production bonuses paid as a result of lower volume of activity.
- Labour efficiency — More effective working.
- Overheads — Ineffective control of overheads.

(d) Clearly, not all of the sales volume variance can be attributed to poor marketing, given a 10 per cent reduction in demand.

It will probably be useful to distinguish between that part of the variance that arose from the shortfall in general demand (a planning variance) and a volume variance, which is more fairly attributable to the manager concerned. Thus accountability will be more fairly imposed.

	£
Planning variance $(10\% \times 4,000) \times £2.24$	896
'New' sales volume variance	
$[4,000 - (10\% \times 4,000) - 3,500] \times £2.24$	224
Original sales volume variance	1,120

Chapter 8

8.1   Beacon Chemicals plc

(a) Relevant cash flows are as follows:

	Year 0 £000	Year 1 £000	Year 2 £000	Year 3 £000	Year 4 £000	Year 5 £000
Sales revenue	–	80	120	144	100	64
Loss of contribution		(15)	(15)	(15)	(15)	(15)
Variable costs		(40)	(50)	(48)	(30)	(32)
Fixed costs (Note 1)		(8)	(8)	(8)	(8)	(8)
Operating cash flows		17	47	73	47	9
Working capital	(30)					30
Capital cost	(100)					
Net relevant cash flows	(130)	17	47	73	47	39

Notes:
1 Only the fixed costs that are incremental to the project (only existing because of the project) are relevant. Depreciation is irrelevant because it is not a cash flow.
2 The research and development cost is irrelevant since it has been spent irrespective of the decision on X14 production.

(b) The payback period is as follows:

	Year 0 £000	Year 1 £000	Year 2 £000	Year 3 £000
Cumulative cash flows	(130)	(113)	(66)	7

Thus the equipment will have repaid the initial investment by the end of the third year of operations.

(c) The net present value is as follows:

	Year 0 £000	Year 1 £000	Year 2 £000	Year 3 £000	Year 4 £000	Year 5 £000
Discount factor	1.00	0.926	0.857	0.794	0.735	0.681
Present value	(130)	15.74	40.28	57.96	34.55	26.56
Net present value	45.09	(That is, the sum of the present values for years 0 to 5.)				

Chapter 9

9.1   Williams Wholesalers Ltd

	£	£
Existing level of debtors (£4m × 70/365)		767,123
New level of debtors: (£2m × 80/365)	438,356	
(£2m × 30/365)	164,384	602,740
Reduction in debtors		164,383
Costs and benefits of policy		
Cost of discount (£2m × 2%)		40,000
Less Savings		
Interest payable (£164,383 × 13%)	21,370	
Administration costs	6,000	
Bad debts (20,000 − 10,000)	10,000	37,370
Net cost of policy		2,630

The above calculations reveal that the business will be worse off by offering the discounts.

Chapter 10

10.1   Andromeda International plc

(a)

Jupiter	Mars
(i) (260/1,330) × 100%	(50/1,380) × 100%
= 19.5%	= 3.6%
(ii) (275/1,420*) × 100%	(80/1,680†) × 100%
= 19.4%	= 4.8%

* The profit will increase by £15,000 ((£250,000 × 0.30) − £60,000). Assets will increase by £90,000.
† Profit will increase by £30,000 (£90,000 − £60,000 depreciation). Assets will increase by £300,000.

(b) The investment opportunity for Jupiter division will result in an ROI of 16.7% (that is, 15/90) which is above the cost of capital for the company. As a result, central management is likely to view the opportunity favourably. However, the effect of taking the opportunity will be to lower the existing ROI of the division. This may mean that the divisional manager will be reluctant to take on the opportunity.

The investment opportunity for the Mars division provides an ROI of 10% (that is, 30/300), which is below the cost of capital of the company. As a result central management would not wish for this opportunity to be taken up. However, the opportunity will increase the ROI of the Mars division overall and, as a result, the divisional manager may be keen to invest in the opportunity.

There may be reasons for investing in each opportunity which are not given in the question but which may be compelling. For example, it may be necessary to introduce the new product into the Jupiter division in order to ensure that the range of products offered to customers is complete. Failure to do so may result in a decline in overall sales. It may be that investment in the Mars division is important to ensure that productivity over the longer term does not slip behind that of its competitors.

(c) Ideally, ROI should be calculated using the current value of the assets employed. By so doing we can see whether or not the returns are satisfactory as compared with the alternative use of those resources. Using costs (or cost less accumulated depreciation) as the basis for ROI will be measuring current performance against past outlays.

Gross book value fails to take account of the age of the assets held. It may be that the assets are all near the end of their useful lives and are, therefore, highly depreciated. In such a case, the gross book value may produce a low ROI and may provide too high a 'hurdle' rate for new investment opportunities. Gross book value in such circumstances would also provide a poor approximation to the current value of the assets.

Using net book value would overcome the problem mentioned above but, during a period of inflation, this measure may be significantly lower than the current value of the assets employed. In addition, there is the problem that ROI can improve over time simply because of the declining value of the assets employed. Divisional managers may be less inclined to replace old assets where this will lead to a decline in ROI.

Chapter 11

11.1 The student is talking about strategic planning, not about assessment of strategic change. Strategic planning is concerned with going through a process of identifying the aim or mission of the business, turning that aim into objectives, assessing the current position of the business (perhaps through a SWOT analysis) and planning strategies to achieve the objectives, given the current position.

On the other hand, assessing strategic change is carrying out an analysis, not unlike variance analysis, to investigate the success of a new strategy, relative to the old one, following the first operating period after the change.

Customer profitability analysis is concerned with assessing how profitable particular customers are to one's own business, as customers. This involves preparing a 'mini profit and loss account (income statement)' for each customer or, perhaps, group of customers. Here all of the costs of providing the business's goods or services to the customer are taken into account. This includes not just the cost of providing the basic goods or service, but also other costs that probably vary between customers, such as delivery costs, warehousing (stores) costs and the costs of providing trade credit. How profitable the customer is as a business is not the subject of customer profitability analysis, though this would be of interest to the supplying business. The student is therefore wrong in stating this.

SVA is an approach to management that focuses on the generally accepted business objective of maximisation of shareholder wealth. It does this by identifying a number of 'value drivers' that are seen as key to delivering value for shareholders. Plans can be made in respect of each of these key value drivers. These plans can be used as the basis of day-to-day management targets, against which managers can be assessed. SVA has little to do with the preferences of individual shareholders for dividends rather than retained profits.

EVA® stands for 'economic value added', not 'equity value analysis'. It tries to measure the extent to which a period of trading has led to value being created for shareholders. It tries to assess whether the profit generated by the business exceeds the minimum required to maintain the shareholders' wealth. The latter is based on the shareholders' required return and a fair assessment of the value of the assets in use in generating that profit. Though SVA and EVA® are quite closely linked, in that they both focus on achieving shareholder wealth maximisation, they approach this in rather different ways and are certainly not the same thing.

The Balanced Scorecard is certainly not another name for the balance sheet. It is an attempt to provide financial and non-financial targets for managing the business. It seeks to strike a balance between financial and non-financial, external and internal, and predictive and historic factors. The balance sheet deals only with financial matters and has no connection with the Balanced Scorecard, except that both use the word 'balance' in their names.

Chapter 1

1.1 Strategic management involves five steps:

1 *Establish mission and objectives.* The mission statement is usually a brief statement of the overall aims of the business. The objectives are rather more specific than the mission and need to be both quantifiable and consistent with the mission or aims.

2 *Undertake a position analysis.* Here the business is seeking to establish how it is placed relative to its environment (competitors, markets, technology, the economy, political climate and so on), given the business's mission and objectives. This is often approached within the framework of an analysis of the business's strengths, weaknesses, opportunities and threats (a SWOT analysis). Strengths and weaknesses are internal factors that are attributes of the business itself, whereas opportunities and threats are factors expected to be present in the environment in which the business operates. The SWOT framework is not the only possible approach to undertaking a position analysis, but it seems to be a very popular one.

3 *Identify and assess the strategic options.* This involves attempting to identify possible courses of action that will enable the business to reach its objectives in the light of the position analysis undertaken in Step 2.

4 *Select strategic options.* Here the business will select what seems to be the best of the courses of action or strategies (identified in Step 3) and will formulate a strategic plan in the form of long- and short-term budgets.

5 *Perform review and control.* Here the business pursues the plans derived in Step 4, using the traditional approach to compare actual performance against budgets, seeking to control where actual performance appears not to be matching plans.

1.2 **SWOT analysis of Jones Dairy Ltd**

Strengths

- A portfolio of identifiable customers who show some loyalty to the business.
- Good cash flow profile. Though credit will be given, a week is the normal credit period.
- An apparently sound distribution system.
- A monopoly of doorstep delivery in the area.
- Barriers to entry. There are probably relatively high fixed costs, which implies a 'critical mass' of volume is necessary.
- Good employees and ease of recruitment.
- Differentiated product; clearly different from what is supplied by the supermarket in that it is delivered to the door.
- Apparently good marketing, since the decline in business is less than the national average.
- Good knowledge of the local market.

- Tendency for people to shop infrequently means that doorstep delivery may be the only practical means of having fresh milk.

Weaknesses

- Ageing managers.
- Success might be dependent on the present management continuing to manage.
- Narrow product range.
- High price necessary to generate acceptable level of profit.
- Available substitute, that is non-delivered milk.
- High operating gearing (probably) means that profit suffers disproportionately with a downturn in demand.
- Single supplier.

Opportunities

- Possibility of extending the product range to include other dairy and non-dairy products to existing customers.
- Possible geographical expansion to cover other local towns and villages.
- Possibly move to act as a wholesaler to local stores at differentiated prices. It is probable that the bottlers would supply Jones more cheaply than they would supply individual small stores.
- Using plant for some other purpose, such as letting coldstore facilities.

Threats

- Apparently strong trend against doorstep delivery driven by price differential.
- Trend away from dairy products for health/cultural reasons.
- The probability that Jones is entirely dependent on the only local bottler. More geographically remote bottlers may not be prepared to supply at an acceptable price.
- Increasing strength of supermarket buying power.

Chapter 2

2.1 Lombard Ltd

Relevant costs of undertaking the contract are:

	£
Equipment costs	200,000
Component X (20,000 × 4 × £5)	400,000
Component Y (20,000 × 3 × £8)	480,000
Additional costs (20,000 × £8)	160,000
	1,240,000
Revenue from the contract (20,000 × £80)	1,600,000

Thus, from a purely financial point of view the project is acceptable. (Note that there is no relevant labour cost since the staff concerned will be paid irrespective of whether the contract is undertaken.)

2.2 The local authority

(a) **Net benefit of accepting the touring company proposal**

		£
Net reduction in ticket revenues (see workings below)		(10,000)
Savings on:	Costumes	2,800
	Scenery	1,650
	Casual staff	1,760
Net deficit		3,790

Since there is a net deficit, on financial grounds, the touring company's proposal should be rejected.

Note that all of the following are irrelevant, because they will occur irrespective of the decision:

- full-time staff salaries;
- artistes' salaries;
- heating and lighting;
- administration costs;
- refreshment revenues and costs; and
- programme advertising.

Workings   £

Normal ticket sales: 200 @ £12 = 2,400
                         500 @ £8 = 4,000
                         300 @ £6 = 1,800
                                     8,200

Ticket revenue at 50 per cent capacity for
  20 performances (£8,200 × 50% × 20)   82,000

Touring company ticket sales:

  Total revenue for each performance for a full house:

                                     £
                    200 @ £11 = 2,200
                    500 @ £7 = 3,500
                    300 @ £5 = 1,500
                                7,200

  Ticket revenues (£7,200 × 10 × 50%)   36,000
                   (£7,200 × 15 × $^{2}/_{3}$ × 50%)   36,000
                                                  72,000

  Net loss of revenue (£82,000 – £72,000)   10,000

(b) Other possible factors to consider include:

- The reliability of the estimations, including the assumption that programme and refreshment sales will not be altered by the level of occupancy.
- A desire to offer theatregoers the opportunity to see another group of players.
- Dangers of loss of morale of staff not employed, or employed to do other than their usual work.

2.3   Andrews and Co. Ltd

Minimum contract price

			£
Materials	Steel core:	10,000 × £2.10	21,000
	Plastic:	10,000 × 0.10 × £0.10	100
Labour	Skilled:		–
	Unskilled:	10,000 × 5/60 × £5	4,167
Minimum tender price			25,267

2.6 **The local education authority**

(a) One-off financial net benefits of closing:

	D only	A and B	A and C
Capacity reduction	800	700	800
	£m	£m	£m
Property developer (A)	–	14.0	14.0
Shopping complex (B)	–	8.0	–
Property developer (D)	9.0	–	–
Safety (C)	–	–	3.0
Adapt facilities	(1.8)	–	–
Total	7.2	22.0	17.0
Ranking based on total one-off benefits	3	1	2

(Note that all past costs of buying and improving the schools are irrelevant.)

Recurrent financial net benefits of closing:

	D only £m	A and B £m	A and C £m
Rent (C)	–	–	0.3
Administrators	0.2	0.4	0.4
Total	0.2	0.4	0.7
Ranking based on total of recurrent benefits	3	2	1

On the basis of the financial figures alone, closure of either A and B or A and C looks best. It is not possible to add the one-off and the recurring costs directly, but the large one-off cost-saving associated with closing schools A and B makes this option look attractive. (In Chapter 8 we shall see that it is possible to add one-off and recurring costs in a way that should lead to sensible conclusions.)

(b) The costs of acquiring and improving the schools in the past are past costs or sunk costs and, therefore, irrelevant. The costs of employing the chief education officer is a future cost, but irrelevant because it is not dependent on outcomes, it is a common cost.

(c) There are many other factors, some of a non-quantifiable nature. These include:

● Accuracy of projections of capacity requirements.
● Locality of existing schools relative to where potential pupils live.
● Political acceptability of selling schools to property developers.
● Importance of purely financial issues in making the final decision.
● The quality of the replacement sporting facilities compared with those at school D.
● Political acceptability of staff redundancies.
● Possible savings/costs of employing fewer teachers, which might be relevant if economies of scale are available by having fewer schools.
● Staff morale.

2.7	**Rob Otics Ltd**

(a) The minimum price for the proposed contract would be:

	£
Materials	
Component X (2 × 8 × £180)	2,880
Component Y	0
Component Z [(75 + 32) × £20] − (75 × £25)	265
Other miscellaneous items	250
Labour	
Assembly (25 + 24 + 23 + 22 + 21 + 20 + 19 + 18) × £48*	8,256
Inspection (8 × 6 × £18)	864
Total	12,515

* £60 − £12 = £48.

The assembly labour cost is irrelevant here because it will be incurred irrespective of which work the members of staff do. The historic cost of the stock (inventory) of component X and the fact that it is not yet paid for are both irrelevant. The historic cost and the £1,500 relating to component Y are also irrelevant. Thus the minimum price is £12,515.

(b) Other factors include:

- Competitive state of the market.
- The fact that the above figure is unique to the particular circumstances at the time – for example, having component Y in stock but having no use for it. Any subsequent order might have to take account of an outlay cost.
- Breaking even (that is, just covering the costs) on a contract will not fulfil the business's objective.
- Charging a low price may cause marketing problems. Other customers may resent the low price for this contract. The current enquirer may expect a similar price in future.

Chapter 3

3.4	**Motormusic Ltd**

(a) Break-even point = fixed costs/contribution per unit
= (80,000 + 60,000)/[60 − (20 + 14 + 12 + 3)] = 12,727 radios.
These would have a sales value of £763,620 (that is, 12,727 × £60)

(b) The margin of safety is 7,273 radios (that is, 20,000 − 12,727). This margin would have a sales value of £436,380 (that is, 7,273 × £60)

3.5	**Products A, B and C**

(a) Total time required on cutting machines is:

$$(2,500 \times 1.0) + (3,400 \times 1.0) + (5,100 \times 0.5) = 8,450 \text{ hours}$$

Total time available on cutting machines is 5,000 hours. Therefore, this is a limiting factor.

Total time required on assembling machines is:

$$(2,500 \times 0.5) + (3,400 \times 1.0) + (5,100 \times 0.5) = 7,200 \text{ hours}$$

Total time available on assembling machines is 8,000 hours. Therefore, this is not a limiting factor.

	A (per unit) £	B (per unit) £	C (per unit) £
Selling price	25	30	18
Variable materials	(12)	(13)	(10)
Variable production costs	(7)	(4)	(3)
Contribution	6	13	5
Time on cutting machines	1.0 hour	1.0 hour	0.5 hour
Contribution per hour on cutting machines	£6	£13	£10
Order of priority	3rd	1st	2nd

Therefore, produce:

3,400 product B using	3,400 hours
3,200 product C using	1,600 hours
	5,000 hours

(b) Assuming that the business would make no saving in variable production costs by sub-contracting, it would be worth paying up to the contribution per unit (£5) for product C, which would therefore be £5 × (5,100 − 3,200) = £9,500 in total.

Similarly it would be worth paying up to £6 per unit for product A – that is, £6 × 2,500 = £15,000 in total.

3.6   Darmor Ltd

(a) Contribution per hour of skilled labour of product X is:

$$\frac{£(30 - 6 - 2 - 12 - 3)}{(6/6)} = £7$$

Given the scarcity of skilled labour, if the management is to be indifferent between the products, the contribution per skilled-labour-hour must be the same. Thus for product Y the selling price must be:

$$[£(7 × (9/6)) + 9 + 4 + 25 + 7] = £55.50$$

(that is, the contribution plus the variable costs), and for product Z the selling price must be:

$$[£(7 × (3/6)) + 3 + 10 + 14 + 7] = £37.50$$

(b) The business could pay up to £13 an hour (£6 + £7) for additional hours of skilled labour. This is the potential contribution per hour, before taking account of the labour rate of £6 an hour.

3.7   Intermediate Products Ltd

(a)

	A £	B £	C £	D £
Total costs per unit	(65)	(41)	(36)	(46)
Less Fixed costs	20	8	8	12
Variable cost per unit	(45)	(33)	(28)	(34)
Buying/selling price per unit	70	45	40	55
Contribution per unit	25	12	12	21
Hours on special machine	0.5	0.4	0.5	0.3
Contribution per hour	50	30	24	70
Order of preference	2	3	4	1

Optimum use of hours on special machine	*Balance of hours*
D 3,000 × 0.3 = 900	5,100 (that is, 6000 – 900)
A 5,000 × 0.5 = 2,500	2,600 (that is, 5,100 – 2,500)
B 6,000 × 0.4 = 2,400	200 (that is, 2,600 – 2,400)
C 400 × 0.5 = 200	–
6,000	

Therefore, make all of the demand for Ds, As and Bs plus 400 (of 4,000) Cs.

(b) The contribution per hour from Cs is £24, and so this is the maximum amount per hour that it would be worth paying to rent the machine, for a maximum of 1,800 hours (that is, 3,600 × 0.5, the time necessary to make the remaining demand for Cs).

(c) Other possible actions to overcome the shortage of machine time include the following:

- Alter the design of the products to avoid the use of the special machine.
- Increase the selling price of the product so that the demand will fall, making the available machine-time sufficient but making production more profitable.

3.8   Gandhi Ltd

(a) Given that the spare capacity could not be used by other services, the standard service should continue to be offered. This is because it renders a positive contribution.

(b) The standard service renders a contribution per unit of £15 (that is, £80 – £65), or £30 during the time it would take to render one unit of the nova service. The nova service would provide a contribution of only £25 (that is, £75 – £50).

The nova service should, therefore, not replace the standard service.

(c) Under the original plans, the following contributions would be rendered by the basic and standard services:

		£
Basic	11,000 × (£50 – £25) =	275,000
Standard	6,000 × (£80 – £65) =	90,000
		365,000

If the basic were to take the standard's place, 17,000 units (that is, 11,000 + 6,000) of them could be produced in total. To generate the same total contribution, each unit of the standard service would need to provide £21.47 (that is, £365,000/17,000) of contribution. Given the basic's variable cost of £25, this would mean a selling price of £46.47 each (that is £21.47 + £25.00).

Chapter 4

4.4 Promptprint Ltd

(a) The budget may be summarised as:

	£	
Sales revenue	196,000	
Direct materials	(38,000)	
Direct labour	(32,000)	
Total overheads	(77,000)	(2,400 + 3,000 + 27,600 + 36,000 + 8,000)
Profit	49,000	

The job may be priced on the basis that both overheads and profit should be apportioned to it on the basis of direct labour cost, as follows:

	£	
Direct materials	4,000	
Direct labour	3,600	
Overheads	8,663	(£77,000 × 3,600/32,000)
Profit	5,513	(£49,000 × 3,600/32,000)
	21,776	

This answer assumes that variable overheads vary in proportion to direct labour cost.

Various other bases of charging overheads and profit loading the job could have been adopted. For example, materials cost could have been included (with direct labour) as the basis for profit loading, or even apportioning overheads.

(b) This part of the question is, in effect, asking for comments on the validity of 'full cost-plus' pricing. This approach can be useful as an indicator of the effective long-run cost of doing the job. On the other hand, it fails to take account of relevant opportunity costs as well as the state of the market and other external factors. For example, it ignores the price that a competitor printing business may quote.

(c) Revised estimates of direct material costs for the job:

	£	
Paper grade 1	1,500	(£1,200 × 125%) This stock needs to be replaced
Paper grade 2	0	It has no opportunity cost value
Card	510	(£640 – £130: using the card on another job would save £640, but cost £130 to achieve that saving)
Inks and so on	300	This stock needs to be replaced
	2,310	

4.5 **Bookdon plc**

(a) To answer this question, we need first to allocate and apportion the overheads to product cost centres, as follows:

Cost	Basis of apportionment	Total	Department			
			Machine shop	Fitting section	Canteen	Machine main'ce section
		£	£	£	£	£
Allocated items:	Specific	90,380	27,660	19,470	16,600	26,650
Rent, rates, heat, light	Floor area	17,000	9,000	3,500	2,500	2,000
			(3,600/ 6,800)	*(1,400/ 6,800)*	*(1,000/ 6,800)*	*(800/ 6,800)*
Dep'n and insurance	Book value	25,000	12,500	6,250	2,500	3,750
			(150/300)	*(75/300)*	*(30/300)*	*(45/300)*
		132,380	49,160	29,220	21,600	32,400
Canteen	Number of employees	–	10,800	8,400	(21,600)	2,400
			(18/36)	*(14/36)*		*(4/36)*
		132,380	59,960	37,620	–	34,800
Machine maintenance section	Specified %	–	24,360	10,440	–	(34,800)
			(70%)	*(30%)*		
		132,380	84,320	48,060	–	–

Note that the canteen overheads were reapportioned to the other cost centres first because the canteen renders a service to the machine maintenance section but does not receive a service from it.

Calculation of the overhead absorption (recovery) rates can now proceed:

(i) Total budgeted machine hours are:

	Hours
Product X (4,200 × 6)	25,200
Product Y (6,900 × 3)	20,700
Product Z (1,700 × 4)	6,800
	52,700

Overhead absorption rate for the machine shop is:

$$\frac{£84,320}{52,700} = £1.60/\text{machine hour}$$

(ii) Total budgeted direct labour cost for the fitting section is:

	£
Product X (4,200 × £12)	50,400
Product Y (6,900 × £3)	20,700
Product Z (1,700 × £21)	35,700
	106,800

Overhead absorption rate for the fitting section is:

$$\frac{£48,060}{£106,800} \times 100\% = 45\% \text{ or } £0.45 \text{ per } £ \text{ of direct labour cost.}$$

(b) The cost of one unit of product X is calculated as follows:

	£
Direct materials	11.00
Direct labour	
Machine shop	6.00
Fitting section	12.00
Overheads	
Machine shop (6 × £1.60)	9.60
Fitting section (£12 × 45%)	5.40
	44.00

Therefore, the cost of one unit of product X is £44.00.

4.6 **Products A, B and C**

Allocation and apportionment of overheads to product cost centres

	Basis of apportionment	Department				
		Cutting £	Machining £	Pressing £	Engineering £	Personnel £
Total		154,482	64,316	58,452	56,000	34,000
Personnel	specified	18,700 (55%)	3,400 (10%)	6,800 (20%)	5,100 (15%)	(34,000)
		173,182	67,716	65,252	61,100	–
Engineering	specified	12,220 (20%)	27,495 (45%)	21,385 (35%)	(61,100)	
		185,402	95,211	86,637	–	–

Note that the personnel overheads were reapportioned to the other cost centres first because the canteen renders a service to the engineering department section, but does not receive a service from it.

Calculation of the overhead absorption (recovery) rates

In both the cutting and pressing departments, no machines seem to be used, and so a direct-labour-hour basis of overhead absorption seems reasonable.

In the machining department, machine hours are far in excess of labour hours and the overheads are probably machine related. In this department, machine hours seem a fair basis for cost units to absorb overheads.

Total planned direct-labour hours for the cutting department are thus:

Product A	4,000 × (3 + 6) =	36,000
Product B	3,000 × (5 + 1) =	18,000
Product C	6,000 × (2 + 3) =	30,000
		84,000

The overhead absorption rate for the cutting department = £185,402/84,000 = £2.21 per direct labour hour.

Total planned machine hours for the machining department are thus:

Product A	4,000 × 2.0 =	8,000
Product B	3,000 × 1.5 =	4,500
Product C	6,000 × 2.5 =	15,000
		27,500

The overhead absorption rate for the machining department = £95,211/27,500 = £3.46 per machine hour.

Total planned direct labour hours for the pressing department are:

Product A	4,000 × 2 =	8,000
Product B	3,000 × 3 =	9,000
Product C	6,000 × 4 =	24,000
		41,000

The overhead absorption rate for the cutting department = £86,637/41,000 = £2.11 per direct labour hour.

(a) **Cost of one completed unit of product A**

		£
Direct materials		7.00
Direct labour		
Cutting department: skilled	(3 × £8)	24.00
unskilled	(6 × £5)	30.00
Machining department	(0.5 × £6)	3.00
Pressing department	(2 × £6)	12.00
Overheads		
Cutting department	(9 × £2.21)	19.89
Machining department	(2 × £3.46)	6.92
Pressing department	(2 × £2.11)	4.22
		107.03

(b) **Cost of one uncompleted unit of product B**

		£
Direct materials		4.00*
Direct labour		
Cutting department: skilled	(5 × £8)	40.00
unskilled	(1 × £5)	5.00
Machining department	(0.25 × £6)	1.50
Overheads		
Cutting department	(6 × £2.21)	13.26
Machining department	(1.5 × £3.46)	5.19
		68.95

* This assumes that all of the materials are added in the cutting or machining departments.

4.7

Offending phrase	Explanation
'Necessary to divide up the business into departments'	This can be done but it will not always be of much benefit. Only in quite restricted circumstances will it give significantly different job costs.
'Fixed costs (or overheads)'	This implies that fixed costs and overheads are the same thing. They are not really connected with one another. 'Fixed' is to do with how costs behave as the level of output is raised or lowered; 'overheads' are to do with the extent to which costs can be directly measured in respect of a particular unit of output. Though it is true that many overheads are fixed, not all are. Also, direct labour is usually a fixed cost. All of the other references to fixed and variable costs are wrong. The person should have referred to indirect and direct costs.
'Usually this is done on the basis of area'	Where overheads are apportioned to departments, they will be apportioned on some logical basis. For certain costs – for example, rent – the floor area may be the most logical; for others, such as machine maintenance costs, the floor area would be totally inappropriate.
'When the total fixed costs for each department have been identified, this will be divided by the number of hours that were worked'	Where overheads are dealt with on a departmental basis, they may be divided by the number of direct labour hours to deduce a recovery rate. However, this is only one basis of applying overheads to jobs. For example, machine hours or some other basis may be more appropriate to the particular circumstances involved.
'It is essential that this approach is taken in order to deduce a selling price'	It is relatively unusual for the 'job cost' to be able to dictate the price at which the manufacturer can price its output. For many businesses, the market dictates the price.

4.8 (a) Charging overheads to jobs on a departmental basis means that overheads are collected 'product' cost centre (department) by 'product' cost centre. This involves picking up the overheads that are direct to each department and adding to them a share of overheads that are general to the business as a whole. The overheads of 'service' cost centres must then be apportioned to the product cost centres. At this point, all of the overheads for the whole business are divided between the 'product' cost centres, such that the sum of the 'product' cost centre overheads equals those for the whole business.

Dealing with overheads departmentally is believed to provide more fair and useful information to decision makers, because different departments may have rather different overheads, and applying overheads departmentally can take account of that and reflect it in job costs.

In theory, dealing with overheads on a departmental basis is more costly than on a business-wide basis. In practice, it possibly does not make too much difference to the cost of collecting the information. This is because, normally, businesses are divided into departments, and the costs are collected departmentally, as part of the normal routine for exercising control over the business.

(b) In order to make any difference to the job cost that will emerge as a result of dealing with overheads departmentally, as compared with a business-wide basis, the following *both* need to be the case:

- The overheads per unit of the basis of charging (for example direct labour hours) need to be different from one department to the next; and
- The proportion (but not the actual amounts) of total overheads that are charged to jobs must differ from one job to the next.

Assume, for the sake of argument, that direct labour hours are used as the basis of charging overheads in all departments. Also assume that there are three departments, A, B and C.

There will be no difference to the overheads charged to a job if the rate of overheads per direct labour hour is the same for all departments. Obviously, if the charging rate is the same in all departments, that same rate must also apply to the business taken as a whole.

Also, even where overheads per direct labour hour differ significantly from one department to another – if all jobs spend, say, about 20 per cent of their time in Department A, 50 per cent in Department B and 30 per cent in Department C – it will not make any difference whether overheads are charged departmentally or overall.

These conclusions are not in any way dependent on the basis of charging overheads or even that overheads are charged on the same basis in each department.

The statements above combine to mean that, probably in many cases in practice, departmentalising overheads is not providing information that is significantly different from that which would be provided by charging overheads to jobs on a business-wide basis.

Chapter 5

5.1 Woodner Ltd

A Output	B Sales price per unit	C Total sales revenue $(A \times B)$	D Marginal unit sales revenue	E Total variable cost $(A \times £20)$	F Total cost (variable cost + £2,500)	G Marginal cost per unit	H Profit/(loss)
units	£	£	£	£	£	£	£
0	0	0	0	0	2,500	–	(2,500)
10	95	950*	95†	200	2,700	20	(1,750)
20	90	1,800	85	400	2,900	20	(1,100)
30	85	2,550	75	600	3,100	20	(550)
40	80	3,200	65	800	3,300	20	(100)
50	75	3,750	55	1,000	3,500	20	250
60	70	4,200	45	1,200	3,700	20	500
70	65	4,550	35	1,400	3,900	20	650
80	60	4,800	25	1,600	4,100	20	700
90	55	4,950	15	1,800	4,300	20	650
100	50	5,000	5	2,000	4,500	20	500

* $(10 \times £95)$

† $((950 - 0)/(10 - 0))$

An output of 80 units each week will maximise profit at £700 a week. This is the nearest, given the nature of the input data, to the level of output where marginal cost per unit equals marginal revenue per unit. (For the mathematically minded, this question could have been solved by using calculus to find the point at which slopes of the total sales revenue and total cost lines were equal.)

5.2   Cost-plus pricing means that prices are based on calculations/assessments of how much it costs to produce the good or service, and includes a margin for profit. 'Cost' in this context might mean relevant cost, variable cost, direct cost or full cost. Usually cost-plus prices are based on full costs.

If a business charges the full cost of its output as a selling price, it will in theory break even. This is because the sales revenue will exactly cover all of the costs. Charging something above full cost will yield a profit. Thus, in theory, cost-plus pricing is logical.

If a cost-plus approach to pricing is to be taken, the issue that must be addressed is the level of profit required from each unit sold. This must logically be based on the total profit that is required for the period. Normally, businesses seek to enhance their wealth through trading. The extent to which they expect to do this is normally related to the amount of wealth that is invested to promote wealth enhancement. Businesses tend to seek to produce a particular percentage increase in wealth. In other words, they seek to generate a particular return on capital employed. It seems logical, therefore, that the profit loading on full cost should reflect the business's target profit and that the target should itself be based on a target return on capital employed.

An obvious problem with cost-plus pricing is that the market may not agree with the price. Put another way, cost-plus pricing takes no account of the market demand function (the relationship between price and quantity demanded). A business may fairly deduce the full cost of some product and then add what might be regarded as a reasonable level of profit, only to find that a rival producer is offering a similar product for a much lower price, or that the market simply will not buy at the cost-plus price.

Most suppliers are not strong enough in the market to dictate pricing; most are 'price takers', not 'price makers'. They must accept the price offered by the market or they do not sell any of their wares. Cost-plus pricing may be appropriate for price makers, but it has less relevance for price takers.

The cost-plus price is not entirely useless to price takers. When contemplating entering a market, knowing the cost-plus price will tell the price taker whether it can profitably enter the market or not. As has been said above, the full cost can be seen as a long-run break-even selling price. If entering a market means that this break-even price, plus an acceptable profit, cannot be achieved, then the business should probably stay out. Having a breakdown of the full cost may put the business in a position to examine where costs might be capable of being cut in order to bring the full cost-plus profit to within a figure acceptable to the market.

Being a price maker does not always imply that the business dominates a particular market. Many small businesses are, to some extent, price makers. This tends to be where buyers find it difficult to make clear distinctions between the prices offered by various suppliers. An example of this might be a car repair. Though it may be possible to obtain a series of binding estimates for the work from various garages, most people would not normally do so. As a result, garages normally charge cost-plus prices for car repairs.

5.3   **Kaplan plc**

(a) At present, the business makes each model of suitcase in a batch. The direct materials and labour costs will be recorded in respect of each batch. To these costs will be added a share of the overheads of the business for the period in which production of the batch takes place. The basis of the batch absorbing overheads is a matter of managerial judgement. Direct labour hours spent working on the batch, relative to total direct labour hours worked during the period, is a popular method. This is not the 'correct' way, however. There is no correct way. If the activity is capital intensive, some machine-hour basis of dealing with overheads might be more appropriate, though still not 'correct'. Overheads might be collected, department by department, and charged to the batch as it passes through each department. Alternatively, all of the overheads for the entire production facility might be totalled and the overheads dealt with more globally. It is only in restricted circumstances that overheads charged to batches will be affected by a decision to deal with them departmentally, rather than globally.

Once the 'full cost' (direct costs plus a share of indirect costs) has been ascertained for the batch, the cost per suitcase can be established by dividing the batch cost by the number in the batch.

(b) The uses to which full cost information can be put have been identified as:

- *For pricing purposes*. In some industries and circumstances, full costs are used as the basis of pricing. Here the full cost is deduced and a percentage is added on for profit. This is known as cost-plus pricing. A solicitor handling a case for a client probably provides an example of this.

    In many circumstances, however, suppliers are not in a position to deduce prices on a cost-plus basis. Where there is a competitive market, a supplier will probably need to accept the price that the market offers – that is, most suppliers are 'price takers' not 'price makers'.

- *For income-measurement purposes*. To provide a valid means of measuring a business's income, it is necessary to match expenses with the revenue realised in the same accounting period. Where manufactured stock (inventory) is made or partially made in one period but sold in the next, or where a service is partially rendered in one accounting period but the revenue is realised in the next, the full cost (including an appropriate share of overheads) must be carried from one accounting period to the next. Unless we are able to identify the full cost of work done in one period, which is the subject of a sale in the next, the profit figures of the periods concerned will become meaningless.

    Unless all related production costs are charged in the same accounting period as the sale is recognised in the profit and loss account (income statement), distortions will occur that will render the profit and loss account much less useful. Thus it is necessary to deduce the full cost of any production undertaken completely or partially in one accounting period but sold in a subsequent one.

(c) Whereas the traditional approach to dealing with overheads is just to accept that they exist and deal with them in a fairly broad manner, ABC takes a much more enquiring approach. ABC takes the view that overheads do not just 'occur', but that they are caused or 'driven' by 'activities'. It is a matter of finding out which activities are driving the costs and how much cost they are driving.

For example, a significant part of the costs of making suitcases of different sizes might be resetting machinery to cope with a batch of a different size from its predecessor batch. Where a particular model is made in very small batches, because it has only a small market, ABC would advocate that this model is charged directly with its machine-setting costs. The traditional approach would be to treat machine setting as a general overhead that the individual suitcases (irrespective of the model) might bear equally. ABC, it is claimed, leads to more accurate costing and thus to more accurate assessment of profitability.

(d) The other advantage of pursuing an ABC philosophy and identifying cost drivers is that, once the drivers have been identified, they are likely to become much more susceptible to being controlled. Thus the ability of management to assess the benefit of certain activities against their cost becomes more feasible.

5.6   **GB Company – the International Industries (II) enquiry**

(a) The minimum acceptable price of 120,000 motors to be supplied over the next four months is:

	£000	
Direct materials	600	(120,000 × £5.00)
Direct labour	720	(120,000 × £6.00)
Variable manufacturing overheads	360	(120,000 × £3.00 (that is, £3.00 for half an hour))
Fixed manufacturing overheads	60	(4 × £15,000)
Total	1,740	

The offer price is:

$$120,000 \times £19.00 = £2,280,000$$

On this basis, the price of £19 per machine could be accepted, subject to a number of factors identified in (b) below.

(b) The assumptions on which the above analysis and decision in (a) are based include the following:

- That the contract can be accommodated within the 30 per cent spare capacity of GB. If this is not so, then there will be an opportunity cost relating to lost 'normal' production, which must be taken account of in the decision.
- That sales commission and freight costs will not be affected by the contract.
- It is unlikely that work more remunerative to GB than the contract will be available during the period of the contract.

There are also some strategic issues involved in the decision, including:

- The possibility that the contract could lead to other and better remunerated work from II.
- A problem of selling similar products in the same market at different prices. Other customers, knowing that GB is selling at marginal prices, may make it difficult for the business to resist demand from other customers for similarly priced output.

5.7   **Sillycon Ltd**

(a)   **Overhead analysis**

	Electronics £000	Testing £000	Service £000
Variable overheads	1,200	600	700
Apportionment of service dept (800:600)	400	300	(700)
	1,600	900	–
Direct labour hours ('000)	800	600	
Variable overheads per direct labour hour	£2.00	£1.50	

		Electronics £000	Testing £000	Service £000
Fixed overheads		2,000	500	800
Apportionment of service dept (equally)		400	400	(800)
		2,400	900	–
Direct labour hours		800	600	
Fixed overheads per direct labour hour		£3.00	£1.50	

Product cost (per unit)

		£	
Direct materials		7.00	
Direct labour:	electronics	40.00	(4 × £10.00)
	testing	18.00	(3 × £6.00)
Variable overheads:	electronics	8.00	(4 × £2.00)
	testing	4.50	(3 × £1.50)
Total variable cost		77.50	(assuming direct labour to be variable)
Fixed overheads:	electronics	12.00	(4 × £3.00)
	testing	4.50	(3 × £1.50)
Total 'full' cost		94.00	
Add Mark-up, say 30%		28.20	
		122.20	

On the basis of the above, the business could hope to compete in the market at a price that reflects normal pricing practice.

(b) At this price, and only taking account of incremental fixed overheads, the break-even point (BEP) would be given by:

$$\text{BEP} = \frac{\text{Fixed costs}}{\text{Contribution per unit}} = \frac{£150,000*}{£122.20 - £77.50} = 3,356 \text{ units}$$

* (£13,000 + £100,000 + £37,000) namely the costs specifically incurred.

As the potential market for the business is around 5,000 to 6,000 units a year, the new product looks viable.

Chapter 6

6.3 Nursing Home

(a) The rates per patient for the variable overheads, on the basis of experience during months 1 to 6, are as follows:

Expense	Amount for 2,700 patients £	Amount per patient £
Staffing	59,400	22
Power	27,000	10
Supplies	54,000	20
Other	8,100	3
	148,500	55

Since the expected level of activity for the full year is 6,000, 3,300 (that is, 6,000 – 2,700) is the expected level of activity for the second six months.

Thus the budget for the second six months will be:

Variable element:	£	
Staffing	72,600	(3,300 × £22)
Power	33,000	(3,300 × £10)
Supplies	66,000	(3,300 × £20)
Other	9,900	(3,300 × £3)
	181,500	(3,300 × £55)

Fixed element:		
Supervision	60,000 ⎫	
Depreciation/finance	93,600 ⎬ 6/12 of the values given in the question	
Other	32,400 ⎭	
	186,000 (per patient = £56.36 (£186,000/3,300))	
Total (second six months)	367,500 (per patient = £111.36 (£56.36 + £55.00))	

(b) For the second six months the actual activity was 3,800 patients. For a valid comparison with the actual outcome, the budget will need to be revised to reflect this activity.

	Actual costs	Budget (3,800 patients)	Difference
	£	£	£
Variable element	203,300	209,000 (3,800 × £55)	5,700 (saving)
Fixed element	190,000	186,000	4,000 (overspend)
Total	393,300	395,000	1,700 (saving)

(c) Relative to the budget, there was a saving of nearly 3 per cent on the variable element and an overspend of about 2 per cent on fixed costs. Without further information, it is impossible to deduce much more than this.

The differences between the budget and the actual may be caused by some assumptions made in framing the budget for 3,800 patients in the second part of the year. There may be some element of economies of scale in the variable costs; that is, the costs may not be strictly linear. If this were the case, basing a relatively large activity budget on the experience of a relatively small activity period would tend to overstate the large activity budget. The fixed-cost budget was deduced by dividing the budget for twelve months by two. In fact, there could be seasonal factors or inflationary pressures at work that might make such a crude division of the fixed cost element unfair.

6.4 Linpet Ltd

(a) Cash budgets are extremely useful for decision-making purposes. They allow managers to see the likely effect on the cash balance of the plans that they have set in place. Cash is an important asset and it is necessary to ensure that it is properly managed. Failure to do so can have disastrous consequences for the business. Where the cash budget indicates a surplus balance, managers must decide whether this balance should be reinvested in the business or distributed to the owners. Where the cash budget indicates a deficit balance, managers must decide how this deficit should be financed or how it might be avoided.

(b) Cash budget to 30 November

	June £	July £	Aug £	Sept £	Oct £	Nov £
Receipts						
Cash sales						
(note 1)	4,000	5,500	7,000	8,500	11,000	11,000
Credit sales						
(note 2)	–	–	4,000	5,500	7,000	8,500
	4,000	5,500	11,000	14,000	18,000	19,500
Payments						
Purchases						
(note 3)	–	29,000	9,250	11,500	13,750	17,500
Overheads	500	500	500	500	650	650
Wages	900	900	900	900	900	900
Commission						
(note 4)	–	320	440	560	680	880
Equipment	10,000					7,000
Motor vehicle	6,000					
Leasehold	40,000					
	57,400	30,720	11,090	13,460	15,980	26,930
Cash flow	(53,400)	(25,220)	(90)	540	2,020	(7,430)
Opening bal.	60,000	6,600	(18,620)	(18,710)	(18,170)	(16,150)
Closing bal.	6,600	(18,620)	(18,710)	(18,170)	(16,150)	(23,580)

Notes:

1 50 per cent of the current month's sales.
2 50 per cent of sales of two months previous.
3 To have sufficient stock to meet each month's sales will require purchases of 75 per cent of the month's sales figures (25 per cent is profit). In addition, each month the business will buy £1,000 more stock than it will sell. In June, the business will also buy its initial stock of £22,000. This will be paid for in the following month. For example, June's purchases will be (75% × £8,000) + £1,000 + £22,000 = £29,000, paid for in July.
4 This is 5 per cent of 80 per cent of the month's sales, paid in the following month. For example, June's commission will be 5% × 80% × £8,000 = £320, payable in July.

6.5 Lewisham Ltd

(a) The finished goods stock (inventory) budget for the three months ending 30 September (in units of production) is:

	July '000 units	Aug '000 units	Sept '000 units
Opening stock (note 1)	40	48	40
Production (note 2)	188	232	196
	228	280	236
Less Sales (note 3)	180	240	200
Closing stock	48	40	36

(b) The raw materials stock (inventory) budget for the two months ending 31 August (in kg) is:

	July '000 kg	Aug '000 kg
Opening stock (note 1)	40	58
Purchases (note 2)	112	107
	152	165
Less Production (note 4)	94	116
Closing stock	58	49

(c) The cash budget for the two months ending 30 September is:

	Aug £	Sept £
Inflows		
Debtors – Current month (note 5)	493,920	411,600
Preceding month (note 6)	151,200	201,600
Total inflows	645,120	613,200
Outflows		
Payments to creditors (note 7)	168,000	160,500
Labour and overheads (note 4)	185,600	156,800
Fixed overheads	22,000	22,000
Total outflows	375,600	339,300
Net inflows/(outflows)	269,520	273,900
Balance c/f	289,520	563,420

Notes:

1 The opening balance is the same as the closing balance from the previous month.
2 This is a balancing figure.
3 This figure is given in the question.
4 This figure derives from the finished stock budget.
5 This is 98 per cent of 70 per cent of the current month's sales revenue.
6 This is 28 per cent of the previous month's sales.
7 This figure derives from the raw materials stock budget.

6.6 Newtake records

(a) The cash budget for the period to 30 November is:

	June £000	July £000	Aug £000	Sept £000	Oct £000	Nov £000
Cash receipts						
Sales (Note 1)	227	315	246	138	118	108
Cash payments						
Administration (Note 2)	(40)	(41)	(38)	(33)	(31)	(30)
Goods purchased	(135)	(180)	(142)	(94)	(75)	(66)
Loan repayments	(5)	(5)	(5)	(5)	(5)	(5)
Selling expenses	(22)	(24)	(28)	(26)	(21)	(19)
Tax paid			(22)			
Shop refurbishment	—	(14)	(18)	(6)	—	—
	(202)	(264)	(253)	(164)	(132)	(120)
Cash surplus (deficit)	25	51	(7)	(26)	(14)	(12)
Opening balance	(35)	(10)	41	34	8	(6)
Closing balance	(10)	41	34	8	(6)	(18)

Notes:
1 (50% of the current month's sales) + (97% × 50% of that sales revenue). For example, the June cash receipts = (50% × £230,000) + (97% × 50% × £230,000) = £226,550.
2 The administration expenses figure for the month, *less* £15,000 for depreciation (a non-cash expense).

(b) The stock (inventory) budget for the six months to 30 November is:

	June £000	July £000	Aug £000	Sept £000	Oct £000	Nov £000
Opening balance	112	154	104	48	39	33
Stock purchased	180	142	94	75	66	57
	292	296	198	123	105	90
Cost of stocks sold						
(60% sales)	(138)	(192)	(150)	(84)	(72)	(66)
Closing balance	154	104	48	39	33	24

(c) The budgeted profit and loss account (income statement) for the six months ending 30 November is:

	£000	£000
Sales turnover		1,170
Less Cost of goods sold		702
Gross profit		468
Selling expenses	(136)	
Admin. expenses	(303)	
Credit card charges	(18)	
Interest charges	(6)	(463)
Net profit for the period		5

(d) We are told that the business is required to eliminate the bank overdraft by the end of November. However, the cash budget reveals that this will not be achieved. There is a decline in the overdraft of nearly 50 per cent over the period, but this is not enough and ways must be found to comply with the bank's requirements. It may be possible to delay the refurbishment programme that is included in the forecasts or to obtain an injection of funds from the owners or other investors. It may also be possible to stimulate sales in some way. However, there has been a decline in the sales since the end of July and the November sales are approximately one third of the July sales. The reasons for this decline should be sought.

The stock levels will fall below the preferred minimum level for each of the last three months. However, to rectify this situation it will be necessary to purchase more stock, which will, in turn, exacerbate the cash flow problems of the business.

The budgeted profit and loss account (income statement) reveals a very low net profit for the period. For every £1 of sales, the business is only managing to generate 0.4p in profit. The business should look carefully at its pricing policies and its overhead expenses. The administration expenses, for example, absorb more than one-quarter of the total sales turnover. Any reduction in overhead expenses will have a beneficial effect on cash flows.

6.7   Prolog Ltd

(a) Cash budget for the six months to 30 June

	Jan £000	Feb £000	Mar £000	Apr £000	May £000	June £000
Receipts						
Credit sales (Note 1)	100	100	140	180	220	260
Payments						
Trade creditors (Note 2)	112	144	176	208	240	272
Operating expenses	4	6	8	10	10	10
Shelving				12		
Taxation			25			
	116	150	209	230	250	282
Cash flow	(16)	(50)	(69)	(50)	(30)	(22)
Opening balance	(68)	(84)	(134)	(203)	(253)	(283)
Closing balance	(84)	(134)	(203)	(253)	(283)	(305)

Notes:

1 Sales receipts will equal the month's sales, but be received two months later. For example, the January sales revenue = £2,000 × (50 + 20) = £140,000, to be received in March.

2 Creditor payments will equal the next month's sales requirements, payable the next month. For example, January purchases = £1,600 × (50 + 40) = £144,000, payable in February.

(b) A banker may require various pieces of information before granting additional overdraft facilities. These may include:

● Security available for the loan.
● Details of past profit performance.
● Profit projections for the next 12 months.
● Cash projections beyond the next six months to help assess the prospects of repayment.
● Details of the assumptions underlying projected figures supplied.
● Details of the contractual commitment between Prolog Ltd and its supplier.
● Details of management expertise. Can they manage the expansion programme?
● Details of new machine and its performance in relation to competing models.
● Details of funds available from owners to finance the expansion.

Chapter 7

7.1 (a) A favourable direct labour rate variance can only be caused by something that leads to the rate per hour paid being less than standard. Normally, this would not be linked to efficient working. Where, however, the standard envisaged some overtime working, at premium rates, the actual labour rate may be below standard if efficiency has removed the need for the overtime.

(b) The statement is true. The action will lead to an adverse sales price variance and may well lead to problems elsewhere, but the sales volume variance must be favourable.

(c) It is true that below-standard materials could lead to adverse materials usage variances because there may be more than a standard amount of scrap. This could also cause adverse labour efficiency variances because working on materials that would not form part of the output would waste labour time.

(d) Higher-than-budgeted sales could well lead to an adverse labour rate variance because producing the additional work may require overtime working at premium rates.

(e) The statement is true. Nothing else could cause such a variance.

7.2 **Pilot Ltd**

(a) and (b)

	Budget			Actual	
	Original	Flexed			
Output (units) (production and sales)	5,000	5,400		5,400	
	£	£		£	
Sales	25,000	27,000		26,460	
Raw materials	(7,500)	(8,100)	(2,700 kg)	(8,770)	(2,830 kg)
Labour	(6,250)	(6,750)	(1,350 hr)	(6,885)	(1,300 hr)
Fixed overheads	(6,000)	(6,000)		(6,350)	
Operating profit	5,250	6,150		4,455	

	£		Manager accountable
Sales volume variance (5,250 – 6,150)	900	(F)	Sales
Sales price variance (27,000 – 26,460)	(540)	(A)	Sales
Materials price variance (2,830 × 3) – 8,770	(280)	(A)	Buyer
Materials usage variance [(5,400 × 0.5) – 2,830] × £3	(390)	(A)	Production
Labour rate variance (1,300 × £5) – 6,885	(385)	(A)	Personnel
Labour efficiency variance [(5,400 × 0.25) – 1,300] × £5	250	(F)	Production
Fixed overhead spending (6,000 – 6,350)	(350)	(A)	Various – depends on the nature of the overheads
Total net variances	(795)	(A)	

Budgeted profit	£5,250
Less Total net variance	(795)
Actual profit	£4,455

7.4 (a) Flexing the budget identifies what the profit would have been, had the only difference between the original budget and the actual figures been concerned with the difference in volume of output. Comparing this profit figure with that in the original budget reveals the profit difference (variance) arising solely from the volume difference (sales volume variance). Thus, flexing the budget does not mean at all that volume differences do not matter. Flexing the budget is the means of discovering the effect on profit of the volume difference.

In one sense, all variances are 'water under the bridge', to the extent that the past cannot be undone, and so it is impossible to go back to the last control period and put in a better performance. Identifying variances can, however, be useful in identifying where things went wrong, which should enable management to take steps to ensure that the same things do not to go wrong in the future.

(b) Variances will not tell you what went wrong. They should, however, be a great help in identifying the manager within whose sphere of responsibility things went wrong. That manager should know why it went wrong. In this sense, variances identify relevant questions, but not answers.

(c) Identifying the reason for variances may well cost money, usually in terms of staff time. It is a matter of judgement in any particular situation, of balancing the cost of investigation against the potential benefits. As is usual in such judgements, it is difficult, before undertaking the investigation, to know either the cost or the likely benefit.

In general, significant variances, particularly adverse ones, should be investigated. Persistent (over a period of months) smaller variances should also be investigated. It should not automatically be assumed that favourable variances can be ignored. They indicate that things are not going according to plan, possibly because the plans (budgets) are flawed.

(d) Research evidence does not show this. It seems to show that managers tend to be most motivated by having as a target the most difficult goals that they find acceptable.

(e) Budgets normally provide the basis of feedforward and feedback control. During a budget preparation period, potential problems (for example a potential stock shortage) might be revealed. Steps can then be taken to revise the plans in order to avoid the potential problem. This is an example of a feedforward control: potential problems are anticipated and eliminated before they can occur.

Budgetary control is a very good example of feedback control, where a signal that something is going wrong triggers steps to take corrective action for the future.

7.5 Bradley-Allen Ltd

(a)

	Budget			Actual	
	Original	Flexed			
Output (units) (production and sales)	800	950		950	
	£	£		£	
Sales	64,000	76,000		73,000	
Raw materials – A	(12,000)	(14,250)	(285 kg)	(15,200)	(310 kg)
– B	(16,000)	(19,000)	(950 m)	(18,900)	(920 m)
Labour – skilled	(4,000)	(4,750)	(475 hr)	(4,628)	(445 hr)
– unskilled	(10,000)	(11,875)	(1,484.375 hr)	(11,275)	(1,375 hr)
Fixed overheads	(12,000)	(12,000)		(11,960)	
Operating profit	10,000	14,125		11,037	

Sales variances

Volume:	$10,000 - 14,125 = £4,125$ (F)
Price:	$76,000 - 73,000 = £3,000$ (A)

Direct materials A variances

Usage:	$[(950 \times 0.3) - 310] \times £50 = £1,250$ (A)
Price:	$(310 \times £50) - £15,200 = £300$ (F)

Direct materials B variances

Usage:	$[(950 \times 1) - 920] \times £20 = £600$ (F)
Price:	$(920 \times £20) - £18,900 = £500$ (A)

Skilled direct labour variances

Efficiency:	$[(950 \times 0.5) - 445] \times £10 = £300$ (F)
Rate:	$(445 \times £10) - £4,628 = £178$ (A)

Unskilled direct labour variances

Efficiency:	$[(950 \times 1.5625) - 1,375] \times £8 = £875$ (F)
Rate:	$(1,375 \times £8) - £11,275 = £275$ (A)

Fixed overhead variances

Spending:	$(12,000 - 11,960) = £40$ (F)

Budgeted profit				£10,000
Sales:	Volume	4,125	(F)	
	Price	(3,000)	(A)	1,125
Direct material A:	Usage	(1,250)	(A)	
	Price	300	(F)	(950)
Direct material B:	Usage	600	(F)	
	Price	(500)	(A)	100
Skilled labour:	Efficiency	300	(F)	
	Rate	(178)	(A)	122
Unskilled labour:	Efficiency	875	(F)	
	Rate	(275)	(A)	600
Fixed overheads:	Expenditure			40
Actual profit				**£11,037**

(b) The statement in (a) is useful to management because it enables them to see where there have been failures to meet the original budget and to quantify the extent of such failures. This means that junior managers can be held accountable for the performance of their particular area of responsibility.

7.7 Varne Chemprocessors

(a) The standard usage rate of UK194 (per litre of Varnelyne) is $200/5,000 = 0.04$.

The standard price = $£392/200 = £1.96$ per litre of UK194.

Materials usage variance (UK194) is:

$$[(637,500 \times 0.04) - 28,100] \times £1.96 = £5,096 \text{ (A)}$$

Materials price variance is:

$$(28,100 \times £1.96) - £51,704 = £3,372 \text{ (F)}$$

(b) The net variance on UK194 was, from the calculations in (a), £1,724 (A) (that is £5,096 – £3,372). This seems to have led directly to savings elsewhere of £4,900, giving a net cost saving of over £3,000 for the month.

Unfortunately things may not be quite as simple as the numbers suggest. Will the non-standard mix to make the Varnelyne lead to a substandard product, which could have very wide-ranging ramifications in terms of potential loss of market goodwill?

There is also the possibility that the material for which the UK194 was used as a substitute was already in stock. If this were the case, is there any danger that this material may deteriorate and, ultimately, prove to be unusable?

Other possible adverse outcomes of the non-standard mix could also arise.

The question is raised by the analysis in part (a) (and by the production manager's comment) of why the cost standard for UK194 had not been revised to take account of the lower price prevailing in the market.

(c) The variances, period by period and cumulatively, for each of the two materials are given as follows:

| | UK500 | | UK800 | |
| | Period | Cumulative | Period | Cumulative |
Period	£	£	£	£
1	301 (F)	301 (F)	298 (F)	298 (F)
2	(251) (A)	50 (F)	203 (F)	501 (F)
3	102 (F)	152 (F)	(52) (A)	449 (F)
4	(202) (A)	(50) (A)	(98) (A)	351 (F)
5	153 (F)	103 (F)	(150) (A)	201 (F)
6	(103) (A)	zero	(201) (A)	zero

Without knowing the scale of these variances relative to the actual costs involved, it is not possible to be too dogmatic about how to interpret the above information.

UK500 appears to show a fairly random set of data, with the period variances fluctuating from positive to negative and giving a net variance of zero. This is what would be expected from a situation that is basically under control.

UK800 also shows a zero cumulative figure over the six periods, *but* there seems to be a more systematic train of events, particularly the four consecutive adverse variances from period 3 onwards. This looks as if it may be out of control and worthy of investigation.

Chapter 8

8.1   Mylo Ltd

(a) The annual depreciation of the two projects is:

$$\text{Project 1: } \frac{(£100,000 - £7,000)}{3} = £31,000$$

$$\text{Project 2: } \frac{(£60,000 - £6,000)}{3} = £18,000$$

Project 1

(i)

	Year 0 £000	Year 1 £000	Year 2 £000	Year 3 £000
Net profit(loss)		29	(1)	2
Depreciation		31	31	31
Capital cost	(100)			
Residual value				7
Net cash flows	(100)	60	30	40
10% discount factor	1.000	0.909	0.826	0.751
Present value	(100.00)	54.54	24.78	30.04
Net present value	9.36			

(ii) Clearly the IRR lies above 10 per cent; try 15 per cent:

15% discount factor	1.000	0.870	0.756	0.658
Present value	(100.00)	52.20	22.68	26.32
Net present value	1.20			

Thus the IRR lies a little above 15 per cent, perhaps around 16 per cent.

(iii) To find the payback period, the cumulative cash flows are calculated:

Cumulative cash flows	(100)	(40)	(10)	30

Thus the payback will occur after about 3 years if we assume year-end cash flows.

Project 2

(i)

	Year 0 £000	Year 1 £000	Year 2 £000	Year 3 £000
Net profit(loss)		18	(2)	4
Depreciation		18	18	18
Capital cost	(60)			
Residual value				6
Net cash flows	(60)	36	16	28
10% discount factor	1.000	0.909	0.826	0.751
Present value	(60.00)	32.72	13.22	21.03
Net present value	6.97			

(ii) Clearly the IRR lies above 10 per cent; try 15 per cent:

15% discount factor	1.000	0.870	0.756	0.658
Present value	(60.00)	31.32	12.10	18.42
Net present value	1.84			

Thus the IRR lies a little above 15 per cent; perhaps around 17 per cent.

(iii) The cumulative cash flows are:

Cumulative cash flows	(60)	(24)	(8)	20

Thus, the payback will occur after 3 years (assuming year-end cash flows).

(b) Presuming that Mylo Ltd is pursuing a wealth-maximisation objective, project 1 is preferable since it has the higher NPV. The difference between the two NPVs is not significant, however.

(c) NPV is the preferred method of assessing investment opportunities because it fully addresses each of the following:

- *The timing of the cash flows*   Discounting the various cash flows associated with each project, according to when they are expected to arise, takes account of the fact that cash flows do not all occur simultaneously. Associated with this is the fact that by discounting, using the opportunity cost of finance (namely the return that the next-best alternative opportunity would generate), the net benefit, after financing costs have been met, is identified (as the NPV).
- *The whole of the relevant cash flows*   NPV includes all of the relevant cash flows irrespective of when they are expected to occur. It treats them differently according to their date of occurrence, but they are all taken into account in the calculation of the NPV and they all have, or can have, an influence on the decision.
- *The objectives of the business*   NPV is the only method of appraisal where the output of the analysis has a direct bearing on the wealth of the business. (Positive NPVs enhance wealth; negative NPVs reduce it.) Since most private sector businesses seek to increase their value and wealth, NPV clearly is the best approach to use.

8.5 Newton Electronics Ltd

(a)   Option 1

	Year 0 £m	Year 1 £m	Year 2 £m	Year 3 £m	Year 4 £m	Year 5 £m
Plant and equipment	(9.0)					1.0
Sales		24.0	30.8	39.6	26.4	10.0
Variable costs		(11.2)	(19.6)	(25.2)	(16.8)	(7.0)
Fixed costs (ex. dep'n)		(0.8)	(0.8)	(0.8)	(0.8)	(0.8)
Working capital	(3.0)					3.0
Marketing costs		(2.0)	(2.0)	(2.0)	(2.0)	(2.0)
Opportunity costs		(0.1)	(0.1)	(0.1)	(0.1)	(0.1)
	(12.0)	9.9	8.3	11.5	6.7	4.1
Discount factor 10%	1.000	0.909	0.826	0.751	0.683	0.621
Present value	(12.0)	9.0	6.9	8.6	4.6	2.5
NPV	19.6					

Option 2

	Year 0 £m	Year 1 £m	Year 2 £m	Year 3 £m	Year 4 £m	Year 5 £m
Royalties	–	4.4	7.7	9.9	6.6	2.8
Discount factor 10%	1.000	0.909	0.826	0.751	0.683	0.621
Present value	–	4.0	6.4	7.4	4.5	1.7
NPV	24.0					

Option 3

	Year 0	Year 2
Instalments	12.0	12.0
Discount factor 10%	1.000	0.826
Present value	12.0	9.9
NPV	21.9	

(b) Before making a final decision, the board should consider the following factors:

- The long-term competitiveness of the business may be affected by the sale of the patents.
- At present, the business is not involved in manufacturing and marketing products. Would a change in direction be desirable?
- The business will probably have to buy in the skills necessary to produce the product itself. This will involve costs, and problems will be incurred. Has this been taken into account?
- How accurate are the forecasts made and how valid are the assumptions on which they are based?

(c) Option 2 has the highest NPV and is therefore the most attractive to shareholders. However, the accuracy of the forecasts should be checked before a final decision is made.

8.6 Chesterfield Wanderers

(a) and (b)

Player option

	0 £000	1 £000	2 £000	3 £000	4 £000	5 £000
Sale of player	2,200					1,000
Purchase of Bazza	(10,000)					
Sponsorship and so on		1,200	1,200	1,200	1,200	1,200
Gate receipts		2,500	1,300	1,300	1,300	1,300
Salaries paid		(800)	(800)	(800)	(800)	(1,200)
Salaries saved		400	400	400	400	600
Net cash received (paid)	(7,800)	3,300	2,100	2,100	2,100	2,900
Discount factor 10%	1.000	0.909	0.826	0.751	0.683	0.621
Present values	(7,800)	3,000	1,735	1,577	1,434	1,801
NPV	1,747					

Ground improvement option

	1 £000	2 £000	3 £000	4 £000	5 £000
Ground improvements	(10,000)				
Increased gate receipts	(1,800)	4,400	4,400	4,400	4,400
	(11,800)	4,400	4,400	4,400	4,400
Discount factor 10%	0.909	0.826	0.751	0.683	0.621
Present values	(10,726)	3,634	3,304	3,005	2,732
NPV	1,949				

(c) The ground improvement option provides the higher NPV and is therefore the preferable option, based on the objective of shareholder wealth maximisation.

(d) A professional football club may not wish to pursue an objective of shareholder wealth maximisation. It may prefer to invest in quality players in an attempt to enjoy future sporting success. If this is the case, the NPV approach will be less appropriate because the club is not pursuing a strict wealth-maximisation objective.

8.7 Simtex Ltd

(a) Net operating cash flows each year will be:

	£000	£000
Sales (160 × £6)		960
Less		
Variable costs (160 × £4)	640	
Relevant fixed costs	170	810
		150

The estimated NPV of the new product can then be calculated:

	£000
Annual cash flows (150 × 3.038*)	456
Residual value of equipment (100 × 0.636)	64
	520
Less Initial outlay	480
Net present value	40

* This is the sum of the discount rates over four years. Where the cash flows are constant, it is a quicker procedure than working out the present value of cash flows for each year and then adding them together.

(b) (i) Assume the discount rate is 18 per cent. The net present value of the project would be:

	£000
Annual cash flows (150 × 2.690)	404
Residual value of equipment (100 × 0.516)	52
	456
Less Initial outlay	480
NPV	(24)

Thus an increase of 6 per cent, from 12 per cent to 18 per cent, in the discount rate causes a fall from +40 to –24 in the NPV, a fall of 64, or 10.67 (that is, 64/6) for each 1 per cent rise in the discount rate. So a zero NPV will occur with a discount rate approximately equal to 12 + (40/11.67) = 15.4%. (This is, of course, the IRR.)

This higher discount rate represents an increase of about 28 per cent on the existing cost of capital figure.

(ii) The initial outlay on equipment is already expressed in present-value terms and so, to make the project no longer viable, the outlay will have to increase by an amount equal to the NPV of the project (that is, £40,000) – an increase of 8.3 per cent on the stated initial outlay.

(iii) The change necessary in the annual net cash flows to make the project no longer profitable can be calculated as follows:

Let Y = change in the annual operating cash flows. Then:

$$(Y \times \text{cumulative discount rates for a four-year period}) - \text{NPV} = 0$$

This can be rearranged as:

$$Y \times \text{cumulative discount rates for a four-year period} = \text{NPV}$$
$$Y \times 3.038 = £40,000$$
$$Y = £40,000/3.038$$
$$Y = \underline{£13,167}$$

In percentage terms, this is a decrease of 8.8 per cent on the estimated cash flows.

(iv) The change in the residual value required to make the new product no longer profitable can be calculated as follows:

Let V = change in the residual value. Then:

$$(V \times \text{discount factor at end of four years}) - \text{NPV of product} = 0$$

This can be rearranged as follows:

$$V \times \text{discount factor at end of four years} = \text{NPV of product}$$
$$V \times 0.636 = £40,000$$
$$V = £40,000/0.636$$
$$V = \underline{£62,893}$$

This is a decrease of 63.9 per cent in the residual value of the equipment.

(c) The NPV of the product is positive and so it will increase shareholder wealth. Thus, it should be produced. The sensitivity analysis suggests the initial outlay and the annual cash flows are the most sensitive variables for managers to consider.

8.8 **Kernow Cleaning Services Ltd**

(a) The first step is to calculate the expected annual cash flows:

Year 1	£	Year 2	£
£ 80,000 × 0.3	24,000	£140,000 × 0.4	56,000
£160,000 × 0.5	80,000	£220,000 × 0.4	88,000
£200,000 × 0.2	40,000	£250,000 × 0.2	50,000
	144,000		194,000

Year 3		Year 4	
£140,000 × 0.4	56,000	£100,000 × 0.3	30,000
£200,000 × 0.3	60,000	£170,000 × 0.6	102,000
£230,000 × 0.3	69,000	£200,000 × 0.1	20,000
	185,000		152,000

The *expected net present value (ENPV)* can now be calculated as follows:

Period	Expected cash flow £	Discount rate 10%	Expected PV £
0	(540,000)	1.000	(540,000)
1	144,000	0.909	130,896
2	194,000	0.826	160,244
3	185,000	0.751	138,935
4	152,000	0.683	103,816
ENPV			(6,109)

(b) The *worst possible outcome* can be calculated by taking the lowest values of savings each year, as follows:

Period	Cash flow £	Discount rate 10%	PV £
0	(540,000)	1.000	(540,000)
1	80,000	0.909	72,720
2	140,000	0.826	115,640
3	140,000	0.751	105,140
4	100,000	0.683	68,300
NPV			(178,200)

The probability of occurrence can be obtained by multiplying together the probability of *each* of the worst outcomes above, that is $0.3 \times 0.4 \times 0.4 \times 0.3 = \underline{0.014}$.

Thus, the probability of occurrence is 1.4%, which is very low.

Chapter 9

9.1 **Hercules Wholesalers Ltd**

(a) The operating cash cycle can be calculated as follows:

No. of days

Average stockholding period:

$$\frac{[(\text{Opening stock} + \text{Closing stock})/2] \times 360}{\text{Cost of sales}} = \frac{[(125 + 143)/2] \times 360}{323} = 149$$

Add Average settlement period for debtors:

$$\frac{\text{Trade debtors} \times 360}{\text{Credit sales}} = \frac{163}{452} \times 360 \qquad = \underline{130}$$

$$= 279$$

Less Average settlement period for creditors:

$$\frac{\text{Trade creditor} \times 360}{\text{Credit purchases}} = \frac{145}{341} \times 360 \qquad = \underline{153}$$

$$= \underline{126}$$

(b) The business can reduce the operating cash cycle in a number of ways. The average stock-holding period seems quite long. At present, average stocks held represent almost five months' sales. This period can be reduced by reducing the level of stocks held. Similarly, the average settlement period for debtors seems long at more than four months' sales. This may be reduced by imposing tighter credit control, offering discounts, charging interest on overdue accounts, and so on. However, any policy decisions concerning stocks (inventories) and debtors (receivables) must take account of current trading conditions.

The operating cash cycle would also be reduced by extending the period of credit taken to pay suppliers. However, for the reasons mentioned in the chapter, this option must be given careful consideration.

9.5

Mayo Computers Ltd
New proposals from credit control department

	£000	£000
Current level of investment in debtors (receivables)		
(£20m × (60/365))		3,288
Proposed level of investment in debtors		
((£20m × 60%) × (30/365))	(986)	
((£20m × 40%) × (50/365))	(1,096)	(2,082)
Reduction in level of investment		1,206

The reduction in overdraft interest as a result of the reduction in the level of investment will be £1,206,000 × 14% = £169,000.

	£000	£000
Cost of cash discounts offered (£20m × 60% × $2^{1}/_{2}$%)		300
Additional cost of credit administration		20
		320
Bad debt savings	(100)	
Interest charge savings (see above)	(169)	(269)
Net cost of policy each year		51

These calculations show that the business would incur additional annual costs if it implemented this proposal. It would therefore be cheaper to stay with the existing credit policy.

9.6 **Boswell Enterprises Ltd**

(a)

	Current policy		New policy	
	£000	£000	£000	£000
Debtors (receivables)				
[(£3m × 1/12 × 30%) + (£3m × 2/12 × 70%)]		425.0		
[(£3.15m × 1/12 × 60%) + (£3.15m × 2/12 × 40%)]				367.5
Stocks (inventories)				
[£3m − (£3m × 20%)] × 3/12]		600.0		
{[£3.15m − (£3.15m × 20%)] × 3/12}				630.0
Cash (fixed)		140.0		140.0
		1,165.0		1,137.5
Creditors (payables)				
[£3m − (£3m × 20%)] × 2/12]	(400.0)			
{[£3.15m − (£3.15m × 20%)] × 2/12}			(420.0)	
Accrued variable expenses				
[£3m × 1/12 × 10%]	(25.0)			
[£3.15m × 1/12 × 10%]			(26.3)	
Accrued fixed expenses	(15.0)	(440.0)	(15.0)	(461.3)
Investment in working capital		725.0		676.2

(b) The forecast net profit for the year

	Current policy		New policy	
	£000	£000	£000	£000
Sales		3,000.0		3,150.0
Cost of goods sold		(2,400.0)		(2,520.0)
Gross profit (20%)		600.0		630.0
Variable expenses (10%)	(300.0)		(315.0)	
Fixed expenses	(180.0)		(180.0)	
Discounts	–	(480.0)	(47.3)	(542.3)
Net profit		120.0		87.7

(c) Under the proposed policy we can see that the investment in working capital will be slightly lower than under the current policy. However, profits will be substantially lower as a result of offering discounts. The increase in sales resulting from the discounts will not be sufficient to offset the additional costs of making the discounts to customers. It seems that the business should, therefore, stick with its current policy.

9.7   Delphi plc

(a) The debtors ageing schedule is:

	Number of months outstanding							
	1 month or less £000	%	1 to 2 months £000	%	2 to 3 months £000	%	Total debtors £000	%
February								
TV and hi-fi	20.0	(22.2)					20.0	(22.2)
Music	30.0	(33.3)					30.0	(33.3)
Retail	40.0	(44.5)					40.0	(44.5)
	90.0	(100.0)					90.0	(100.0)
March								
TV and hi-fi	20.8	(12.5)					20.8	(12.5)
Music	31.8	(19.2)	30.0	(18.1)			61.8	(37.3)
Retail	43.2	(26.1)	40.0	(24.1)	—	—	83.2	(50.2)
	95.8	(57.8)	70.0	(42.2)	—	—	165.8	(100.0)
April								
TV and hi-fi	21.6	(10.0)					21.6	(10.0)
Music	33.7	(15.6)	31.8	(14.7)			65.5	(30.3)
Retail	46.7	(21.4)	43.2	(19.9)	40.0	(18.4)	129.9	(59.7)
	102.0	(47.0)	75.0	(34.6)	40.0	(18.4)	217.0	(100.0)
May								
TV and hi-fi	22.5	(9.6)					22.5	(9.6)
Music	35.7	(15.4)	33.7	(14.6)			69.6	(30.0)
Retail	50.4	(21.7)	46.7	(20.1)	43.2	(18.6)	140.2	(60.4)
	108.6	(46.7)	80.4	(34.7)	43.2	(18.6)	232.3	(100.0)

We can see that the debtors figure will increase substantially in the first four months. The retail chains will account for about 60 per cent of the total debtors outstanding by May as this group has the fastest rate of growth. There is also a significant decline in the proportion of total debts outstanding from TV and hi-fi shops over this period.

(b) In answering this part of the question, you should refer to the 'five Cs of credit' that were discussed in detail in the chapter.

9.8 Goliath plc

(a) (i) The existing operating cash cycle can be calculated as follows:

	Number of days
Stockholding period $= \dfrac{\text{Stock at year end}}{\text{Cost of sales}} \times 365$	
$= \dfrac{560}{1{,}440} \times 365 =$	142
Add Debtors settlement period $= \dfrac{\text{Debtors at year end}}{\text{Sales}} \times 365$	
$= \dfrac{565}{2{,}400} \times 365 =$	86
	228
Less Creditors settlement period $= \dfrac{\text{Creditors at year end}}{\text{Purchases}} \times 365$	
$= \dfrac{451}{1{,}450} \times 365 =$	(114)
Operating cash cycle	114

The new operating cash cycle is:

	Number of days
Stockholding period $= \dfrac{(560 \times 1.15)}{(2{,}400 \times 1.10) \times 0.60} \times 365 =$	148
Debtors settlement period $= 86 + 20$	106
	254
Less Creditors settlement period $= 114 + 15$	(129)
	125
New operating cash cycle	125
Existing operating cash cycle	(114)
Increase in operating cash cycle (days)	11

(ii)

	£000
Increase (decrease) in stock held [(560 × 1.15) – 560]	84.0
Increase (decrease) in debtors {[(2,400 × 1.1) × (106/365)] – 565}	201.7
	285.7
(Increase) decrease in creditors [1,668 × (129/365) – 451]	(138.6)
Increase (decrease) in net investment	147.1

(iii)

	£000	£000
Gross profit increase [(2,400 × 0.1) × 0.40]		96.0
Adjust for		
Admin. expenses increase (15%)	(45.0)	
Bad debts increase	(120.0)	
Interest (10%) on borrowing for increased net investment in working capital (147.1)	(14.7)	(179.7)
Increase (decrease) in net profit before tax		(83.7)
Decrease in tax charge for the period (25% × 83.7)		20.9
Increase (decrease) in net profit after tax		(62.8)

(b) There would be an increase in the operating cash cycle and this will have an adverse effect on liquidity. The existing debtors and stockholding periods already appear to be quite high. Any increase in either of these must be justified. The planned increase in the creditors (payables) period must also be justified because it may risk the loss of goodwill from suppliers. Though there is an expected increase in turnover of £240,000 from adopting the new policy, the net profit after taxation will decrease by £62,800. This represents a substantial decrease when compared with the previous year. (The increase in bad debts is a major reason why the net profit is adversely affected.) There is also a substantial increase in the net investment in stocks (inventories), debtors (receivables) and creditors (payables), which seem high in relation to the expected increase in sales. The new policy requires a significant increase in investment and is expected to generate lower profits than are currently being enjoyed. It should, therefore, be rejected.

Chapter 10

10.1 (a) A divisional organisation is one which divides itself into operating units in order to deliver its range of products or services. Divisionalisation is, in essence, an attempt to deal with the problems of size and complexity.

Autonomy of action relates to the amount of discretion the managers of divisions have been given by central management over the operations of the division. Two popular forms of autonomy are profit centres and investment centres. Though divisionalisation usually leads to decentralisation of decision making, this need not necessarily be the case.

(b) The benefits of allowing divisional managers autonomy include:

- Better use of market information.
- Increase in management motivation.
- Providing opportunities for management development.
- Making full use of specialist knowledge.
- Giving central managers time to focus on strategic issues.
- Permitting a more rapid response to changes in market conditions.

(c) There are certain problems with this approach which include:

- Goal conflict between divisions or between divisions and central management.
- Risk avoidance on the part of divisional managers.
- The growth of management 'perks'.
- Increasing costs due to inability to benefit from economies of scale.

Transfers between divisions can create problems for a business. Managers of the selling division may wish to obtain a high price for the transfers in an attempt to achieve certain profit objectives. However, the managers of the purchasing division may wish to buy as cheaply as possible in order to achieve their own profit objectives. This can create conflict and central managers may find that they are spending time arbitrating disputes. It may be necessary for central managers to impose a solution on the divisions where agreement cannot be reached which will, of course, undermine the divisions' autonomy.

10.2 (a) *Contribution* represents the difference between the total sales of the division and the variable expenses incurred. This is a useful measure for understanding the relationship between costs, output and profit. However, it ignores any fixed expenses incurred and so not all aspects of operating performance are considered.

The *controllable profit* deducts all expenses (variable and fixed) within the control of the divisional manager when arriving at a measure of performance. This is viewed by many as the best measure of performance for divisional managers as they will be in a position to determine the level of expenses incurred. However, in practice, it may be difficult to categorise expenses as being either controllable or non-controllable. This measure also ignores the investment made in assets. For example, a manager may decide to hold very high levels of stock, which may be an inefficient use of resources.

Return on investment (ROI) is a widely used method of evaluating the profitability of divisions. The ratio is calculated in the following way:

$$ROI = \frac{\text{Division profit}}{\text{Divisional investment (assets employed)}} \times 100\%$$

The ratio is seen as capturing many of the dimensions of running a division.

When defining divisional profit for this ratio, the purpose for which the ratio is to be used must be considered. When evaluating the performance of a divisional manager, the controllable contribution is likely to be the most appropriate, whereas for evaluating the performance of a division, the divisional contribution is likely to be more appropriate. Different definitions can be employed for divisional investment. The net assets or total assets figure may be used. In addition, assets may be shown at original cost or some other basis such as current replacement cost.

(b) There are several non-financial measures available to evaluate a division's performance. Examples of these measures have been cited in the chapter. Further example include:

- Plant capacity utilised
- Percentage of rejects in production runs
- Ratio of customer visits to customer orders
- Number of customers visited.

By using a broad range of financial and non-financial measures covering different time horizons there is a better chance that all of the major dimensions of management and divisional performance will be properly assessed. By focusing on a few short-term financial objectives there is a danger that managers will strive to achieve these at the expense of the longer-term objectives. Clearly, ROI can be increased in the short term by cutting back on discretionary expenditure such as staff training and research and development and by not replacing heavily depreciated assets.

10.4 **ABC Corporation**

(a) (i) Residual income calculation – original plan:

	£000
Sales	1,200
Less Variable costs	800
Contribution	400
Fixed costs	250
Divisional profit	150
Capital charge (£500,000 × 20%)	100
Residual income	50

(ii) Residual income calculation – original plan and option I:

	£000
Sales [(100,000 × £12) + (20,000 × £11)]	1,420
Less Variable costs (120,000 × £8)	960
Contribution	460
Fixed costs [250,000 + (80,000/4)]	270
Divisional profit	190
Capital charge (£580,000 × 20%)	116
Residual income	74

(iii) Residual income calculation – original plan and option II:

	£000
Sales [(80,000 × £12) + (20,000 × £10)]	1,160
Less Variable costs	800
Contribution	360
Fixed costs	250
Divisional profit	110
Capital charge (£500,000 × 20%)	100
Residual income	10

(b) Division A is unlikely to find the price reduction for division B attractive. Division B, on the other hand, will benefit by £40,000 (20,000 × £2) from the price reduction. However, overall, the total profits of the business will be unaffected as the increase in Division B's profits will be cancelled out by the decrease in Division A's profit.

If an outside supplier is used, the profits of the business overall will fall by the amount of the lost contribution (20,000 × (£10 – £8) = £40,000).

Another option would be to allow the outsiders to supply Division B and to use the released production capacity to sell outside customers 20,000 units at £11 per unit. In this way, additional equipment costs would be avoided.

10.5 **Telling Company**

(a) (i)

$$\text{ROI} = \frac{\text{Division profit}}{\text{Divisional investment (assets employed)}} \times 100\%$$

$$= \frac{25,000}{150,000} \times 100\%$$

$$= 16.7\%$$

(ii)

	£
RI = Divisional profit	25,000
Required return 20% × £150,000	30,000
Residual income (loss)	(5,000)

(iii) The results show that the ROI is less than the required return of 20 per cent and the residual income is negative. The results must therefore be considered unsatisfactory.

(b)

	£
Increase in sales (£7.5 × 10,000)	75,000
Increase in variable costs (£6 × 10,000)	60,000
Increase in contribution	15,000
Increase in fixed costs	5,000
Increase in divisional profit	10,000
Increase in cost of capital (20% × £20,000)	4,000
Increase in RI	6,000

(c) Though the divisional profits of Goodman and Sharp will each be affected by a change in the transfer price, the total profits of Telling Co. will be unaffected. The increase in profit occurring in one division will be cancelled out by the decrease in profit in the other division and so the overall effect will be nil.

If the work goes outside, Goodman would lose £20,000 in contribution (that is, 10,000 × £2) and Sharp would gain £8,000 by the reduction in the buying-in price (that is, 10,000 × (£8 − £7.20)). The net effect on the business as a whole will therefore be a loss of £12,000 (that is, £20,000 − £8,000).

10.6 Glasnost plc

(a)

	West £000	East £000
Residual income:		
300 − (2,500 × 10%)	50	
100 − (500 × 10%)		50
Return on investment (ROI):		
Based on net profit		
(250/2,500) × 100%	10%	
(80/500) × 100%		16%
Based on divisional profit		
(300/2,500) × 100%	12%	
(100/500) × 100%		20%
Expenses to sales ratio:		
Direct manufacturing	30%	53%
Indirect manufacturing	22%	12%
Selling and distribution	18%	10%
Central overhead	5%	5%

(b) The ROI ratios indicate that East is the better performing division. However, we are told in the question that East has older plant than West, which has recently modernised its production lines. This difference in the age of the plant is likely to mean that the ROI of East is higher due, at least in part, to the fact that the plant has been substantially written down. Some common base is required for comparison purposes (for example, unadjusted historical cost).

We are told that ROI is used as the basis for evaluating performance. We can see that, whichever measure of ROI is used, the two divisions meet the minimum returns required. If ROI is being used to assess managerial performance then the divisional profit rather than net profit figure should be used in the calculation. This is because the net profit figure is calculated after non-controllable central overheads have been deducted.

The business should consider the use of RI as another measure of divisional performance. This measure reveals the same level of performance for the current year from each division.

The expenses to sales ratios are revealing. West has a lower direct manufacturing cost to sales ratio but a higher indirect manufacturing cost to sales ratio than East. This is consistent with the introduction of modern labour-saving plant.

West has a higher selling expenses to sales ratio than East. This is probably due to the fact that inter-business transfers are minimal whereas for East they represent 50 per cent of total sales.

Chapter 11

11.1 Aires plc

(a) The SVA approach to determining shareholder value will be as follows:

Year	FCF	Discount rate	Present value
	£m	12%	£m
1	28.0*	0.89	24.9
2	28.0	0.80	22.4
3	28.0	0.71	19.9
4	28.0	0.64	17.9
	Total business value		85.1
	Less Loan capital		24.0
	Shareholder value		61.1

* The free cash flows will be the operating profit after tax *plus* the lease depreciation charge (that is, £12.0m + £16m).

(b) The EVA®approach to determining shareholder value will be as follows:

Year	Opening capital invested(C)	Capital charge (12% × C)	Operating profit after tax	EVA®	Discount rate 12%	PV of EVA®
	£m	£m	£m	£m		£m
1	64.0*	7.7	12.0	4.3	0.89	3.8
2	48.0	5.8	12.0	6.2	0.80	5.0
3	32.0	3.8	12.0	8.2	0.71	5.8
4	16.0	1.9	12.0	10.1	0.64	6.5
						21.1
			Opening capital			64.0
						85.1
			Less loan capital			24.0
			Shareholder value			61.1*

11.3 Sharma plc: Analysis of trading with Lopez Ltd during last year

		£
Gross sales revenue	(40,000 × £20)	800,000
Discount allowed	(£800,000 × 5%)	40,000
Manufacturing cost	(40,000 × £12)	480,000
Sales order handling	(22 × £75)	1,650
Delivery costs	(22 × 120 × £1.50)	3,960
Customer sales visits	(30 × £230)	6,900
Credit costs	[(£800,000 − £40,000) × $^2/_{12}$ × 2%]	2,533
		535,043
Net profit from the customer for the year		264,957

11.4 Vitality Ltd

(a) The income statements for the two years are as follows:

	Year 2 £	Year 3 £
Sales	50,000	49,200
Cost of bottles	30,000	34,440
Contribution	20,000	14,760

The change in strategy led to a decline in contributions of £5,240 (that is, £20,000 − £14,760).

(b) This change in contribution can be analysed as follows:

Growth aspect

1 Revenue growth is the effect of the growth in revenues arising from the volume growth: (units sold in Year 3 less units sold in Year 2) × Year 2 selling price per unit = (123,000 − 100,000) × £0.50 = £11,500 (F) (it is 'favourable' because it represents a contribution increase arising from the change in strategy).

2 Cost of growth is the effect on costs of the sales volume growth: (number of bottles for Year 3 less number of bottles in Year 2) × price per bottle in Year 2 = [(123,000 − 100,000)] × £0.30 = £6,900 (A) (it is 'adverse' because it represents a contribution decrease arising from the change in strategy).

		£
Summary of growth aspect	Revenue growth	11,500 (F)
	Cost growth	6,900 (A)
		4,600 (F)

Price aspect

1 Revenue price is the effect of the decrease in revenues arising from the price reduction: (selling price per bottle in Year 3 less selling price per bottle in Year 2) × Year 3 sales volume = (£0.40 − £0.50) × 123,000 = £12,300 (A)

2 Cost price decrease effect on costs: (cost per bottle of DM in Year 3 less cost per bottle of DM in Year 2) × number of bottles sold in Year 3 = (£0.28 − £0.30) × 123,000 = £2,460 (F)

		£
Summary of price aspect	Revenue price	12,300 (A)
	Cost price	2,460 (F)
		9,840 (A)

Usage (or productivity) aspect

Since the number of bottles needed to make each sale remained at one (as it had to), there is no usage aspect to this analysis.

		£
Overall summary:	Growth aspect	4,600 (F)
	Price aspect	9,840 (A)
	Usage aspect	zero
		5,240 (A)

(c) The change in strategy was clearly a mistake. Though making extra sales taken alone generated an additional £4,600 of contribution, this was overwhelmed by the effect of the lower price, even taking account of the benefit of the reduced cost price to the business. This led to a reduction of more than 25 per cent of the Year 1 contribution.

Clearly for this strategy to work at the selling and cost prices applying in Year 2, rather greater sales volume was required than was able to be generated. Possibly with more determined marketing, highlighting to customers the low price, it could be made to work.

11.5 Virgo plc

There is no single correct answer to this problem. The suggestions set out below are based on experiences that some businesses have had in implementing a management bonus system based on EVA® performance.

In order to get the divisional managers to think and act like the owners of the business, it is recommended that divisional performance, as measured by EVA®, should form a significant part of their total rewards. Thus, around 50 per cent of the total rewards paid to managers could be related to the EVA® that has been generated for a period. (In the case of very senior managers it could be more and for junior managers less.)

The target for managers to achieve could be a particular level of improvement in EVA® for their division over a year. A target bonus can then be set for achievement of the target level of improvement. If this target level of improvement is achieved, 100 per cent of the bonus should be paid. If the target is not achieved, an agreed percentage (below 100 per cent) could be paid according to the amount of shortfall. If, on the other hand, the target is exceeded, an agreed percentage (with no upper limits) may be paid.

The timing of the payment of management bonuses is important. In the question it was mentioned that Virgo plc wishes to encourage a longer-term view among its managers. One approach is to use a 'bonus bank' system whereby the bonus for a period is placed in a bank and a certain proportion (usually one-third) can be drawn in the period in which it is earned. If the target for the following period is not met, there can be a charge against the bonus bank and so the total amount available for withdrawal is reduced. This will ensure that the managers try to maintain improvements in EVA® consistently over the years.

In some cases, the amount of bonus is determined by three factors: the performance of the business as a whole (as measured by EVA®), the performance of the division (as measured by EVA®) and the performance of the particular manager (using agreed indicators of performance). Performance for the business as a whole is often given the most weighting and individual performance the least weighting. Thus, 50 per cent of the bonus may be for corporate performance, 30 per cent for divisional performance and 20 per cent for individual performance.

11.6 Leo plc

Free cash flows

	Yr 1	Yr 2	Yr 3	Yr 4	Yr 5	After Yr 5
	£m	£m	£m	£m	£m	£m
Sales	30.0	36.0	40.0	48.0	60.0	60.0
Operating profit (20%)	6.0	7.2	8.0	9.6	12.0	12.0
Less						
Cash tax (25%)	1.5	1.8	2.0	2.4	3.0	3.0
Operating profit less cash tax	4.5	5.4	6.0	7.2	9.0	9.0
Less						
ANCAI (15%)	(4.5)*	(0.9)	(0.6)	(1.2)	(1.8)	
AWCI (10%)	(3.0)*	(0.6)	(0.4)	(0.8)	(1.2)	–
Free cash flows	(3.0)	3.9	5.0	5.2	6.0	9.0
12% discount factor	0.893	0.797	0.712	0.636	0.567	0.567
Present value	(2.7)	3.1	3.6	3.3	3.4	42.5†
	53.2					

* In the first year, the additional sales will be £30m and so the calculations for non-current (fixed) assets and working capital must be based on this figure.

† The terminal value is $(9.0/0.12 \times 0.567) = 42.5$.

Total business value will increase by £53.2m. As there has been no change to the level of borrowing, shareholder value should increase by this amount.

Appendix D
Present value table

Present value of £1, that is, $1/(1 + r)^n$

where r = discount rate
n = number of periods until payment

Periods					Discount rates (r)						
(n)	1%	2%	3%	4%	5%	6%	7%	8%	9%	10%	
1	0.990	0.980	0.971	0.962	0.952	0.943	0.935	0.926	0.917	0.909	1
2	0.980	0.961	0.943	0.925	0.907	0.890	0.873	0.857	0.842	0.826	2
3	0.971	0.942	0.915	0.889	0.864	0.840	0.816	0.794	0.772	0.751	3
4	0.961	0.924	0.888	0.855	0.823	0.792	0.763	0.735	0.708	0.683	4
5	0.951	0.906	0.863	0.822	0.784	0.747	0.713	0.681	0.650	0.621	5
6	0.942	0.888	0.837	0.790	0.746	0.705	0.666	0.630	0.596	0.564	6
7	0.933	0.871	0.813	0.760	0.711	0.665	0.623	0.583	0.547	0.513	7
8	0.923	0.853	0.789	0.731	0.677	0.627	0.582	0.540	0.502	0.467	8
9	0.914	0.837	0.766	0.703	0.645	0.592	0.544	0.500	0.460	0.424	9
10	0.905	0.820	0.744	0.676	0.614	0.558	0.508	0.463	0.422	0.386	10
11	0.896	0.804	0.722	0.650	0.585	0.527	0.475	0.429	0.388	0.350	11
12	0.887	0.788	0.701	0.625	0.557	0.497	0.444	0.397	0.356	0.319	12
13	0.879	0.773	0.681	0.601	0.530	0.469	0.415	0.368	0.326	0.290	13
14	0.870	0.758	0.661	0.577	0.505	0.442	0.388	0.340	0.299	0.263	14
15	0.561	0.743	0.642	0.555	0.481	0.417	0.362	0.315	0.275	0.239	15

(continued over)

Periods (n)	Discount rates (r)										
	11%	12%	13%	14%	15%	16%	17%	18%	19%	20%	
1	0.901	0.893	0.885	0.877	0.870	0.862	0.855	0.847	0.840	0.833	1
2	0.812	0.797	0.783	0.769	0.756	0.743	0.731	0.718	0.706	0.694	2
3	0.731	0.712	0.693	0.675	0.658	0.641	0.624	0.609	0.593	0.579	3
4	0.659	0.636	0.613	0.592	0.572	0.552	0.534	0.516	0.499	0.482	4
5	0.593	0.567	0.543	0.519	0.497	0.476	0.456	0.437	0.419	0.402	5
6	0.535	0.507	0.480	0.456	0.432	0.410	0.390	0.370	0.352	0.335	6
7	0.482	0.452	0.425	0.400	0.376	0.354	0.333	0.314	0.296	0.279	7
8	0.434	0.404	0.376	0.351	0.327	0.305	0.285	0.266	0.249	0.233	8
9	0.391	0.361	0.333	0.308	0.284	0.263	0.243	0.225	0.209	0.194	9
10	0.352	0.322	0.295	0.270	0.247	0.227	0.208	0.191	0.176	0.162	10
11	0.317	0.287	0.261	0.237	0.215	0.195	0.178	0.162	0.148	0.135	11
12	0.286	0.257	0.231	0.208	0.187	0.168	0.152	0.137	0.124	0.112	12
13	0.258	0.229	0.204	0.182	0.163	0.145	0.130	0.116	0.104	0.093	13
14	0.232	0.205	0.181	0.160	0.141	0.125	0.111	0.099	0.088	0.078	14
15	0.209	0.183	0.160	0.140	0.123	0.108	0.095	0.084	0.074	0.065	15

Index